MODELS IN PROCESS:

A
Rhetoric
and
Reader

William J. Kelly

Bristol Community College

Macmillan Publishing Company
New York

Macmillan Publishing Company
866 Third Avenue, New York, New York 10022

Library of Congress Cataloging-in-Publication Data

Kelly, William J.
  Models in process.

  Includes index.
  1. English language — Rhetoric.   2. College readers.
I. Title.
PE1408.K474   1988   808'.0427   87-15215
ISBN 0-02-363090-6

Printing: 1 2 3 4 5 6 7   Year: 8 9 0 1 2 3 4

Acknowledgments:

Richard Armour, "Money." Published with permission of the author.

Arthur Ashe, "A Black Athlete Looks at Education." Copyright © 1977 by The New York Times
    Company. Reprinted by permission.

Isaac Asimov, "The Nightmare of Life Without Fuel." Copyright © 1977 Time Inc. All rights
    reserved. Reprinted by permission from TIME.

Stephen Birmingham, "Dallas vs. Dynasty: Which Show is Better?" Copyright © 1983 by Triangle
    Publications, Inc. Radnor, Pennsylvania. Reprinted with permission from TV Guide ® Maga-
    zine, reprinted by permission of Brandt & Brandt Literary Agents, Inc.

Frank DeFord, "Cystic Fibrosis," from *Alex: The Life of a Child* by Frank DeFord. Copyright © 1983
    by Frank DeFord. Reprinted by permission of Viking Penguin, Inc.

Ellen Goodman, "The Workaholic." Copyright © 1986, Washington Post Writers Group, The
    Boston Globe Newspaper. Reprinted with permission.

Allan J. Hamilton, "Who Shall Live and Who Shall Die." Copyright 1984, by Newsweek, Inc. All
    Rights Reserved. Reprinted by Permission.

Helen Keller, "Everything Has a Name," from *The Story of My Life.* Copyright © 1902, 1903, 1905
    by Helen Keller. Reprinted by permission of Doubleday & Company, Inc.

William J. Kelly, "Aleksandr *Who?*" Copyright © *The Leaflet,* Journal of the New England Associa-
    tion of Teachers of English. Published with permission.

William J. Kelly, "The Advent of Glory, the Death of a Church." Copyright © 1983 by Providence
    Journal Company. Published with permission of the author.

William J. Kelly, "A Life Unfolds Under Dad's Workbench." Copyright © 1983 by Providence
    Journal Company. Published with permission of the author.

Harold S. Kushner, Reprinted by permission of Schocken Books Inc. "Why Do Bad Things Happen
    to Good People?" from *When Bad Things Happen to Good People* Copyright © 1981 by Harold S.
    Kushner. Reprinted with permission from the January 1983 Reader's Digest.

Ed Lowe, "Adrift on a Sea of Words." Copyright © 1980, Newsday Inc. Reprinted by permission.

George Orwell, "Shooting an Elephant," from *Shooting an Elephant and Other Essays.* Copyright ©
    1950 by George Orwell. Reprinted by permission of Harcourt Brace Jovanovich, Inc.

ISBN 0-02-363090-6

Charles Osgood, "It's New! It's Improved! You Get to Carry It Yourself!" Published with permission of the author.

Andrew A. Rooney, "Republican or Democrat?" from *And More by Andy Rooney*. Copyright © 1982 by Andrew A. Roony. Reprinted by permission of Atheneum Publishers.

Roger Rosenblatt, "Oops! How's That Again?" Copyright © 1981 Time, Inc. All rights reserved. Reprinted by permission from TIME.

Howard Silverman, "A Ghost of Christmas Past." Copyright © 1983 by Providence Journal Company. Published with permission of the author.

Carla Stephens, "Drownproofing." Copyright © 1976 by CBS Magazines, the Consumer Publishing Division of CBS. Reprinted by permission of the author and Woman's Day Magazine, Inc.

Judy Syfers, "I Want a Wife." Copyright © 1972 by Judy Syfers. Published with permission of the author.

Jonathan Walters, "To This Hurler, Throwing Is an Art Form, Not a Hit-or-Miss Proposition," from the January 16, 1984, *Sports Illustrated*. Published with permission from the author.

E. B. White, "Once More to the Lake," from *Essays of E. B. White*. Copyright © 1941, 1969 by E. B. White. Reprinted by permission of Harper & Row Publishers Inc.

*To Michelle,
for her love,
support,
and friendship*

Preface

Writing a paper for an introductory composition class is among the biggest challenges beginning college students face. The writing process itself sometimes seems confusing and intimidating. These students know that for each assignment they must generate ideas and then specify and clarify them — but how?

This is the question about writing that most troubles beginning college students, and this is essentially the question *Models in Process: A Rhetoric and Reader* answers. *Models in Process* shows students plenty of examples of what the finished paper — the product — should look like, but its major focus is on how to get to that finished paper — the process. Throughout the text, various student models — some in facsimile form — illustrate the various steps of the writing process. And the material is presented in tone and style that talks directly to the students. There's no dry theory here, no explanation without illustration. Basically *Models in Process* uses student models to support a simple, highly readable explanation of the writing process. Product and process are both clearly illustrated. Students are, therefore, effectively guided from idea to finished draft.

Models in Process is divided into two sections, rhetoric and reader. The strength of both sections springs from the various models. The student models — twenty-one complete papers as well as numerous partial writings, all shown in various stages of development — illustrate how a writing develops from beginning to end.

The fourteen professional writings by some of today's top writers — two per chapter in the reader — are outstanding examples of the various modes in practice. Three of the chapters in the reader — Chapter 7, "Narration"; Chapter 8, "Description"; and Chapter 15, "Argument" — also contain an additional section entitled "How I Wrote It." Each of these sections presents one of my own published essays featuring the mode discussed and then my explanation of how the piece developed. The idea behind these sections is to give students a window into the writing process by giving them a firsthand explanation of how a paper developed from idea to published essay.

The first section of *Models in Process* (the rhetoric) presents writing as a recursive process involving three basic steps — prewriting, composing, and revising — and provides numerous practical exercises to reinforce the lessons presented. Additional exercises are included in the Instructor's Manual.

Once the students have read these first five chapters, they'll have the basic information needed to complete whatever writing assignments they'll face. More important, though, the confusion and intimidation they may have felt earlier will have disappeared, and they'll have the confidence they need to become effective collegiate writers.

Chapter 1, "The First Steps," presents an overview of the writing process and introduces freewriting as a means of liberating ideas. Chapter 2, "Prewriting: Moving Forward," illustrates a four-step prewriting technique that shows how to move from unfocused freewriting to clear thesis. Chapter 3, "Composing: From One Stage to the Next," illustrates how to turn the freewriting material into sentences and paragraphs to support that thesis. Chapter 4, "Drafting: Considering Your Reader," focuses on the reader and the reader's needs in the writing process, and Chapter 5, "Revising: Refining for Your Reader," divides the revising stage into three steps and illustrates both the minor tinkering and the wholesale changes that occur in this stage of writing. And all the chapters feature models; after each point is presented, it is then illustrated with a model. The result is a rhetoric that takes the confusion and intimidation out of writing.

The reader section of *Models in Process* begins with Chapter 6, 'Cross-modes: Fulfilling Your Purpose." This chapter discusses the traditional division of modes but identifies them as labels for general patterns of arrangement rather than as all-inclusive categories of reasoning. Chapters 7–14 cover narration, description, process, example, definition, comparison and contrast, cause and effect, and division and classification. Chapter 15 introduces argument, which, in this text, is presented as an aim or intent in writing that the writer fulfills by using the various modes.

Each chapter in the reader provides a clear, thorough introduction to the particular mode. Then, two writing assignments are presented, each of which is clearly divided into five sections: "Reason" elaborates on the topic presented. "What Your Reader Needs" specifies what strategies to follow so that the writing produced will meet the needs of the reader. "Model" gives the writers a concrete example to follow — a model essay written to the exact assignment they face. "Follow-through" discusses the model, explaining and illustrating the process by which it developed. "Checklist" presents a series of questions on which to base a revision. The Instructor's Manual provides other possible topics for writing.

Each chapter in the reader also contains at least two professional models, with discussion questions and alternate writing assignments. Some of these essays are old favorites and some are fresh offerings, but they are all excellent starting points for additional papers. Therefore, although *Models in Process* focuses primarily on college-level writing, it also contains a selection of outstanding professional essays.

ACKNOWLEDGMENTS

Many people deserve thanks for their assistance and support in helping me finish this book. In particular, I owe John Michael Lannon of Southeastern Massachusetts University a great deal. He first suggested that I turn these materials into a textbook, and he always made time to discuss some aspect of my proposal, even as he dealt with his own writing projects. He richly deserves his fine reputation as a teacher and writer. I value his friendship greatly.

I am also grateful to Robert A. Schwegler of the University of Rhode Island. Besides helping to strengthen my background in the field, he examined various drafts of the proposal and generously offered advice and assistance. His comments truly helped me shape the text.

My reviewers also provided outstanding advice and encouragement; their suggestions definitely improved the book, and for that I thank them:

At Macmillan, English Editor Jennifer Crewe deserves special thanks. From the moment she received the proposal, she gave it — and me — her complete support. Her relaxed guidance, genuine enthusiasm, and poet's attention to detail made my work much easier. And current English Editor Barbara Heinssen has provided invaluable help as well.

My colleagues at Bristol Community College provided invaluable support, especially Paul Fletcher and Debbie Lawton, of the English Department, and Patricia Darcy, Director of Testing, who read large parts of text and offered suggestions and encouragement. Special thanks should also go to Stuart Bellman, Black Hills State College; Nina

Chasteen, Louisiana State University at Alexandria; Kathleen E. Dubs, Cedar Crest College; Edward C. Nolte, Norfolk State University; Patricia Owen, Nassau Community College; David Shimkin, Queensborough Community College; and Thelma B. Thompson, University of the District of Columbia. I owe special thanks to Bernard F. Sullivan, Massachusetts News Editor for *The Providence Journal.* By giving me the opportunity to be a weekly columnist, he gave me the chance to apply and refine the principles underlying the text.

Of course, my strongest support has come from my family. My parents, Mary and Edward Kelly, and my in-laws, Flo and Leo Nadeau, offered their unwavering support throughout the whole process. My children, Nicole and Jacqueline, cheerfully tolerated hundreds of "Not now—I have to work on the book" answers in response to their requests.

But most of all, I'm indebted to my wife, Michelle. She's read and commented on every word of the text; the book would not have appeared in its present form without her valuable assistance, her support, and her strength. She deserves more thanks than could ever be given in a few sentences.

W.J.K.

Contents

4   DRAFTING: CONSIDERING YOUR READER ————— 32

5   REVISING: REFINING FOR YOUR READER ————— 42

6 CROSS-MODES: FULFILLING YOUR PURPOSE _____ 63

7 NARRATION _____ 78

8 DESCRIPTION _____ 98

11 DEFINITION —————— 171

Chapter 1

—— THE FIRST STEPS ——

INTRODUCTION

> WRITE*EASE, the new, simple, painless, proven method to write anything from a grocery list to a short story to a doctoral dissertation is now available at fine stores everywhere! Yes, now you too can be like William Shakespeare, Ernest Hemingway, and Erma Bombeck. Today's technology makes it all easy. WRITE*EASE has been tested and approved by Underwriters' Laboratory and it's fully guaranteed. *Consumer Reports* has given WRITE*EASE a five-star rating.

If you saw this advertisement, would you be tempted to try this product?

Most people probably would, and that's because writing seems like such hard work. Most of the time, you struggle with part or maybe all of a writing assignment. You start, you stop, you crumple up the paper, and then you start again. The entire process is frustrating. Unlike a mathematical equation or a recipe, writing has no step-by-step approach — that's why most of us would welcome any program that provides a shortcut without shortchanging anyone.

Unfortunately, no product exists that will give you much of a shortcut. Writing seems to be hard work because it is hard work. But you can make the work easier for yourself if you study the process of writing. You need to take your first steps: learning what writing is and recognizing how it comes to be.

1

OVERVIEW OF THE WRITING PROCESS

What happens when you write? Yes, you sit down (or stand up or lie down) someplace and put words on your paper, but how do your ideas end up in a form that (you hope, anyway) is both effective and acceptable? In other words, what is good writing and how does it develop?

Defining Writing

First, let's define what happens when you write: Writing is a type of communication through which you use the written or printed word to convey a message to your reader. Put in the form of an illustration, writing looks like this:

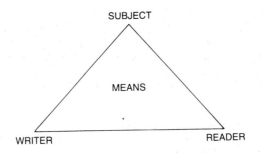

This figure, called **the communications triangle,** shows in symbolic terms the four main elements of writing: the **writer,** the **reader,** the **subject** you are writing about, and the **means** you use to communicate. Writing is effective and acceptable when these four elements interact and produce communication. In other words, when you write anything, your purpose is to make your ideas (the subject) understandable for somebody else (your reader). And the words you put on paper are your means of accomplishing your task.

Expanding on Common Information

You and your reader probably share some common information about your subject. Look, for example, at these sentences, which contain information that is probably common between you and your reader:

> MTV is cable television programming that specializes in video performances of today's top music.
>
> *The Godfather* is a movie that deals with organized crime in America.

To write successfully, you use the means — words — to expand on that common information:

> Some pop stars feel that MTV has actually hurt the music industry because it puts more emphasis on the musicians as actors than as artists.
>
> The brutal murders ordered by former innocent war hero Michael Corleone in *The Godfather* (including that of his own brother-in-law, the father of the

child he sponsors for baptism) symbolize the infection of evil bred by organized crime.

As you can see, the interaction of the four elements produces even more information to be shared with your reader.

Explaining Writing

If writing is the interaction of the four elements of writing, how does that interaction develop? To answer this question, we need to divide the writing process into stages.

Writing occurs in three general stages: **prewriting, composing,** and **revising.** Because writing is not a strict, step-by-step process, these stages overlap. And within any stage, you may repeat a part or parts of the other stages.

Prewriting. Prewriting includes all the work you do before you actually begin to arrange your ideas into formal sentences and paragraphs. Prewriting includes thinking, doodling, talking, list making, and some forms of outlining. Sometimes, it also includes reading and formal researching. It depends in part on how well you know the subject. If, for example, you're discussing the effect that a recent horror movie had on you, you probably won't have to run to the library. If, however, you are writing about how the moviemaker produced the special effects, you should begin your prewriting by reading.

Composing. Once you have sifted through your ideas and have decided on a focus for your writing, you begin the composing stage. This is probably the stage that you think of right away when told to write something. Composing basically means completing draft versions of your paper, that is, arranging your ideas on a subject in some order and in sentences and paragraphs.

Revising. The next stage of writing is revising — refining your writing by adding, deleting, and rearranging information. Many beginning writers mistake revising for **editing,** a step that is actually only the last part of revising. Revising is a great deal more than merely correcting technical errors; in fact, it is in some cases the most important stage of writing.

Unlike preparing a special meal, writing isn't a step-by-step process. Writing is recursive; rather than a straight line, the writing process is more like a series of loops that brings you back through different stages of the writing process.

In that paper about the special effects in that recent horror movie, for example, maybe you (or another reader) will discover places where you moved away from your main idea or find spots needing more specific information. Or maybe the paragraph explaining your response should come before the paragraph explaining how the moviemaker made the dismembered corpse move. Perhaps the introduction doesn't provide a clear direction for your reader.

Revising means reworking these parts of your draft — and doing this brings you back to the other stages of the writing process, always with the intent to change and mold that draft so that it better reflects your ideas on your subject.

LIBERATING IDEAS

When faced with a writing assignment, many people immediately move to the composing stage. And often they quickly become miserable because they don't know what to write.

Why? They can think about a subject; chances are they could talk about it. Why, then, can't they write about it?

Part of the problem has to do with intent. Except for those occasions when you're unprepared to write about a subject (as on an essay test you haven't studied for), you want to express your ideas the way you understand them— completely and clearly. And you want to express those ideas right the first time. As a result, your expectations of the finished paper actually inhibit your ability to write; your ideas become prisoners.

You need to liberate your ideas, and one of the best ways to do so is **freewriting.** A technique made popular by such successful writing teachers as Ken Macrorie and Peter Elbow, freewriting involves pouring all your thinking on a subject onto your paper. In literature, **stream-of-consciousness** is the name given to this type of freewheeling writing. Look, for instance, at this passage about a funeral from James Joyce's classic *Ulysses*. Here, Leopold Bloom, Joyce's protagonist, ponders funerals and death as he stands in the graveyard after the service:

> Your heart perhaps but what price the fellow in the six feet by two with his toes to the daisies. No touching that. Seat of the affections. Broken heart. A pump after all, pumping thousands of gallons of blood every day. One fine day it gets bunged up and there you are. Lots of them lying around here: lungs, hearts, livers. Old rusty pumps: damn the thing else. The resurrection and the life. Once you are dead you are dead. That last day idea. Knocking them all up out of their graves. Come forth, Lazarus! And he came fifth and lost the job. Get up! Last day! Then every fellow mousing around for his liver and his lights and the rest of his traps. Find damn all of himself that morning. Pennyweight of powder in a skull. Twelve grammes one pennyweight. Troy measure. (Joyce, James. *Ulysses.* New York: Random House, 1961, pp. 105–106)

Notice how Bloom's ideas shift around, just as your own thoughts on a subject wander.

But stream-of-consciousness writing in literature is not the same as freewriting, because in fiction, the writer consciously molds the ideas to resemble a thought pattern. You will not be molding anything when you freewrite. Instead, you will record your ideas as they create their own form.

USING THE TECHNIQUE

Although you may find it awkward at first, freewriting is actually very simple. Once you have a subject, either one assigned to you or one chosen by you, begin writing for ten minutes or so without stopping. Put down every word, phrase, sentence, and idea that comes to mind. Don't worry if it doesn't make sense immediately; don't worry if you spell something wrong. Just don't stop —and don't cross anything out.

If you get stuck and can't think, write "Can't think" or "Don't know" or something like that until a word or words come to mind. Don't worry about repeating yourself—that's fine. Write what you see, what you smell, what you feel. Just don't stop.

Examining a Sample

Look at this freewriting on funerals:

> *Cold, sad, people crying—so much money—ideas of the dead coming back. The priest and the holy water altarboys all those dirges. Movie versions of death— most of them are gruesome but sometimes it's funny too. That undead guy in American Werewolf in London said "I'm not having a fun time here"—cracked me up. That baby's funeral was probably the worst I ever went to. So much money Steve and Donna were devestated. Caskets and all that bullshit—what a rippoff casket—a fancy word for coffin I guess. Those funeral directors constantly solemn. How can they go through it over and over? I can never look at the families again without pity. My old man How Great Thou Art now that he's said he wants that played at his funeral, everytime I hear it I think about when he goes. Goes—we never want to say Dies Pall bearers my first time was for my father's Aunt Helen. I never even met her. I was about 12 with all my cousins from Boston "Mac" was really "Mark" what an accent. My old Uncle Jack was funny that time. He kept crying and trying to make everybody feel better by telling jokes. He's deaf so he was telling the jokes so loud. It was like the stories I've heard of Irish wakes—stand the body up and have a hell of a party. I hate sitting in the funeral home. Watching the people walk up to the body and kneel. What the hell do you say when you go through the line? Most times I don't even know the people I always feel stupid. Then carrying the body out—always feel a shift inside. How about the guy who drives the hearse. Great job he has to drive stiffs around all day everyday. Get to the cemetery and some front-end loader has dug the hole and they cover the giant pile of dirt with a green cloth as if you're not going to notice it. My aunt Mary's funeral—we all had to put flowers on the casket and then they lowered it.*

Identifying a Focus

As you can see, this freewriting covers plenty of territory. Like Bloom's thoughts in *Ulysses,* this freewriting contains plenty of words, phrases, sentences, and ideas directly related to funerals and death:

- *Casket—a fancy word for coffin I guess*
- *Those funeral directors constantly solemn. How can they go through it over and over?*
- *Goes—we never want to say Dies*

But another angle, more specific, appears, too—humor:

- *That undead guy in American Werewolf in London said "I'm not having a fun time here"—cracked me up.*
- *My old uncle Jack was funny that time. He kept crying and trying to make everybody feel better by telling jokes. He's deaf so he was telling the jokes so loud.*
- *How about the guy who drives the hearse. Great job he has to drive stiffs around all day every day.*

There is potential in this freewriting for several focuses, including this idea of some of the funny points associated with death and funerals.

Discovering Useful Information in Your Freewriting

Particularly for the first few times that you try it, freewriting may seem awkward. The ten minutes you spend may seem more like ten hours, and the result may look something like this:

> *Death what an awful topic. Jesus she knows how to pick them O.K. how about that lady down the street who died—no that's too gross they didn't find her for a week. Can't think—no idea I must be blocking this out. How about that dead dog in the road on the way to school—I wonder if she wants stuff on dead dogs—like that song a few years ago Dead Skunk in the Middle of the Road. I don't know—how much time left? I can't believe this. I feel so stupid I guess I just don't like to think about it like when Regina Spokes drowned in grammar school—we all had to go to the wake. I remember how scared I was. Now whenever I smell flowers I think of her in the box. Isn't that stupid—well it was stupid to send little kids like us to a wake. Teachers and parents are stupid sometimes. They don't think of what kids feel they treat them like little adults. How much time is left! I don't know anything about this stuff Look at this junk—I can't even stick to a subject what else can I say. Death? That's it, man close the door. I hope things get easier in the course I just can't think.*

As you can see, this freewriting doesn't seem nearly as successful as the earlier one. "Can't think" and "don't know" appear a few times, and overall the freewriting doesn't seem to flow as well as the first one did.

But this second freewriting is still successful. In fact, some of these starts and stops represent interesting possibilities for writing:

- *Like when Regina Spokes drowned in grammar school—we all had to go to the wake. I remember how scared I was. Now whenever I smell flowers I think of her in the box.*
- *Well it was stupid to send little kids like us to a wake. Teachers and parents are stupid sometimes. They don't think of what kids feel they treat them like little adults.*

The first snippet from the freewriting hints of a powerful subject for writing: the trauma of facing a wake and funeral as a child. And although it is just a minor point in the freewriting, the detail about the fragrance of the flowers being forever associated with the whole ritual of death is exactly the kind of specific image that will make a paper on this aspect of death clear for a reader.

Further, the second quote from the freewriting, although not directly associated with death, could be an even richer subject for writing: Too often, adults do forget that children are children, not miniature men and women. Maybe this second freewriting doesn't contain as many obvious ideas for development, but it is still successful: useful information is there, waiting to be mined.

Don't be surprised sometimes if some or maybe most of a freewriting seems like garbage. Remember, however, that the ideas that are left after you go "barrel-picking" aren't garbage; they are good ideas that have been liberated, kernels of thought that probably wouldn't have appeared otherwise because your desire to say it right the first time would have been in your way.

WRITING RITUALS

Writing is a private act made public. And because it's a private act, everyone works through it a bit differently. If you learn to recognize what conditions help you write better, you can use this information to make your job easier.

When you have an out-of-class assignment, where do you complete it? Do you head to your room for quiet and privacy, or do you spread everything you could possibly need to write a paper—dictionaries, old magazines, newspaper clippings, and so on—across the table in your crowded kitchen? Because writing is an individual enterprise, your answer can't be wrong; wherever is right for you is right!

But other things besides location make you comfortable. Some people prefer quiet and so head to the library or another quiet study area; others need noise. Many students say that they actually change clothes to write. (Although I don't go that far, I do like to write with my shoes off. As I write, I scrunch them up with my feet and play with them as I work on my writing.) The time of day may be a factor, too. "Morning" people probably do their best writing during the morning hours, "evening" people in the evening. Many people definitely prefer pencil to pen, green ink to black, loose paper to spiral bound, yellow legal ruled to white lined paper. How about you?

Do you enjoy food or drink while you work? (I seem to make cup after cup of instant coffee—in my special mug, of course—as I write.) Do you work at a desk or a table, or do you balance your pad on your lap? A few students have said that they write best sitting in the middle of the bed. They claim it's actually comfortable.

Trivial points? Maybe, but because the very act of writing can be so intimidating and difficult, you may find it helpful and productive to uncover the most comfortable atmosphere for you to write. Of course, sometimes we set up certain unreasonable guidelines to avoid getting down to work: "Oh, I just can't write unless I use a fountain pen." Check yourself—don't use some element of your writing ritual as a convenient excuse to put off writing. Instead, concentrate on the parts of your writing ritual that truly make you comfortable so that you can do what you are supposed to do: to write.

SUMMARY

Writing is communication using the written or printed word to convey a message through the interaction of the four **elements of communication: writer, reader, subject,** and **means.** Writing occurs in three general stages—**prewriting, composing,** and **revising**—but it isn't a step-by-step process.

Too often, people try to start writing without doing any prewriting. This planning stage is crucial, however. One way to do some of this important planning is to freewrite. Freewriting is a pouring out of all your ideas on a subject without concern for logic or form.

Writing is intimidating; finding out what makes you comfortable may make the time you spend working on a paper more productive. Learn if you have a particular time, place, or other condition that puts you at ease when you write.

EXERCISES

1. What do you find most difficult about writing? Do a ten-minute freewriting on this subject and then save it. You'll be able to use it later on in the course.

2. Take a look at this poem by Richard Amour:

"Money"

Workers earn it,
Spendthrifts burn it,
Bankers lend it,
Women spend it,
Forgers fake it,
Taxes take it,
Dying leave it,
Heirs receive it,
Thrifty save it,
Misers crave it,
Robbers seize it,
Gamblers lose it . . .
I could use it.

Now it's your turn. Take the topic of money and freewrite for ten minutes.

3. After you have completed your freewriting, go back over it. You may also pair up with a classmate. Try to identify related ideas; circle or underline them.

4. The freewriting on death and funerals (p. 5) contains many related ideas; the humor indirectly associated with death is just one possible focus. Identify other related ideas from that freewriting.

5. Where do you write? Do you go through any rituals when you write? Make a list and prepare to discuss it with your classmates.

Chapter 2

PREWRITING: MOVING FORWARD

INTRODUCTION

> Sing in me, muse, and through me tell the story
> of that man skilled in all ways of
> contending . . .

In these first lines of *The Odyssey* (Robert Fitzgerald's translation), Homer asks the special goddess of poetry to inspire him to tell the story of Odysseus, among the greatest of Greek heroes. Obviously his request worked: *The Odyssey* remains today one of literature's greatest works.

Although asking for inspiration was a good technique for Homer, don't expect it to work for you when you have to complete an essay answer in your psychology class or a letter of application for your first full-time job. You'll need more than the help of a muse in most writing situations.

Does inspiration play a part in writing? Yes, Sometimes you will be inspired and then, without being able to explain how you did it, produce something excellent. Former Beatle Paul McCartney, for instance, says that he woke up one morning and simply knew the entire melody for "Yesterday," one of the biggest popular hits in the last thirty-five years. Unwilling at first to believe that the song was the result of a sudden burst of inspiration, McCartney reportedly spent several days playing the song for friends and asking them what old song it was before finally recording it. He just wouldn't believe that the song had come to him that easily.

Of course, it wasn't an old song; it was an original. McCartney knew, however, that inspiration usually isn't the reason for success in music—and the same is true for writing. Rather than waiting for the muse, you, like the rest of us mortal writers, will simply have to work your way through the writing process.

A MODEL PAPER: THE COMPLETED DRAFT

A good way to study the process of writing is first to look at a product of that process — an essay — and then to look at how that draft developed. Here, for instance, is an effective essay on computers:

COMPUTERS: CURE-ALL OR CURSE

If there is one invention that has truly changed the lives of the people of the twentieth century, it is the computer. With it, our fast-paced society has been speeded up even more. Business transactions occur in the blink of an eye. Libraries rest inside tiny bits of silicon. Personal amusement and entertainment center on electronic games. These scenes, once present only in science fiction, are now commonplace, all because of the development of computers. They may be our cure-all. Ironically, they may also be our curse.

Saying that computers are destroying civilization, however, is unfair and misleading. For example, as labor-saving devices, computers are without parallel. What once took hundreds of people hundreds of hours to do, such as a complete inventory at a manufacturing plant, can be completed in a fraction of the time originally needed, thanks to computerization. As a result of this streamlining in all fields, the quality of life that we enjoy has definitely improved.

Yet this improvement has not been without drawbacks, the chief of which is the depersonalization that accompanies computerization. More computers means less human contact. The result may be a society that deals more with microchips and floppy disks than with other people, to the detriment of us all.

In industry, computers have brought about a rapid evolution. For example, standard in even small offices now are personal or business computers. These units, which resemble overgrown typewriters, enable workers to tap into networks of information as numerous as the wires in the telephone cable they often use. But this setup denies personal communication, replacing it with the person-to-machine kind. In some cases, workers spend much of their workday with only a glowing computer screen as a companion. Many won't have to suffer long, however, because increased computerization often means job loss, too; one operator and a computer can replace entire departments in some cases.

Our schools are also redirecting their curriculums to keep pace with the rapid growth in computerization. Today mathematics is king. But as math becomes our new language, will reading and writing become secondary skills? Will literature be buried deep inside some obscure memory bank?

As schoolchildren struggle to learn about computers,

the rest of us wrestle with another effect of the increased presence of computers: computer errors that plague us in all areas of our lives. For example, hardly a week goes by during which we can't read a story in the newspaper (itself marred by errors, compliments of the computers that have replaced human proofreaders) about some poor soul who is trying to convince some agency that he has not died or that he has not run up a $1 million credit-card bill. Computer wands now read the pricing codes at the grocery store, but they present the consumer with the exact breakdown of the order <u>after</u> the total price is indicated, and detecting an error <u>may</u> mean unbagging the entire order.

Even in the home, the fortress of the family, the computer intrudes. For years the television has been the center of entertainment in many homes, and with the introduction of affordable home computers and entertainment centers, this is even more the case. Again, however, the threat is depersonalization. Competition and learning become human versus machine. In the one place where people should be able to count on human comfort and communication, a computer may create a subtle isolation.

Of course, suggesting that we return to simpler times is ridiculous. The computer and the lifestyle it has spawned are here to stay. And they should be. Thanks to the advances in computerization, our lives are better. What we should strive for, however, is an awareness of the problems, both actual <u>and</u> potential, that this growth brings on. Whether at work, in our schools, or at home, computers should serve us. They should be our cure-all, and they will be, if we remember who should run whom.

PREWRITING: FOUR PRELIMINARY STEPS

This draft is fairly well done, typical of the writing you will complete during the drafting stages of your writing. Certainly it could be improved through revising; in fact, you will see a revised version of it in Chapter 5, "Revising: Refining for Your Reader." Still, even as it stands now, it's a good draft.

How did this writing develop? The best way to answer this question is to go back to the very beginnings of the draft of this paper and examine the preliminary steps that had to be taken to create it: (1) **freewriting;** (2) **statement of purpose;** (3) **focused freewriting;** and (4) **thesis.**

Step One: Prewriting

As you saw in the first chapter, freewriting is a technique that helps you start writing by liberating your ideas. Freewriting is easy, too. All you need to do is choose a topic, set aside ten minutes or so, and write down everything that comes to mind about your subject. You don't worry about form — spelling, grammar, punctuation, and so on — because nobody but you needs to see the result. When you freewrite, you accumulate plenty of information, as much as you can manage in the period of time that you set aside. Although you won't use all the material you generate, this information becomes a starting point for your writing. Look for instance, at this freewriting on computers:

> *Computers do everything so quickly — even t.v's are computerized, cars, etc —*
> *like the space shuttle has so many computers. Each system is run by its own*
> *computer — it almost eliminates people from the whole process. But all the*
> *takeoffs before challenger blew up had been delayed because of computer break-*
> *down, so they're also bad at the same time. So many places have gone computer*
> *with tv screens on And auto workers were complaining because of computers*
> *taking over their jobs. But computers can't do some things like close hand work*
> *on clothes and furniture. They can't do farming either — so I guess there'll*
> *always be plenty of work for people. Computers can do great things too. The way*
> *a company can get information on a person so quickly so that they can check*
> *credit. I went shopping last night and watched as the salegirl called in all these*
> *charge card numbers. But what was funny was one of the ladies tried to buy*
> *something with her card but the girl said that she couldn't because there was*
> *already a big charge on it. The lady kept saying she hadn't bought anything with*
> *the card ever, but she couldn't argue with the computer. If they say you're*
> *wrong, I guess you're wrong. How can a machine do everything so quickly and*
> *still screw it up? Computer games are fun but they're expensive to buy or play*
> *and they're addictive too. What's scary about computers is there's all kinds of*
> *informaton recorded on it. One surge of electricity can wipe it all out — that*
> *happened to my friends last semester.*

As you can see, there is plenty of information here — in fact, too much to deal with in the relatively short papers (500 – 800 words) you'll be preparing. And as you can also see, not all of the information deals with one idea. The freewriting looks like what it is: a pouring out of information about computers. It is simply your starting point.

Step Two: Statement of Purpose

Before you can use the information from your freewriting, you need to filter it and to decide what bits of information you will use. The next step, developing a statement of purpose, does exactly this. A statement of purpose is a summary of either the main, related ideas in your freewriting or the one point that you would like to develop. Remember, your freewriting is probably a rambling list of ideas. To make your freewriting useful, you need to identify and isolate some ideas that you consider connected, connectable, or potentially interesting.

Filtering Your Freewriting.   Look again at the freewriting on computers. Notice, however, that this time some of the related ideas have been isolated:

> *Computers do everything so quickly — even t.v's are computerized, cars, etc —*

like the space shuttle has so many computers. Each system is run by its own computer—it almost eliminates people from the whole process. But all the takeoffs before challenger blew up had been delayed because of computer break-down, so they're also bad at the same time. So many places have gone computer with tv screens on And auto workers were complaining because of computers taking over their jobs. But computers can't do some things like close hand work on clothes and furniture. They can't do farming either—so I guess there'll always be plenty of work for people. Computers can do great things too. The way a company can get information on a person so quickly so that they can check credit. I went shopping last night and watched as the salegirl called in all these charge card numbers. But what was funny was one of the ladies tried to buy something with her card but the girl said that she couldn't because there was already a big charge on it. The lady kept saying she hadn't bought anything with the card ever, but she couldn't argue with the computer. If they say you're wrong, I guess you're wrong. How can a machine do everything so quickly and still screw it up? Computer games are fun but they're expensive to buy or play and they're addictive too. What's scary about computers is there's all kinds of informaton recorded on it. One surge of electricity can wipe it all out—that happened to my friends last semester.

These circled ideas, all dealing with the darker side of computerization, represent a much narrower focus, one easily summarized so that it reflects your intent, your statement of purpose:

> I want to tell my reader about the drawbacks of computers.

Directing Your Statement of Purpose. Notice that your statement of purpose contains the words "I want" (or "I intend" or "I plan"). That's because a statement of purpose is directed to you, the writer. Basically it reminds you exactly what you're supposed to be doing; writing something for another person.

Yes, there will be some times when you will write for yourself only—a diary is a good example—and in these cases, you probably won't need to be as careful to provide complete details. After all, whatever appears in your diary or journal will have involved you in some way, so you won't need to tell yourself as much as you would have to tell somebody else.

But for the most part, your writing will be reader-centered, and by the time you're ready to prepare a draft, you'll have a good idea of what you intend to tell your reader. Therefore you probably won't include these directions to yourself. A statement of purpose is an indication of your intent—a plan for you to follow as you write.

Step Three: Focused Freewriting

Your statement of purpose narrows your subject so that you're prepared to generate more ideas. You do this by completing a **focused freewriting**. Like your initial freewriting, a focused freewriting is an outpouring of information;

unlike the first freewriting, however, a focused freewriting has a much narrower, more specific starting point.

Narrowing Your Focus.   The following focused freewriting deals with a specific idea—the dark flipside of computers, the drawbacks—rather than with computers in general:

I want to tell my reader about the drawbacks of computers

A lot of people don't think about the drawbacks of computers like computer error. I got charged for calls I didn't make on my phone two months ago. When I called the girl told me it was computer error. What's funny is the computer people always say there's no such thing as computer error—it's operator error Also stories about people who are notified by Social Security that they're dead then they have a hard time proving they're not. I also read a story about a lady who received a box weighing ten pounds' full of incorrect long distance charges—I'd go nuts if somebody ever rang my doorbell with a mistake like that. All the computers at work. Almost every office has a computer—even the little construction company that built our house had one in the office. But all the people who run them do is sit in front of that t.v. screen and push keys. It's weird to think of a big office—maybe 20 people all working at computers without talking to each other all day. And some of them probably know that as soon as the computers get smarter, they'll replace their jobs. It's like working to replace yourself. Radiation from the screens I read where it might hurt pregnant women. Must be the same reason kids aren't supposed to sit so close to the set. For awhile everyone got video games—pac man fever. I'd rather go out and ski or bowl than play the computer versions. No computers for me. My calculator, though? I guess I wasted all that time in math class. Now teachers let kids use calculators in math—how are little kids ever going to add without a calculator if they don't practice times tables and other stuff. Like telling time—all the new clocks are digital so kids will be confused when they see one with hands. Now new cars have computers that talk to you and tell you to buckle your seat belt or take your keys—what a pain. Funny voices, too. The phone company's voice is one lady she had to say number and they recorded each one. Then the computer combined the recordings so the same lady's voice says every single phone number in the country.

As you can see, this focused freewriting is far more restricted and specific than the initial freewriting on computers in general. Yes, some of the ideas listed don't seem very connected yet, but much of the focused freewriting deals with the narrowed subject. A focused freewriting, then, is particularly useful because it provides more specific information related to a narrower topic.

Your focused freewriting will probably contain much more information than you can use. You might save some of this leftover material in a folder to draw on for another paper. Remember, however, that some of your initial material will be repetitive or uninformative. Don't preserve this type of material; give it a decent burial in the wastebasket and turn your attention to the material that will meet the needs of your reader.

Step Four: Thesis

From your focused freewriting, you develop your main idea for your writing: your **thesis.** Like your statement of purpose, your thesis is a sentence. Unlike your statement of purpose, though, your thesis is a cue for your reader; it's a street sign that announces to your reader what you are presenting.

Distinguishing Between a Statement of Purpose and a Thesis. As you can see, a statement of purpose is a note that you write to yourself; it's a way for you not only to decide on your main focus but also to stick with that focus during the rest of the prewriting stage. A thesis, however, is a statement for your reader that not only says what your subject is but also explains what point you are making about that subject. Unless your paper has a thesis, it won't provide the direction that your reader needs to understand the significance of your essay.

Developing a Thesis. You develop a thesis in much the same way that you develop a statement of purpose. You identify main ideas and summarize them in a single sentence. Look at the focused freewriting below, this time with the main ideas circled:

I want to tell my reader about the drawbacks of computers

A lot of people don't think about the drawbacks of computers like computer error. I got charged for calls I didn't make on my phone two months ago. When I called the girl told me it was computer error. What's funny is the computer people always say there's no such thing as computer error — it's operator error Also stories about people who are notified by Social Security that they're dead then they have a hard time proving they're not. I also read a story about a lady who received a box weighing ten pounds' full of incorrect long distance charges — I'd go nuts if somebody ever rang my doorbell with a mistake like that. All the computers at work. Almost every office has a computer — even the little construction company that built our house had one in the office. But all the people who run them do is sit in front of that t.v. screen and push keys. It's weird to think of a big office — maybe 20 people all working at computers without talking to each other all day. And some of them probably know that as soon as the computers get smarter, they'll replace their jobs. It's like working to replace yourself. Radiation from the screens I read where it might hurt pregnant women. Must be the same reason kids aren't supposed to sit so close to the set. For awhile everyone got video games — pac man fever. I'd rather go out and ski or bowl than play the computer versions. No computers for me. My calculator, though? I guess I wasted all that time in math class. Now teachers let kids use calculators in math — how are little kids ever going to add without a calculator if they don't practice times tables and other stuff. *Like telling time — all the new clocks are digital so kids will be confused when they see one with hands. Now new cars have computers that talk to you and tell you to buckle your seat belt or take your keys — what a pain. Funny voices, too. The phone company's voice is one lady she had to say number and they recorded each one. Then the computer combined the recordings so the same lady's voice says every single phone number in the country.*

There are a number of possibilities for development here including the effect that computers have on various industries or the impersonality often associated with computers. Most of the information in the focused freewriting, however, deals in some way with the drawbacks of computers; these circled ideas represent the major drawbacks.

Once these points have been identified, a summarizing statement — a thesis — can be developed:

> Computers have made our lives much easier, but sometimes their drawbacks make day-to-day living harder for us.

This draft thesis is effective because it presents the subject (the impact of computers on our lives) and the point that is to be made about the subject (that computers complicate our lives as well as help us). Rather than an unfocused general idea, a thesis presents a specific direction for you as the writer to fulfill and for your reader to follow.

Writer-Centered Versus Reader-Centered. Unlike your statement of purpose, your thesis doesn't usually contain something like the words "I intend." Because a thesis is **reader-centered,** your intent is implied rather than stated directly, as it is the **writer-centered** statement of purpose. With a thesis, you no longer have to remind yourself of your purpose; your purpose should be clear. If your statement of purpose is "I want to tell my reader about the drawbacks of computers," and you've followed through on that intent in your focused freewriting, the words "I want" or "I intend" are unnecessary; your thesis — "Computers have made our lives much easier, but sometimes their drawbacks make day-to-day living harder for us" — proves that you've done what you set out to do.

Making Your Thesis Match Your Essay. Of course, like any other part of your writing, a thesis should be revised so that it better reflects your ideas. For example, the wording of the thesis that appeared in the draft version of the computer paper at the beginning of this chapter is somewhat different from — and more effective than — this draft version.

After you complete a draft of your paper, you may find that it reflects a view different from what you set out to present. There's nothing necessarily wrong with this; writing is often an act of discovery. Changing the focus in your paper, however, means adapting your thesis to reflect this new focus. If, for example, rather than dealing with the drawbacks, this draft dealt with some of the great advantages of computerization, the thesis must be changed to reflect this focus:

> Even when the drawbacks are considered, however, nobody can argue with the tremendous steps forward in industry and our personal lives because of computers.

Your thesis provides direction for your reader. Therefore, to improve your paper, you must make sure that your thesis truly reflects the paper that follows and supports it.

Identifying an Effective Thesis

A paper without an effective thesis will fail because it won't meet the needs of your reader. An effective paper deals with a limited subject; your thesis is the result of the filtering that occurs during freewriting, so the thesis helps make sure that you will stick to a manageable topic. To write effectively, you must therefore be able to judge whether your thesis is effective or not.

A thesis is a statement that provides a clear direction for your reader. It doesn't announce what you are planning to say; you do this with a statement of purpose, a sentence that sets the guidelines for you as the writer. Nor is it a simple statement of fact. A thesis is a statement for your reader that presents your subject and your attitude or opinion about that subject. A fact is a verifiable truth; by itself, therefore, it leaves no room for discussion, and for that reason, it isn't a thesis.

Sometimes students also make the mistake of relying on the title of the paper to direct their readers. A paper dealing with sightseeing in America, for example, might appropriately be entitled "From Sea to Shining Sea: Sightseeing in America." Unless it contains a sentence that specifically prepares the reader for the rest of the paper, however, the paper will not be effective. But if your introduction contains a clear thesis—A driving vacation across the United States will take about a month, but in that time you'll have the chance to see a number of beautiful spots, including three that should be classified as true wonders of the world"—your reader knows right from the start of your paper specifically what your paper is about.

A good title can help, so do spend some time developing the title. But spend that time once your paper is done—after you have clearly established that direction by preparing an effective thesis.

SUMMARY

Inspiration does occasionally play a part in your writing, but rather than waiting for inspiration, generate ideas through the preliminary steps of writing: **freewriting, statement of purpose, focused freewriting,** and **thesis.** An initial freewriting on a subject unlocks ideas. From this freewriting, isolate the main, connected ideas or some specific, promising aspect and then summarize this focus in a statement of purpose, usually containing the works "I intend" or "I want." From this statement of purpose, complete a focused freewriting beginning with a more specific starting point: the statement of purpose. From this focused freewriting, isolate the main focus and express it in one sentence: your thesis.

EXERCISES

1.   Take one of the freewritings you have already completed (See exercises 1 and 2 at the end of Chapter 1), and identify the main related ideas or the idea you feel has the most promise. If you don't feel comfortable with either of those freewritings, complete another ten-minute freewriting on one of the following topics, and then identify what you would like to focus on. Save all your work!

> movies
> prejudice
> college
> embarrassment
> music
> dishonesty

If you wish, team up with a classmate and work with each other throughout these exercises.

2.   Now write a statement of purpose that summarizes the main ideas you have identified or that specifies the one idea you want to focus on.

3.   Using your statement of purpose as a starting point, complete a ten-minute focused freewriting.

4.   Identify the main points in your focused freewriting, those you think are the most connected or that you think will be the easiest to develop later on.

5.   Summarize your main focus — your thesis — in a single sentence.

6.   Team up with some classmates and decide which of the following statements would be effective theses. Identify the effective theses and rewrite the ineffective ones:

> a.   Johnny Carson has maintained his popularity as a late-night television host for more than twenty years.
> b.   The physical contact in professional basketball today is out of control.
> c.   I intend to explain the difficulty of being a single parent in modern American society.
> d.   Physically capable people caught parking in handicapped parking spaces should have their names published in the newspaper.
> e.   Money is the Name of the Game: Fairness in Our Legal System
> f.   There are many serious problems in higher education.

    g.   The movie rating system contains four general categories: P, PG, R, and X.

    h.   My paper is going to deal with the abuses of the welfare system.

    i.   Drugs are a terrible problem.

    j.   One reason that alcoholism is more socially acceptable than other forms of drug addiction is that television commercials make drinking look glamorous.

Chapter 3

COMPOSING: FROM ONE STAGE TO THE NEXT

INTRODUCTION

Once you have developed a thesis that you feel you can work with, you are ready to move to the composing stage of writing. You have filtered your ideas on a subject, focused your topic, and then refiltered it until you have created a sentence expressing your main point: your **thesis.** At the same time, you have accumulated a more focused list of supporting ideas. Now you are ready to compose an initial draft of your paper.

CHANGING GEARS

In the last chapter, you followed the steps in the prewriting stage, during which you first try to accumulate plenty of information and eventually to center on specific points. The idea is to focus your ideas directly and, at the same time, to narrow the list of information to points that you may be able to use. The following figure gives you a sense of this process:

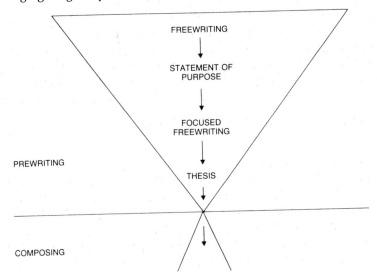

FREEWRITING

↓

STATEMENT OF
PURPOSE

↓

FOCUSED
FREEWRITING

↓

PREWRITING

THESIS

↓

COMPOSING

↓

As this figure shows, in prewriting you move from the general to the specific, from unfocused ideas to thesis. But once you develop a thesis, you begin to reverse that process somewhat. Rather than continuing to narrow your ideas, you begin to arrange the main ideas you have identified and to expand or illustrate — **amplify** — them with specific information.

SENTENCES AND PARAGRAPHS: YOUR BUILDING BLOCKS

One of the major differences between prewriting and composing is with form. In prewriting, you pour out your ideas with little conscious attention to structure, but in composing you deliberately arrange your ideas in sentences, combine these sentences into paragraphs, and then arrange the paragraphs so that they effectively support, illustrate, or explain your thesis.

Defining a Sentence

A sentence is the basic unit of writing. It contains a **subject** (a person, place, thing, or idea that acts or is acted on or focused on) and a **predicate** (a verb expressing action or state of being or otherwise helping to make a statement), **and** it expresses a complete thought.

Topic Sentences and Their Placement in a Paragraph

In an essay, sentences are arranged in paragraphs — groups of sentences, with each group covering a specific topic. Generally a paragraph has one idea expressed in a topic sentence supported, explained, or illustrated by the other sentences in the paragraph.

A topic sentence can appear anywhere in a paragraph. In an introductory paragraph, for instance, the topic sentence (which is also the thesis) is often the last sentence. In the paragraphs in the body of the paper, however, the topic sentence frequently appears first, as it did in the seventh paragraph of the computer paper you studied in the last chapter:

```
(TOPIC SENTENCE)  1 Even in the home, the fortress of the
family, the computer intrudes.  2 For years the television
has been the center of entertainment in many homes, and
with the introduction of affordable home computers and
entertainment centers, this is even more the
case.  3 Again, however, the threat is
depersonalization.  4 Competition and learning become
human versus machine.  5 In the one place where people
should be able to count on human comfort and communication,
a computer may create a subtle isolation.
```

The topic sentence says that computers disrupt even our home lives. Then sentences 2, 3, 4, and 5 illustrate this point by using the examples of home computers and home video games as devices that isolate people without their being aware of it.

Of course, a topic sentence can also appear at the end of a paragraph, as it does in this example:

```
1 We weren't moving.  2 Instead we seemed to hang in
midair.  3 Yet, when I finally had the courage to look over
the side, I could see that we had moved and were moving, both
forward and up.  4 The occasional scalding burst from the
heater was the only sound.  5 I couldn't believe that I
could be so far away from everyone and not care.  6 It was as
if I had never received that early phone call saying the
weather was picture-perfect for my long-awaited trip.  7 I
guess I had only dreamed that a hot-air balloon ride could
be so wonderful. (TOPIC SENTENCE)
```

In this paragraph, as in the previous example, the rest of the sentences support the topic sentence. But in this example, these supporting sentences lead up to the topic sentence—"I guess I had only dreamed that a hot-air balloon ride could be so wonderful"—by giving specific details that illustrate the unusual nature of the experience.

Choosing where to place the topic sentence is your decision as the writer. Basically, you make your decision according to how this sentence will best communicate your ideas to your reader; that's always your top priority.

Using Complete Sentences

Is your idea any better in complete sentences than in its freewriting state? Yes and no. Though it may seem a bit different down on paper, your idea probably means the same to you. In sentence form, however, that idea will be in a more complete, detailed state than it was in your freewriting.

Further, writing is more formal than speech, and it has more formal conventions; in an essay, your reader expects writing to be in complete sentences. To write a paper that not only captures the wealth of important information from the prewriting stage but also communicates those ideas to your reader, you must arrange your ideas in sentences and paragraphs.

THE STRUCTURE OF THE ESSAY

All writings should have a beginning, a middle, and an end—and **introduction**, a **body**, and a **conclusion**. The introduction is a paragraph (sometimes more than one paragraph) that features the thesis and provides a clear direction for your reader. The body is a series of paragraphs that explains, supports, or illustrates your thesis. And the conclusion is a paragraph (sometimes more than one) that usually restates or sums up the significance of what you have told your reader. Basically, then, all the parts of an effective paper are connected; all share common information.

TRACING THE COMMON THREAD

Imagine, for example, that you are writing about current alternatives for single people to meet. Your paper would begin with an introduction that features a thesis like this:

> Today, however, single people have a variety of ways to meet other eligible single people.

You would then provide paragraphs in the body of the paper that support this thesis; each paragraph could deal with one available alternative for dating — the common thread. The following figure illustrates this relationship:

THESIS

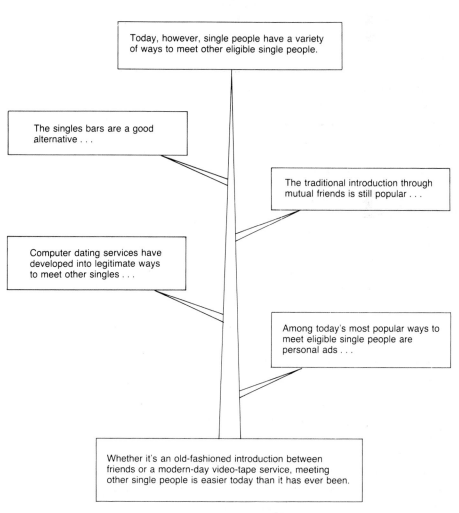

Today, however, single people have a variety of ways to meet other eligible single people.

The singles bars are a good alternative . . .

The traditional introduction through mutual friends is still popular . . .

Computer dating services have developed into legitimate ways to meet other singles . . .

Among today's most popular ways to meet eligible single people are personal ads . . .

Whether it's an old-fashioned introduction between friends or a modern-day video-tape service, meeting other single people is easier today than it has ever been.

The thesis states that there are many alternatives for singles to meet, and then the paragraphs of the body give examples of alternatives: meetings in singles bars; introductions between friends; computer dating services; and personal columns.

As the illustration shows, each example is tied to the common thread; each presents one way for singles to meet. And the conclusion restates the significance of the paper and thus reinforces the common thread.

When you write a paper, you must establish and support the common thread. In other words, you must express your thesis in clear, direct terms. Then you must use examples that reinforce some aspect of that thesis and sum all the material up with a concluding paragraph.

SYNTHESIS: THE COMPOSING STAGE ILLUSTRATED

Although a picture may be worth a thousand words, the figures in this chapter are obviously only simple representations of a far more complex process. Rather than relying on these visuals to explain composing, let's take a look at an example.

Moving to the Composing Stage

As the last chapter demonstrated, prewriting is the stage during which you narrow your ideas down to a thesis by isolating the main ideas from both your freewriting and your focused freewriting. When you put these ideas in sentence form, you have moved to the composing stage, during which you develop these ideas fully so that they support that thesis.

One way to amplify the ideas you've developed in prewriting is to use the *key questions:* who, what, where, when, how, and (often) why. The first few sentences of any good news story result from using the key questions, as this example shows:

```
     WHEN           WHERE            WHO
Last night at Camp David, the President signed the
                    WHAT                        HOW/WHY
controversial $7.6 billion defense plan against the advice
of his chief aides.
```

Providing facts — getting to the heart of any story — is a journalist's job, and the answers to the key questions provide the information needed.

Amplifying by Using the Key Questions

You can use these same questions to amplify or specify your main ideas. Look, for instance, at this sentence developed from ideas presented in the freewriting and focused freewriting shown in Chapter 2 (pp. 12–13, 14–16):

```
Computer errors seem to affect us all, even in our personal
lives.
```

Six incidents or ideas associated with computer error appear in these two prewritings: (1) the writer's fouled-up phone bill; (2) a space shuttle delay; (3) a credit-card mix-up; (4) a lost computer-class project; (5) ten pound's worth of incorrect phone bills; and (6) a social security mistake. Now the key questions can be used to make ideas more specific, as Table 3.1 on the next page shows. In their freewriting form, these ideas are general. But the key questions make it easy to specify the information.

Turning Memories into the Written Word

Look at the information listed about the woman with the enormous phone bill. The reason behind the mistake—a computer accidentally assigning hundreds of long-distance calls to her credit-card number—wasn't even given in the freewritings. Instead, only the result—the enormous bill—was presented. That's because you as the writer work in an individualized shorthand; you rely on memory to fill in the rest when it comes time to write. Using the key questions helps you to turn these memories into the written word.

Obviously every result has a cause, and using the key questions makes it easy to "fill in the blanks" that is to amplify any bit of information. When you freewrite, you won't record all the specific information about an idea. But when you take that freewriting and use the key questions, those blanks are far easier to fill in.

Deciding Which Answers to Use

Once you have used the key questions, will you use all the information you have listed? No; writing is a process of making statements and supporting, illustrating, and explaining them. Therefore, you should use the information that best supports your main ideas because those ideas will probably become the topic sentences of your paragraphs.

Narrowing Your Information. Consider the sentence that reflects the ideas from the chart:

```
Computer errors seem to affect us all, even in our personal
lives.
```

Of the ideas dealing with computer error originally isolated in the freewritings, five deal with computer errors in our personal lives. You can thus discard the material about the space shuttle because it deals with the effort of an agency rather than of an individual.

Choosing Your Strongest Examples. Of the remaining five examples, two are especially startling: (1) a man, alive and well, notified by Social Security that he is dead, must prove that he isn't; and (2) a woman receives a ten-pound, $1 million phone bill because a computer incorrectly assigned hundreds of long-distance calls to her credit-card number. These examples

Table 3.1 Key Questions

Who	What	When	Where	Why/How
Me	Phone bill	last month	–	I was over charged for calls I didn't make.
Space shuttle	Delays	2 weeks ago?	Florida	One of the computer systems shut the whole thing down one minute from launch.
Lady at mall	Credit-card sale rejected	Last week (Wed.)	Filene's	They said she had already exceeded her charge limit–she said she had never even used the card.
Michelle	Lost her whole computer program	Fall semester	Computer lab (Wang) at school	Surge of electricity wiped out her whole program after she worked three weeks!
Lady in newspaper story	10 pounds of incorrect phone bills	Tuesday Times	Philadelphia	Phone company charged long-distance calls incorrectly to her credit card.
Man in newspaper story	Social Security said he was dead	Friday USA Today	Boston	Computer said he was dead and discontinued his benefits. Social Security said he had to prove he was alive!

clearly point out how extensive the damage from computer errors can be, and so they are good choices to support the main idea.

Adding New Information.   If you reread the paragraph from the draft of the computer paper in Chapter 2, you will notice that these two examples are included. But you should also notice that another example—computer error at the grocery store—has been added. As you will see when we talk about drafting and revising in the next chapters, not all the information you use in your final draft comes from your free writing. As you prepare different drafts of your paper, you may add information that you discover after you have completed a draft, or you may delete some material that you decide is weak or ineffective.

SPECIAL PARAGRAPHS: INTRODUCTIONS AND CONCLUSIONS

Your thesis is the main idea of your paper. Although this idea appears in some way in each paragraph, it generally appears most directly and completely in two places: the **introduction** and the **conclusion.** For this reason, these two types of paragraphs deserve special attention.

Introductions

For some people, the best part of going to the movies is seeing the trailers for the coming attractions, brief scenes that are supposed to give an accurate idea of what a movie is about. Of course, moviemakers don't always play fair; sometimes the trailers don't match the movie. But most trailers do a good job, inspiring patrons to risk their money and see the movie by showing **what is to come.** Telling what is to come is basically your job with the introduction.

Providing Direction.   Take a look at this second paragraph from an essay by Andy Rooney, well-known television ("60 Minutes") and newspaper essayist:

> If it isn't our fault—the fault of the American people—whose fault is it? Who is it that makes so many bad television shows so popular? Why were *Life, Look,* and *The Saturday Evening Post* driven out of business in their original forms while our magazine stands are filled with the worst kind of junk? Why are so many good newspapers having a tough time, when the trash "newspapers" in the supermarkets are prospering? No one is forcing any of us to buy them.

Based on what you've read, what is this essay about? Television? Magazines? Newspapers? After all, those are the subjects covered in this paragraph.

Now look at the actual introduction and see the real focus:

> It is increasingly sickening to see someone make a bad product and run a good one out of business. It happens all the time, and we look around to see whose fault it is. I have a sneaking feeling we aren't looking hard enough. It's *our* fault, all of us. (Andrew A. Rooney "Quality" from *And More by Andy Rooney,* New York: Atheneum, 1982, p. 28)

Rooney was writing not only about the media but about the poor quality of many products; further he stated that the public must accept the responsibility for the poor quality of such things as paper towels, chain drugstores, automobiles, and homes. The introduction, therefore, presents his purpose: it provides a clear direction for the reader. Without this introductory paragraph, you would not necessarily see that Rooney planned to talk about the quality of many things, not just the quality of today's television shows or journalism.

Placing your Thesis Effectively. In order to make your introduction effective, you must place your thesis so that your introduction showcases it. Look, for example, at this paragraph from the Chapter 2 draft of the computer paper:

```
1 If there is one invention that has truly changed the
lives of the people of the twentieth century, it is the
computer.  2 With it, our fast-paced society has been
speeded up even more.  3 Business transactions occur in
the blink of an eye.  4 Libraries rest inside tiny bits of
silicon.  5 Personal amusement and entertainment center on
electronic games.  6 These scenes, once present only in
science fiction, are now commonplace, all because of the
development of computers.  7 They may be our
cure-all.  8 Ironically, they may also be our curse.
(THESIS)
```

The thesis is expressed in the final two sentences: computers have disadvantages that may complicate our lives. The thesis is often the last sentence in an introduction so that it acts as a lead-in to the body of the paper.

But this isn't always the case. Sometimes the thesis is at the very beginning of the paper. For example, if you were writing about the embarrassment you felt when you criticized a classmate, only to discover that you were talking to that person's cousin, you might start with your actual words to your classmate. Likewise, a paper about making a stained-glass "sun-catcher" might begin with a description of the finished piece and the ease with which it was made. Remember: how you structure your introduction depends on your purpose.

Because the computer paper presents an unusual, perhaps controversial, position about computerization, placing the thesis at the end of the introductory paragraph is effective; it catches the reader by surprise.

Even though the thesis appears at the end of the introduction, the reader still gains a clear direction from the paragraph. Sentences 3, 4, and 5 indicate the areas — business, school, and home — that the writer will focus on. And true to the promise put forth in the introduction, the computer paper does present the drawbacks of computerization as they appear in these areas.

As you compose and revise, experiment. Try setting up your introduction in different ways until you find the best way to preview the writing that follows.

Conclusions

Besides providing a clear direction for your reader through an introduction, you also usually need to sum up the writing you have completed. In other words, you need to tie up the different pieces of information you have explained, supported, or illustrated in the body of the paper.

Restating the Significance of Your Paper.   Look at the conclusion from the computer paper in Chapter 2:

> 1 Of course, suggesting that we return to simpler times
> is ridiculous. 2 The computer and the lifestyle it has
> spawned are here to stay. 3 And they should be. 4 Thanks
> to the advances in computerization, our lives are
> better. 5 What we should strive for, however, is an
> awareness of the problems, both actual and potential, that
> this growth brings on. 6 Whether at work, in our schools,
> or at home, computers should serve us. 7 They should be
> our cure-all, and they will be, if we remember who should
> run whom.

Sentences 5 and 7 — underlined here — restate the thesis: computerization has draw-backs that we should recognize. At the same time, though, the conclusion also restates what was originally expressed in the first and second paragraphs: the benefits of computerization make the risks worthwhile because once we are aware of the potential dangers, we can begin to combat them.

Summing up Versus Presenting New Information.   Notice, however, that no new information is added in the conclusion. New ideas generally belong in the body of the paper, where they can be explained, supported, or illustrated. If an idea has enough potential or connection with your subject to be mentioned, it deserves a more thorough presentation, and the place for this additional material is the body of your paper. For the most part, use your conclusion to restate rather than to present.

A concluding paragraph, then, is much like an introduction; both present the thesis of an essay. But a conclusion is likely to contain more information than an introduction. It captures the significance of the entire writing; that is, it is another, more concise version of what you have presented. With a conclusion, you have another chance to hammer home your point, to reinforce your purpose in writing.

SOME CAUTIONS

You will not always have an introduction that clearly directs your reader. Sometimes you will not have a conclusion that neatly summarizes what you have presented. And at other times you won't have either, at least not as they have been described here.

For example, a paper about teenage drinking might begin with a graphic description of an accident rather than with an explicitly stated thesis. And the conclusion of this same paper might contain a list of recommendations to help teenagers handle alcohol—information that has not been presented in the body of the paper. Still, this paper might be a brilliant piece of writing, even without a more conventional introduction and conclusion.

The guidelines you've read about introductions and conclusions in this chapter are just that: guidelines. They are not rules but suggestions. As you become a more experienced writer, you should experiment with these parts of your papers. For now, however, rely on these guidelines. By doing so, you will increase the chances of communicating your ideas to your reader. And because communicating these ideas is what you are trying to do when you write, it makes sense to do whatever you must to reach this goal.

SUMMARY

During the composing stage, you make the ideas you've generated during the prewriting stage more complete by transforming them into sentences and then arranging those sentences into paragraphs. Each paragraph must have a topic sentence that embodies the main idea of the paragraph and the other sentences that support, illustrate, or explain it.

Your draft should have an **introduction,** a **body,** and a **conclusion.** The introduction features your thesis and indicates the direction of the writing. The body is composed of paragraphs that explain, support, or illustrate that thesis. The conclusion restates the significance of what you've told the reader.

One way to develop the ideas originally generated during prewriting is to use the **key questions:** who, what, when, where, why, and how. By applying the key questions to your main ideas, you specify them and thus better your chances of communicating your ideas to your reader.

Introductions and conclusions deserve special attention because each presents the thesis more completely than the paragraphs in the body do. The introduction provides the direction of your paper; the conclusion restates the main idea of your paper.

EXERCISES

1.   In the exercises at the end of chapter 2, you worked your way through the prewriting stage of writing. You generated a freewriting, a statement of purpose, a focused freewriting, and a thesis.

Now take that thesis and identify the main ideas that you want to use to support your ideas from your freewriting and focused freewriting. (You may also have ideas that you did not develop during the prewriting stage but that still support your thesis. Of course, use these ideas, too!) Put these ideas in sentence form.

If you'd prefer to start with a new idea, choose one of the following alternatives and then work through the prewriting stage. After identifying the main ideas, put them in sentence form and then complete the rest of these exercises:

    a.   Take a walk through the campus bookstore, a local supermarket, or a department store, for example, and note how people react as they wait in line; maybe you could question some of them about their feelings.

    b.   Choose a normally crowded spot, for example, a stadium, a lounge area, or a fast-food restaurant. Visit it at a busy hour and then return at a quiet time when it is nearly deserted.

    c.   Walk by an elementary-school or preschool center during recess and watch the children at play.

    2.   Using the key questions, make a chart like the one in this chapter for your main points.

    3.   Decide what specific information best explains, supports, or illustrates your main ideas (topic sentences). After you make your decision, show your paper to your instructor. Or if you have been working with another student, ask your partner to take a look at your choices: Will your examples make your ideas clear for somebody else?

    4.   Turn the details you have chosen into complete sentences and combine them with your main ideas in paragraphs.

    5.   After you have completed all your supporting paragraphs, arrange them in an order that you think is effective. You'll see in the next few chapters that this order is probably temporary; as you complete additional drafts of the paper, you will very likely change the order that you initially set. For now, though, set up your ideas the way you think works best.

    6.   Reread the body of your paper and then reread your thesis. Compose an introduction of four or five sentences that includes your thesis and that also indicates what your paper presents.

    7.   Complete a conclusion that restates the thesis as well as the significance of your paper. Remember: you don't need to repeat ideas word-for-word in order to reinforce your message. Don't include any new information, however.

Chapter 4

DRAFTING: CONSIDERING —— YOUR READER ——

INTRODUCTION

"What we got here is failure to communicate."

In the movie *Cool Hand Luke*, Paul Newman, playing the small-time crook of the title, hears this statement from the warden of a small southern prison. In Luke's case, the not-so-subtle message suggests that he had better begin to listen to what the warden and the prison guards tell him or continue to face their unbridled punishment. Though only eight words long, the message is effective, in large part because the intimidation and physical abuse Luke has experienced in prison illustrate exactly what failure to communicate with those that run the prison means.

Failure to communicate is the problem that many beginning writers also face. In order to be effective, your writing must communicate your ideas to your reader. True, your reader, like Luke, must listen, but you must present your case so that there is no doubt about what is being expressed. Unlike the warden, however, you must rely on your words alone.

OBSTACLES TO COMMUNICATION

The problem with much writing is that it doesn't say what it was intended to say. For example, have you ever had a conversation like this:

"Are you gonna see Cheryl today?"

"Cheryl who?"

"You know, Cheryl—I don't remember her last name. You were just talking to her after class yesterday!"

"Which class? I don't know what you're talking about. I got five classes, y'know!"

"C'mon, how many classes are we in together, huh? Don't you even remember yesterday? Whatsamatter with you anyway?"

"I'm telling you—I didn't talk to any Cheryl yesterday!"

"C'mon—CHERylll"
"You mean SHAR on?"
"Oh."

The problem with this conversation is that the two individuals fail to communicate. Each individual believes that the other individual understands; therefore, neither speaker considers the possibility that his explanation might not be complete. Instead of communication, these two individuals have frustration.

Communication is even more difficult when it is written, because written communication lacks the benefits of the various physical cues, such as eye contact and gestures, usually present in spoken communication. Particularly in writing, when you fail to explain yourself fully, you will not communicate.

RECOGNIZING YOUR READER'S NEEDS

As curious as it may sound, having an idea of what you want to say may actually get in the way when you try to write. You know what you intend to say—at least, once you've done your initial prewriting. You feel comfortable with your chosen subject, and you feel confident that you have a fairly good way to express your ideas.

After all, you think, it is simple enough. And if you understand it, then anyone will be able to—at least, that's what you think.

Amplifying Content

Of course, expressing your ideas so that your audience can understand them isn't that simple. You don't think in grammatically correct sentences, so you must somehow organize your ideas in a form that conveys them in terms your reader can understand.

And simply putting your ideas in complete sentences is not enough. You must also explain them fully: you must amplify the **content** by providing significant information for your reader.

For example, the conversation about Cheryl and Sharon would have been successful immediately if the participants had simply amplified some of their ideas (shown here in italics):

"Are you gonna see Cheryl today?"
"Cheryl who?"
"You know, Cheryl—I don't remember her last name. She's the one with the *red hair*. You were talking to her after *Western Civ* yesterday."
"Cheryl? There's no Cheryl in Western Civ. You mean Sharon?"
"Oh."

With more significant information—in this case, *red hair* and *Western Civ*—there is communication.

Providing the Whole Picture

Sometimes knowing your subject well can also cause you to leave out material that you don't think is significant but that a newcomer needs in order to understand your point. Without this essential material, however, your reader hears only half the story. This selection from a children's reading primer illustrates the confusion that can result when essential material is left out of a story:

> Judy said, "Look mother. That is Puff. Look at Puff run. Look at that."
> Mother said, "Oh Judy. Puff is here with me."
> Judy said, "Puff! Puff! Get down. I want you to jump down. I want you to run and play. Jump down, Puff."
> "Oh Judy," said Mother. "Puff did jump down. Come here, Judy. Come here and play with Puff."
> (*Fun with Our Family,* Glenview: Scott, Foresman, 1963, 31–34)

As the text appears here, the story is confusing. But if you had seen the pictures that accompany the story, you would understand that the child Judy is watching another kitten on television. Puff is actually sitting with Judy's mother on a chair. Without the crucial information about the cat on the television, the reader can't fully understand the story.

Summarizing and Paraphrasing

Providing the crucial information is precisely your task when you summarize or paraphrase what someone else has written. A **summary** is a greatly reduced version of the original in your own words; a **paraphrase** is also a reduced version, but it more closely follows the wording of the original. In both a summary and a paraphrase, you focus on the essence of the original.

Look at this writing, for instance:

According to recent statistics, more than 50 percent of all marriages in the United States end in divorce. In plain terms, one out of every two of the married couples you know are destined to break up. This phenomenon has far-reaching implications, especially for the children of these broken families.

For one thing, many of these children experience trouble in school. Counselors have reported cases of elementary-school children who were formerly outgoing and affectionate with teachers and other children becoming distant and cold. At the high-school level, challenges to authority and physical aggressiveness are two of the signs often associated with youngsters whose parents have recently divorced.

Youngsters whose parents divorce also frequently suffer academically. Although some children actually improve their grades, either because they are no longer distracted by the unrest and fighting that had occurred before the

divorce or because they choose to become wholly involved in
schoolwork to avoid the pain they would feel otherwise,
<u>divorce usually spells at least a temporary drop in
classroom productivity.</u>

These underlined phrases represent the crucial information of these paragraphs. Once you've identified these points, you can use your own words and
provide a much shorter version — a summary:

Half of all marriages in the United States end in
divorce, a situation that greatly affects the children
involved. Some of them develop problems relating to their
friends and teachers. Others have trouble with academics,
at least temporarily.

Although the essential information is retained, the wording is different, and
the resulting paragraph is a great deal shorter than the original. A paraphrase is
a bit different, as this version shows:

More than 50 percent of all marriages in the United
States end in divorce, which has far-reaching implications
for the children of these broken families. Many of them
have trouble in school. Some elementary-school children
who have experienced divorce reportedly become distant and
cold; some high-school students react by challenging
authority and becoming physically aggressive. Although
some children actually improve their grades as a reaction
to the divorce, it usually spells at least a temporary drop
in classroom productivity.

Like the summary, this paraphrase presents the essential information from the
original. The paraphrase follows the original wording more closely, however.
 A summary is especially helpful when you want to condense in a few
sentences and in your own words some long or complex point that has no
particularly striking phrasing. A paraphrase is useful, however, when you
want to preserve as much of the original phrasing as possible, for the impact
that the original wording has, but still to reduce its length. As you go through
college, you will prepare both summaries and paraphrases, particularly when
you are writing academic papers. They are ways for you to focus on essential
information, and that's exactly the information your reader needs.

SHOWING RATHER THAN TELLING

Your job as the writer is to give your reader all those pictures — in words, of
course. You shouldn't assume that your audience will understand what you
mean; **show** as well as **tell** through specific examples.
 Consider this example. You have written a paper defining friendship. You
found the writing easy because you simply summed up the characteristics of

your best friend. You mentioned her compassion, explaining that it was she who comforted you after the death of your grandmother. You also mentioned her generosity, citing how just the previous week she had lent you twenty dollars to buy the book for your writing course.

Failing Your Reader

Both these examples are good because they draw a clear picture for your reader. But another characteristic you illustrated simply didn't come across to your reader:

```
    Jacqueline is always there when I need her. It doesn't
matter what it is; I know I can count on her. In the last
year, I've really counted on her a lot. Never once did she
refuse. One time I was really embarrassed because I
inconvenienced her. It didn't bother Jacqueline. As she
always says, ''No problem.''
```

You have locked out your reader by not supplying enough specific information. You as the writer understand what you mean because you know Jacqueline. Your reader, however, doesn't know Jacqueline. And even if your reader
did know her, the information your reader has would be different from your
information; you are each separate individuals and you each observe different
details and draw different conclusions.

Recognizing the Gaps

No doubt Jacqueline is a fine person — and the other paragraphs in the paper
help to prove this by giving specific examples. But in this paragraph, you have
used the expression "always there when I need her," a phrase that means
different things to different people. Do you mean that Jacqueline spends all her
time with you? Do you mean she is available twenty-four hours a day? Do you
mean if you call her, she'll help you immediately?

And what do you mean when you say you can count on her? Does she drive
you to school? Does she agree with you even when you might be wrong? Do
you trust her with something confidential?

What exactly did you do to inconvenience Jacqueline? Did you make her
break a date so that she could counsel you? Did you leave her stranded at the
mall? Did you forget to give her an important message from her boss?

These are the types of questions your reader will have. Your job is to
anticipate these questions and to provide suitable, specific details to answer
them.

Filling the Gaps

Here is the same paragraph, this time with the necessary details to communicate your ideas to your reader:

> Jacqueline is always available to talk to when I need
> her. Just last week, I called her at midnight after a fight
> with my boyfriend. I knew I'd woken her up, but she didn't
> complain. She just listened. She is there to support me for
> more than boyfriend problems, though. Last year when I
> thought I might not pass psychology, she tutored me for five
> weeks and helped me get a C for the course. The day I found
> out I passed, I was so excited that I drove right home from
> school, forgetting that she had ridden in with me. When I
> remembered, I was so embarrassed I broke down and cried. But
> being left at school didn't bother Jacqueline. When I
> called her on the phone to explain, she just laughed and
> then congratulated me. As she always says, ''No problem.''

This version obviously paints a clearer picture of a good friend, a person who will take midnight phone calls, help another person out with schoolwork, and hitch her own ride without a complaint when she is forgotten. Now the reader isn't locked out. Your details have turned the key for your reader.

ADDRESSING THE READER'S POINT OF VIEW

No doubt your job as a writer would be a good deal easier if you were only writing to yourself, as you do in a diary. But there would still be problems.

Recognizing Differences in Points of View

Think back to the last time you came upon school notes that you had not bothered to decipher right away. You probably puzzled over some part of the notes because you couldn't remember why you'd made them.

You can imagine, then, why writing to someone else can be so complicated. After all, you had written your own notes; you at least understood your own point of view (at the time when you took the notes, anyway). But no two people are alike; more important, no two people share the same **point of view** — accumulated knowledge and attitudes. If there are times when you can't remember why you made a notation for yourself, it is easy to understand why someone else can be so easily confused by things that you write.

You may get lucky and communicate your entire set of ideas in the first draft, but don't count on it. It's much more likely that at least a part of a very important point you want to make will be lost unless you take the time to address your reader's point of view.

Defining, Explaining, and Illustrating

The first-draft paragraph from the story of Jacqueline illustrates what happens when you fail to consider your reader's point of view. The ideas necessary for an effective paragraph are present, but they're not stated explicity.

Even though they are common expressions, phrases like "always there when I need her" and "I can count on her" mean something different for everybody. For this reason, the first-draft version of this paragraph isn't effective. But the redrafted version explains these terms by using examples that define the components of friendship, for instance, a willingness to accept late-night telephone calls and to volunteer study help. Now, instead of a fuzzy, incomplete picture, your reader has a sharp, detailed portrait of a special person.

Remember, writing means making statements and defining, explaining, and illustrating them. When you simply make the statements without amplifying them, you are doing only half the job.

Deciding How Much Information is Enough

Considering the reader's point of view means facing yet another problem: How much information is needed to provide a suitable background for your reader? Unfortunately there is no set answer. You will have to make a different decision each time you write. There are, however, a couple of guidelines that will help you provide the necessary, significant information for your reader each time.

Simplifying Complex Information.   Recheck your subject. If it is complex to any degree — if an average person, someone like a family member or a friend from school, might not understand it — provide some type of definition or explanation.

For example, you wouldn't expect the average person to know the difference between *nuclear fission* and *nuclear fusion*. And, although it is probably common knowledge that most cars have spark plugs, a mention of the *gap* of any spark plug deserves some explanation. Remember, the more obscure or technical the point, the more elaborate the definition should be.

Providing Sufficient Information.   Check to make sure you have provided enough information to illustrate what you are trying to say. In other words, make sure you have amplified. You are not supposed to provide a bare outline; instead, you want your reader to view your ideas fully.

For instance, the first-draft paragraph about Jacqueline tells the reader that Jacqueline was inconvenienced on one occasion. From this hint, the reader can't see to what degree she was inconvenienced. But the final draft shows that after Jacqueline spent five weeks tutoring you, you left her stranded at school. The redrafted version, then, doesn't hint; if presents the points directly, thus underscoring what a fine friend Jacqueline is.

Remember, how much information you present also depends on your choice of subject and your thesis as well as on the focus and organization you follow. In other words, **what** you have to say and **whom** you have to say it to will help you decide **how** to say it, that is, how much information to provide and how to arrange it.

Providing Transitions

Your reader needs to see the connections between your information and illustrations. Without this **transition,** your writing will not flow, and your paragraphs may look more like lists of sentences than units of ideas.

Transitions include single words and word groups, as well as synonyms and pronouns. Here are some common transitional devices and examples as they appear in the paragraphs from the paper on computers from Chapter 2:

TO ILLUSTRATE OR SPECIFY

accordingly, after all, as a result, because, consequently, for example, for instance, indeed, in fact, of course, particularly, specifically, therefore, thus

- *For example,* as labor-saving devices, computers are without parallel.
- *Of course,* suggesting that we return to simpler times is ridiculous.

TO ADD OR RESTATE

again, also, and, besides, finally, further, in addition, in conclusion, in other words, moreover, next, too, to sum up

- Our schools are *also* redirecting curriculums to keep pace with the rapid growth in computerization.
- *Again,* however, the threat is depersonalization.

TO SHOW TIME OR PLACE

after, as soon as, below, currently, earlier, here, immediately, lately, once, now, presently, since, soon, then, there, until, when, where

- These scenes, *once* present only in science fiction, are *now* commonplace, all because of the development of computers.
- Computer wands now read the pricing codes at the grocery store, but they present the consumer with the exact breakdown of the order *after* the total price is indicated, and detecting an error may mean unbagging the entire order.

TO COMPARE OR CONTRAST

although, and, yet, as, at the same time, but, despite, even though, however, in contrast, in spite of, likewise, nevertheless, on the other hand, regardless, still, though, yet

- *But* as math becomes our new language, will reading and writing become secondary skills?
- What we should strive for, *however,* is an awareness of the problems, both actual and potential, that this growth brings on.

Transitions are vital; without them, communication is shut down. Defining terms and providing information is not enough. Everything must be tied together through transitions.

As you write, focus in on your reader. Remember; your writing won't be successful unless it meets your reader's needs. If you make sure your writing meets the the guidelines, chances are that your reader will be able to understand what you are trying to say.

In that case, congratulations: "what we got here" *is* communication.

SUMMARY

Failure to communicate results when you don't take into account the difference between writer and reader. Unlike spoken communication, written communication lacks the benefit of physical cues to indicate whether or not your reader understands your point.

To overcome this problem, you must amplify with **specific, significant** information. Your reader's **point of view** is different from your own, and you overcome this barrier by **explaining, illustrating,** or **supporting** your ideas.

If your subject is complex to any degree, provide some type of **definition** or explanation for the potentially confusing points, and provide sufficient illustration for the points you make. Finally, make sure to tie all your ideas together with **transition.** These words, phrases, and ideas ensure that your writing will flow by showing how the various ideas are connected.

EXERCISES

1. Reread the draft you completed at the end of Chapter 3. Identify points that might be confusing to your audience. If you are working with a partner, exchange papers and identify the confusing parts of each paper.

2. Identify and make a list of the transitional elements in your draft. Then check for any points in your paper that need additional transitions. If you are working with a partner, check each other's papers and indicate the problem spots.

3. Sit down with a few friends or classmates and, as they talk, summarize what they say and make a list of some of the physical cues that they use as they speak. Then reconstruct some portion of the conversation based solely on the words used and ask the speakers to explain the differences between what your transcript says and what they meant. Bring your results to class to compare with your classmates' results.

4. Take one of the books from a current college class and write a summary of one of the chapters for two of the following readers. Remember, provide the type of detail that will meet the needs of that particular reader.

    a. An exchange student with limited abilities in English.
    b. An academic adviser, a professor of the subject that you are dealing with.
    c. An academic adviser, a professor of a subject different from the one you are dealing with.
    d. A high-school-aged brother or sister.
    e. A person at least seventy years old with no college background.
    f. A classmate who missed that particular class.

5. Read the following three paragraphs and make a list of the unfamiliar terms. Working with a partner or a group, define and amplify the various unfamiliar terms so that you and your partner(s) understand the passage:

    a. Various forms of soft accretions occur upon the teeth and are generally indicative of malhygiene. All areas of the mouth are subject to the deposition of soft accretions made up of varying amounts of mucin, bacteria, food debris, and epithelial calls. Soft organic accretions on the teeth include materia alba, mucinous and bacterial plaques, and the "pigmented pellicle." (Donald A. Kerr and Major M. Ash, *Oral Pathology*, 3rd ed., Philadelphia: Lea & Febiger, 1971, p. 200)

    b.   Lay a stretcher block in mortar inside each end pilaster and on both sides of the pilasters, centering the stretcher blocks on the point between the two pilaster blocks—use the inside chalk line as a guide. After the mortar has begun to set, use two pins stuck in the vertical points between the pilasters and the stretcher blocks to run a mason's line to establish a guideline for the rest of the stretchers to be laid between each pair of pilasters. Fill in the blocks for each section and point up the holes in the mortar left by the line pins. (*Outdoor Structures*, New York: Time-Life Books, 1978, p. 58)

    c.   Multiple embedded metaphor is elaborately illustrated in Chapter 7, with three entire case transcripts and the discussions of the work and the results. Chapter 8 looks at self-image thinking and other work that is directed at changing unconscious emotional conflict. Again, this is done in the context of the multiple embedded metaphor. Chapter 9 concludes with a discussion of terminating theory. (Stephen R. Lankton and Carol H. Lankton, *A Clinical Framework of Ericksonian Hypnotherapy*, New York: Brunner/Mazel, 1983, p. xviii–xix)

Chapter 5

REVISING: REFINING FOR YOUR READER

INTRODUCTION

Revising is a key stage in the writing process. In fact, it is probably the most important stage, at least if you want the paper you hand in to the instructor to be a complete reflection of what you think about a subject. The draft you have completed following the prewriting and composing stages is probably already good. But good isn't what you're after. What you're after is the best, most detailed, and most effective writing you can create, and you achieve that goal through revision.

A THREE-STEP PROCESS

Too often students think that revising is no more than reading over their papers before they hand them in to their instructors. Yes, checking your paper over for problems with **form** — misspellings, incorrect punctuation, faulty parallelism, and so on — is definitely important because these errors distract your reader and keep your message from being as clear and direct as you want it to be.

But this step, called *editing*, is actually the third step in the revising process. Before you get to that point, you must first **reassess** what you've written. Next you must **redraft**, based on what parts of your draft need more work. When you've completed this second step, then you **edit.**

Reassessing

Once you have a sound draft of your paper, the real work in writing begins. Now you have to take that completed draft and begin to **refine** it so that it communicates your ideas clearly in terms that somebody else — your reader — will understand.

You must not assume that your reader will automatically understand what you mean. Each of us is an individual, each with different pieces of information and different attitudes about those pieces of information. Therefore, if you want to communicate most effectively, you must identify your reader and anticipate the questions that the reader may have.

Remember; your reader has a perspective different from your own. Your job as the writer is to communicate your ideas by recognizing that different perspective so that you can meet your reader's needs. You do this by defining, illustrating, or explaining the points you are making.

For instance, if you use the term *writ*, define it as a formal legal document prohibiting some action; if you say an individual became belligerent during a confrontation with police, illustrate by showing how he swore and tried to punch one of the officers and then kicked out the window of the cruiser; if you say that a piece of abstract sculpture is complex, explain the complexity by showing how the various shapes symbolize emotions or experiences. In short, provide enough specific details to enable your reader to use your words to see through your eyes.

But who is your reader? And what information is detailed enough to allow your reader to see things as you see them? These are the questions you need to answer before you can be sure your writing will be effective.

Identifying Your Reader.   In your writing class, identifying your reader is easy, right? Your instructor will read your paper, so you have found your reader.

But wait a minute — do you have a partner in class who reads your papers? Or a friend who isn't in your writing class but whom you have coffee with after class and who also reads your papers? Or somebody at home who doesn't attend college (or at least is not in your class) but who reads your work? All these people have very different needs; if you write to meet the needs of only your instructor, you probably won't be meeting the needs of these other readers.

Underestimating Your Reader's Needs.   You've probably suffered through this situation before. You've written a paper for some class — let's say, "Introduction to Sociology" — and you've really worked hard at it. When your instructor originally assigned this paper, you chose a topic from your reading that you had found riveting: child abuse as it relates to the sociological setting. What you learned from your reading is that all forms of child abuse occur at all sociological levels, a finding that surprised you. As many people do, you figured that child abuse was the sole property of the lower classes.

After slaving away for many hours, you produced what you felt was a prize-winning paper on exactly that aspect of child abuse. Just to make sure it worked, however — just to make sure your ideas were clear — you discussed it with your friend or brother or sister and asked that person to read it over. "Looks good to me," your reader told you, and so, smiling at your anticipated success, you turned in the document, which featured paragraphs like this:

```
The kids who are abused are always the victims, though. A
lot of people don't really realize that they come from all
```

over, too. When I started reading about it, I was surprised.
No matter where you're thinking about, it happens. It's
important that the public recognize this, too, so that we
can do more to support the victims.

But at least we have started being more sensitive to the
needs of the victims. For example, they have developed a
number of techniques designed to make it easier for the
victims to talk about what happened to them. The victims
are often unable, afraid, or ashamed to talk about what has
happened. These new techniques have been tested and even
used in the courtroom. We need to do more of this.

When you received the paper back a few weeks later, instead of the good grade you expected, you received a disappointing mark accompanied by these comments from your instructor: "I can see you put a great deal of effort into this paper, but I'm afraid I frequently can't see what point you are trying to make. *Child abuse cuts across all sociological levels* — is this what you're trying to say? I can't quite tell, in part because you don't specify what you mean."

It doesn't add up, you thought. My first reader thought it was great, but my instructor thinks it stinks. What went wrong?

Focusing on the Average Reader.   The simple answer, at least according to your sociology instructor, is that you didn't provide enough specific information. Maybe your first reader understood what you meant because she had discussed the matter with you or had read the same articles and chapters; maybe she even asked you questions. As a result, she had a built-in background to help her understand your thesis and to evaluate your paper. Or maybe she was being nice; maybe she was trying to say what she felt you wanted to hear.

But the situation is different with your instructor. The broad knowledge your instructor possesses doesn't provide the ability to see inside your head and understand your ideas as you understand them. Further, in an academic paper, your instructor is essentially testing your mastery of the subject; if your paper doesn't communicate your ideas so that it indicates that mastery, your instructor will mark your paper accordingly. And your instructor isn't going to be nice; on this paper, for example, your instructor's comments indicate compassion, but the grade indicates an objective assessment.

With all the differences between writer and reader, it's simply not practical to assume that your reader will understand what you write because you understand it. Instead, set your expectations of what your reader will know a bit lower. Write for the **average reader,** an individual who, like a good "Trivial Pursuit" player, knows a little — general information — about many subjects.

Therefore, if you're discussing the effect of cable television on traditional television programming, assume that your reader at least knows that cable television is alternative programming available in some areas at the viewer's expense. But don't assume that the reader will have seen "The Karate Kid" on cable or even will automatically know that "ShowTime" (or "Preview" or whatever name this type of feature may go by in your area) is a cable television feature that brings first- or second-run movies into your home. Unless you know for sure that your reader has expert information equal to your own and wants you to deal with a subject in expert terms (as would be the case if your Asian history instructor asked you to prepare a research paper on the Vietnamese "boat people," from which you will lecture to your classmates, who have also been doing research on the subject), figure that the reader knows as much as you did *before* you gained that expert information.

Meeting Your Reader's Needs

As an example, imagine that your hobby is running. You are a former high-school middle-distance runner. Even though you are not competing collegiately, you've kept up your interest in running; as a result, you subscribe to a few running magazines and follow new developments in the sport.

You were all set, then, when your writing teacher offered you the option of discussing some controversy in sports. After a little thought, you decided you would deal with a subject you had recently read about: blood doping, a questionable technique allegedly used by some world-class athletes to increase their endurance.

Blood doping entails withdrawing a pint of the athlete's blood some weeks before a race and then reinjecting the blood just before to the event. The idea behind it, according to some experts, is to increase the oxygen-carrying capacity of the blood, thus giving the athlete more endurance. Some European athletes had been accused of blood doping in the 1970s; and according to some reports, member's of the U.S. Olympic bicycling team had used the technique in the 1984 Olympics. You decide, therefore, to focus on blood doping and its relationship to amateur athletics.

Identifying What Information Your Reader Needs. Now you have to focus in on the needs of your reader: How much does your instructor know about running itself, never mind blood doping? True, one of the reasons you chose the subject in the first place is that you know your instructor also has an interest in running because you've heard him speak about it in class. You just don't know how extensive his interest or knowledge is.

From what you have gathered, he's more of a recreational jogger than a competitive runner, so as a result you decide that you and your reader don't share a common level of knowledge on running. For example, you've never heard your instructor talk "runner's talk" — chatter about such insider's terms as *intervals* or *splits* or *carbohydrate loading,* which serious runners use among themselves — so you've guessed his interest is purely recreational.

Playing it Safe. Therefore, if your instructor doesn't seem familiar with these terms, it's not likely that he'll know much about out-of-the-ordinary practices such as blood doping. Based on the information you have gathered through observation, you decide to explain the situation much as you would for a nonrunner. With this information about your reader in mind, you prepare this introductory paragraph:

> The Olympic Games are supposed to be a showcase for the
> world's best amateur athletes. But today working to the
> very best of their own natural abilities is no longer enough
> for some of these athletes and their coaches. Winning is
> what's now most important, and in order to win, many top
> amateurs and their coaches have looked beyond the natural
> range of the human body. Some have turned to drugs like
> steroids, which unnaturally increase the body's ability to
> build muscle tissue. Drugs like steroids are illegal, and
> Olympic officials have set up extensive drug-testing
> programs to combat their use. But Olympic officials don't
> really have a test to check on whether athletes have been
> blood doping, withdrawing some of their own blood and then
> reinjecting it to give them an added boost. Unlike using
> steroids, blood doping may not yet be illegal, but it still
> seems like cheating to me.

The rest of the paper goes on to explain the point that amateur athletes have lost perspective when it comes to the ethics of competition, by citing some specific examples, including stories of one Finnish runner who earned three medals in middle- and long-distance events in five days in an earlier Olympics and the members of the 1984 U.S. bicycling team who claim to have performed better than they would have without the injection of their own blood.

Your paper also explains the actual procedure and points out that although it isn't technically illegal—your own blood is hardly an illegal drug—it is regarded by many athletes and coaches as unethical. Your paper also indicates that some noted exercise specialists feel that the boost is merely psychological; no concrete evidence shows that blood doping positively helps.

In terms of your reader, you've played it safe. You haven't spoken down to the reader, for example, explaining what the Olympic Games are or what a long-distance event is or that running is a sport recognized worldwide. Nor have you spoken above your reader, by, for instance, putting forth all the expert information about running as a sport that you have acquired through years of competition and research. Instead, you've simply explained the concept of blood doping and its implications for amateur athletics so that even someone unfamiliar with running as a sport will be able to understand it.

Assessing Your Effectiveness.   Imagine, then, that it is now a week or so later and you have received your paper back with these comments: "Good job—you've explained the complex technique of blood doping very well. As a former half-miler on the U.S. Olympic team—1964—I had heard about the practice, but your paper presented a good update on how widespread a practice it is today. If you get the chance, look at this month's *Runner's Digest.* There's a new study out about some newly discovered dangers of both blood doping and steroid use."

Have you failed? Should you be embarrassed because you gave your instructor information that he obviously already knew? No. The fact that he knew already did not take away from the effectiveness of the paper. Instead, you explained a complex and, if not illegal, unethical practice that some amateur athletes use to give themselves an unfair edge over their opponents to someone who you thought had a general knowledge of the subject. Your reader's knowing more than you thought does not make your paper less effective.

Practice meeting the needs of different readers. How would you explain affirmative action to a ten-year-old student? How would you explain heavy metal music to someone your grandmother's age? How would you explain the binary system that computer function is based on to a classmate with no computer background? What information will these different audiences need to know? Being able to recognize different audiences and then being able to write for different audiences will make you better able to communicate what you have to say.

Providing the Right Kinds of Information

Once you have focused in on your reader, you need to elaborate the information you have already used in your draft in relation to your reader. Is the information general (broad or unfocused) or specific (detailed and to the point)?

Using a Classification Tree. One way to find out how specific an idea or term is is to plot it in a **classification tree,** an informal list that allows you to see how specific a term is in relation to items of the same class. For example, one reason the paper on child abuse discussed earlier wasn't successful is that the reader couldn't see the point being made about child abuse. One reason is that what child abuse means to you as the writer was not clear; it must be made more specific.

A classification tree can help you judge how specific the terms you use are. Here's how child abuse might fit in a quick classification tree:

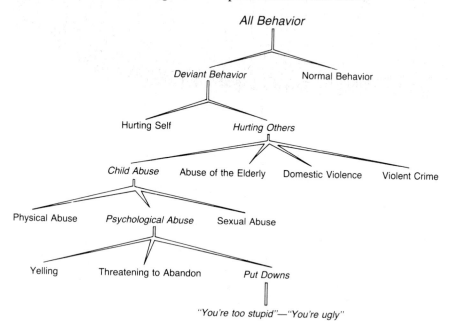

As you can see, the tree "grows" downward. The root — "All Behavior," in this case — is at the top. As the tree grows, the terms become increasingly specific.

Although this tree could grow in any number of directions — you could follow any term on this tree (or any tree) to its most specific state — the italics here show it following one idea: from the general "All Behavior" to the more specific "Deviant Behavior" to the even more specific "Child Abuse" and eventually to the most specific, an actual example of psychological abuse: "You're too stupid — ugly," used to hurt a child.

Surely saying something as insulting and hurtful as this is child abuse; and how much better a picture does it show the reader than just the fairly general term *child abuse* or even *psychological abuse,* a term more specific than *child abuse* but still less specific than *putdowns,* terms that are still more general than the quotes themselves.

Once you have completed a good draft, take a look at the terms you've included. Try to place these terms on a classification tree, and see if you can make them even one level more specific. Remember; the more specific the information, the more likely it is that your reader will understand it.

Using Appropriate Diction. Another point to consider once you have focused in on your reader is **diction,** that is, your choice and use of words. Of course, in the college classroom, you can be fairly sure that your instructor will be able to handle a higher level of vocabulary (at least, we instructors like to think we can handle it), but rather than flipping through a thesaurus in order to impress your instructor, concentrate on meeting the needs of the general reader.

In the famous writing text *The Elements of Style,* the late Professor William Strunk offered this bit of advice about selecting the proper word:

> Avoid the elaborate, the pretentious, the coy, and the cute. Do not be tempted by a twenty-dollar word when there is a ten-center handy, ready and able. . . . If you admire fancy words, if every sky is *beauteous,* every blonde *curvaceous,* if you are tickled by *discombobulate,* you will have a bad time with [this suggestion]. (3rd ed. New York: Macmillan, 1979, pp. 76–77)

Here's a good way to establish an appropriate level of diction. Think for a moment of a person you know — but not well. You like, maybe even admire, this individual and would like to express yourself to this person in such a manner that you create a good impression. But because you don't know this person well, you'll want to be careful to avoid words and terms that this person may not understand; you don't want to make this listener uneasy or embarrassed. Even if you're fairly certain that your reader would understand the words and terms, you wouldn't want to appear to be showing off — to sound pompous or pretentious.

Adjusting Your Language. In a case such as this, what type of words would you use? The words appropriate for this situation would also be appropriate for college-level writing for a number of reasons:

1. It wouldn't be slang—"insider's" talk.
SLANG: That nerd must have felt wicked baked.
TRANSLATION: That fool must have felt really embarrassed.
2. It wouldn't be jargon—"specialist's" talk.
JARGON: In-stack electrostatic precipitators ionize the escaping gas, thus trapping particulates.
TRANSLATION: Special devices electronically attract tiny particles of material escaping in the gas and keep them from leaving the exhaust stack and entering the atmosphere.
3. It wouldn't be bombast—"windbag's" talk.
BOMBAST: A bevy of health-care specialists executed acts of wellness-giving upon the unwitting subject of fate.
TRANSLATION: The emergency room staff worked quickly on the unconscious accident victim.

Remember, of course, that these guidelines are not absolute rules but suggestions. If you and your readers (including your instructor) think that using any of these types of language in combination will help you to write a more effective paper, do so. Anything that enables you to communicate your ideas more clearly is definitely a good idea.

Redrafting

Once you have done your reassessing, it's time to do some **redrafting,** going back through the various parts of the writing process to create new material to replace or improve any weak areas. Up to this point, you may have got the sense that writing is a step-by-step process with no deviation from the path.

In fact, this isn't the case at all: writing is a **recursive** act. Basically this means that instead of following a lockstep process, you may begin, then create, then check, then create some more, then check again, and so on. Rather than a straight line, your actions may look more like a series of gentle loops that bring you back, when necessary, to prewriting, then up to revising, then back to composing, and so on.

Going Back Through the Stages.   Look at these paragraphs from that unsuccessful paper on child abuse:

> The kids who are abused are always the victims, though. A
> lot of people don't really realize that they come from all
> over, too. When I started reading about it, I was surprised.
> No matter where you're thinking about, it happens. It's
> important that the public recognize this, too, so that we
> can do more to support the victims.
>   But at least we have started being more sensitive to the
> needs of the victims. For example, they have developed a
> number of techniques designed to make it easier for the
> victims to talk about what happened to them. The victims
> are often unable, afraid, or ashamed to talk about what has

happened. These new techniques have been tested and even used in the courtroom. We need to do more of this.

These paragraphs are not effective because they are too general. But a quick trip back to the prewriting stage can produce the following bits of specific information:

> *Chapter 6 says that there are thousands of documented child abuse cases from middle-class and rich families too—last week that trial for that old man who molested those two girls put the kids on tv in another part of the courthouse so they wouldn't be embarrassed or scared—the* Time *article about that massive California sexual abuse case with the child care workers she talked about in class, they used special dolls with all the parts so the little kids could show how they were molested.*

This new information specifically notes that child abuse is a problem for society at large rather than just for one segment. It also provides the specific example of the use of videotaped testimony by victims of child abuse to illustrate the point that society is now less likely to ignore a child's complaint about sexual abuse. And the information about the anatomically correct dolls used by some therapists to enable even young children to explain in what way they were molested backs up the idea that we, as a society, are making a conscious effort to punish wrongdoers but, more important, to protect the victims and help them begin to adjust to more normal lives. With a few changes in phrasing, the information italicized here can be added to the original paragraphs to make them more effective:

> The kids who are abused are always the victims, though. A lot of people don't really realize that they come from all levels of society, too. Chapter 6 of Deep in the Shadows (pp. 65-66) explained that there are thousands of documented child-abuse cases from middle- and upper-class homes. It's important the the public recognize this, too, so that we can do more to support the victims.
>
> But at least we have started being more sensitive to the needs of the victims. For example, an article in the March 31, 1987, issue of Time (pp. 38-39) explained how psychologists have developed dolls with sexual parts. This way, even if they don't know the words to explain it, little children can show what a molestor has done to them.
>
> Also, as we talked about in class last week, in the trial going on right now in this city of a man accused of sexually assaulting two young girls, law-enforcement officials have used for the first time a closed-circuit television setup so that the two girls can testify without being afraid or ashamed to talk about what has happened.

These paragraphs incorporate the new information, and they also tell the reader where you found the information. Even though these three paragraphs contain the same basic information as the two earlier paragraphs, these new paragraphs are clearly better because they communicate your ideas clearly to your reader.

Reworking Your Introduction and Conclusion. Incidentally, remember that once you've completed your redrafting, you may have to rewrite part (or all) of your introduction and conclusion. These parts of your paper are crucial in making your paper effective. When you adjust some of the material in the body of your paper, you have a slightly new story to introduce and conclude. Make a special effort, therefore, to alter both these parts of your paper so that they still fit the body of your paper glove-tight.

Even if a paper is already acceptable, it can be improved through redrafting. It's more work, yes, but if it helps you to communicate your ideas more clearly and directly, the extra work makes sense.

Editing

Once you've gone through the redrafting stage and identified which information you should include, you're ready to turn that good draft into an even better paper. You face two main steps in editing: tightening and proofreading. **Tightening** means going through your paper word for word to eliminate any unnecessary words, ideas, or phrases. It also means making sure that you've expressed your sentences in the most effective way.

Once you've done this tightening, you **proofread** to find and correct errors in form: spelling, grammar, punctuation, and so on. Actually you proofread your work all the way through the writing process; therefore, it is among the first steps in the entire writing process. More important, though, it is always the last step.

Tightening. Sharpen your pencil; that's the best way to prepare to tighten your paper (unless you're working on a word processor, in which case you'll want to warm up the finger you use on the delete key). Tightening is changing your writing so that you take those great ideas you've discovered and developed and express them in the most efficient, effective way.

Part of tightening has to do with **style,** probably the hardest element of writing to define or explain. Style is how you say what you have to say, and it is as individual as people are. However, you can improve your individual style by eliminating whatever will keep your reader from seeing your ideas clearly.

Using the Active Voice. As you revise, write in the **active voice** — the subject as the doer of the action rather than being acted on. Look at these two sentences, both containing the same information:

ACTIVE VOICE: Dr. Howard performed the heart transplant.
PASSIVE VOICE: The heart transplant was performed by Dr. Howard.

As you can see, the active voice is shorter (five words compared to seven in the passive voice), and the active voice is more direct. As often as possible, use action verbs and use the active voice to paint a clearer picture for your reader. That's your job.

Eliminating Deadwood.   Another way to tighten your writing is to eliminate any **deadwood** — words, phrases or ideas that won't be missed from your paper.

If you read your draft quickly, you probably won't see any deadwood — but it's probably there. Take a look, for example, at this paragraph from a paper on CPR (cardiopulmonary resuscitation):

> Finding the sternum is a crucial step when you are trying to perform the lifesaving act of giving CPR. The sternum is essentially between the breasts, and you find it by using the fingers on your hand to trace the sternum. Once you find the sternum, you need to find its tip, which is at its end, which you can find just above where the ribcage starts. Once you've found the tip, use two fingers on your hand to help you measure back from the tip. This is the point at which you will begin the process that will help the unfortunate individual, man and woman or child, who needs your help.

In terms of content, this paragraph isn't bad, but it is filled with deadwood. A sharp pencil allows you to make these kinds of changes:

> Finding the sternum is a crucial ~~step~~ when you ~~are trying~~
>
> to perform ~~the lifesaving act of giving~~ CPR. The sternum is
>
> ~~essentially~~ between the breasts, *Use your* ~~and you find it by using~~
>
> ~~the~~ fingers ~~on your hand~~ to trace *it until you* ~~the sternum. Once you find~~
>
> ~~the sternum, you need to~~ find its tip, ~~which is at its end,~~
>
> *the start of the ribcage* ~~which you can find~~ just above ~~where the ribcage starts.~~
>
> ~~Once you've found the tip, use two fingers on your hand to~~
>
> ~~help you~~ Measure back from ~~the~~ tip, *this using the width of your*
>
> *index and middle fingers together* ~~This is the point at~~
>
> ~~which~~ You will begin *CPR at this point* ~~the process that will help the~~
>
> ~~unfortunate individual, man and woman or child, who needs~~
>
> ~~your help.~~

Shift a few words around, change some others, and that paragraph filled with deadwood ends up looking like this:

> Finding the sternum is crucial when you perform CPR. The sternum is between the breasts. Use your fingers to trace it until you find its tip, just above the start of the rib cage. Measure back from this tip, using the width of your index and middle fingers together. You will begin CPR at this point.

As you can see, by cutting out unnecessary words and phrases — cutting back from 112 words to 56 — you've preserved the original content of the paragraph, but you've made the entire paragraph much clearer and thus more effective. With a subject like CPR, you want to make sure that your paragraphs are as efficient as possible; it might literally be a matter of life or death, so the more efficient your writing is, the more likely your reader will be able to carry out your instructions.

Even if you're not explaining such an important process, however, you still want to make your ideas as clear and understandable as possible for your reader. That's your purpose, the reason you have written in the first place. Tightening is therefore a crucial step in fulfilling your purpose.

Proofreading.   We should never judge a book by its cover, we're told, and yet, particularly when it has to do with writing, human nature says people do judge the message by its form. "But that's not fair," you protest, and you're right. Unfortunately, life isn't always fair. Your work will often be judged by what people see first — and that's its form. Once you have tightened your paper, you are ready for the last step in the writing process, **proofreading,** that is, checking for errors in form.

If you question whether proofreading is all that necessary, you can provide the answer yourself. When you read a book, magazine, or a newspaper, aren't you always a little surprised when you see a mistake that has slipped by the writers and editors? Well, that moment of surprise takes you away from the subject matter, at least for a moment. If you come across a few more errors in the same article, you will probably end up concentrating more on the mistakes than on the content of the article or chapter.

Finding and Correcting Common Errors.   Your reader will be at least as adept as you are at finding errors, maybe even better. Therefore ask yourself the following questions and change your paper if necessary based on the answers:

1.   Are all your ideas expressed in complete sentences?

In order for your ideas to be wholly effective, they must appear in complete sentence form. Although some professional writers occasionally disregard this standard, as a beginning writer you should adhere to it.

Three main errors plague writers as they try to put their ideas in complete sentence form: fragments, comma splices, and run-on sentences.

Fragments are incomplete sentences. The simplest way to correct a sentence fragment is to complete the thought:

FRAGMENT: Opening day for the Red Sox scheduled for early April.
CORRECTED: Opening day for the Red Sox *is* scheduled for early April.
By adding the verb *is,* you turn the fragment into a sentence.

Sometimes you can correct a fragment by adding it to the sentence coming before or after it:

FRAGMENT: After the state police had cleared away all the debris from the accident.

CORRECTED: I could finally see the oil slick that made me skid after the state police cleared away the debris from the accident.

or

CORRECTED: After the state police cleared away the debris, traffic began to flow more regularly.

A **comma splice** occurs when you use a comma to connect two sentences. Commas can't connect; commas separate. You correct a comma splice by adding a conjunction after the comma or by changing the comma to either a semicolon or a period:

COMMA SPLICE: Reruns of "I Love Lucy" and "Leave It to Beaver," two television shows from the '50s and '60s, are still being shown throughout the country, both shows seem to be just as popular today as they were originally.

CORRECTED: Reruns of "I Love Lucy" and "Leave It to Beaver," two television shows from the '50s and '60s, are still being shown throughout the country, and both shows seem to be just as popular today as they were originally.

or

CORRECTED: Reruns of "I Love Lucy" and "Leave It to Beaver," two television shows from the '50s and '60s, are still being shown throughout the country; both shows seem to be just as popular today as they were originally.

or

CORRECTED: Reruns of "I Love Lucy" and "Leave It to Beaver," two television shows from the '50s and '60s, are still being shown throughout the country. Both shows seem to be just as popular today as they were originally.

A **run-on sentence** is similar to a comma splice in that it, too, is the incorrect combination of two sentences. In a run-on sentence, however, no attempt is made to connect the two sentences; one sentence just runs into the next. You correct a run-on sentence by adding a comma and a conjunction or by placing a semicolon between the sentences to connect them or a period between them to make two separate sentences.

RUN-ON SENTENCE: Racquetball and handball are both difficult games you have to have strength, speed, and agility to succeed.

CORRECTED: Racquetball and handball are both difficult games, and you have to have strength, speed, and agility to succeed.

or

CORRECTED: Racquetball and handball are both difficult games; you have to have strength, speed, and agility to succeed.

or

CORRECTED: Racquetball and handball are both difficult games. You have to have strength, speed, and agility to succeed.

2.   Is anything you've written ambiguous or awkward?

Have you ever made an innocent enough statement, only to end up blushing at the implications that you never intended but that your listener's discovered? It happens in writing, too, and not just to amateur writers, either. In fact, because they have to work with words every day, professional writers are probably sometimes more liable to mental lapses that lead to awkward or ambiguous or downright silly writing.

One of the best collections of blunders in writing is *Squad Helps Dog Bite Victim,* a collection of mistakes from the nation's press (Garden City, N.Y.: Dolphin Books, Doubleday & Company, 1980). Many of the mistakes are headlines that accidentally say more than the writer intended. The title of the book, for example, is a headline that conjures up a picture of people helping a dog bite its victim; the headline should read "Squad Helps Dog-Bite Victim." Another seems like a "fashion" story from the world of sports: "Complaints About NBA Referees Growing Ugly" (How do their wives and children feel about this new look?).

The mistakes are not limited to headlines, either. These passages, for instance, come from news articles themselves: "After years of being lost under a pile of dust, Walter P. Stanley III . . . found all the old records of the Bangor Lions Club at the Bangor House" (Is Walter's new nickname "Dusty"?); "By then, she will have shed 80 of the 240 pounds she weighed in with when she entered Peter Bent Brigham hospital obesity program. A third of her left behind!" (Is it harder for her to sit now?).

As you might imagine, the people who wrote these passages or phrases were certain that their words conveyed only the idea they intended their readers to receive. You are probably just as certain when you write, so carefully reread what you've written: Is there any word, phrase, idea, or sentence that may have more than the meaning you intended?

If you're not sure yourself, ask somebody else to read over your paper. If you're comparing different brands of jeans, for instance, you wouldn't want to use *overall* as a transitional element because jeans are sometimes called *overalls.* Although you might not notice the potential unintentional humor, another reader might.

Finding misplaced modifiers is often hard. But as you saw in the examples dealing with awkward or ambiguous phrasing, putting your modifiers in the wrong places can distort your message and distract your reader. Therefore, difficult or not, finding misplaced modifiers is crucial.

3.   Is the spelling correct throughout?

Spelling counts! Your readers are aware of spelling only when it's incorrect. Therefore a dictionary is a crucial part of your writing equipment.

But if you aren't a good speller, a dictionary isn't always helpful. If you don't know how to spell the word, how do you look it up? The simple answer to this question is to sound the word out and search in the dictionary a bit. But in English, words aren't always spelled the way the sound: *chronological, sophomore, psychology,* and hundreds more like them have silent letters. And that's just the beginning. Is it *ie* or *ei;* Do you change the *y* to *i* or keep it the same? What do you do with a prefix? A suffix? The list goes on and on.

There are no easy answers. If you are a poor speller, work on your spelling. Pick up a spelling guide or the spelling section in a handbook and start memorizing. Keep a "backward" dictionary; that is, as you find you've misspelled a word, enter the corrected version in alphabetical order in a notebook. By keeping such a list, you will always have the solution to your previous spelling mistakes with you. And if you make additional errors, enter those words, too. With a little work, you can master the spelling of all these words and, as a result, cut down or even eliminate those glaring errors that readers notice right away.

Besides these ordinary spelling problems, you face another, more serious type of spelling error, one that can cause a sentence error. *Your* and *you're,* for instance, may look almost the same, but the second one contains a verb. If you use the first one when you mean the second one, you will have written a fragment. Here are few more of these **homonyms** to watch out for:

its — it's   whose — who's
where – were   there, their, they're

Once you have completed and checked your final draft, check the spelling one more time by reading your paper backward — from the last word to the first. When you check your paper from the beginning to the end, you may be distracted by the content of what you've written. But when you read your paper from last word to the first, you'll be better able to concentrate on the words themselves rather than on the content — your ideas.

4.   Have you been consistent in your use of verb tense throughout?

Tense means time: past, present, or future. If you begin writing in one tense, stay with that tense at least in the same sentence, unless you have a valid reason for switching. Remember; any change distracts your reader, so if you're considering changing tenses, ask yourself whether the change is worth the chance that you might confuse your reader:

MIXED TENSE: After our first meeting, Jerry and I *became* close friends. Day after day, he *says* that we *weren't* being smart about our relationship. I *hated* the way we *fought;* he *does,* too.

CORRECTED: After our first meeting, Jerry and I *became* close friends. Day after day, he *said* that we *weren't* being smart about our relationship. I *hated* the way we *fought;* he *did,* too.

5. Are the appropriate words, phrases, clauses, and ideas parallel?

Parallelism means presenting similar ideas, words, phrases, and clauses in a balanced fashion. You correct faulty parallelism by putting connected items in a similar form:

> FAULTY PARALLELISM: Even though she is in a wheelchair, Marsha still *dresses* herself, she *drives* her car, *handles* a high-pressure position, and she *volunteers* at the hospital.
>
> CORRECTED: Even though she is in a wheelchair, Marsha still *dresses* herself, *drives* her car, *handles* a high-pressure position, and *volunteers* at the hospital.
>
> FAULTY PARALLELISM: The tornado dropped debris *in* the Quinesit River, *across* Highway 14A, and there were pieces found in communities eighty-five miles away.
>
> CORRECTED: The tornado dropped debris *in* the Quinesit River, *across* Highway 14A, and *throughout* communities eighty-five miles away.

6. Do all subjects and verbs, as well as the pronouns and antecedents, agree?

You need a singular form of a verb for a singular subject, a plural form of a verb for a plural subject; that sums up subject–verb agreement. You correct faulty subject–verb agreement by identifying the actual subject and adjusting either the subject or the verb:

> FAULTY SUBJECT/VERB AGREEMENT: The *Grammy,* given to top performers, *are* among the most prestigious music awards.
>
> CORRECTED: The *Grammy,* given to top performers, *is* among the most prestigious music awards.

or

> CORRECTED: The *Grammies,* given to top performers, *are* among the most prestigious music awards.

Pronouns take the place of nouns, and the pronouns must agree in number and gender with the nouns they replace, their **antecedents.** You correct faulty pronoun–antecedent agreement by first identifying the actual antecedents, then establishing whether the antecedents are singular or plural, and then adjusting either the pronoun or its antecedent:

> FAULTY PRONOUN/ANTECEDENT AGREEMENT: *Nobody* should complain about having to wear *their* seatbelts; seatbelts save lives.
>
> CORRECTED: *Nobody* should complain about having to wear *his or her seatbelt;* seatbelts save lives.

or

> CORRECTED: *People* should not complain about having to wear *their seatbelts;* seatbelts save lives.

Of course, this list is not all-inclusive. If your instructor hasn't assigned a handbook, find out where the handbooks are kept in your library, or buy one. A handbook will cover all these points plus many others.

Proofreading may be the last step in the revising stage, but it is nevertheless vital. When you don't catch your errors, you lessen the effectiveness of your paper; your reader won't concentrate on your content because of the distracting errors in form. Proofreading can help you correct these errors. It's therefore worth the effort.

APPLYING THE STEPS: AN EXAMPLE

If you revise an already good paper, will you improve it? Don't look for a guarantee; sometimes a paper doesn't hold much more promise than you've drawn from it in earlier drafts. But most times you will improve a draft when you go through the various steps outlined in this chapter and revise a solid essay.

Look, for instance, at this revised version of the computer essay presented in Chapter 2. This draft is clearer, more direct, more specific, and more understandable, thanks to a thorough revision:

COMPUTERS: CURE-ALL OR CURSE

One invention that has truly changed the lives of the people of the twentieth century is the computer. With it, our fast-paced society has picked up even more speed. Companies are bought and sold and millions of dollars exchanged, all in the blink of an eye. Entire libraries are stored inside bits of plastic and silicon. Elaborate electronic games featuring fast action and brilliant graphics provide entertainment and personal amusement. Through the development of computers, these scenes, once present only in science fiction, are now commonplace. These electronic wizards may be our cure-all. Ironically, they may also be our curse.

Saying that computers are destroying civilization, however, is unfair and misleading. For example, as labor-saving devices, computers are without parallel. A complete inventory at a manufacturing plant, for instance, that once took hundreds of people hundreds of hours to do, can be completed in a fraction of the time originally needed, thanks to computerization. Computers have helped streamline just about every aspect of our lives; as a result, the quality of life that we enjoy has definitely improved.

Yet this improvement has not been without drawbacks. First of all, more computers usually mean less contact with other people. Unfortunately, the result may be a society that deals more with microchips and floppy disks than with other people.

In industry, computers have brought about a rapid evolution. For example, now even small offices have personal or business computers. Resembling overgrown typewriters, these units perform a variety of tasks, including bookkeeping and other forms of record keeping and word processing. Also, using a modem, a device that connects a computer to a telephone, workers are able to tap into networks of information as numerous as the wires in the telephone cable.

But for the worker, this setup means less contact with other people. In some cases, workers spend much of their workday with only a glowing computer screen as a companion. Many won't have to suffer long, however, because increased computerization often means job loss, too; one word-processing secretary and a computer, for example, may replace an entire secretarial pool.

Computers have drastically affected our educational system, too. Now schools are redirecting their curriculums to keep pace with the rapid growth in computerization; today mathematics is king. But as the binary code and other elements from the world of math become our new language, will reading and writing be treated as secondary skills? Will literature and the lessons we learn from it be buried deep inside some obscure memory bank?

As schoolchildren struggle to learn about computers, the rest of us wrestle with another problem brought about by increased computerization: computer errors. For example, hardly a week goes by during which we can't read a story in the newspaper (itself marred by errors, as more computerization means less human proofreading) about some poor soul who is trying to convince some agency that he has not died or run up a $1 million credit-card bill. Computer wands read the pricing codes at the grocery store so quickly that the consumer may not be able to detect an error until the order is totaled up. Proving that an error has been made may mean unbagging all those groceries.

Even in the home, the fortress of the family, the computer intrudes. In many homes, the television has been the center of entertainment for a number of years. Now, with the introduction of affordable home computers and entertainment centers that hook right up to a set, the television is even more popular. But as people pay more attention to their television sets, they pay less attention to other people. Competition and learning become human versus machine. In the one place that people should be able to count on human comfort and communication, a computer may create a subtle isolation.

```
    Of course, suggesting that we return to simpler times is
ridiculous. The computer and the lifestyle it has spawned
are here to stay. And they should be. Thanks to the advances
in computerization, our lives are better. What we should
strive for, however, is an awareness of the problems, both
actual and potential, that this growth brings on. Whether
at work, in the office, or at home, computers should serve
us. They should be our cure-all, and they will be, if we
remember who should run whom.
```

As you can see, this draft is definitely better than the earlier, already good draft. It is clearer, more direct, less awkward, and thus more effective. It contains more specific information and less deadwood.

In addition, words are again spelled correctly and are arranged in complete sentences. Subjects and verbs again agree, as do pronouns and antecendents. Verb tense is again consistent throughout. Words, phrases, clauses, and ideas are expressed in parallel form.

A display case should never be so broken or flawed that it attracts attention to itself, because then the attention is focused on the case rather than on the valuables within. The same is true of your writing; make its display case (its **form**) effective, and you'll find that your reader will give the proper attention to the valuables (the **content**).

SUMMARY

Revising, maybe the most important stage in writing, involves three steps: **reassessing, redrafting,** and **editing.**

Reassessing means refining your draft so that it better communicates your ideas to your reader. To do this, write to a general reader, an individual who knows a bit about many topics.

Once you've focused in on your reader, reevaluate the information you've already included in your draft and make sure it is specific. You can use a **classification tree**—an informal list on which you plot a term in relation to other terms in its class—to check how specific the information is.

Check the diction, avoiding slang, jargon, and bombast because these types of diction can confuse, distract, or annoy your reader. Instead, write in simple, direct terms.

Once you have reassessed your paper, redraft, that is, go back through the various steps in the writing process. Writing is a recursive activity, so that rather than following a strictly forward movement, you may loop back through some stages.

After you have redrafted, edit. First, tighten your writing by eliminating any unnecessary words. Using the active voice trims unnecessary words. Cutting out deadwood is another trimming device.

The final part of editing is proofreading, which helps you detect errors that would otherwise distract your reader from your content. Use these questions — and a handbook, if necessary—as a guide when your proofread:

1. Are all your ideas expressed in complete sentences?
2. Is anything you've written ambiguous or awkward?
3. Is the spelling correct throughout?
4. Have you been consistent in your use of verb tense throughout?
5. Are the appropriate words, phrases, clauses, and ideas parallel?
6. Do subjects and verbs, as well as the pronouns and antecendents, agree?

EXERCISES

1. Take one of the following subjects that you understand and make a list of what types of information the general reader needs to know to understand the topic. Next make a list of the answers:

astrology	myopia
recreational vehicles	claustrophobia
mortages	photosynthesis

Then choose one topic you don't know and prepare the questions you need answered to understand the topic. Once you've prepared the questions, head to the library and, using a dictionary, an encyclopedia, or other reference book, answer the questions.

2. Choose two very different readers — a grade-school child, for instance, and a physician, or a elderly grammar-school dropout and a business executive. Then write a hundred-word paragraph to each explaining one of the terms you've studied. Don't forget to meet the needs of your readers.

3. Take two terms from an earlier paper (or two terms from the list in Exercise 1) and plot them on classification trees. If you're working with a partner, do independent trees and then compare your results.

4. Identify the weaknesses in a paragraph from an earlier paper; if your instructor or another reader hasn't already specified which paragraph you should work on, reevaluate the paper yourself, using what you've read in this chapter concerning who your reader is and how specific your information should be. Make a list of the weak or unclear spots, and do some prewriting to develop material to remedy the weaknesses. Once you're done, check with your instructor (or a partner, if you're working with one) to see if any questions still remain.

5. Find a 150- to 250-word example of what you feel is writing in need of tightening. It can be a portion of a textbook, part of a magazine or a newspaper article, or one of your own papers. See how many words you can eliminate *without* changing the meaning of the original. Look for instances of needless passive voice and deadwood. If you're working with a partner, exchange your edited versions and decide whether further editing is possible. At the same time, make sure that the meaning of the original is still intact. Be sure to explain to your partner why you made your changes.

6. Proofread and correct the following paragraph. If necessary, use the hints presented on pp. 53–58 as guidelines:

The trouble began just about when I got to the door. There, waiting on the porch, is the biggest doberman pincer I had ever seen, I didn't know whether to go ahead or turn back so I just froze. Meanwhile, snarling and barking and pulling on a chain that didn't look strong enought to hold back a chihuaha, I watched Spot. I could feel my clean shirt soaking up the sweet as I squealed, "Julia! I'm here. It's me—Robert."

It was embarasing enough to be stuck on the porch like some little coward all I wanted was for Julia to come out so we could leave. Instead, though, her little brother. Who was about six years old, comes out and told the dog to be quite. I felt ridiculous. But I felt even worse when the rest of her family came out to, looked at me, and they began laughing about how I was afraid of such a gentle animal as their Fluffy.

Chapter 6

CROSS-MODES: FULFILLING ═══ YOUR PURPOSE ═══

INTRODUCTION

Throughout the rest of this text, writing is discussed in terms of **modes.** If you've looked ahead or through the table of contents, you've seen the names: "Narration," "Description," "Process," "Example," "Definition," "Comparison and Contrast," "Cause and Effect," "Division and Classification," and "Argument."

But what do these titles mean? Will you be preparing a paper that is somehow *all* description or comparison and contrast or process? After all, that doesn't seem to be what you've done before. When you wrote an essay about an outstanding teacher, for instance, you probably didn't set out to write a definition paper. You probably just told your reader who the teacher was and why he or she was outstanding.

Yet your portrait was a definition paper because it delineated the qualities that a top teacher should have. At the same time, however, your paper was also narration because it related a sequence of events or incidents. And it was also description because it presented specific details that helped your reader to picture that ideal teacher. In fact, whenever you write, you probably use several modes at one time to communicate your ideas to your reader, that is, to fulfill your purpose.

REASONS WE WRITE

We write for three general reasons: to **inform,** to **entertain,** and to **persuade.** A newspaper story or a textbook informs; a novel or short story entertains; a television advertisement or a political position paper persuades. (In fact, because writing that persuades—*argument,* as it is usually called—is so commonly expected of college students, all of Chapter 15 deals with preparing this type of paper.)

Of course, we write for other reasons, too. In a hypothesis or a theoretical discourse — an extension of the philosophical point concerning the possibility of a Utopian society, for instance — you attempt to discover something.

Further, you could write an essay that informs *and* entertains *and* persuades. Any mixture is possible. Remember, communicating your ideas to your reader is your primary concern, so whatever is necessary to communicate those ideas is correct.

Techniques in Action

In order to communicate your ideas to your reader, you use certain techniques; in this text, these techniques are called *modes.* They are general titles that identify strategies that you use in combination when you write.

For instance, when you relate an event or a series of incidents — some sequence — you use **narration.** When you use words in order to re-create the sense of what someone or something was, you use **description.** When you tell how something occurs, how to do something, or how you did something, you use **process.** When you explain something by referring to other instances, individuals, or items like it, you use **example.** When you specify the elements or components of a person, place, event, or idea, you use **definition.** When you show the similarities of or differences between people, places, things, ideas, or events, you use **comparison and contrast.** When you show that one point has led to another or has produced another, you use **cause and effect.** When you group individuals, concepts, or occurrences based on common points or when you divide groups into their individual parts, you use **division and classification.**

Do you use modes when you write? Yes. You may not have been aware of the names of the techniques when you used them before, but you have used them because they helped you fulfill your purpose. These two case studies show how the modes are used in combination to fulfill the writer's purpose.

Case Study One

Imagine for a moment that you've been given this writing assignment:

> Most students find history dull and uninteresting. The problem is one of perspective, however. Ask people about a historic event and they'll probably mention the signing of the Declaration of Independence or the fall of the Roman Empire. Yet history is what happened – not just major events.
> For this assignment, take a bit of history that <u>you</u> honestly think is interesting or important. Don't worry if you think others might find your choice silly or trivial. In any case, make your paper five hundred to seven hundred words long.

After some thought, you decide to focus on the musical "British invasion" of 1964, a subject you read a few articles about last summer. During 1964, English rock groups such as the Beatles came to the United States and changed American music and popular culture quickly and dramatically. The British invasion was not an event that many people would think of as history. Nevertheless, it had long-range effects on society, even if the effects were not on the same scale as the assassination of Abraham Lincoln or Neil Armstrong's first step on the moon.

After you complete the initial sequence — freewriting, then statement of purpose, then focused freewriting, then thesis — you develop an initial draft. After reworking the draft a few times, you end up with the following version.

Where are the modes? Take a look at the analysis of the essay in the left column:

When historians record important events that have changed life in the twentieth century, they will probably ignore the so-called British invasion of 1964, when English rock groups such as the Beatles were catapulted into the limelight.

Definition: The British invasion is identified and explained.

The British invasion doesn't rank with the invention of the automobile or the dropping of the atomic bomb at Hiroshima; still, it did bring about widespread changes in our lifestyles.

Division and classification: Other historical events are presented.

Along with new music, the British invasion inspired new fashions and the idea that life was for the young. It also acted as a catalyst for the antiwar movement and the sexual revolution, and it made generation gap a familiar household expression.

Example: The various changes that evolved because of the British invasion are listed.

The British invasion began with a Sunday-night television appearance of the Beatles, four young musicians from Liverpool, England, on the ''Ed Sullivan Show'' in New York City.

Narration: The sequence of the British invasion is given to provide background.

From the moment that John Lennon, Paul McCartney, George Harrison, and Ringo Starr stepped before the TV cameras for the nationwide broadcast, America exploded with excitement and change.

Cause and effect: The initial results of the British invasion are presented.

Description: Specific details of the British invasion are given.

It was Beatle mania. Their music, their dress, their disdain for authority, and, most startling of all, their long hair were all exactly what a restless population of teenagers needed.

Narration: The sequence of the British invasion continues.

Cause and effect: Additional results of the British invasion are given.

In the weeks that followed the appearance of the Beatles, the changes began to flower. From coast to coast, girls screamed and fainted at the sounds of their young heartthrobs on the radio. Throughout the country, sons fought their parents and combed their hair across their foreheads in bangs and down over their collars in the back.

Comparison and contrast: The new music is examined next to earlier popular music.

These young people also moved to a new beat. The music was different from the sultry rhythm of their parents' Sinatra and Crosby but also different from the driving intensity of their older siblings' Elvis. The new lyrics and harmonies were as fresh and exciting as the Beatles themselves were. John, Paul, George, and Ringo were bright and brash, and in love with their fame and their fans.

Description: Additional specific details of the British invasion are given.

Narration: The sequence of the British invasion continues.

The Beatles sparked the interest and appetite of America's young people. Before long, they were followed across the Atlantic by other groups of young Englishmen with names like the Animals, the Dave Clark Five, the Who, the Rolling Stones, the Kinks, Freddie and the Dreamers, Herman's Hermits, Gerry and the Pacemakers, Billy J. Kramer and the Dakotas, and the Yardbirds. During the next few years, these groups made

Example: Other musical groups taking part in the British invasion are listed.

music that America moved to and grew with.

The incredible success of many of these groups sent shock waves throughout the country. Suddenly the world belonged to the young and it began to cater to them. Fashions changed to reflect this movement to youth. Besides long hair, men began sporting beards, moustaches, and sideburns. Wide, bell-bottomed pants and wildly colored shirts became commonplace. For women, skirts went up and up, becoming mini- and then micro-miniskirts. For all young people, blue jeans became a national uniform.

Along with these surface changes came some others that were not so visible. The most dangerous of these was an increase in drug use. It is unfair to put the entire responsibility for this increase on the British invasion. Yet the British invasion was fueled by rebellion against authority. One way the musician heroes of this revolution showed their disdain for the ''Establishment'' was through drug use; if the leaders of the revolution reacted this way, why shouldn't the followers? Within a few years, drugs such as marijuana and LSD became more and more available on city streets and college campuses.

Rebellion surfaced in other ways, too. For example, a few years after the Beatles arrived, an unpopular war in Vietnam

Narration: The sequence of the British invasion continues.

Cause and effect: Additional results of the British invasion are presented.

Division and classification: The various changes brought about by the British invasion are separated into categories.

Description: Additional specific details of the British invasion are given.

Narration: The sequence of the British invasion continues.

Cause and effect: Some reasons for the changes are given; less visible results of the British invasion are presented.

Narration: The sequence of the British invasion continues.

Cause and effect: Further results of the British invasion are presented.

became the perfect target for unleashing the distrust of a political system. Campus riots and demonstrations against the war erupted throughout the country.

Narration: The sequence of the British invasion continues.

Through all of this chaos, the beat went on. Not all the musicians whose sound fed the rebellion survived, though. Some, like Freddie and the Dreamers and the Dave Clark Five, disappeared almost overnight. Others, like the Rolling Stones and the Who, made it through and continued to make hits throughout the 1970s and early 1980s, but not without paying a heavy price; drugs claimed a member each of the Who and the Rolling Stones.

Comparison and contrast: The fates of the various rock groups are examined in relation to each other.

Example: Specific rock groups from the British invasion are listed.

Narration: The sequence of the British invasion continues.

And what about the leaders of the British invasion? Ironically, they didn't survive the revolution they helped to start. After turning out some of the greatest popular music of their age, Lennon and McCartney, the artistic masters behind the Beatles, could no longer work together. It was as if they had been defeated by the fame they had pursued so fervently. The split of the Beatles, made official in 1971, marked the end of the British invasion.

Cause and effect: The reasons that the Beatles split up are presented.

Narration: The sequence of the British invasion is completed.

From 1964 to 1971, America underwent some massive changes in fashions, attitudes, and music. Was the British invasion, sparked by the appearance of the Beatles on the ''Ed Sullivan Show'' in 1964, directly responsible for these changes? Of course, it

Narration: The sequence of the British invasion is recapped.

Example: The various changes that occurred during the British invasion are recounted.

wasn't. The British invasion did, however, give the youth of America the knowledge that their world was ripe for change. The new music and style that the Beatles brought across the Atlantic during the British invasion were just starting points. Seven years later, the Beatles were dissolved, but the effects on popular culture that they and their counterparts inspired remain today.

Analysis

As the comments in the left column show, seven modes — narration, cause and effect, example, description, division and classification, comparison and contrast, and definition — are used to explain the British invasion. The purpose of the essay is to tell about a historical event that was somehow significant; these modes are the means of achieving this purpose.

Incidentally, the analysis you see in the left column is quite general. Maybe you see techniques not mentioned, or maybe you feel that a passage labeled "description" should be called "example" or vice versa. Don't be concerned; the labels are broad, and there is overlap from one category to the next.

Noting the Dominant Mode. The paper presents the sequence of the British invasion as it progressed from beginning to end. Not surprisingly, there are more instances of narration — ten — than of any other mode. In each instance in which it appears, narration *frames* the story.

For example, in the second paragraph, the 1964 appearance of the Beatles on the "Ed Sullivan Show" is noted as the beginning of the British invasion, and in the concluding paragraph, the sequence is restated to begin a recap of the overall significance of the British invasion.

In between the second and final paragraphs, the sequence of the British invasion is set forth. For instance, in the third paragraph, the scene moves forward through the weeks following the Beatles' initial appearance on national television. In fact, except for the introduction and the fourth paragraph, each paragraph shows the sequence of the British invasion until the tenth paragraph, which ends the sequence.

Noting the Supporting Modes. Although narration may be the dominant mode, it does not appear alone. Several other modes appear as support.

For instance, the mode of cause and effect appears six times in the essay. The use of this mode is no surprise because the significance of the British invasion comes down to one word: *change.* Therefore, the instant result —

Beatle mania—is mentioned in the second paragraph, and other immediate results are given in the third paragraph. The sixth paragraph presents the swing to youth in hair style and clothing attributable to the British invasion. The seventh and eight paragraphs illustrate the more insidious changes associated with the British invasion: increased drug use and political unrest. And the tenth paragraph presents the most ironic effect of the British invasion; the team in the vanguard of the British Invasion, Lennon and McCartney, was creatively torn apart by its own success.

Example appears four times in the essay, too. This mode also helps to fulfill the purpose of the essay by providing concrete references to illustrate the point being made. In the introduction, for instance, example is used to identify the types of changes that resulted from the British invasion. Besides this use in the introduction, example appears entensively in the fifth paragraph with a listing of the various rock groups that capitalized on the interest the Beatles generated. Later, in the ninth paragraph, some of these same groups are mentioned again as either successes or failures. An example is used in the conclusion to restate the types of changes that occurred during the British invasion.

As the left-column notes indicate, description is used three times in the writing. In the second, fourth, and sixth paragraphs, specific details illustrate the scenes, whether the subject is clothing, fashion, or hair styles.

Besides these modes, division and classification, comparison and contrast, and definition appear once each. Whether ideas connected with the British invasion are separated or grouped, judged to be similar or different, or explained, the passages that result all have one thing in common; they all serve the purpose of the paper.

This essay on the British invasion illustrates the historical significance of the event through the use of various modes. The paper is largely narrative; however, six other modes are used in combination so that the purpose—to draw a complete picture of the British invasion of 1964 for the reader—is fulfilled.

Case Study Two

Imagine for a moment that you've been given this writing assignment:

> When the television special on nuclear holocaust, ''The Day After,'' was originally broadcast, several opinion polls showed that the greatest fear of American young people is nuclear extinction. But is this our only worry? What other threats do we face; more specifically, what other problem do you feel is a major threat to our life here on earth? Is it dumping of industrial waste? Euthanasia? Wholesale illiteracy? Uncontrolled chemical engineering? Decide on a danger that you think we should all be alerted to, and tell your reader about it in detail. Make your paper five hundred to seven hundred words long.

After some thought, you decide to write about acid rain, a very real threat to waterways and therefore to the life in them. When you were in high school, you had been part of a summer science program that monitored water pollution in your area. During that summer, you and your classmates learned a great deal about the phenomenon of acid rain, thanks to frequent lectures from a college professor who specializes in this area of study.

Although a great deal has been written in newspapers and magazines about the dangers of acid rain, you still feel that the public does not know enough to be as alarmed as they should be.

After you complete the initial sequence — freewriting, then statement of purpose, then focused freewriting, then thesis — you develop an initial draft. After reworking the draft a few times, you end up with the following version.

Where are the modes? Take a look at the analysis of the essay in the left column:

Description: Specific details are used to set the scene. ————	Picture a small cottage at the edge of a mirrorlike lake. Picture it hundreds of miles from any city. There are no cars, trucks, or factories belching out pollution. It's like a step into another world, one filled with peace and tranquility. Everything about this scene is perfect, except for one fact: that beautiful, mirrorlike lake is dead, no longer able to support aquatic life. Acid rain, a frightening
Definition: Acid rain is explained. —	consequence of burning fossil fuels, has killed it. Although these sentences may sound like the script of a
Cause and effect: The reason for acid rain is explained. ————	science-fiction movie, the scenario is true. Right now, thousands of waterways around the world are dying. They are the victims of the fallout created when fossil fuels are burned.
Process: How acid rain forms is detailed. ————	Acid rain actually begins after fossil fuels like oil and coal have been burned. Once the fuel has been expended, leftover gases drift out as exhaust and rise up into the atmosphere. Two of the elements in the leftover gases, sulfur

Division and classification: The by-product of fossil fuel that causes acid rain is separated into the specific pollutants.

Process: How acid rain forms is detailed.
Narration: The sequence of acid rain as it develops is stated.

Comparison and contrast: The element shared by urban and rural areas — both suffer from acid rain — is stated.

Cause and effect: The results of acid rain are outlined.

Example: Types of property damage are highlighted.

Cause and effect: Further results of acid rain are detailed.

Process: How acid rain destroys a waterway is presented.

dioxide and nitrogen oxide, go through a chemical change over a few days and become sulfuric and nitric acid.

When these compounds combine with normal moisture in the air, the rain that results contains diluted quantities of these acids. As an added twist, this transformation takes place as the gases drift hundreds, sometimes thousands, of miles from their source. Therefore areas without industrial centers nearby, like that beautiful cottage, are as vulnerable to damage as the urban areas.

The property damage from acid rain can be extensive. It can corrode paint, metal, and some stone used for building. In some cities in the United States—Boston, for example—acid rain has eroded some priceless monuments, statues, and architectural carvings beyond repair. And acid rain is a silent threat; people don't really notice it because its effects are gradual. Unfortunately, the effects are cumulative, too. One dose of acid rain may have little effect on anything, but repeated soakings with even a weak solution of acid cause permanent damage. Every little sprinkle of acid rain, is part of that silent threat.

Yet, as bad as the destruction of property can be, the damage to waterways and the life they support is far worse. That's because acid rain changes the pH level—the chemical balance—

Definition: pH level is explained. —— | of the water. The pH scale runs from 0 to 14; 7 is neutral. Readings above 7 are increasingly alkaline, and readings below 7 are increasingly acidic. For

Example: pH levels for various liquids are given. —— | example, household ammonia has a pH reading of 11; lemon juice has a pH reading of 2. Normal rainfall already has a pH level of around 5.6 because of the elements naturally present in the atmosphere. In some areas affected by acid rain, the precipitation has a pH reading between 4.5 and 4, nearly a thousand times more acid than distilled water, which has a pH level of 7.

Cause and effect: Further results of acid rain are detailed; reasons for—— decreased reproduction are given.

Process: How acid rain destroys a waterway is further detailed. ——

When a lake or river shows a pH reading of 5.4 or lower, some species stop reproducing; once the pH level hits 4.5, no fish reproduce. With the constant bathing of acid rain, the pH level gradually drops until species after species stops reproducing. Because each

Cause and effect: Further results of acid rain are detailed. ——

creature is a link in the food chain, even a slight increase in acidity can affect the entire ecosystem.

Comparison and contrast: Acid rain is examined in relation to acid snow.

In parts of the northeastern United States and Canada, the damage is heightened by the effects of acid snow. Although acid rain affects the earth it falls on immediately, acid snow has a delayed reaction. All during the cold months, the snow accumulates, and except for some evaporation,

Definition: Acid snow is explained.——

Description: Specific details are used to illustrate the scene. ——

it stays on the ground until spring. When the spring thaw comes, the amount of acid released into the waterways increases dramatically. This ''knockout punch'' can

Process: The altering of the chemical balance of a waterway affected by acid snow is detailed. ————

Cause and effect: Further results of acid rain and snow are given. ————

Narration: The sequence of destruction of acid rain is restated. ————

Description: Specific details are used to illustrate the scene. ————

Cause and effect: The reason that acid rain develops is restated. ——

Narration: The initial scenario is restated. ————

Cause and effect: The ultimate result of acid rain is restated. ————

increase the acid level of a river or stream a hundred times within a few weeks. To make matters worse, this increase coincides with the beginning of the reproductive cycle of many creatures, and the result is fewer or, in some cases, no offspring. Those that do survive may be deformed or incapable of reproducing.

Right now irreparable damage is being done to rivers, lakes, ponds, and streams. These waterways don't look different, but the destruction is occurring nevertheless. Until we begin to require that industries and power plants burning fossil fuels install adequate antipollution devices, the damage will continue. People will continue to row across that mirror-like lake near their vacation cottages deep in the woods and wonder why the fish aren't biting as much as the year before. And each little shower will continue to bring that lake and thousands more like it closer to their end as life-supporting bodies of water.

Analysis

As the comments in the left column show, eight modes — cause and effect, process, description, definition, narration, example, comparison and contrast, and division and classification — appear. The purpose of the paper is to inform the reader of a threat to humanity, and through these modes, the writer's purpose is fulfilled.

As always, some overlap in indentifying or labeling the modes occurs, so don't be surprised if your analysis of the acid rain paper differs somewhat from the analysis in the left column. Whether you feel that a passage is more specifically cause and effect or process is less important than the recognition that a technique is being used to fulfill the purpose: to communicate ideas to the reader.

Noting the Dominant Mode. The dominant mode in this acid rain paper is cause and effect which appears nine times. The thesis is that acid rain is a major threat to people; therefore, a mode that explains what brings acid rain about and how it affects our world is a natural choice.

In the introduction and again in the conclusion, the mode of cause and effect is used to show the reasons for the results of acid rain. Then, in the fourth, sixth, and seventh paragraphs, more specific details about the origin of acid rain and the destruction it brings about to property and waterways are presented. The cause-and-effect passages thus effectively illustrate the far-reaching consequences of acid rain.

Noting the Supporting Modes. Of the other modes used in this paper, process appears most often: five times. Process is also a natural choice for explaining the threat of acid rain because process explains how to do something or how something happens or is done. For example, in the second and third paragraphs, process is used to explain how acid rain develops and spreads. Then, in paragraph five, process is used to illustrate how acid rain destroys waterways: the increased acidity changes the delicate chemical balance of the water. Process is used again in the sixth paragraph to show how the increase in acidity reduces or eliminates the reproduction of some species and then, in the seventh paragraph, to illustrate how the runoff from acid snow destroys by radically altering the pH level of a waterway over a brief period of time that ironically coincides with the beginning of the reproductive cycle of many species.

Description appears three times in the paper. It is used in both the introduction and the conclusion to illustrate the scene from which the explanation of acid rain develops: the waterway that appears to be no different but that nevertheless is suffering severe damage with each rain shower. And in the seventh paragraph, description underscores the irony of acid rain: a pristine winter scene masks a chemical nightmare.

Definition also appears three times. In the introduction, it is used to specify what acid rain is. In the fifth paragraph, definition is used to explain pH level; because the disruption of the pH level is precisely how acid rain destroys, the use of definition at this point is vital if the reader is to understand the full significance of the threat. Definition also appears in the seventh paragraph to explain what acid snow is and how its delayed effect occurs during the spring thaw.

Narration is used three times in the essay as well. In the third paragraph, narration is used to illustrate another facet of acid rain: the transformation from leftover gases to sulfuric and nitric acids, a process that takes place over several days hundreds of miles from the source of the gases. In the concluding paragraph, narration is used both to restate the chronology of acid rain and to indicate the constant threat of acid rain: even at this moment, acid rain is damaging the world around us.

Example is used twice in the paper to explain or illustrate some aspect of acid rain. For instance, in the fourth paragraph, example is used to specify the types of property damage resulting from acid rain; and in the fifth paragraph, example is used to illustrate the pH scale through references to specific familiar liquids.

Comparison and contrast, as well as division and classification, are used in the paper, too. The mode of comparison and contrast is used first to illustrate that both rural areas and urban centers are affected by acid rain (in the third paragraph) and then to distinguish between acid rain and acid snow (in the seventh paragraph). Division and classification are used to specify which elements of fossil-fuel exhaust — sulfur dioxide and nitrogen oxide — develop into acid rain.

The original assignment called for a paper that discusses and explains some threat to humanity. The resulting paper on acid rain tells about the threat largely by emphasizing the cause-and-effect elements of acid rain: how it develops and what it does. But various other modes are also used so that the threat of acid rain comes across clearly to the reader. In other words, the modes help the writer to fulfill her or his purpose.

STUDYING THE MODES: A RATIONALE

When you write, you use several modes in combination in order to fulfill your purpose; that's what the analysis of these two paper shows. And if you're going to be prepared to use the modes in combination, you need to recognize the characteristics of each mode and to practice writing papers that will emphasize these characteristics.

Each of the next eight chapters focuses primarily on one mode, and each chapter follows basically the same pattern. (Chapter 15, "Argument," deals with argument as an aim of purpose you fulfill by using the various modes in conbination.) First, the various characteristics and uses of the mode in question are presented. Then two assignments calling for the use of that mode are presented, with model papers written on the same assignment.

Studying another paper written on the same set of guidelines that you face will give you a concrete sense of what to write about and how to write about it. In other words, the model essays will help you to identify and fulfill the purpose of the writing. In addition, part of each model is also shown in some stage of development, so that you will also be able to see how a paper progresses from draft to draft until it becomes a fully developed final paper.

Each chapter also contains sample essays written by professional writers. Like the other models, these professional samples contain the mode discussed in the chapter. Each chapter thus presents plenty of concrete, relevant examples of what you need to do to master writing.

Of course, when you write your paper, you will use *many* modes. As the two papers in this chapter show — and as you've no doubt seen already as you've begun writing papers — you never write a paper that is wholly narrative or wholly cause and effect, for example; you combine techniques in a natural, functional way to fulfill your purpose. As the analysis shows, the modes can appear in individual paragraphs as a means of developing or supporting your thesis.

A FINAL CAUTION

As you read the following nine chapters, remember this important point: no matter what mode you concentrate on, you will also be using other modes to support or illustrate your thesis. Although you may not have been aware of it, you have already been using these techniques. All the next nine chapters do is give you an opportunity to study and thus master these modes so that you will be better able to communicate your ideas to your reader, that is, to fulfill the purpose you set whenever you write.

SUMMARY

One way to study writing is to classify it in terms of **modes,** that is, techniques or patterns that enable you to fulfill your purpose as a writer: **narration, description, process, example, definition, comparison and contrast, cause and effect, division and classification,** and **argument.**

Although writing can be classified in terms of modes, you don't write papers that are wholly one type, for example, all definition or all comparison and contrast. Instead, the modes are functional; they serve the writer's purpose. Generally we write to **inform** or to **entertain** or to **persuade** (or any combination of the three).

The modes are used in combination to fulfill your purpose as a writer, and analysis of any piece of writing would show several modes at work. One mode may predominate, but other modes will be used to support, explain, or illustrate. Studying the individual modes in action and mastering their characteristics will prepare you to communicate your ideas to your reader, that is, to fulfill your purpose.

EXERCISES

1.   Using the models on pp. 64 – 69 and 70 – 74 as examples, analyze one of your writings. Make a list of the modes you've used based on the brief explanation on p. 64. If you're working with a partner, discuss your findings; see if you agree with your partner's assessment.

2.   Using the models on pp. 66 – 69 and 70 – 74 as examples, analyze the revised computer paper presented at the end of Chapter 5.

3.   Choose one of the topics listed below and make a list of the modes you'd be likely to use if you wrote a paper on it. For each mode you list, note the reason; in other words, tell what points you would make and how or why that particular mode would help you fulfill your purpose:

a beach party   police brutality
the dangers of smoking   outlandish Christmas or birthday gifts
depression   a professional wrestling match

Chapter 7

_____ NARRATION _____

INTRODUCTION

"Once upon a time . . ." How many times do you think you have heard a story that begins with these words? Of course, this expression is the traditional beginning for fairy tales, but we probably use variations of the same words to tell true stories, too:

> One time when I was at the beach with a bunch of kids from
> my school, my best friend got caught in the undertow.
> Before anybody realized it, he was trapped out there. Then
> the lifeguards headed out and pulled him in . . .

or

> I remember a time when I was so embarrassed I thought I would
> never be able to face my family again. I was reading in my
> uncle's yearbook about how college students back in the early
> 1970s used to go streaking–running across campus without any
> clothes. I didn't think anyone was home, so I decided to take a
> quick streak around the backyard. But when I got out there, I
> found my parents and my brother entertaining our minister . . .

These are obviously abbreviated versions of the stories, but as you can see, they would probably make great papers once they were fleshed out with details.

Each passage contains a compacted **sequence**—a series of events making up the story—that follows through on or otherwise illustrates or supports a thesis: the horror of a near drowning in the first and the embarrassment of being caught in a prank in the second. Basically you must do the same when you write a narrative paper: you must provide a thesis and then back it up with the appropriate sequence of events.

THE MAKEUP OF A NARRATIVE PAPER

Narrative papers are often written in the **first person;** that is, you will often write about something that you did or witnessed or had happen to you. Therefore the pop fly you missed at second base, causing your little-league team to lose the championship, and the fatal accident you witnessed one morning on your way to school are both potentially great narrative papers. For each scenario, you could easily develop a thesis and then present the sequence; in other words, you would tell the story as it occurred.

Of course, in a narrative paper, you might also write about something that happened to someone else. You might, for example, tell about an acquaintance who had to wrestle with the ideas of either having a baby or having an abortion, finally discovering that she wasn't pregnant. Certainly you'd be able to develop a thesis:

> Marlese wasn't prepared for the prospect that she and her boyfriend had started a life that maybe neither of them wanted, but she came face to face with it on that December morning when she missed her second period.

And certainly you'd have a powerful sequence to relate as you tell how she was forced to grow up fast: how alone she felt at the prospect of telling her parents and how ashamed she felt at giving a false name and then running out of an abortion clinic at which she had stopped to ask questions; how angry she felt at her boyfriend for blaming her and then walking out; and how drained she was when she finally discovered that she wasn't pregnant.

USING THE TECHNIQUE

As you can see, then, in a narrative paper, you can tell your own story or you can tell somebody else's. No matter what story you're telling, however, you'll want to make certain that you follow through on these points:

1. Make sure your reader can follow your sequence.

In a narrative paper, you need to be particularly careful about presenting your story in some recognizable order. The most obvious choice for a narrative paper is **chronological order,** the actual order of time.

For example, imagine you are writing a story about the time in grammar school when you and your classmates got back at the class "apple polisher" by filling his school bag with cow chips. After your introduction, you would first tell some of his antics: how he always told on the other children in class, how he always brought little gifts for the teacher, and how he always volunteered to stay in at recess and help the teacher grade tests. Then you would tell about the lunchtime meeting during which you and your classmates decided how to get back at him. Next you would detail how two of your classmates sneaked off at lunch and brought back several cow chips and then sneaked into the coatroom and loaded up his schoolbag. Finally, you would tell how, when she investigated the foul odor, the teacher sent her pet off to the office, schoolbag under arm.

Because this story is told in chronological order, your reader sees the series of events as they actually unfolded. And because your reader sees the sequence after you have presented the background, your story will no doubt be better understood.

Of course, you don't always tell a story in chronological order. Sometimes you use **flashbacks,** episodes from the past presented out of sequence. For example, in a story about finally having that dream date, only to discover that your ideal partner is nothing like what you thought he or she would be, you might not follow a strict chronological order. Instead, in the middle of the story, you might include a paragraph like this:

> It took us about twenty minutes to get settled in at the restaurant. She sat directly across from me, and when I looked at her up close, I could still see the look that had intrigued me from the first. It was a Friday afternoon in October of our freshman year, and I had just left algebra when I first saw her. She held the door for me, and when I thanked her, she gave me that look. It was a cross between a frown and a smirk, and it really intimidated me. Now it was our senior year, and that look still intimidated me.

As you can see, this paragraph starts at one point in time, and then it regresses to a time four years earlier. Finally it returns to the initial time. That step into the past is a flashback.

Flashbacks are useful tools for any writer. Make sure, however, that your switch to the past is clearly signaled for your reader. If, during a story about a dream vacation, you suddenly turn to a terrible vacation that you went on when you were seven years old, your reader is going to be confused unless you tie the two points together clearly.

2.   Make sure you tell your story without becoming sidetracked.

In one of his writings, Mark Twain tells the story of a man who had a perfect memory. Ordinarily, you'd think having a perfect memory would be an asset, but as Twain told it, it was a curse for this man (and anyone caught listening to him) because as he would tell a story, he'd be reminded of another story that was somehow related to the first one, and he'd begin telling that story until he remembered another related incident; with a perfect memory, he could never finish any story he started.

You face the same danger. As you are planning your paper, examine the details of the sequence very carefully. Have you included something in the sequence that might confuse your reader? If you are talking about the time when the child you were baby-sitting with disappeared for a half an hour or so, you wouldn't want to mention other baby-sitting jobs or bratty children you have known unless these points are directly related to the story. Doing so might distract your reader from your subject. Therefore, as you write, make sure you haven't included details that take your reader down another avenue of adventure.

3.   Make sure you've told your story thoroughly.

Because a narrative paper often recounts an event that you feel strongly about, you are at a slight disadvantage: you know your story too well, and the danger is that you will consider an important point somehow less significant than it actually is.

For instance, if you are telling your reader about the time when you were driving and showing off, racing the engine of your brother's car at a traffic light, only to stall, you need to explain why the car stalled. Don't forget that not everyone drives a car with a standard transmission, and those readers unfamiliar with a standard will miss a key point—that you had the car in fifth gear instead of first, a mistake that only a real novice at the wheel of a standard should make—unless you explain it.

Without this information, your reader might not understand your embarrassment. After all, cars stall for a variety of reasons. But when you point out that just as you were imitating a race-car driver, you stalled the car and ended up dead in the road in front of the same people whose attention you had been seeking, the reason for the embarrassment will come across clearly for your reader.

Narrative writing makes for good reading because we all generally like to see how other people handle situations that we have faced or may face. And if your paper is accurate and detailed, if it is presented in some recognizable order, and if it is focused, you will be successful because your reader will be able to relive your experience as you went through it.

ASSIGNMENT 1

Take a "first-time" experience, and in a 500 to 750-word essay, tell your reader this story.

Reason

Among the most interesting reading are stories about a first-time experience. That's probably because plenty of common elements are at work.

Let's face it; most of us are not immediately adept at handling something new, whether it's a new skill at work (the time you had to face a Christmas crowd with a brand-new, highly computerized, and highly confusing cash register), a new social custom (the time you were invited to a party at the home of someone whose social or financial class was above your own), or a new duty (the time you were put in charge of keeping all the financial records for your church group).

Of course, you aren't restricted to writing about your own experiences. If, for instance, you watched as a new parking-lot attendant looked at an expensive Porsche boxed in between a Mercedes Benz and a BMW, sighed, got behind the wheel of the Porsche, and meticulously maneuvered back and forth until he moved one $30,000 car from in between $60,000 worth of fancy automobiles without a scratch, you've got the makings of a great paper.

Whether you are writing about yourself or someone else, remember that most of us don't immediately welcome change; when the new replaces the old, nervousness, awkwardness, and confusion usually accompany it. Join the crowd; that's what being human means. And write about it. Whether you made gigantic errors or just spent the time gingerly carrying out something new, your audience will be interested because your audience has probably been through something similar.

What Your Reader Needs

Whenever you tell a story, your reader needs first to be able to trace the progression. If you are talking about that beeping computer that refused to cooperate on Christmas Eve, you should first explain that the training you had received was quick and probably less than adequate. Then you need to move to the beginning of your shift to explain any other points, like last-minute price reductions, a co-worker who called in sick, or a headache that made it hard for you to concentrate. Next, you might tell about the sudden rush at your register and the line of about twenty people, all irritable and anxious to go home. Finally, you would present the episode involving the balky computerized register and the trouble it caused. If you follow this process, your reader will be better able to understand the story because the progression of episodes is clear.

Of course, at the same time, you need to make sure that all the information you include in the story is indeed necessary. Don't include any information about a flirting supervisor, for instance, if that individual isn't directly connected to this particular story.

But if the supervisor *is* involved—if that flirtation was what distracted you so that you pushed the wrong buttons on the register and accidentally destroyed the customer's receipt and locked the cash drawer—tell your reader. In fact, as in any writing, make sure you provide plenty of detail. Just make sure that the details you include are necessary for your reader. Your reader depends on you to draw a complete picture, so once you've worked your way through the initial prewriting steps, amplify the bits of information you have generated, isolated, and decided to use.

Model

MY KINGDOM FOR A MAP

Any change is difficult to handle. Changing schools is no different, especially when the new one is so much more complex than the last one. I don't think I'll ever forget my first day as a high-school student. By the end of that school day, I was so frustrated and embarrassed that I never wanted to return.

All during the summer before I began high school, my older friends told me these horror stories about how awful the school was, how mean the teachers were, and how tough the older kids were. By the end of August, I was convinced that I wouldn't last through the first day, so I didn't exactly start school with the best attitude.

At eight o'clock on that first morning, I entered the imposing building and went to the bulletin board to find my homeroom. In spite of my nervousness, I managed to read through the list and find my homeroom. I asked a teacher nearby where Room 491 was, and following her directions, I found the room and took a seat.

At this point, just as I was beginning to think I would make it through the day, my teacher entered and convinced me that I probably wouldn't. First, he ordered us to be quiet, and then he barked instructions for the rest of the period. Any mistakes on the nine or ten forms he gave us meant we had to begin all over again. By the time I finished, my shirt was soaking wet.

The rest of the morning was a series of mishaps. Between periods I got lost in the halls, so I was late for each class. By the time I made it into the rooms, my teachers had already begun their presentations, and everyone just stared at me. I began to know what a rat feels like in a maze.

The final blow was lunch. First, I couldn't find the cafeteria. Then, when I finally arrived there, I got in the teachers' line. As I realized my mistake and turned to get out of line, I bumped into my homeroom teacher and knocked his lunch on the floor.

At this point, I felt the end of the day would never come. I spent two more periods getting lost and arriving late for class before the final bell sounded and I headed for my locker. Twenty-five minutes later, I finally found it and headed for home. At least I knew where that was.

After that start, it is hard to believe that I became an expert on the school. Within a couple of days, I knew my way around the building, and I even managed to help some of the other kids. I also found out that most of my classmates were too nervous to notice how late I had been for class that first day. Like me, they were intimidated at the prospect of change. Our experiences just show that although any change is upsetting, thank goodness the effects are temporary.

Follow-through

The biggest advantage you'll have in this paper is the subject; it has great appeal. For that reason, you'll want to pay close attention to the planning you do before you write, so that the thesis you develop and present in the introduction and then restate in the conclusion will be supported in the body of your paper.

After you've decided on your first-time experience and you've done your prewriting, you must decide which details your reader needs to know to understand your story and the order in which you should present them. In the example story about a first-day experience, these are the crucial details:

- *Lunch-line mess with Mr. Harolds*
- *Mr. Harolds yelling about forms in homeroom*

- *Friends telling me stories ahead of time*
- *Couldn't find my locker after school*
- *Scared of the building itself*
- *Late for class so missed lessons*

But that initial list also included these details:

- *Mrs. Lys gave forty pages of reading*
- *Auditorium was comfortable*
- *Vice-principal had a stern voice*
- *Gym class had three kids I knew*
- *At least I could walk each morning*
- *Couldn't believe all the stuff in lab*

This second list contains ideas that aren't directly connected. For instance, that a teacher gave forty pages of homework or that the auditorium was comfortable may have been first-day observations, but they don't have nearly the impact of the first group, which includes such details as being lost in the building, being late for class, and bumping into the homeroom teacher who had made such an impression in the morning.

As the writer, you must be selective. If your initial steps in the writing process have been successful, you'll have far more information than you need or can use. You mustn't get sidetracked; your reader is depending on you to present your story in simple, direct terms. Anytime you turn away from your main subject, you will confuse your reader. For example, the condition of the science laboratories is not crucial to the story unless it somehow affected your first-day journey through high school. Therefore make sure that the details you choose will make it easier for your reader to see your point.

Once you've decided which details you want to include, you have to set up the sequence. For the most part, this kind of assignment makes setting the sequence easy. Unless you plan to use flashbacks — and you should use them if they are appropriate (see the example on p. 80 of this chapter), you will probably tell your story in chronological order, that is, in the same order that it occurred. For example, if you took the same list of details that became the essay about the first day at school and numbered them to indicate the chronological order, the order would look like this:

5. *Lunch-line mess with Mr. Harolds*   6. *Couldn't find my locker after school*
3. *Mr. Harolds yelling about forms in*   2. *Scared of the building itself*
   homeroom   4. *Late for class so missed lessons*
1. *Friends telling me stories ahead of*
   time

As the essay shows, the actual story begins the summer before, when playground buddies told of the terrors awaiting the unwitting freshman in September (1). Then the story moves to the morning of the first day, when the very building intimidated the newcomer (2). A difficult homeroom period (3), followed by a pattern of arriving late for class (4), leads to an unfortunate cafeteria encounter with a gruff homeroom teacher (5). The final indignity of the day is the frustration of seeking out the locker that seemed so easy to find that morning (6). Chronological order makes this story clear and easy to understand.

Once you have established which details to include and the sequence within which you will present them, you're on your way to telling that first-time experience. And if your introduction and conclusion are effective, your reader will soon be enjoying walking in your footsteps — or in somebody else's — on that first day.

Checklist

Use the answers to the following questions to help you revise your first draft:

1. Does your paper have a thesis? Write it down.
2. Does your paper have enough specific examples? List the main examples.
3. Have you provided enough support for each of these details?
4. Have you followed chronological order? And if you have used flashbacks or otherwise altered the order you initially set, have you made the switch in time clear for your reader?
5. Does your introduction provide a clear direction for your reader?
6. Does your conclusion restate the significance of what you have told your reader?

ASSIGNMENT 2

Take a traumatic experience, and in a 500- to 750-word essay, tell your reader this story.

Reason

Thank goodness our daily lives aren't filled with traumatic incidents; there's no way we could handle the pressure. A traumatic incident is one during which we face severe anxiety, paralyzing fear, or potential or actual danger. Unfortunately, each of us has been through at least one such experience. For that reason, a traumatic incident is an excellent subject to write about because of the common ground involved.

For instance, many of us have been involved in or have witnessed a car accident. And because the event was so traumatic, we remember a great deal about it. Think for a moment: Do you remember on what day of the week the accident happened or who was sitting where in the car or what any bystanders may have said? The sound of metal against metal or of glass breaking?

You are not unusual if you remember many details; the event was probably frightening enough to almost etch those details into your permanent memory. The same is true of your reader, so a built-in attraction exists in a paper about a traumatic incident. Your reader has no doubt had to face a trauma at some time and will therefore be interested in seeing how you handled your incident.

But you aren't restricted to writing about something that happened to you. Do you remember, for instance, an occasion at the beach when you heard that a child was missing? You looked several blankets over and saw the father—a man in his early twenties, head in hands, crying. Although you weren't directly involved, you remember the incident as if it just happened, and as a result, you'll be able to record it in detail.

Because of his or her memory bank of details about traumatic incidents, your reader will be interested in the depth and accuracy of your details. Therefore, whether you are writing about a traumatic incident that happened to you or that occurred around you, you can be sure of reader interest.

What Your Reader Needs

When you think back to that traumatic incident, no doubt the details are all jumbled up. Although you remember the events clearly, you don't always remember them in the direct order in which they occurred. Therefore, before you can effectively record the traumatic incident, you have to sort out the details and establish the order in which they happened.

For example, think back to that episode on the beach. You probably recall most clearly the sheer emotion expressed by the father as he sat hoping that his daughter wasn't drowned and trying to figure out how he would deal with the loss if she were dead. Yet other events happened first (hearing about the lost child and noticing the crowd three deep along the edge of the water), and other events occurred afterward (the arrival of the police and the discovery of the child, alive and digging in the sand fifty yards away from her father, oblivious to all the fuss).

Even though the father's initial reaction is what you remember best, you must still provide a time frame for the story so that your reader can clearly see the progression of events. And you must provide specific examples. In a paper such as this, description is particularly useful because the vivid details you generate will provide excellent support. If, for example, the extremely hot weather and the extraordinary size of the Fourth of July crowd combined to make it easier for the child to slip off by herself, provide this information in specific detail. By paying close attention to sequence and detail, you will better meet the needs of your reader.

Model

THE SQUEEZE OF MY LIFE

There is at least one therapist who travels around the country lecturing that the best cure for human ills is hugging. I'm not sure if he is right, but I do know that one type of hugging <u>does</u> save lives: the hugging that is integral in the Heimlich maneuver. In fact, if it wasn't for one of these hugs, I probably wouldn't be here today.

My experience actually occurred because I talk when I eat, a bad habit I developed as a child. A few times while I was growing up, my habit caused me some problems. Usually I would almost seem to inhale a bit of food, and then, after a coughing fit and a lecture from my parents, everything would return to normal.

Because of my childhood experiences, nobody at my table seemed to react right away when I began to choke last fall. My whole family was celebrating my parents' anniversary at a local restaurant. My older brother and his wife were there from New York, and my sister had come home from college just for the occasion. It had been almost two years since we had all been together, so there was plenty to talk about. As usual, I seemed to be doing most of the talking. In between all my yapping, though, I managed to order my favorite, filet mignon with all the trimmings.

During the appetizers and salads, I caught up on the news about my nieces from my brother and my sister-in-law and about college life from my sister the freshman. My parents were just glowing with pride and happiness as we chattered on.

The first break in the conversation appeared when the main course arrived. I guess all our talking had helped us work up our appetites. My filet was cooked just the way I like it—medium rare—and the first piece almost melted in my mouth. But as I took my second bite and looked up to tell my family how delicious it was, I felt that familiar inhaling sensation. This time, though, it was different. When I tried to cough, no sound came out, and I couldn't breathe. I knew I was choking to death.

Everything seemed to be going in slow motion. I looked from face to face at the table, and I could see their confusion and horror. I distinctly remember watching the color drain out of my mother's face.

But if they were frozen, I certainly wasn't. I could feel myself thrashing around as I tried to stand. Just as I got to my feet, however, my sister dodged the chair I had knocked over, rushed behind be, locked her arms around my waist, and squeezed as hard as she could.

The pressure I felt was incredible. For a second, I felt as if I would split. Then, just as suddenly, I felt a release as the piece of meat shot out of my mouth. I was alive again.

After the shock wore off, I was as embarrassed as I had ever been. This time my parents didn't lecture me. Instead, they tried to calm me down and convince me that I hadn't ruined their night. They also praised my sister for recognizing the problem and reacting so quickly, even though it seemed like forever to me. She laughed and told us that she had just finished studying the Heimlich maneuver in a health class but that she had received a D-minus on her practical exam on the procedure. She

jokingly suggested that I write to her professor and ask
him to reconsider her grade, and then we finished our meal.
   Bad habits are hard to break, but after this experience
I don't think I'll have much trouble. The vision of my
family frozen as I fought to breathe is hard to forget. And
although I love my sister, I hope she never gives me a hug
like that one again – or has reason to.

Follow-through

In a story about a traumatic incident, you already have a head start toward
success. Most people enjoy reading about struggling with or overcoming tragedy, probably because it reminds them of their own struggles, successes, and
failures in dealing with traumatic events.

   To take advantage of your reader's natural interest, you must tell your story
in a recognizable order with enough specific examples to re-create the tension
and emotion of the original event. Once you have done your initial prewriting,
you should have a suitable list of examples and details from which to draw the
specific points to illustrate your story. This initial list will also help you develop
your thesis — a crucial step, as this thesis gives your reader much-needed
direction.

   Once you have a clearly stated thesis, you need to sort through the details
you have generated in order to decide which ones will draw the clearest picture
for your reader. For example, look at this preliminary list of details accumulated for this paper:

> *Julia was home from school, the first time in two years we are all together and I
> almost ruined the night—I choked once at Aunt Regina's and then at
> Grandma's when I was a kid, and Mom and Dad yelled, but this time they were
> super—it was their anniversary, too—I couldn't remember the universal sign
> for choking; who remembers stuff like that under pressure?—my mother's face
> was absolutely white—last time I saw that was when I split open my head in the
> yard and walked in with a face full of blood—I wasn't able to order filet mignon
> for months afterward—Julia made me laugh; she said she nearly flunked the
> practical exam on the Heimlich maneuver last week and told me I should drop a
> line to her Health Prof—my brother and his wife were so upset they couldn't
> even finish their meals; I felt so guilty—here Bob works all day and drives four
> hours to be here and he can't even eat—at least it didn't cost them anything for a
> baby-sitter—his wife's parents took the girls, otherwise that would be even
> more expense—Julia moved so fast—no wonder she has the girls 50-yard
> record from high school—she practically jumped over that chair and then
> squeezed—the pressure was so painful, and then the meat just shot out—what
> a feeling it is when you choke like that, I couldn't make a sound—it was a little
> like the time Bobby held me under water in the pool two summers ago—you
> want to breathe but you can't and you don't have any control.*

As you can see, this preliminary list contains the main details appearing in the final draft, but it also includes plenty of details that would serve little purpose and might well confuse the reader. The edited list from which the various drafts were developed looked like this:

> *Julia was home from school; the first time in two years we are all together and I almost ruined the night—I choked once at Aunt Regina's and then at Grandma's when I was a kid, and Mom and Dad yelled, but this time they were super—it was their anniversary, too—my mother's face was absolutely white—Julia made me laugh; she said she nearly flunked the practical exam on the Heimlich maneuver last week and told me I should drop a line to her Health Prof—Julia moved so fast—she practically jumped over that chair and then squeezed—the pressure was so painful, and then the meat just shot out—what a feeling it is when you choke like that; I couldn't make a sound.*

This edited listing contains the ideas that were later adapted and amplified in the drafts. They become the means of illustrating the trauma of nearly choking to death.

As they appear in these lists, however, the events are out of sequence. In terms of chronological order, this is how the details are arranged:

> *(3) Julia was home from school; the first time in two years we are all together and I almost ruined the night—(1) choked once at Aunt Regina's and then at Grandma's when I was a kid, and Mom and Dad yelled, (7) but this time they were super—(2) it was their anniversary, too—(5) my mother's face was absolutely white—(3) Julia made me laugh; she said she nearly flunked the practical exam on the Heimlich maneuver last week and told me I should drop a line to her Health Prof—(6) Julia moved so fast—she practically jumped over that chair and then squeezed—the pressure was so painful, and then the meat just shot out—(4) what a feeling it is when you choke like that; I couldn't make a sound.*

The numbers added here indicate the chronological order. But if you look back at the final draft on the previous pages, you'll see that the story isn't told in absolute chronological order. The third paragraph begins with this sentence. sentence.

        Because of my childhood experiences, nobody at my table
     seemed to react right away when I began to choke last fall.

This point is definitely out of sequence; the actual choking doesn't occur until the end of the fifth paragraph:

     When I tried to cough, no sound came out, and I couldn't
     breathe. I knew I was choking to death.

Even though the sentence in the third paragraph is out of chronological order, this information is vital; it helps to explain the initial hesitation on the part of other family members. After all, they had experienced other episodes of choking that were not serious (as the second paragraph illustrates), and they therefore had no special reason to think that this choking episode would be any different.

The secret to writing an effective paper about a traumatic incident isn't very secret. It's the principle behind all good writing: provide an introduction with a thesis to direct your reader, tell your story in some logical order and in specific detail, and sum up the significance of the experience in a concluding paragraph. If you follow this formula, chances are good that your reader will get a real sense of the emotion you felt during this experience.

Checklist

Use the answers to the following questions to help you revise your first draft:

1. Does your paper have a thesis? Write it down.
2. Does your paper have enough specific examples? List the main examples.
3. Have you provided enough support for each of these details?
4. Have you followed chronological order? And if you have used flashbacks or otherwise altered the order you initially set, have you made the switch in time clear for your reader?
5. Does your introduction provide a clear direction for your reader?
6. Does your conclusion restate the significance of what you have told your reader?

FOR FURTHER STUDY

Certainly among the most inspirational figures of our time is Helen Keller. Struck with deafness and blindness as an infant, she might never have escaped from the darkness that was her world if it had not been for the efforts of her dedicated teacher, Anne Mansfield Sullivan. The story of their first encounters has been dramatized in the play and movie *The Miracle Worker.* The following passage is actually an excerpt from Keller's book, *The Story of My Life.* It recalls that monumental moment in her life when she first became aware of the connection between words and objects.

Everything Has a Name

HELEN KELLER

The most important day I remember in all my life is the one on which my teacher, Anne Mansfield Sullivan, came to me. I am filled with wonder when I consider the immeasurable contrast between the two lives which it connects. It was the third of March, 1887, three months before I was seven years old.

On the afternoon of that eventful day, I stood on the porch, dumb, expectant. I guessed vaguely from my mother's signs and from the hurrying to and fro in the house that something unusual was about to happen, so I went to the door and waited on the steps. The afternoon sun penetrated the mass of honeysuckle that covered the porch, and fell on my upturned face. My fingers lingered almost unconsciously on the familiar leaves and blossoms which had just come forth to greet the sweet southern spring. I did not know what the future held of marvel or surprise for me. Anger and bitterness had preyed upon me continually for weeks and a deep languor had succeeded this passionate struggle.

Have you ever been at sea in a dense fog, when it seemed as if a tangible white darkness shut you in, and the great ship, tense and anxious, groped her way toward the shore with plummet and sounding-line, and you waited with beating heart for something to happen? I was like that ship before my education began, only I was without compass or sounding-line, and had no way of knowing how near the harbour was. "Light! give me light!" was the wordless cry of my soul, and the light of love shone on me in that very hour.

I felt approaching footsteps. I stretched out my hand as I supposed to my mother. Some one took it, and I was caught up and held close in the arms of her who had come to reveal all things to me, and, more than all things else, to love me.

The morning after my teacher came she led me into her room and gave me a doll. The little blind children at the Perkins Institution had sent it and Laura Bridgman [the first deaf and blind person to be educated in the United States] had dressed it; but I did not know this until afterward. When I had played with it a little while, Miss Sullivan slowly spelled into my hand the word "d-o-l-l." I was at once interested in this finger play and tried to imitate it. When I finally succeeded in making the letters correctly I was flushed with childish pleasure and pride. Running downstairs to my mother I held up my hand and made the letters for doll. I did not know that I was spelling a word or even that words existed: I was simply making my fingers go in monkey-like imitation. In the days that followed I learned to spell in this uncomprehending way a great many words, among them *pin, hat, cup,* and a few verbs like *sit, stand* and *walk.* But my teacher had been with me several weeks before I understood that everything has a name.

One day, while I was playing with my new doll, Miss Sullivan put my big rag doll into my lap also, spelled "d-o-l-l" and tried to make me understand that "d-o-l-l" applied to both. Earlier in the day we had had a tussle over the words "m-u-g" and "w-a-t-e-r." Miss Sullivan had tried to impress it upon me that "m-u-g" is *mug* and that "w-a-t-e-r" is *water,* but I persisted in confounding the two. In despair she had dropped the subject for the time, only to renew it at the first opportunity. I became impatient at her repeated attempts and, seizing the new doll, I dashed it upon the floor. I was keenly delighted when I felt the fragments of the broken doll at my feet. Neither sorrow nor regret followed my passionate outburst. I had not loved the doll. In the still, dark world in which I lived there was no strong sentiment or tenderness. I felt my teacher sweep the fragments to one side of the hearth, and I had a sense of satisfaction that the cause of my discomfort was removed. She brought me my hat, and I knew I was going out into the warm sunshine. This thought, if a wordless sensation may be called a thought, made me hop and skip with pleasure.

We walked down the path to the well-house, attracted by the fragrance of the honeysuckle with which it was covered. Some one was drawing water and my teacher placed my hand under the spout. As the cool stream gushed over one hand she spelled into the other the word *water,* first slowly, then rapidly. I stood still, my whole attention fixed upon the motions of her fingers. Suddenly I felt a misty consciousness as of something forgotten — a thrill of returning thought; and somehow the mystery of language was revealed to me. I knew then that "w-a-t-e-r" meant the wonderful cool something that was flowing over my hand. That living word awakened my soul, gave it light, hope, joy, set it free! There were barriers still, it is true, but barriers that could in time be swept away.

I left the well-house eager to learn. Everything had a name, and each name gave birth to a new thought. As we returned to the house every object which I touched seemed to quiver with life. That was because I saw everything with the strange, new sight that had come to me. On entering the door I remembered the doll I had broken. I felt my way to the hearth and picked up the pieces. I tried vainly to put them together. Then my eyes filled with tears; for I realized what I had done, and for the first time I felt repentance and sorrow.

I learned a great many new words that day. I do not remember what they all were; but I do know that *mother, father, sister, teacher* were among them — words that were to make the world blossom for me, "like Aaron's rod, with flowers." It would have been difficult to find a happier child than I was as I lay in my crib at the close of that eventful day and lived over the joys it had brought me, and for the first time longed for a new day to come.

Questions for Study

1. Is there a recognizable sequence in this story? Briefly outline the sequence as you see it.
2. What are the main details Keller used to re-create the experience? List them.
3. Which incident illustrates the moment of awareness — the climax — for Keller? Write it down.
4. In the next-to-the-last paragraph, Keller wrote about feeling repentance over breaking the doll earlier. What details help explain how she now knew that what she had done was wrong? Or are other details necessary to make this clear? In a brief paragraph, explain how you feel about this point.

ALTERNATE ASSIGNMENT A

Thank goodness most of us have not faced such a dramatic turning point in our lives as Keller faced. However, each of us has experienced a moment or event that turned us about a little or had some meaningful impact on our lives. For this assignment, tell the story of an experience that somehow altered your view of life.

The cruelty of children often has an impact that lasts a lifetime. In this essay, Howard D. Silverman, a retired retailer, recalled one such episode. Silverman's story has a Christmas setting, but it is less a Christmas story than it is the story of one classmate victimized by another and the effect that has lingered for over sixty years as a result.

A Ghost of Christmas Past

Howard D. Silverman

This Christmas story, unlike most, is not a happy one. It is, however, true. It happened in 1923, in the fourth grade classroom at the Spring Street School, now long-since gone. In its place is an empty field that must echo with the ghostly shouts of hundreds of East Greenwich schoolchildren.

In that innocent era, Christmas was Christmas, a joyous time anticipated by everyone, and the school Christmas party was for everyone.

There was a tree, of course, decorated by the class. Names had been picked for gift-giving. No gift was to cost more than 25 cents, and nobody knew the name of the giver. Remember?

It's time to introduce the two characters in my story: our teacher, Miss Grace Shippee, whose family was among the town's earliest settlers, and Charlie Moore, our protagonist. By the way, all names and places in this story are real, too: my memory of the events is so poignant that I cannot change them.

I can see Charlie now as though it were yesterday, and 1923 was 60 years ago. Charlie was taller than most of us and, like many children whose growth is early, he was awkward. Perhaps "gangly" would describe him better: he had an uncoordinated walk that made him different.

Charlie came from the other side of the tracks. More important to this story, he usually came to school dirty. His face and hands could have used soap and water, and his clothes, too, were dirty and often torn.

So, Charlie stood out and he knew it. He had no friends. In fact, he did not allow us to get close. It was as though he knew that none of us would take him into our homes. Sadly enough, he was probably right.

Came the day of the Christmas party, and Charlie's appearance both amazed and delighted me.

He was scrubbed to a shine; his clothes, although old, were clean. But Charlie's face fascinated me even more than his new-found cleanliness: He had a tight-lipped smile and a look in his eyes that said, clearly, "Here I am. Look at me. Today I'm one of you."

Names were called and, one by one, presents were opened. There was an air of excitement that one would expect from a class of eight- and nine-year-olds. Then came Charlie's turn.

He ambled up the aisle and, reaching the tree, slowly opened his small gift. Removing the gift-wrapping with care, he gradually revealed his present and showed it to the class—a bar of soap!

The class was totally silent, almost as though the room were empty. From someone there was a small titter, then another, and suddenly the whole class was laughing. And there was Charlie, immobile, holding the bar of soap aloft.

His face haunts me to this day. Charlie stood there, soap in hand, trying desperately to smile, trying even more desperately not to cry.

I hardly dared to look up, yet I was totally mesmerized by Charlie's weirdly contorted appearance. And then it happened. Suddenly, all I saw was Charlie's face, as if suspended in midair, separated from his body. His features were torn between two overwhelmingly opposed feelings, and he seemed to hang there forever, smiling strangely through brimming eyes.

I wanted so much to turn away, but I couldn't. Then I heard a quiet voice say, "Charles, you may be seated."

It was Miss Shippee's voice, and all at once it was over. But was it? As you can tell it wasn't for me, so how could it have been over for Charlie?

I have thought of Charlie at Christmas every year since that distant fourth-grade Christmas party, and many other times when I have watched children at play.

At some time during the school year, the Moore family moved away; I never saw Charlie again. But I have often wondered what became of him and what that Christmas party did to his soul, to his character, to his feelings toward his fellow man.

I often wonder if he has forgiven us.

Questions for Study

1. Is there a recognizable sequence in this story? Briefly outline the sequence as you see it.
2. The narrative itself is rather brief. What background details help you understand the story better? List them.
3. The climax of the story occurs halfway through the story. In a brief paragraph, explain why you think Silverman spent nearly the rest of the essay talking about the moments following the climax.
4. This incident changed the way Silverman looked at life. List the details that show this change.

ALTERNATE ASSIGNMENT B

As Silverman's story shows, childhood is not always the simple, easy, happy time that television shows and movies would lead us to believe. And because childhood is a period during which most of us are especially sensitive to slights and hurts, the memories of these bad times stay with us for a lifetime. For this assignment, tell of a time that you were hurt yourself or helped, either willingly or unknowingly, in hurting someone else, and tell of the effect it's had on you.

HOW I WROTE IT

A Life Unfolds Under Dad's Workbench

William J. Kelly

Well, you see, my father has this old workbench in the cellar of his house, and I have asked him to leave it to me in his will.

It's kind of a family joke, except I'm not really kidding. But if you're going to understand any of this, you need to know about my father, and you need to know about his workbench.

First, my father. He is a dedicated husband and the father of four sons. The ultimate civil servant, he has performed his current job faithfully and expertly for more than 20 years.

For me, he has been disciplinarian, provider, teacher, tyrant — all those things that a father might feel are necessary to guide four sons.

My father is a straight arrow. He doesn't drink, unless you count the glass of wine he has been drinking nightly for 20-odd years. He hates the taste of the stuff, but some doctor told him to drink a glass every night, so he does.

My father is disciplined. For example, he used to be a two-packs-a-day smoker — Camels — but he quit about 15 years ago; he stopped his 35-year habit in *two* days.

All in all, my father is a model citizen. Except if you consider his workbench. I suppose every rock has its crack. My father's is in the cellar.

More than likely, the workbench was there when my parents bought the house. It looks like most workbenches, four legs supporting a three-by-six-foot working surface. It also has a shelf underneath, and in this space lies the dark side of this model citizen. In here is an enormous collection of . . . well, it's kind of hard to say exactly.

Some of it is in groups. For example, my father probably has the world's largest collection of broken portable shower hoses. You know the type — nearly guaranteed to come off the faucet exactly when the shampoo lather has dripped into your eyes.

How about empty coffee cans? Maxwell House. If you ever decide to begin refilling cans, let me know and I'll give you my father's address. You'd better plan on sending a truck.

Tell the truth now: How many of you find that the quality of bags at the supermarket has slipped terribly? No problem. My father has a bunch of vintage ones. With these, you could be the darling of the cash-register set. Instead of waiting for some surly bagger to stick your groceries in the store's flimsy sacks, you could hold your head high and say, "No, I'll put my groceries in *these*, thank you."

Of course, this listing is by no means all-inclusive. Besides the collections, there are the individual items, and these reflect something more specific about my father.

Take, for example, the baseball-size roll of blue-chalked twine. When I was seven, my parents prepared an apartment upstairs for my grandmother, and my father decided to put down a new plywood floor.

This is where the chalked string comes in. My father turned the new floor into a giant checkerboard of blue squares by having one of us kids hold an end of the string while he snapped the other end. Then he gave the four of us hammers, and for the next few nights, we whacked the blazes out of that plywood.

There were rules, though; my father *always* has rules. We could hammer nails only in the four corners of each square. And we had to hold the hammers from the end of the handles *only* because, my father said, "If you're going to learn something, learn it the right way."

This took some of the fun, to say nothing of our individual aim, out of the project. But we *did* learn to hammer.

I'm also sure that buried somewhere under that workbench are some bricks, symbols of my father's greatest project. He got a pile of them from the local gas company one spring, and it didn't take him long to decide what we would do with them: pave the slope above the small basketball court in the backyard.

My father had us dig up the slope to a depth of four inches. Then he had a load of sand delivered, which we spread as a bed for the bricks.

All summer, we placed the bricks in neat rows in the sand, tapped them so they were firmly set in the bed, and dribbled soupy cement between the rows. We worked in shifts, and although our masterpiece has a few wrinkles where one shift of brothers ended and another began, it stands (or, rather, lies) today as testimony to my father's projects.

Junk, you say? Maybe so. But it's my father's junk. If you're confused by this, remember that most people know only the model-citizen side of my father. But the real knowledge of my father comes when you blend that with his other side — his junk side, I guess.

My father casts an enormous and admirable shadow. Seeing his other side makes it a bit easier to live up to his standards. After all, it's more difficult to love a statue on a pedestal than a man who saves rubber shower hoses.

I first came up with the idea of writing this story about my father one night in early December of 1982. As I was driving, I heard a song by Dan Fogelberg, "The Leader of the Band," a tune dedicated to his father. In his song, Fogelberg used the image of his father as a bandleader whose time is almost gone. In the refrain of the song, Fogelberg referred to himself as "a living legacy to the leader of the band" and used the song to tell a little of his father's life. Although I had often warned my students about how difficult it can be to write about someone close, Fogelberg's song reminded me again that doing so is not impossible.

Because the following February would mark my father's sixty-fifth birthday, I wanted to write a story about him as a birthday tribute. I needed a starting point — an angle — which eventually became my father's workbench. My father is a great believer in the idea of saving something because it might be needed someday. He stores many of these things under his workbench, so I headed to his cellar to look around. Basically, I tried to tie the objects I found, including boxes of grocery bags and coffee cans and a couple of shower hoses, to past events to illustrate what my father is like.

As I searched for other objects, I also began to remember more incidents, including preparing an apartment for my grandmother and the last summer project I completed with my brothers: the bricked slope in the backyard.

Once I had accumulated these tidbits of information, I began to focus in on my specific angle. To the public at large, my father seems a man who "goes by the book," highly logical and highly organized. My intent was to use the objects and episodes to show the slightly eccentric side of my father — to poke some gentle fun at him — but at the same time to say, "I love you because you are both organized and slightly eccentric."

The editor clipped some incidents from my original story. For example, the final version tells that he quit smoking in two days, but it doesn't give the story behind that incident as the original version had. Another episode originally included involved another of my father's projects: portable tent poles that he had us make by shaving the ends of lengths of wood with rectangles of window glass, as the local carpenter had recommended.

I can't say I was happy with the deletions — no more than you are when someone suggests that you change or leave something out of a paper you've written. But I must also confess that this editor improved my article by cutting off my original conclusion and ending the paper with what was actually the next-to-the-last paragraph. I had originally concluded the story with a funny twist because I didn't want to appear to be needlessly sentimental. But when I reread the final ending, I could see that it showed the love and respect I have for my father far better than my original ending, which made my father look a little too silly.

ALTERNATE ASSIGNMENT C

Write an essay about an influential person in your life. As you plan your paper, remember the built-in problems: the strong feelings you have for that person may initially make it difficult for you to express the way you feel. The task isn't impossible, however, and the result will no doubt be worth the extra work you'll have to do in the initial stages of your writing.

Chapter 8

DESCRIPTION

INTRODUCTION

Your writing is a camera lens through which your reader views the experiences you've witnessed or been through, and description is among the best types of writing for focusing in on the scene through that lens. After all, description makes your writing vivid and clear for your reader. Without it, your writing seems vague and unclear. Look at this passage, for instance:

> When the hurricane finally hit, everybody was excited. The wind blew strongly and we couldn't see much outside. After the telephone pole outside snapped in half, the lights went out, and all we could hear was the wind and the rain.

These sentences **tell** about the hurricane, but they provide very little specific information **showing** what the experience was actually like. Compare that passage to this one, which provides the all-important descriptive details:

> When the hurricane finally hit, everybody was excited. My roommate's fifteen-year-old sister began to cry out loud, her face pale and tight. My roommate kept walking from window to window, shaking his head and whistling, and my friend John and I kept talking about nothing just to try to keep calm. The force of the wind was unbelievable: we could see the windows bend under the strain. Only the masking tape that criss-crossed the panes seemed to keep the glass from shattering. Even though it was 2 P.M., it was as dark as midnight. Through the picture window, though, we could see several of the oak trees on the lawn bend at nearly forty-five-degree angles and then spring back as if they were being pulled by giant invisible elastic bands. Suddenly there was a tremendous crack and hiss. Our lights went out, and for a moment, nobody in the room could see. When our eyes adjusted, we could see the telephone pole across the street broken nearly in half, with the wire that used to supply electricity to the house sparking in the puddle in the

driveway. We sat in the deathly quiet, interrupted only by
Sheila's whimpers and the freight-train roar of the
hurricane winds.

The initial version of the story **told;** it didn't **show** because it didn't provide the necessary description. The first version says people were excited, but it doesn't describe how they were excited. Like many words, *excited* has several possible meanings.

As the second version shows, however, the excitement in this case was nervousness and fear: one person crying, one pacing back and forth and nervously whistling, and two others trying to make small talk in order to calm themselves. The original version said that visibility was poor; the descriptive version calls it "dark as midnight." The original version says, "The wind blew strongly"; the second version describes the sound as a "freight-train roar."

Descriptive writing is the difference between telling and showing. Showing communicates your ideas to your reader; that's why descriptive writing is so important.

THE MAKEUP OF A DESCRIPTIVE PAPER

Although description is often used as a supporting technique, sometimes the subject you choose to write about will demand a more thorough descriptive treatment. Of course, as in any paper that you write, a descriptive paper must have a thesis that is supported, explained, or illustrated.

For instance, if you are writing about an outdoor rock concert at which over 100,000 people crowded in a stadium, you would definitely use description to tell your reader about this huge chunk of humanity. But description alone will not make your paper effective. With a thesis like "I just expected to sit around and listen to the music, but the real show was watching the audience," however, description would illustrate the activities of the crowd during the concert and thus support the thesis.

Description may be among the most important techniques available to you as a writer. You are writing about something that your reader has not experienced, at least not in the exact way you have re-created it on paper. For example, your reader has no doubt seen a circus performance, but has your reader seen the same activities in the same order and with the same intensity as you did? Maybe the erection of the tent itself struck you:

The football-field-long, yellow-and-white-striped
canvas seemed suddenly alive as the troupe of five
straining elephants, heeding the shouted commands of their
handlers, slowly raised the massive thirty-foot varnished
post that supported the center of the big top. When the post
was set, the small crowd, mostly about twenty older men
with a few smaller children, cheered. The elephant
handlers, seemingly oblivious to the applause, patted the
elephants and led them to their reward: an extra bale of hay
and a wet-down with a leaking garden hose.

Your reader may also have been fascinated by the raising of the circus tent, but it is unlikely that your reader saw the same details in the same way that you did. Therefore, by meticulously describing the scene—"football-field long," "thirty-foot varnished post," "twenty older men"—you communicate your ideas more completely for both the newcomer to circus life and the veteran of countless tent-raisings.

USING THE TECHNIQUE

No matter what subject you choose to write a descriptive paper about, your writing will be more successful if you pay attention to the following suggestions:

    1.   Use your senses to record descriptive details.

One of the greatest ways to develop descriptive details is to use your five senses—touch, taste, hearing, sight, and smell—to generate them. What does milk taste like? What does velvet feel like? What does a vacuum cleaner sound like? No single answer to any of these questions is correct because we each feel, taste, and smell things slightly differently.

You should still use sensory details, however. We may all experience things differently, but the differences still share a common base. At a sad scene in a movie or play, for instance, some people may cry out loud; others may not cry, but they still may feel saddened.

Of course, in most of the papers you will write, you won't describe something for the sake of the beauty of the description. In a story about a skiing trip when you got off the trail by accident and then fractured your leg, though, you might describe how cold you felt. In this case, the description of this sensation would have a purpose: to support the thesis.

The difficulty in describing sensory details is finding words that will accurately illustrate what you experienced. One way to deal with this problem is to show the results of the sensation. This paragraph, for instance, describes the cold experienced following that skiing accident:

> Once I realized that nobody was going to find me right away, I started to panic a little. Then I also began to feel colder than I had ever felt. My insulated ski boots didn't seem to be able to help my feet; I couldn't feel my toes at all and there was a dull pain across the balls of my feet. Below the elbows, I couldn't feel my arms. It was so frightening to have to look to see if I was moving my arms. Every breath was a knifelike sensation through my nose and throat, but what scared me the most was the overwhelming urge to close my eyes and sleep. I knew I shouldn't, but the throbbing in my injured leg and the overall numbness made it hard to stay awake.

Because everyone feels warmth and cold and pain differently, you make your reader better able to understand the way you felt these sensations by explaining the sensations themselves or presenting the effects the sensations brought about.

2. Use a mixture of objective and subjective (or impressionistic) description.

Primarily, two types of description are available to you: **objective** and **subjective.** Objective description is the type of information you might expect to find in a newspaper story, the observable or verifiable characteristics: size, shape, color, speed, weight, and so on. Subjective description, however, is phrasing that shows how you felt and what impression the experiences created for you.

Think of a place where you were frightened to go as a child — a cellar, for instance. That cellar was a room about ten by fifteen feet with unfinished, whitewashed walls and a dirt floor; it was lit by a single light bulb hanging from a wire. In the dim light, you could see boxes of old magazines, broken tools, and assorted odds and ends. All in all, it was a pretty ordinary cellar.

But the way it used to make you feel! It was cold and clammy, and although you never saw any, you were sure there were giant insects — or worse — down there. And you could always see shadows. Your father had told you that it was only your own shadow, thanks to the poor lighting, but it always seemed as if there was someone hiding behind you. And you always wondered what was buried under the dirt — there was such a musty smell, like what a mausoleum must smell like.

The first paragraph about the cellar is objective description. It deals with the actual elements of the cellar. The second paragraph, however, is subjective description; its focus is on impressions, not facts.

An explanation of how to perform a chemistry experiment, would be primarily objective description — the color the solution in the test tube should turn when it is cooled to twenty degrees centigrade, for instance — whereas a short story or poem about a near-death experience would be mostly subjective description.

But you should probably use a mixture of both types in most of the writings you'll complete. Your reader gets a better picture of what your cellar was like when both the types are used because you show both what it was actually like and what it made you think.

3. Make your description clear and specific.

"Muriel is such a beautiful person!" The descriptive information given in this sentence doesn't provide much of a picture of Muriel. *Beautiful* is a descriptive word, but it is also abstract. Abstract words are those that name intangibles, such as ideas, feelings, and impressions, and as a result, their meanings are relative. For example, although you might find a classroom cool, the person sitting next to you might feel that it was a uncomfortably warm.

Abstract terms affect clarity because they mean something special to you but they don't always carry the same meaning for your reader. For your reader, *beautiful* may conjure up ideas of physical beauty — itself an abstract term because definitions of physical beauty differ from time to time, culture to culture, and country to country. But your definition of *beautiful* is different. To you, Muriel is a person so generous that she regularly donates 10 percent of her pay to the local center for the homeless, so kind that she spends each weekend with a "Little Sister," and so dedicated to the patients she cares for at the nursing home that she has received two achievement awards in the last six months from the nursing-home administration — that's what *beautiful* means to you as you relate the word to Muriel.

The solution is to amplify, that is, to explain what the abstract terms mean. Whenever you can, back up the abstract words with **concrete** language, that is, words that name tangibles, things recognizable through our senses. Saying that you felt "strange" the morning after your first-ever drinking spree is not enough. If by *strange* you mean physically cold and sweaty and dizzy, then use these concrete terms to explain the abstract one.

You face a similar problem with **general** words, terms that name groups or classes of things, such as *animal, school,* and *person.* If you saw an advertisement in the paper listing a "sportscar" for $5,000, you would want to know a number of things before you gave any serious thought to buying it. What kind of sportscar is it? A $25,000 Porsche for $5,000 would seem to be a bigger bargain that a $10,000 Triumph at that same price. And what year is the car? Maybe a ten-year-old car is no bargain at $5,000, regardless of its type.

Remember, too, that a word can be specific in one context but general in another. As with abstract terms, the solution to having an abundance of general information is to amplify it, that is, to make it specific enough so that your reader understands what you mean. *Triumph* may be specific as it is used to name the brand of sportscar mentioned in the previous paragraph, but if the reader needs to know which style of Triumph it is — a Spitfire or a TR-6, for example — in order to understand your point, *Triumph* alone would be too general. This additional information makes your description that much more specific and therefore that much more likely to communicate your ideas to your reader.

Whether you use it as the main technique or to support other techniques in writing, description is among the modes you use most often. But no matter how you use it, make sure your description draws from your senses, includes both objective and subjective details, and uses clear and specific language. In description, you are writing so that your reader will see something as you saw it, and following through on these points will help you meet your reader's needs.

ASSIGNMENT 3

In a five hundred- to seven hundred-word essay, describe a unique experience you've been through.

Reason

For a number of reasons, people can't always experience life to the fullest, at least not to the extent they would if they won $1 million, for instance, and were able to spend their days thinking up and then fulfilling adventures. But the inability to fulfill their wildest dreams doesn't mean that people aren't interested in reading about the adventures that other people have had. For this reason, a paper about a unique experience makes good reading.

If, for example, you haven't been on a helicopter ride over Niagara Falls, would you like to go on one? After all, the ride would take you right above one of the greatest natural wonders of the world in an open-doored helicopter; you can almost reach out and touch the mist rising from millions of gallons pouring over the edge to the rocks below.

Even if you haven't been through anything as captivating as a helicopter "buzz" around Niagara Falls, you have had experiences that could tax your descriptive abilities. What is it like to water-ski? What sensations do you get when you finally rise up out of that crouching position and begin actually skiing? And what does it feel like when you hit the water full speed and fail to let go of the tow rope right away? What is it like to face a television camera or to help backstage at a play? True, people perform these acts every day, but every person doesn't, and even those who have done so will probably welcome a chance to see how someone else handled the situation. Therefore, whether it's a riveting trip in a helicopter or a chaotic visit backstage on opening night, you've got the basis for a fine paper.

What Your Reader Needs

In any descriptive writing, you need to give your reader plenty of specific details that support the thesis. Take the example about water-skiing, for instance. It might begin with this thesis:

> From the moment you break free of the water around your waist and knees until you fall and hit that wall of water coming at your face full speed, water skiing is as exciting an experience as you can get on a summer afternoon.

This thesis dictates a framework that presents the experience step by step and gives you a chance to tell your reader about the sound of the engines as they strained to accelerate, about the feeling of being pulled in two directions as the rope yanked on your arms while the water held you down, about the exhilarating chill you felt as you cut through the wind, about the painful impact you felt as you hit the choppy wake created by the boat, and about the strangling sensation you felt as you instinctively clung to the tow bar and were dragged through the churning water for a few more seconds.

Because the experience was so vivid for you, it is easy to forget that it can't be as vivid for your reader. You were there; your reader was not. But if you are thorough with your description, your paper will seem almost to put the tow rope in your reader's hands.

Model

RIDE INTO SPACE

Although space exploration is dangerous, few people would dispute that it is exciting and captivating. However, traveling to Cape Canaveral and hoping to be picked as an astronaut is not the only way to get the sense of what space travel is like. Instead of heading to mission control, plan a trip to Disneyworld in Florida and ride on Space Mountain, one of the Magic Kingdom's most popular attractions.

Even with all the stunning buildings in Disneyworld, visitors can't miss Space Mountain. From a distance, the building looks like an enormous white circus tent. When the bright Florida sun shines on it, the glare from the roof is almost overpowering. On top is a flagpole towering over the area, beckoning the park-goers to stop.

Even though Space Mountain is popular and the lines are long, the average fifteen-minute wait doesn't seem bad because the path to where you board the ride winds around inside the building and keeps everyone moving. The interior of the building is white, too, and the air-conditioning makes it about fifteen degrees cooler than the usual eighty-plus-degree Florida weather outside.

As they wait to board the ride, people walk up ramps that rise gradually, maybe half as steep as the average set of stairs that takes them to the loading zone. As if to heighten the nervousness and anticipation, throughout the building are signs warning anyone with a heart condition to beware. The whole place is as clean as the inside of a hospital or a laboratory, so it is easy to imagine that it is actually NASA headquarters rather than an amusement park ride.

The ramps continue to lead the riders upward, and within five minutes or so, the loading zone appears. This part of the building is darker, so those waiting can't help focusing on the roar of spaceships taking off and the flash of lights from meteors and asteroids that role across the immense ceiling. Lights near the end of the rampway ahead flash red and green. Behind a glass wall is the control room. The workers inside are all dressed in tan uniforms, with insignias and headsets completing their outfits. As the people wait at this point, they can see the ships moving quickly through the first part of their flight patterns. The tiny spaceships, each carrying at least two persons and sometimes as many as four, fade into the darkness; only a trace of light can be seen as they roar above the waiting crowd.

Actually, the ride is similar to a roller coaster, but the people ride in small, separate cars and they ride pretty much in darkness. Without lights, the cars seem to blast along, free in space. For the riders, there is no way to prepare for the steep hills or sharp corners because they can't be seen ahead of time. The most amazing part of all this is that it takes place inside a building, an enormous planetarium; it just seems as if it happens in outer space.

After the ride is over, the people are quickly helped from the little bullet ships and sent toward a rubber beltway to the exit. One big difference here is that there are no warning signs on the way out. Five minutes later, the individuals who were zooming through space are facing the hot Florida sun. Most head off to other attractions, but there are always those three or four who walk around the building to the entrance so that they can blast off again.

Space Mountain isn't the <u>Apollo</u> lunar lander or the space shuttle, but it is the closest that most people will come to experiencing a ride in space. Disneyworld is filled with fantastic rides, but Space Mountain should be ranked as the best one because for a few minutes, the people in those tiny spaceships almost seem to get the chance to leave the earth and experience space travel.

Follow-through

Although descriptive writing may initially seem difficult, it is sometimes quite easy if the subject you write about gives you a head start. With a unique experience as a subject, you certainly have that head start.

Once you've established your thesis, you're ready to select the details you'll use to make your description come alive for your reader. With a unique experience, you'll probably have a scrapbook full of details. In fact, you'll probably find your freewritings full of verbal pictures. Take a look at this list taken from the freewriting for this paper:

- *excitement near the takeoff point*
- *rubber belts — no noise*
- *long lines*
- *like a roller coaster*
- *hot as hell outside*
- *about thirty warning signs*
- *great air-conditioning*
- *cars look like bullets*
- *clean as a lab — almost sterile*
- *workers all in uniform*
- *control room behind glass*
- *building looks like a big metal tent*
- *it's weird riding in the dark*
- *get in by yourself or in twos*

As you can see, there are plenty of details here, but as they appear on this list, they don't paint complete pictures. They need to be fleshed out.

You do the fleshing out by amplifying them, sometimes by relying on sensory impressions. For instance, "hot as hell outside" and "great air-conditioning" aren't specific; what's hot for one person may be comfortably tropical for somebody else. The final version not only identifies these temperatures by drawing on the senses but also specifies them with actual temperatures: "the air-conditioning makes it about fifteen degrees cooler than the usual eighty-plus-degree Florida weather outside."

You can also amplify the descriptive details you wish to use by making them clearer and more specific. For example, "it's weird riding in the dark" and "excitement near the takeoff point" don't show anything. *Weird* and *excitement* are abstract terms. You make them clearer and more specific by amplifying them. In this case, *excitement* is illustrated through the various activities and actions happening at one time: the roaring of spaceships, the flashing of lights, and the fading of spaceships into the darkness. And *weird* is illustrated and specified by the explanation that the darkness makes it impossible to brace yourself for the turns and dips. With this additional information, the reader is that much more likely to find the description clear.

Notice, too, that the final version contains both subjective description:

> When the bright Florida sun shines on it, the glare from the roof is almost overpowering. On top is a flagpole towering over the area, beckoning the park-goers to stop.

and objective description:

> The ramps continue to lead the riders upward, and within five minutes or so, the loading zone appears. This part of the building is darker, so those waiting can't help focusing on the roar of spaceships taking off and the flash of lights from meteors and asteroids that roll across the immense ceiling.

Although there are always exceptions, you should usually try to include both types of description: you'll give your reader a more complete picture.

Writing about a unique experience has its advantages. One advantage is the plentiful details available to you in your memory. To communicate these ideas clearly to your reader, make them clear and specific by amplifying them. Like any other good writing, a successful descriptive paper needs an introduction with a clear thesis and a conclusion that restates that idea. But a successful descriptive paper demands specific details throughout the body because these details are what makes your experience come alive for your reader.

Checklist

Use the answers to the following questions to help you revise your first draft:

1. Does your paper have a thesis? Write it down.
2. What descriptive details have you included? Make a list of them.
3. Do these details support your thesis?
4. Have you made these details clear and specific by supporting or explaining them?
5. Have you included both objective and subjective description?
6. Does your introduction provide a clear picture of your purpose?
7. Does your conclusion sum up or restate the experience?

ASSIGNMENT 4

In a 500- to 700-word paper, describe the most unusual room you've ever been in.

Reason

Can where a person lives tell us what that person is like? In any case, people still generally enjoy peeking behind closed doors for a little while. People will gladly invest a few dollars to tour a historical mansion, for instance, and few people tour Washington, D.C., without taking the opportunity to walk through the White House.

But it isn't just splendor that attracts us. Many of us stay glued to the television as we see a documentary about Mother Teresa that shows the terrible living conditions that the people she cares for in India must endure, even though we may want to forget that such poverty exists.

Unusual places leave us with vivid impressions. For example, have you been in a hospital emergency room? What did it smell like? What was hanging on the walls? What colors did you notice? Was it warm or cold? What was the atmosphere — in other words, were people calm or frantic or somewhere in between? And how did all the activity make you feel?

Like many other writing assignments, a descriptive paper dealing with an unusual room has automatic attraction for your reader. If your reader hasn't been through the White House, for instance, your description will provide an open window to the pomp and splendor of our presidential mansion. And if your reader has been through the White House, your description will conjure up your reader's memories of the same room. What color was the rug? Did it have a pattern? Did you see any dust? A cobweb in the corner? Were the walls freshly painted? Your reader will want to read in order to compare mental notes.

The unusual room you have to tell about has appeal. It makes no difference whether your reader has been through or seen this room — or a similar one; the details you focus on are sure to provide a different view.

What Your Reader Needs

In a paper about an unusual room, your reader basically needs to see two things: the reason you have written about the room — your thesis — and a series of specific details that illustrate that thesis. This is your formula for success.

Imagine that the hospital emergency room is your subject. You'll have no problem coming up with details. You had to wait nearly forty-five minutes for the doctor to stitch up the cut in your hand. As you waited in a curtained-off cubicle, you became more and more apprehensive about the extent of the injury that had been so hastily wrapped up when you first stepped through the emergency room doors. You were shivering, but you couldn't be sure if your shivering was due to the actual temperature in the room or your nervousness. The glistening white tiles and dull brown linoleum floor just made you feel more uncomfortable—they were so cold. The curtain that surrounded the examining table reminded you of one of those moldy old canopied beds in all those ghost stories you read as a kid.

But the basis for the story is your annoyance at being kept waiting and the negative effect the wait had on your physical condition: "The forty-five-minute wait for the doctor that I faced in the emergency room did more to frighten me than the injury itself." Once this direction is provided by the thesis, your reader will be able to appreciate the description that supports it.

Model

MY NIGHT IN JAIL

My father had warned me several times during my high school years that if I ever got picked up by the police for anything, I could expect to spend the night in jail. He told me he wasn't about to get out of bed to bail a jackass out of trouble he'd made for himself. I never paid much attention because I never planned to get into any trouble with the cops. But the night I got arrested for loitering and illegal possession of an alcoholic beverage, I found out how serious my father had been about his warning. I got to spend a night in a place I hope I never have to return to: a jail cell.

Larry, Junior, Steve, and I had been warned many nights by the local cops not to hang around the park after hours. Most of the time we'd agree, drive off, and return a few minutes later, this time parking the car a block away. It would be a big game for us. The cops would come back, and we'd run for the woods. We figured they were too fat and lazy to chase us; most of the time we were right.

One night they decided to get tough, however. We were all under age, but Junior had managed to get served at a liquor store. We were sitting in a little clearing in the woods drinking when these bright lights exploded on us. The four of us took off in different directions, but I tripped over one of the six packs, and two cops grabbed my arms, whipped them so far behind my back that I had to blink back tears, and pulled me up.

The light they shone in my face blinded me, but I heard one of the cops say, ''That's one of 'em! Hey, kid, you wouldn't listen to us last week. Had to screw around, right? I'll bet you wanna go home now, don't you, kid. But you're comin' to <u>our</u> house.'' They read me my rights and then put me in the back of the police car.

By the time we got to the station, I was shaking so much I almost couldn't walk, and I was afraid to say anything because I thought I'd start crying. They took me in through the police garage and sat me in front of the booking sergeant. After he took all my information, he called my house. Like an emotionless tape recording, he told my father what had happened. Then he asked my father if he would come down and get me. I couldn't hear the answer, but I saw the sergeant's eyebrows move a little. Then he said, ''Yessir, we'll keep him overnight. We'll release him in your custody tomorrow.'' That's when I couldn't stop the tears.

The booking sergeant took my belt and shoelaces and then brought me back to the cell block. The lighting was poor, but I could make out eight cells altogether, four cells on one tier and four on another. He walked me up this metal ramp and put me in the cell in the far right-hand corner. He opened the door of the cell, gently pushed me in, and closed the barred door. With the click of the lock, I realized fully where I was and just how horrible it was.

The cell was about five paces deep and eight across; I remember so clearly because I spent the night pacing. I was afraid to do anything else. The bed was a thin mattress on a plywood platform, and I thought I saw something moving on it; I didn't dare sit down. In the corner behind the bed was a cracked toilet bowl with no seat. In the top center of the back wall was a tiny window. Even if I had stood on the edge of the toilet bowl, I still couldn't have looked out. The window was so filthy I don't think anybody could see through it anyway. The other three walls were bars with what looked like chicken wire in between. The only light came from a recessed fixture in the ceiling.

I couldn't believe how dirty the place seemed. First of all, it smelled just like a public restroom. The ammonia-like stink was enough to make me throw up, and the odor in my cell told me that the last occupant had done just that. The back wall was covered with four-letter words in pen, pencil, and magic marker. The ceiling was even covered: some creative inmate had apparently sneaked a cigarette lighter in, and he had left his jailer an obscene message traced out in smoke just the way the high-school kids used to do in the boys' locker room.

All night long there was noise. There were two people in the tier below. Both were drunk and both were abusive. I don't know how the cops kept themselves from opening the cell door and smashing the occupants with their billy clubs. The cops just laughed at them, which made the drunks even louder and more abusive. I didn't think there were that many swear words.

At 7 A.M., the booking sergeant came up to my cell, unlocked the door, and told me my father was outside. When we walked back to the booking room, I could see that my father hadn't slept all night either. His face looked gray, and his eyes had a dull, glazed look in them. I looked at him, and he said, ''I told you.'' I started crying and told him I was sorry. He said he knew it and that it was all right.

As we walked out, I looked back through the door into the

```
cell block, and it made me shiver. The door of the cell I had
spent the night in was still open, and I could see streaks of
bright sunshine trying to break through the dirt on the
tiny window. I knew then that I'd learned my lesson. I'd
never do anything that would put me in a room like that again.
```

Follow-through

A paper about an unusual room will be appealing to your reader if the reason for the story is clear and if the details show the reader why the room is unusual. Fulfilling these two requirements is your job as the writer.

Focusing your main ideas into a thesis is one of the most important steps in the writing process. Subjects that call for a descriptive treatment need particular attention because the various details could almost swallow up your intent.

This paper on a night in jail is a good example. Surely being arrested and having to spend the night locked up are traumatic; surely a jail cell causes an overpowering pile of sensations (most of them unpleasant). The danger is that the description will become more a grocery list of shocking details than the means of supporting the story of the trauma.

In the case of this paper, the thesis provides direction for the reader:

```
I got to spend a night in a place I hope I never have to
return to: a jail cell.
```

The next three paragraphs explain the reason for the trauma and bring the reader to the point where the description can do what it is supposed to do: illustrate why the experience was traumatic.

But before the initial details can be useful, they must be made more specific. This is how some of the details for this story looked initially:

- *what an awful smell*
- *too much noise to stand*
- *the cell was so small*
- *cell was filthy*
- *my father looked terrible*

The details are not effective because words like *awful*, *small*, and *terrible* don't paint a specific picture for your reader. The versions in the final draft are much better:

- *. . . it smelled just like a public restroom. The ammonia-like stink was enough to make me throw up, and the odor in my cell told me that the last occupant had done just that.*
- *Both were drunk and both were abusive. I don't know how the cops kept themselves from opening the cell door and smashing the occupants with their billy clubs. The cops just laughed at them, which made the drunks even louder and more abusive. I didn't think there were that many swear words.*

- *The cell was about five paces deep and eight across; I remember so clearly because I spent the night pacing.*
- *The bed was a thin mattress on a plywood platform, and I thought I saw something moving on it. . . . The window was so filthy I don't think anybody could see through it anyway. . . . The back wall was covered with four-letter words in pen, pencil, and magic marker. The ceiling was even covered: some creative inmate had apparently sneaked a cigarette lighter in, and he had left his jailer an obscene message traced out in smoke just the way the high-school kids used to do in the boys' locker room.*
- *His face looked gray, and his eyes had a dull, glazed look in them.*

These versions are clear and specific because they show rather than tell. And the overall description effectively supports the thesis.

Notice that even though there are touches of subjective description — the emotionless booking sergeant, the horror that stepping into the cell created, the sensation that something was crawling on the bed — most of the description is objective. But these objective details fulfill the thesis because they help to paint the picture of horror that a night in a police cell must be.

Notice, too, that this essay is heavily narrative. This is not a problem: as a writer, you will always use modes in combination. A paper that presented the sensations alone *without* the explanation of how those sensations were experienced wouldn't be effective.

You can take advantage of the appeal that a paper about an unusual room has by first providing an introduction with a thesis to direct your reader. Then use the descriptive details to support that thesis — to put that unusual room on display. Finally, sum up the significance of the room in a concluding paragraph. That's your formula for success in a descriptive paper.

Checklist

Use the answers to the following questions to help you revise your first draft:

1. Does your paper have a thesis? Write it down.
2. What descriptive details have you included? Make a list of them.
3. Do these details support your thesis?
4. Have you made these details clear and specific by supporting or explaining them?
5. Have you included both objective and subjective description?
6. Does your introduction provide a clear picture of your purpose?
7. Does your conclusion sum up or restate the experience?

FOR FURTHER STUDY

If you've ever wanted to return to a place you visited and enjoyed as a youngster, you'll particularly enjoy this writing by E. B. White. In this essay, White, a writer whose works are marked by clarity and insight, used description to explain the almost timeless nature of a vacation spot that his father had taken the family to years before and that White himself finally returned to some years later with his own son.

Once More to the Lake

E. B. WHITE

August 1941

One summer, along about 1904, my father rented a camp on a lake in Maine and took us all there for the month of August. We all got ringworm from some kittens and had to rub Pond's Extract on our arms and legs night and morning, and my father rolled over in a canoe with all his clothes on; but outside of that the vacation was a success and from then on none of us ever thought there was any place in the world like that lake in Maine. We returned summer after summer — always on August 1 for one month. I have since become a salt-water man, but sometimes in summer there are days when the restlessness of the tides and the fearful cold of the sea water and the incessant wind that blows across the afternoon and into the evening make me wish for the placidity of a lake in the woods. A few weeks ago this feeling got so strong I bought myself a couple of bass hooks and a spinner and returned to the lake where we used to go, for a week's fishing and to revisit old haunts.

I took along my son, who had never had any fresh water up his nose and who had seen lily pads only from train windows. On the journey over to the lake I began to wonder what it would be like. I wondered how time would have marred this unique, this holy spot — the coves and streams, the hills that the sun set behind, the camps and the paths behind the camps. I was sure that the tarred road would have found it out, and I wondered in what other ways it would be desolated. It is strange how much you can remember about places like that once you allow your mind to return into the grooves that lead back. You remember one thing, and that suddenly reminds you of another thing. I guess I remembered clearest of all the early mornings, when the lake was cool and motionless, remembered how the bedroom smelled of the lumber it was made of and of the wet woods whose scent entered through the screen. The partitions in the camp were thin and did not extend clear to the top of the rooms, and as I was always the first up I would dress softly so as not to wake the others, and sneak out into the sweet outdoors and start out in the canoe, keeping close along the shore in the long shadows of the pines. I remembered being very careful never to rub my paddle against the gunwale for fear of disturbing the stillness of the cathedral.

The lake had never been what you would call a wild lake. There were cottages sprinkled around the shores, and it was in farming country although the shores of the lake were quite heavily wooded. Some of the cottages were owned by nearby farmers, and you would live at the shore and eat your meals at the farmhouse. That's what our family did. But although it wasn't wild, it was a fairly large and undisturbed lake and there were places in it that, to a child at least, seemed infinitely remote and primeval.

I was right about the tar: it led to within half a mile of the shore. But when I got back there, with my boy, and we settled into a camp near a farmhouse and into the kind of summertime I had known, I could tell that it was going to be pretty much the same as it had been before—I knew it, lying in bed the first morning smelling the bedroom and hearing the boy sneak quietly out and go off along the shore in a boat. I began to sustain the illusion that he was I, and therefore, by simple transposition, that I was my father. This sensation persisted, kept cropping up all the time we were there. It was not an entirely new feeling, but in this setting it grew much stronger. I seemed to be living a dual existence. I would be in the middle of some simple act, I would be picking up a bait box or laying down a table fork, or I would be saying something and suddenly it would be not I but my father who was saying the words or making the gesture. I gave me a creepy sensation.

We went fishing the first morning. I felt the same damp moss covering the worms in the bait can, and saw the dragonfly alight on the tip of my rod as it hovered a few inches from the surface of the water. It was the arrival of this fly that convinced by beyond any doubt that everything was as it always had been, that the years were a mirage and that there had been no years. The small waves were the same, chucking the rowboat under the chin as we fished at anchor, and the boat was the same boat, the same color green and the ribs broken in the same places, and under the floorboards the same fresh water leavings and débris—the dead helgramite, the wisps of moss, the rusty discarded fishhook, the dried blood from yesterday's catch. We stared silently at the tips of our rods, at the dragonflies that came and went. I lowered the tip of mine into the water, tentatively, pensively dislodging the fly, which darted two feet away, poised, darted two feet back, and came to rest again a little farther up the rod. There had been no years between the ducking of this dragonfly and the other one—the one that was part of memory. I looked at the boy, who was silently watching his fly, and it was my hands that held his rod, my eyes watching. I felt dizzy and didn't know which rod I was at the end of.

We caught two bass, hauling them in briskly as though they were mackerel, pulling them over the side of the boat in a businesslike manner without any landing net, and stunning them with a blow on the back of the head. When we got back for a swim before lunch, the lake was exactly where we had left it, the same number of inches from the dock, and there was only the merest suggestion of a breeze. This seemed an utterly enchanted sea, this lake you could leave to its own devices for a few hours and come back to, and find that it had not stirred, this constant and trustworthy body of water. In the shallows, the dark, water-soaked sticks and twigs, smooth and old, were undulating in clusters on the bottom against the clean ribbed sand, and the track of the mussel was plain. A school of minnows swam by, each minnow with its small individual shadow, doubling the attendance, so clear and sharp in the sunlight. Some of the other campers were in swimming, along the shore, one of them with a cake of soap, and the water felt thin and clear and unsubstantial. Over the years there had been this person with the cake of soap, this cultist, and here he was. There had been no years.

Up to the farmhouse to dinner through the teeming dusty field, the road under our sneakers was only a two-track road. The middle track was missing, the one with the marks of the hooves and the splotches of dried, flaky manure. There had always been three tracks to choose from in choosing which track to walk in; now the choice was narrowed down to two. For a moment I missed terribly the middle alternative. But the way led past the tennis court, and something about the way it lay there in the sun reassured me; the tape had loosened along the backline, the alleys were green with plantains and other weeds, and the net (installed in June and removed in September) sagged in the dry noon, and the whole place steamed with midday heat and hunger and emptiness. There was a choice of pie for dessert, and one was blueberry and one was apple, and the waitresses were the same country girls, there having been no passage of time, only the illusion of it as in a dropped curtain—the waitresses were still fifteen; their hair had been washed, that was the only difference—they had been to the movies and seen the pretty girls with the clean hair.

Summertime, oh, summertime, pattern of life indelible with fade-proof lake, the wood unshatterable, the pasture with the sweetfern and the juniper forever and ever, summer without end; this was the background, and the life along the shore was the design, the cottages with their innocent and tranquil design, their tiny docks with the flagpole and the American flag floating against the white clouds in the blue sky, the little paths over the roots of the trees leading from camp to camp and the paths leading back to the outhouses and the can of lime for sprinkling, and at the souvenir counters at the store the miniature birchback canoes and the postcards that showed things looking a little better than they looked. This was the American family at play, escaping the city heat, wondering whether the newcomers in the camp at the head of the cove were "common" or "nice," wondering whether it was true that the people who drove up for Sunday dinner at the farmhouse were turned away because there wasn't enough chicken.

It seemed to me, as I kept remembering all this, that those times and those summers had been infinitely precious and worth saving. There had been jollity and peace and goodness. The arriving (at the beginning of August) had been so big a business in itself, at the railway station the farm wagon drawn up, the first smell of the pine-laden air, the first glimpse of the smiling farmer, and the great importance of the trunks and your father's enormous authority in such matters, and the feel of the wagon under you for the long ten-mile haul, and at the top of the last long hill catching the first view of the lake after eleven months of not seeing this cherished body of water. The shouts and cries of the other campers when they saw you, and the trunks to be unpacked, to give up their rich burden. (Arriving was less exciting nowadays, when you sneaked up in your car and parked it under a tree near the camp and took out the bags and in five minutes it was all over, no fuss, no loud wonderful fuss about trunks.)

Peace and goodness and jollity. The only thing that was wrong now, really, was the sound of the place, an unfamiliar nervous sound of the outboard motors. This was the note that jarred, the one thing that would sometimes break the illusion and set the years moving. In those other summertimes all motors were inboard; and when they were at a little distance, the noise they made was a sedative, an ingredient of summer sleep. They were one-cylinder and two-cylinder engines, and some were make-and-break and some were jump-spark, but they all made a sleepy sound across the lake. The one-lungers throbbed and fluttered, and the twin-cylinder ones purred and purred, and that was a quiet sound, too. But now the campers all had outboards. In the daytime, in the hot mornings, these motors made a petulant, irritable sound; at night in the still evening when the afterglow lit the water, they whined about one's ears like mosquitoes. My boy loved our rented outboard, and his great desire was to achieve single-handed mastery over it, and authority, and he soon learned the trick of choking it a little (but not too much), and the adjustment of the needle valve. Watching him I would remember the things you could do with the old one-cylinder engine with the heavy flywheel, how you could have it eating out of your hand if you got really close to it spiritually. Motorboats in those days didn't have clutches, and you would make a landing by shutting off the motor at the proper time and coasting in with a dead rudder. But there was a way of reversing them, if you learned the trick, by cutting the switch and putting it on again exactly on the final dying revolution of the flywheel, so that it would kick back against compression and begin reversing. Approaching a dock in a strong following breeze, it was difficult to slow up sufficiently by the ordinary coasting method, and if a boy felt he had complete mastery over his motor, he was tempted to keep it running beyond its time and then reverse it a few feet from the dock. It took a cool nerve, because if you threw the switch a twentieth of a second too soon you would catch the flywheel when it still had speed enough to go up past center, and the boat would leap ahead, changing bull-fashion at the dock.

We had a good week at the camp. The bass were biting well and the sun shone endlessly, day after day. We would be tired at night and lie down in the accumulated heat of the little bedrooms after the long hot day and the breeze would stir almost imperceptibly outside and the smell of the swamp drift in through the rusty screens. Sleep would come easily and in the morning the red squirrel would be on the roof, tapping out his gay routine. I kept remembering everything, lying in bed in the mornings — the small steamboat that had a long rounded stern like the lip of a Ubangi, and how quietly she ran on the moonlight sails, when the older boys played their mandolins and the girls sang and we ate doughnuts dipped in sugar, and how sweet the music was on the water in the shining night, and what it had felt like to think about girls then. After breakfast we would go up to the store and the things were in the same place — the minnows in a bottle, the plugs and spinners disarranged and pawed over by the youngsters from the boys' camp, the Fig Newtons and the Beeman's gum. Outside, the road was tarred and cars stood in front of the store. Inside, all was just as it had always been, except there was more Coca-Cola and not so much Moxie and root beer and birch beer and sarsaparilla. We would walk out with the bottle of pop apiece and sometimes the pop would backfire up our noses and hurt. We explored the streams, quietly, where the turtles slid off the sunny logs and dug their way into the soft bottom; and we lay on the town wharf and fed worms to the tame bass. Everywhere we went I had trouble making out which was I, the one walking at my side, the one walking in my pants.

One afternoon while we were at that lake a thunderstorm came up. It was like the revival of an old melodrama that I had seen long ago with childish awe. The second-act climax of the drama of the electrical disturbance over a lake in America had not changed in any important respect. This was the big scene, still the big scene. The whole thing was so familiar, the first feeling of oppression and heat and a general air around camp of not wanting to go very far away. In midafternoon (it was all the same) a curious darkening of the sky, and a lull in everything that had made life tick; and then the way the boats suddenly swung the other way at their moorings with the coming of a breeze out of the new quarter, and the premonitory rumble. Then the kettle drum, then the snare, then the bass drum and cymbals, then crackling light against the dark, and the gods grinning and licking their chops in the hills. Afterward the calm, the rain steadily rustling in the calm lake, the return of light and hope and spirits, and the campers running out in joy and relief to go swimming in the rain, their bright cries perpetuating the deathless joke about how they were getting simply drenched, and the children screaming with delight at the new sensation of bathing in the rain, and the joke about getting drenched linking the generations in a strong indestructible chain. And the comedian who waded in carrying an umbrella.

When the others went swimming my son said he was going in, too. He pulled his dripping trunks from the line where they had hung all through the shower and wrung them out. Languidly, and with no thought of going in, I watched him, his hard little body, skinny and bare, saw him wince slightly as he pulled up around his vitals the small, soggy, icy garment. As he buckled the swollen belt, suddenly my groin felt the chill of death.

Questions for Study

1. The thesis of White's essay appears in the second paragraph: "On the journey over to the lake I began to wonder what it would be like. I wondered how time would have marred this unique, this holy spot — the coves and streams, the hills that the sun set behind, the camps and the paths behind the camps." Choose one of the features of the area White wrote about — for example, the camp, the lake itself, or the pathways — and make a list of the descriptive details he used to follow through on his thesis.
2. White used both objective and subjective description. Give an example of each type.
3. White wrote that he began to associate himself with his father. Which details trigger these ideas? List them.
4. "You can't go home again": Thomas Wolfe's words sum up what most of us feel about trying to return to the past. Did White feel the same way, or does his essay show that sometimes a trip back in time is possible? Express your opinion in a paragraph or so.

ALTERNATE ASSIGNMENT D

In this essay, E. B. White wrote about what happened when he did what so many of us would like to do: go back to a place that we visited when we were young and try to experience once again the sensations we remember so well. If you've done what White wrote about, tell what happened when you returned. If you haven't, write about a place that you would like to revisit, explaining how you think it might have changed.

Imagine for a moment that you're the lone figure of authority facing over two thousand people who really don't want you to be in charge, and you will begin to understand the position George Orwell wrote about in "Shooting an Elephant." Orwell is noted for his fine attention to detail, as this picture he drew of life and death in Burma shows. This essay is far more than the retelling of his killing an elephant; it is also the story of a testing of wills that left Orwell the loser.

Shooting an Elephant

GEORGE ORWELL

In Moulmein, in Lower Burma, I was hated by large numbers of people—the only time in my life that I have been important enough for this to happen to me. I was sub-divisional police officer of the town, and in an aimless, petty kind of way anti-European feeling was very bitter. No one had the guts to raise a riot, but if a European woman went through the bazaars alone somebody would probably spit betel juice over her dress. As a police officer I was an obvious target and was baited whenever it seemed safe to do so. When a nimble Burman tripped me up on the football field and the referee (another Burman) looked the other way, the crowd yelled with hideous laughter. This happened more than once. In the end the sneering yellow faces of young men that met me everywhere, the insults hooted after me when I was at a safe distance, got badly on my nerves. The young Buddhist priests were the worst of all. There were several thousands of them in the town and none of them seemed to have anything to do except stand on street corners and jeer at Europeans.

All this was perplexing and upsetting. For at that time I had already made up my mind that imperialism was an evil thing and the sooner I chucked up my job and got out of it the better. Theoretically—and secretly, of course—I was all for the Burmese and all against their oppressors, the British. As for the job I was doing, I hated it more bitterly than I can perhaps make clear. In a job like that you see the dirty work of Empire at close quarters. The wretched prisoners huddling in the stinking cages of the lock-ups, the grey, cowed faces of the long-term convicts, the scarred buttocks of the men who had been flogged with bamboos—all these oppressed me with an intolerable sense of guilt. But I could get nothing into perspective. I was young and ill-educated and I had had to think out my problems in the utter silence that is imposed on every Englishman in the East. I did not even know that the British Empire is dying, still less did I know that it is a great deal better than the younger empires that are going to supplant it. All I knew was that I was stuck between my hatred of the empire I served and my rage against the evil-spirited little beasts who tried to make my job impossible. With one part of my mind I thought of the British Raj as an unbreakable tyranny, as something clamped down, in *saecula saeculorum*, upon the will of prostrate peoples; with another part I thought that the greatest joy in the world would be to drive a bayonet into a Buddhist priest's guts. Feelings like these are the normal by-products of imperialism; ask any Anglo-Indian official, if you can catch him off duty.

One day something happened which in a round-about way was enlightening. It was a tiny incident in itself, but it gave me a better glimpse than I had had before of the real nature of imperialism—the real motives for which despotic governments act. Early one morning the sub-inspector at a police station the other end of town rang me up on the phone and said that an elephant was ravaging the bazaar. Would I please come and do something about it? I did not know what I could do, but I wanted to see what was happening and I got onto a pony and started out. I took my rifle, an old .44 Winchester and much too small to kill an elephant, but I thought the noise might be useful *in terrorem*. Various Burmans stopped me on the way and told me about the elephant's doings. It was not, of course, a wild elephant, but a tame one which had gone "must." It had been chained up, as tame elephants always are when their attack of "must" is due, but on the previous night it had broken its chain and escaped. Its mahout, the only person who could manage it when it was in that state, had set out in pursuit, but had taken the wrong direction and was now twelve hours' journey away, and in the morning the elephant had suddenly reappeared in the town. The Burmese population had no weapons and were quite helpless against it. It had already destroyed somebody's bamboo hut; killed a cow and raided some fruit-stalls and devoured the stock; also it had met the municipal rubbish van, and, when the driver jumped out and took to his heels, had turned the van over and inflicted violences upon it.

The Burmese sub-inspector and some Indian constables were waiting for me in the quarter where the elephant had been seen. It was a very poor quarter, a labyrinth of squalid bamboo huts, thatched with palm-leaf, winding all over a steep hillside. I remember that it was a cloudy, stuffy morning at the beginning of the rains. We began questioning the people as to where the elephant had gone, and, as usual, failed to get any definite information. That is invariably the case in the East; a story always sounds clear enough at a distance, but the nearer you get to the scene of events the vaguer it becomes. Some of the people said that the elephant had gone in one direction, some said that he had gone in another, some professed not even to have heard of an elephant. I had almost made up my mind that the whole story was a pack of lies, when we heard yells a little distance away. There was a loud, scandalized cry of "Go away, child! Go away this instant!" and an old woman with a switch in her hand came round the corner of a hut, violently shooing away a crowd of naked children. Some more women followed, clicking their tongues and exclaiming; evidently there was something that the children ought not to have seen. I rounded the hut and saw a man's dead body sprawling in the mud. He was an Indian, a black Dravidian coolie, almost naked, and he could not have been dead many minutes. The people said that the elephant had come suddenly upon him round the corner of the hut, caught him with its trunk, put its foot on his back and ground him into the earth. This was the rainy season and the ground was soft, and his face had scored a trench a foot deep and a couple of yards long. He was lying on his belly with arms crucified and head sharply twisted to one side. His face was coated with mud, the eyes wide open, the teeth bared and grinning with an expression of unendurable agony. (Never tell me, by the way, that the dead look peaceful. Most of the corpses I have seen looked devilish.) The friction of the great beast's foot had stripped the skin from his back as neatly as one skins a rabbit. As soon as I saw the dead man I sent an orderly to a friend's house nearby to borrow an elephant rifle. I had already sent back the pony, not wanting it to go mad with fright and throw me if it smelled the elephant.

The orderly came back in a few minutes with a rifle and five cartridges, and meanwhile some Burmans had arrived and told us that the elephant was in the paddy fields below, only a few hundred yards away. As I started forward practically the whole population of the quarter flocked out of the houses and followed me. They had seen the rifle and were all shouting excitedly that I was going to shoot the elephant. They had not shown much interest in the elephant when he was merely ravaging their homes, but it was different now that he was going to be shot. It was a bit of fun to them, as it would be to an English crowd; besides, they wanted the meat. It made me vaguely uneasy. I had no intention of shooting the elephant—I had merely sent for the rifle to defend myself if necessary—and it is always unnerving to have a crowd following you. I marched down the hill, looking and feeling a fool, with the rifle over my shoulder and an ever-growing army of people jostling at my heels. At the bottom, when you got away from the huts, there was a metalled road and beyond that a miry waste of paddy fields a thousand yards across, not yet ploughed but soggy from the first rains and dotted with coarse grass. The elephant was standing eight yards from the road, his left side towards us. He took not the slightest notice of the crowd's approach. He was tearing up bunches of grass, beating them against his knees to clean them and stuffing them into his mouth.

I had halted on the road. As soon as I saw the elephant I knew with perfect certainty that I ought not to shoot him. It is a serious matter to shoot a working elephant—it is comparable to destroying a huge and costly piece of machinery— and obviously one ought not to do it if it can possibly be avoided. And at that distance, peacefully eating, the elephant looked no more dangerous than a cow. I thought then and I think now that his attack of "must" was already passing off; in which case he would merely wander harmlessly about until the mahout came back and caught him. Moreover, I did not in the least want to shoot him. I decided that I would watch him for a little while to make sure that he did not turn savage again, and then go home.

But at that moment I glanced round at the crowd that had followed me. It was an immense crowd, two thousand at the least and growing every minute. It blocked the road for a long distance on either side. I looked at the sea of yellow faces above the garish clothes—faces all happy and excited over this bit of fun, all certain that the elephant was going to be shot. They were watching me as they would watch a conjurer about to perform a trick. They did not like me, but with the magical rifle in my hands I was momentarily worth watching. And suddenly I realized that I should have to shoot the elephant after all. The people expected it of me and I had got to do it; I could feel their two thousand wills pressing me forward, irresistibly. And it was at this moment, as I stood there with the rifle in my hands, that I first grasped the hollowness, the futility of the white man's dominion in the East. Here was I, the white man with his gun, standing in front of the unarmed native crowd—seemingly the leading actor of the piece; but in reality I was only an absurd puppet pushed to and fro by the will of those yellow faces behind. I perceived in this moment that when the white man turns tyrant it is his own freedom that he destroys. He becomes a sort of hollow, posing dummy, the conventionalized figure of a sahib. For it is the condition of his rule that he shall spend his life in trying to impress the "natives," and so in every crisis he has got to do what the "natives" expect of him. He wears a mask, and his face grows to fit it. I had got to shoot the elephant. I had committed myself to doing it when I sent for the rifle. A sahib has got to act like a sahib; he has got to appear resolute, to know his own mind and do definite things. To come all that way, rifle in hand, with two thousand people marching at my heels, and then to trail feebly away, having done nothing—no, that was impossible. The crowd would laugh at me. And my whole life, every white man's life in the East, was one long struggle not to be laughed at.

But I did not want to shoot the elephant. I watched him beating his bunch of grass against his knees, with that preoccupied grandmotherly air that elephants have. It seemed to me that it would be murder to shoot him. At that age I was not squeamish about killing animals, but I had never shot an elephant and never wanted to. (Somehow it always seems worse to kill a *large* animal.) Besides, there was the beast's owner to be considered. Alive, the elephant was worth at least a hundred pounds; dead, he would only be worth the value of his tusks, five pounds, possibly. But I had got to act quickly. I turned to some experienced-looking Burmans who had been there when we arrived, and asked them how the elephant had been behaving. They all said the same thing: he took no notice of you if you left him alone, but he might charge if you went too close to him.

It was perfectly clear to me what I ought to do. I ought to walk up to within, say, twenty-five yards of the elephant and test his behavior. If he charged I could shoot, if he took no notice of me it would be safe to leave him until the mahout came back. But also I knew that I was going to do no such thing. I was a poor shot with a rifle and the ground was soft mud into which one would sink at every step. If the elephant charged and I missed him, I should have about as much chance as a toad under a steam-roller. But even then I was not thinking particularly of my own skin, only of the watchful yellow faces behind. For at that moment, with the crowd watching me, I was not afraid in the ordinary sense, as I would have been if I had been alone. A white man mustn't be frightened in front of "natives"; and so, in general, he isn't frightened. The sole thought in my mind was that if anything went wrong those two thousand Burmans would see me pursued, caught, trampled on and reduced to a grinning corpse like that Indian up the hill. And if that happened it was quite probable that some of them would laugh. That would never do. There was only one alternative. I shoved the cartridges into the magazine and lay down on the road to get a better aim.

The crowd grew very still, and a deep, low, happy sigh, as of people who see the theatre curtain go up at last, breathed from innumerable throats. They were going to have their bit of fun after all. The rifle was a beautiful German thing with cross-hair sights. I did not then know that in shooting an elephant one would shoot to cut an imaginary bar running from ear-hole to ear-hole. I ought, therefore, as the elephant was sideways on, to have aimed straight at his ear-hole; actually I aimed several inches in front of this, thinking the brain would be further forward.

When I pulled the trigger I did not hear the bang or feel the kick—one never does when a shot goes home—but I heard the devilish roar of glee that went up from the crowd. In that instant, in too short a time, one would have thought, even for the bullet to get there, a mysterious, terrible change had come over the elephant. He neither stirred nor fell, but every line on his body had altered. He looked suddenly stricken, shrunken, immensely old, as though the frightful impact of the bullet had paralyzed him without knocking him down. At last after what seemed a long time—it might have been five seconds, I dare say—he sagged flabbily to his knees. His mouth slobbered. An enormous senility seemed to have settled upon him. One could have imagined him thousands of years old. I fired again into the same spot. At the second shot he did not collapse but climbed with desperate slowness to his feet and stood weakly upright, with legs sagging and head drooping. I fired a third time. That was the shot that did for him. You could see the agony of it jolt his whole body and knock the last remnant of strength from his legs. But in falling he seemed for a moment to rise, for as his hind legs collapsed beneath him he seemed to tower upwards like a huge rock toppling, his trunk reaching skywards like a tree. He trumpeted, for the first and only time. And then down he came, his belly towards me, with a crash that seemed to shake the ground even where I lay.

I got up. The Burmans were already racing past me across the mud. It was obvious that the elephant would never rise again, but he was not dead. He was breathing very rhythmically with long rattling gasps, his great mound of a side painfully rising and falling. His mouth was wide open—I could see far down into the caverns of pale pink throat. I waited a long time for him to die, but his breathing did not weaken. Finally I fired my two remaining shots into the spot where I thought his heart must be. The thick blood welled out of him like red velvet, but still he did not die. His body did not even jerk when the shots hit him, the tortured breathing continued without a pause. He was dying, very slowly and in great agony, but in some world remote from me where not even a bullet could damage him further. I felt that I had got to put an end to that dreadful noise. It seemed dreadful to see the great beast lying there, powerless to move and yet powerless to die, and not even to be able to finish him. I sent back for my small rifle and poured shot after shot into his heart and down his throat. They seemed to make no impression. The tortured gasps continued as steadily as the ticking of a clock.

In the end I could not stand it any longer and went away. I heard later that it took him half an hour to die. Burmans were bringing dahs and baskets even before I left, and I was told they had stripped his body almost to the bones by the afternoon.

Afterwards, of course, there were endless discussions about the shooting of the elephant. The owner was furious, but he was only an Indian and could no nothing. Besides, legally I had done the right thing, for a mad elephant has to be killed, like a mad dog, if its owner fails to control it. Among the Europeans opinion was divided. The older men said I was right, the younger men said it was a damn shame to shoot an elephant for killing a coolie, because an elephant was worth more than any damn Coringhee coolie. And afterwards I was very glad that the coolie had been killed; it put me legally in the right and it gave me a sufficient pretext for shooting the elephant. I often wondered whether any of the others grasped that I had done it solely to avoid looking a fool.

Questions for Study

1. Orwell stated that the Burmese were unhappy with the British occupation. Make a list of the details Orwell included to illustrate this unhappiness.
2. Orwell's story is actually a statement against the British imperialism of the time. In a paragraph, explain how the episode of shooting the elephant helps to illustrate that occupying a nation against the wishes of its people is eventually a hopeless task?
3. Probably the most descriptive part of the story is the section that begins with the actual shooting of the elephant (the eleventh paragraph). Reread this section and then make two columns, listing the objective details in one and the subjective details in another.
4. In this essay, Orwell's descriptive skills are especially on target in dealing with the killing of the elephant. Take one of the details from this section of the essay — the description of the blood as red velvet, for instance — and explain why you feel it is particularly effective.

ALTERNATE ASSIGNMENT E

"As soon as I saw the elephant I knew with perfect certainty that I ought not to shoot him." Yet Orwell did shoot the elephant, even though he knew that shooting it was unnecessary. He felt trapped by the crowd; he felt that to walk away without shooting the elephant would somehow compromise his authority with the Burmese. In other words, Orwell suffered from a variation of a force that we are all quite familiar with: peer pressure. Write about a time when you yielded to peer pressure. Tell the story but explain also how giving in to the pressure of others made you feel. In particular, what did you feel (both emotionally and physically) *before* you did what you were actually very much against doing? And what feelings did you experience *after* you had done what you really didn't want to do?

How I Wrote It

The Advent of Glory, the Death of a Church

WILLIAM J. KELLY

At the corner of Dover and Snell Streets in Fall River is a parking lot. Eleven years ago, a green-domed, Spanish-style church, squat yet majestic, stood there, overlooking the place where first the Quequechan River and later Route 195 cut through the heart of the city.

SS. Peter and Paul Church, dedicated in 1900, was a mile from the center of the city, and the lines of the parish encompassed some of the poorer neighborhoods. The church struggled for life, and it survived, perhaps because of the loyalty and sheer tenacity of its parishioners.

The church building is gone now, the victim of a fire that destroyed it in 1973. But to me the site is much more than the former location of SS. Peter and Paul Church: It is the symbol of Christmas.

Early in Advent, the inside of the church was decorated, and the pattern was always the same: Two Christmas trees in the sanctuary, one on either side of the altar, and two wreaths on the light, inlaid woodwork behind the altar, with evergreen garlands framing the scene. To the left of the main sanctuary, a creche dominated the St. Mary's altar.

Of course, while the decorations looked the same year after year, the church itself did not. It simply grew more shopworn.

In its last years, the church suffered badly from leaks that stained to a dirty beige large areas of the once-salmon walls. The frescoes, particularly the ones around the inside of the great dome, had faded and were beginning to crumble.

The linoleum flooring throughout the church had long ago lost its sheen, and the pews sagged and squeaked at every move of the worshippers.

At the back of the church, the framed honor rolls listing parishioners who had served in the two World Wars were yellowed with age and neglect. Even the bas-relief Stations of the Cross had faded to a uniform dullness, their once-beautiful colors now darkened as if to match their surroundings.

There were only a few windows, and they were so dark and dirty that it was often difficult to distinguish the stained glass from the lead that enclosed it. Compounding the sense of age and decay, the lighting throughout the church was meager except above the sanctuary, where it was fair.

The hallmark of the Christmas celebration was Midnight Mass. One Christmas Eve in particular, in 1966, my first year as an altar boy, stands out in memory.

By 11 that night, we were all in the sacristy, where we added freshly ironed surplices to scarlet cassocks and lined up for the procession that would snake along the side aisles to the back of the church for our march down the center aisle.

At midnight, the organ blared and the four acolytes led us through the sacristy door and into the church by the St. Joseph's altar at the east side of the main sanctuary. We squeezed between the crowded pews until we reached the back of the church, where we struggled past the late-comers who were jammed against the back wall, under the choir loft.

As we walked from the sacristy to the back of the church, I was too nervous to look at much more than the backs of the altar boys in front of me. Once I reached the center aisle, though, I relaxed a little, and as I looked around I was overwhelmed by a sense that something was different: This tired church — the same church I had always found dingy and decayed — was now, suddenly, beautiful.

The pews leading to the altar seemed filled with splashes of color rather than people. Light was cast on the Stations but, mercifully, away from the crumbling plaster.

The sanctuary, decorated just as it had been for the last three weeks, now shone brilliantly, the muted light throughout the rest of the church providing a perfect contrast. The great dome looked awesome in the half-light.

All the way up the aisle, I tried to figure out why the church, decorated almost a month ago, now looked transformed. Finally, as the brass gates in the middle of the marble altar rail grated shut, I figured it out.

There was no miracle; the difference had nothing to do with any solemnity or sacredness. The rich darkness of midnight had, for a brief time, simply obscured all the defects and so restored dignity to that weary church.

After mass, I left to walk the half-mile home. As I crossed Dover Street, I turned to look back at the church.

At that point, I saw that it was not yet willing to give up its reign, for around the great dome, the stained-glass windows glowed in the early morning darkness, illuminating the scenes captured in the glass as I had never seen before. I looked for a moment, then turned and walked home.

The night the church burned down, seven years later, I didn't go to watch the fire, even though I lived within walking distance. The next morning, as I drove to school along Route 195, I looked up the hill and saw that the great dome had fallen into the smoking shell of the building. I knew the church was dead.

For a while, Mass was held in the basement of the separate parish school. Later, the ruins were leveled. The first floor of the school was converted into a new church.

In the end, though, the new cannot replace the old; for me, a part of Christmas died when that church did.

I originally wrote this piece as an entry in a Christmas essay contest sponsored by the *Providence Sunday Journal Magazine*. I didn't win, although they accepted this slightly changed version as a free-lance piece a few years later.

I began my planning of the story with the end: the "trick" of stained glass. During the day, when light shines through a stained-glass window, the colors show up if you are inside the church; at night, when the inside illumination is greater than the light outside, the colors are more visible outside. When I remembered how poor the interior lighting was in the church, I also realized why the church looked so much better at midnight than it looked during the day. So it was a descriptive detail that provided the climax of the story.

Once I had that bit of information, it was easy to backtrack and use description to illustrate the surprise I felt when I discovered the difference in the church that Christmas Eve. I made a list of the details I could remember about the interior of the church by mentally walking back through it. Some of the little things, like the honor rolls in the back of the church, were pretty easy to remember. Others details, like the number of windows and the types of stations of the cross were more difficult. Eventually I developed a decent list of details — information like the frescoes around the dome, the color of the walls, and the marble altar rail with the twin brass gates — that became the supporting description in the story.

In between the time I originally wrote the story and its publication, I revised it several times. In addition, the editor made some changes that initially disappointed me. The third paragraph of the published version reads this way:

> The church building is gone now, the victim of a fire that destroyed it in 1973. But to me the site is much more than the former location of SS. Peter and Paul Church. It is the symbol of Christmas.

I liked (and I still do like) my original wording:

> The church is gone now, the victim of a fire that first humbled and then destroyed it. But, to me, the site is much more than the former location of SS. Peter and Paul Church. It remains the symbol of Christmas, more capable of evoking a sense of this season than anything I can think of.

Obviously, the changes are minor, but I still prefer the word *humbled* to explain how I felt when I saw the ruins of this once-mighty building. And I wanted to make sure my reader understood that the location had a particular significance concerning Christmas only for me. Even if other people see the parking lot and remember that a church used to be there, I'm sure their memories wouldn't automatically focus on Christmas.

The editor saw things otherwise. As you've already found out with your own papers, you may not like the changes your "editor" suggests, but you should remember this: if what you've written somehow doesn't meet the needs of your reader, it isn't your reader's fault; it's your fault. As you can see, the changes don't ultimately worsen the story, and although I hate to admit it, the changes probably improve it.

ALTERNATE ASSIGNMENT F

Special ceremonies or occasions leave vivid memories because of the splendor, solemnity, or significance associated with them. Write an essay about one of the special occasions of your life — your high school prom, for instance, or your bar mitzvah or confirmation or wedding — using the descriptive details about yourself and the place in which it took place to put your reader right out there in the crowd watching.

Chapter 9

════════ PROCESS ════════

INTRODUCTION

It's fifteen minutes before midnight on Christmas Eve, and you're looking at several piles of parts that, totaled up, are supposed to become the beautiful bicycle pictured on the carton. Luckily for you, there's a set of instructions right in the box.

Your luck runs out, however, as soon as you begin looking at the instructions. For one thing, none of the reference points mentioned in the instructions seem to be present on the bicycle frame: there's no Tab B to insert in Slot O, and so on. And the hardware described doesn't match the equipment provided. For instance, carriage bolts are mentioned, but none are included, and as far as you can tell, none should be required.

The clock continues to tick as you struggle with the directions. Finally, working from the illustration on the carton and your own experience, you manage to get the bike together just in time to put it next to the Christmas tree early Christmas morning. As you collect your tools, you think to yourself, "What I would have given for a set of directions that made sense!"

Everyone would agree that poorly written directions complicate a job — and that well-written ones make that job easier. A set of directions is one example of process writing. But you don't use process solely to tell how to do things; you also use it to explain how something occurs (sometimes called **process analysis**) and to explain how something was done (sometimes called **process narrative**).

How, for instance, do plants convert sunlight into energy? The explanation of this process, known as *photosynthesis*, would be a process analysis, as would be a paper that explains how instant film develops or how beaches erode. A lab report that records an experiment that you performed in biology, however, an account of an investigation of a car crash, and a paper explaining how a battle was won would all be process narrative.

But no matter what type, process deals with **how** — how you do it or how it was done or how it works — in a step-by-step method, with plenty of specific details at each step in the sequence, as well as clear connections between those steps. Because it enables you to present instructions, relate the procedures that individuals undertake, and explain the workings of devices, process is a valuable technique to master.

THE MAKEUP OF A PROCESS PAPER

Process appears frequently in your writing. Sometimes, it's the supporting technique. For example, in a paper about the various problems associated with human organ transplants, you might include a passage that explains the process of rejection by which the body seeks to protect itself from what it perceives as an invading foreign object.

At other times, however, the subject you choose to write about requires a more thorough use of process. A "how-to" writing is a good example. A successful process paper of this type begins with a clear thesis. For instance, for a paper explaining how to perform CPR (cardiopulmonary resuscitation), the thesis would be something like this:

> As the Red Cross says, performing CPR is as simple as ABC:
> open the Airway, provide Breath, and restore Circulation.

This thesis provides a direction for your reader; it clearly states what the paper will cover. Then the body follows through on this direction by presenting the various steps in the process: opening an airway, identifying a lack of breathing or circulation or both, and beginning timed artificial breathing and circulation —artificial respiration and chest compressions.

Of course, a process paper must inform, not confuse. Therefore each step of a relatively simple process such as CPR must be presented clearly and directly so that someone with little or no experience could perform the various steps. Look, for instance, at these paragraphs explaining the first steps in CPR:

> When you discover someone passed out, always assume that
> person might need CPR; therefore, check for breathing and
> circulation. First, (1) with one hand under the neck of
> the victim and (2) another on his or her forehead,
> (3) bend the neck back gently to provide a generous airway,
> and (4) open the victim's mouth. (5) insert two fingers
> into the victim's mouth and quickly clear out any debris.
>   (6) Then move your fingers midway down the side of the
> neck until you reach the carotid artery, the main blood
> vessel that runs to the brain. (7) Pressing slightly with
> the same two fingers, feel for a pulse, a throbbing against
> your fingers. Don't use your thumb because it has its own
> pulse.
>   At the same time, (8) turn your head to the side near
> the individual's mouth in order to feel any breath. If the
> individual doesn't have a pulse or isn't breathing, you
> must act very quickly; once oxygen is cut off, brain damage
> will begin and will eventually lead to death unless the
> oxygen supply is restored.

As the numbers show, these paragraphs present this part of the process in eight steps, each relatively simple to perform. It therefore follows through on the thesis. The other paragraphs in the body would present the other steps involved in CPR—administering artificial respiration and chest compressions —each of which is actually a series of steps itself.

Of course, the same principle would hold if you were explaining how air-conditioning works or how a dancer has recovered from an Achilles tendon injury. You would still explain by dividing the process or event into its various steps. Whatever process you write about, the paper must begin with a clear thesis and must be supported by the body of the paper that presents the steps of the process. The result is a paper that will make the subject—some process —clear and understandable to your reader.

USING THE TECHNIQUE

If your process paper is to be effective, the process you present must be clear and understandable to your reader. The following suggestions will help you meet your reader's needs:

1. Don't confuse a list of hints or suggestions with a process paper.

In the strictest sense, a process paper presents a series of steps that, followed in sequence, explain how to do something or how something is done. A paper that presents independent guidelines, hints, or suggestions, however, is not a process paper.

Of course, a paper that provides hints or guidelines would still be good. A paper about studying in college, for example, might begin with a thesis like this:

```
Overall, though, you'll find studying for your college
classes easier if you follow these steps.
```

This thesis could be supported by a body featuring such suggestions as recopying notes in order to remember the information, studying with classmates in a study group, preparing for examination questions similar to those expected, and working for no more than two hours at a time without a break.

A paper featuring this type of information would obviously have merit; the suggestions make sense, and students would no doubt benefit from them. But because each major suggestion could be performed independently of the others or in a completely different order without alteration of the outcome, it wouldn't be a process paper.

You will have occasion to use both writing that actually presents a process and writing that presents some guidelines or hints. Both are important types of writing, and both have specific purposes. One is process, however, and one isn't.

2. Use the second person—*you*—when it is appropriate.

Although sometimes you won't want to address your reader directly, consider using the second person pronoun *you* in a process paper, particularly in a how-to paper. In a set of directions, you are essentially telling someone to do something. Therefore address your reader directly; indirect instructions increase the chances of confusion. Consider this paragraph from a paper on changing a tire:

```
     Once the hubcap has been removed, the driver should take
the lug wrench and begin loosening the lug nuts. The driver
should start with the lug nut closest to the ground; then
the driver should loosen the lug nut diagonally across from
the nut just loosened. The driver should follow a star
pattern until all the nuts are removed; when all the lug
nuts are removed, the driver should store them in the hubcap
until the tire is changed and the lug nuts must be put back on.
```

Compare that version with this version, which features the second person:

```
     Once the hubcap has been removed, take the lug wrench and
begin loosening the lug nuts. Start with the lug nut
closest to the ground, and then loosen the lug nut
diagonally across from the nut just loosened. Follow a star
pattern until all the nuts are removed. When all the lug
nuts are removed, store them in the hubcap until you've
finished changing the tire and then put the lug nuts back on.
```

The second version is both shorter and more direct. The instructions are the same in both, but the second version addresses the reader directly.

Sometimes, of course, the second person would be inappropriate. For instance, using *you* as an indefinite pronoun could be both awkward and confusing. A sentence like — You will spend several years in prison when you rob a bank and are caught and convicted — labels your reader a bank robber and convict-to-be, and a sentence like — You had a tough life back in Shakespeare's time — gives your reader a life span of over 350 years. Eliminate the problem by rewriting the sentences:

```
A person faces several years in prison after being
convicted for bank robbery.
```

```
Life was difficult in Shakespeare's time.
```

As long as you are clearly addressing your reader, *you* is appropriate.

    3.   Separate the process into small, understandable units.

Because you understand the process you're writing about, you can sometimes forget how complex it actually is for somebody else. An old joke illustrates this problem:

A tourist comes upon a sculptor standing next to a full-scale statue of an elephant carved from a single block of granite. The tourist, fascinated with the detail, can't resist asking, "How did you do that?" "Easy," the artist replies, "I simply chipped away everything that didn't look like an elephant."

What makes the joke funny is the sculptor's oversimplification of carving a statue by overlooking one crucial aspect: artistic talent, a quality people do not possess in equal amounts.

In a process paper, you may fall into the same trap that the sculptor fell into because you are writing about something you understand. For example, you have tied shoelaces thousands of times in your life; there's nothing to it, you think. But imagine for a moment that you are explaining how to tie shoelaces to someone who has never before seen them. Directions like these wouldn't be effective:

> First, take a shoelace in each hand. Next, cross them over and put one underneath the other and pull both ends tight. Then, form two loops with the ends and cross them over each other, feeding one loop under the other. Pull on the two loops, and your shoe is tied.

These directions are obviously written for someone who has a great deal of experience in tying shoelaces. But for the individual who lacks that experience, these instructions would be hard to follow because they don't contain enough specific information. Compare that version with this amplified paragraph:

> First, take the end of a shoelace in each hand. Next cross the shoelaces over, right lace on top, switching hands as you cross the laces. Take the end you are now holding with your right hand and wrap it under the one you are holding in your left hand; pull the ends out straight to tighten the first part of the knot. While holding the laces tight, form two loops, leaving about two inches on the end of each loop. Then take the loop in your right hand, cross it over the loop in your left hand, and leave a space as big around as your index finger. Finally, wrap this right-hand loop around the left-hand loop and then push it through the space you left. Pull slowly and firmly on the two loops, and the knot will tighten.

The second version provides more specific directions. For instance, the first version says "cross over"; the second version tells how to do so and which hands to use when you do. Perhaps the second version of the directions still isn't foolproof—somebody without any experience still might struggle—but these instructions are much better.

Of course, it's unlikely you'll ever have to write an explanation of how to tie a shoelace. But you might have to explain how the human circulatory system works. If you wrote, "The heart pumps blood throughout the body; the blood then returns to the heart," your sentence would grossly understate the complex steps in circulation: the heart pumps oxygenated blood to body tissues through the arteries and capillaries and eventually, through the veins, back to the heart, where it is first sent to the lungs to be oxygenated again and, once the blood is oxygen-rich again, from the lungs to the heart again to be sent back through the body.

Consider the needs of your reader. Don't assume that your reader has your level of expertise. Admittedly, your reader may know something about your subject, but because you can't be certain that this is so, present your process so that anyone — especially someone with no experience — could understand your presentation.

4.   Keep the order of the process consistent.

In a process paper, the order that you choose is crucial. Process writing is supposed to present steps that are **linear,** in which one thing leads to the next. Therefore you must arrange your paper consistently so that you present the process step-by-step.

Imagine, for example, that you are writing instructions for changing the washer in a faucet. The process includes removing the handle of the faucet, pulling out the stem, taking out the old washer, inserting a new washer, and putting the stem back in and the handle of the faucet back on.

Oh yes — there is one other step: Turn off the water *before* you start. That's the first step. If you follow these instructions without first turning off the water, you had better make your plumbing repair in your bathing suit.

If you've had any experience following a recipe, you know how a change in the order called for can affect the meal you prepare. If the set of directions you prepare explaining how to get to a wedding reception mentions one highway exit out of order, for instance, your guests may never find the reception hall. No matter what subject you are talking about, you must make sure that you present the steps in the exact order.

5.   Alert your reader to the need for any special equipment or to the potentials for difficulty.

Some of the processes you write about will be relatively simple and straightforward; subjects such as how to tie a neck tie, for instance, or how a bean develops from seed to plant are fairly uncomplicated.

A subject like felling a tree with a chainsaw is a different matter, however. For one thing, a chainsaw is among the most dangerous of power tools; if the operator makes even a small mistake in judgment, permanent disfigurement, maybe death, could result. Therefore provide some warnings about potential problems:

```
     From the moment that blade touches the tree, beware of a
kickback, the saw's sudden jolt toward you caused when the
saw hits a foreign object or some particularly hard spot in
the wood. To guard against being hurt by one of these
kickbacks, never lean against the saw to help it through
the wood. If your saw cuts too slowly, have it sharpened or
consider buying another, larger chain saw. Also, always
keep your fingers at least eight inches away from the blade
whenever the saw is running. Straying fingers are easy
victims of chain-saw kickback.
```

This paragraph serves the needs of the reader by pointing out potential dangers. As a result, it makes the paper more effective.

Even if the subject you write about is not dangerous, it may be potentially confusing or may require some special equipment. In these cases, you should also alert your reader. In a paper about taking an intravenous blood sample, for example, a paragraph such as the following will prepare your reader for a difficult step:

```
    Once you have applied a tourniquet and identified the
vein from which you will draw your sample, insert the
needle. This step is probably the most difficult, as you
must insert the needle into the vein-but not through it-at
the right angle and reasonably quickly so that you don't
add to the patient's discomfort.
```

This paragraph is a caution flag for your reader because it indicates a potential difficulty. Notice that it doesn't give any specific instructions; the paragraphs that follow take care of the instructions. This paragraph simply underscores the potential for difficulty.

Sometimes a process you write about will require special equipment. In these cases, you'll want to provide a listing of this information near the beginning of the paper — if not right in the introduction. In a paper about replacing a pane of glass, you might begin with a paragraph like this:

```
    The next time a foul ball wipes out one of your windows,
don't call a carpenter. Instead of spending twenty dollars
or more for labor and materials, fix it yourself for a
fraction of the cost. To complete the repair job yourself,
you'll need a one-inch putty knife, a can of window putty,
and a replacement pane cut to the proper size. You'll
probably have some of the needed equipment at home; the
rest is available at your local hardware store.
```

This paragraph designates exactly what equipment is needed and where it might be available. As a result, the reader knows right from the beginning what is necessary to complete the process.

A process paper shouldn't contain any surprises concerning what is difficult or what is needed to complete the steps presented. Give your reader any warnings and a listing of the special equipment necessary to understand the process you are presenting.

Process is an important technique to master because it explains what your reader needs to know: how to do something or how something occurs or works. No matter what your subject is, as long as you present the sequence directly, in manageable units, in a consistent order, and with warnings about any potential problems, your paper will be successful.

ASSIGNMENT 5

In a 400- to 600-word essay, explain how to perform some routine household or maintenance task.

Reason

People spend their lives simultaneously performing a variety of tasks and learning to do a variety of others. A process paper can therefore review a well-known process or present a whole new method or technique for some task. Both types of papers will have an obvious appeal to your reader.

A paper dealing with planting a lawn, for instance, would interest many readers, even those who already have established lawns. After all, a luxuriant lawn adds to the value of the property it showcases, and knowing how a lawn develops may better enable a person to care for that valuable green stuff. But for the person who is looking out on patches of dirt, with an occasional weed here and there, a paper that explains how to turn that rough into a fairway would be immediately popular.

As any good writing should, a process paper such as this would begin with a clear thesis:

```
Although at first thought it might not seem possible,
planting and raising the lawn of your dreams is a task you
can complete in one weekend, with a month afterward of
maintenance of forty-five minutes a day.
```

Once this thesis is introduced, the sequence of steps is presented. In this case, the first step is preparing the soil, a step that involves a variety of possibilities.

If the soil in the yard is suitable — and you can establish this by taking a soil sample to a local agricultural school or to a garden-supply company — you can rake out the soil, removing any rocks, and then loosen the soil to the depth of a few inches. Or you can use a rototiller, a device about the size and shape of a snowblower that loosens the soil and prepares it for seed. But if the soil is poor, you will have to add nutrients or bring in and spread new topsoil. Even though your reader will follow only one of these options, you must explain each in the appropriate detail.

The next step is spreading the fertilizer. In most cases, this should be done with a spreader, a device similar to a push lawnmower that evenly distributes preset amounts of powdered fertilizer, ensuring that the proper amounts of nutrients will nurture the soil. The fertilizer shouldn't be spread by hand because there is no way to tell whether the target area has been properly covered. Too much fertilizer may actually kill the seed; at the least, the grass may grow up in uneven clumps and stripes because the fertilizer wasn't evenly distributed.

The ground must next be moistened, and seed must be put down. Because it gives more control in terms of the area to be moistened and the amount of water applied, a hose rather than a sprinkler should be used. A generous amount of seed must then be put down by hand. Finally the lawn must be thoroughly soaked, again by hose, and the lawn must be watered in the same way at least every other day for the following month.

A paper on this topic would definitely be effective. It would provide clear information about a task for those people who want to start a lawn, as well as for those who have tried and failed because they didn't completely understand the process. And knowing how a lawn develops would also be useful for those who already have lawns and are concerned about keeping those lawns healthy. In any case, a process paper like this would be successful because it would meet the needs of the reader — and that's what any paper you write is supposed to do.

What Your Reader Needs

From a "how-to" paper, your reader needs to know two things: (1) exactly what the process is and (2) exactly how to complete it. You take care of the first requirement with a clear thesis, and you fulfill the second with a series of clear, simple, and understandable steps in the body of your paper.

To meet the needs of your reader, you first need to spell out what process you are writing about. If you are going to show how to get up on water skis successfully, your introduction should make this process clear for your reader. Your thesis shouldn't say you are going to explain a summertime activity, because it might mislead your reader; there are many summertime activities. And it shouldn't say that you are going to explain how to water-ski, because it would be unrealistic to expect to teach such a complex activity in one short paper.

If your intent is to teach someone how to get up out of the water — to start water-skiing — then your thesis should make this clear:

```
If you follow these few easy steps, with a little practice
you'll be able to perform the most difficult part of water-
skiing: getting up on the skis.
```

Once your reader has this clear direction, provide the series of steps making up the process. Unless you are writing a process paper for an advanced audience, you should present your steps for the beginner. This means not only breaking the process down into steps that can be completed by someone with no particular experience in the process but also using simple, clear, and understandable examples.

To get up on water skis, for example, you must perform these steps in sequence: (1) check the buckles on the safety vest or lifebelt to make sure the flotation device is securely fastened as you get in the water behind the boat; (2) put your feet in the rubber "boots" on the skis; (3) grasp the handle of the towline overhand, not underhand; (4) bring your knees up to your chest between your arms so that the tips of the skis are out of the water; (5) hold the handle of the towbar firmly as the boat takes up the slack in the tow rope; (6) signal the pilot of the boat when you are ready to start; (7) hold your back stiff and use your feet and flexed knees to "fight" the water as the boat picks up speed; and (8) lean back slightly as the power of the boat pulls you and the skis up out of the water.

But getting up on skis that first time is much more difficult than these simple statements suggest. Therefore your reader needs each step explained in simple, clear, and understandable terms. To be suitable for the reader, the fourth step of this paper would need to be amplified:

> Once your feet are in the ''boots'' and you have an overhand grip on the handle of the towline, shift around in the water to get in the proper position to be pulled up out of the water. Many people fall back into the water or never really get up on skis because they aren't prepared for the sudden pull forward as the boat accelerates. Compensate for this pulling by using the position of your body to ''fight'' the water. Bring your knees between your arms almost up to your chest and lean back a little as if you were in a reclining chair. Don't worry about sinking; the flotation belt or vest will keep your head above the surface of the water. As you lean back, the tips of the skis will come out of the water, and you'll be in the perfect position to get up on your skis.

This paragraph communicates the process to the reader because the process is broken down into simple steps; it provides clear understandable directions, explanations, cautions, and reassurances, so that the average person with no experience could complete this step of the process.

Your reader always depends on you to provide clear and understandable writing; this dependence is particularly strong in a process paper. Your process paper presents a series of steps with which your reader may have little or no experience. Therefore, you must present the steps so that this inexperienced reader will be able to perform the process.

Model

FENCE PAINTING THE EASY WAY

One of the most boring jobs facing a property owner is painting a fence, particularly a chain-link fence. Because of the way it's made, this type of fence requires careful attention so that all its surfaces will be adequately protected. However, you can make the work easier by following a few simple steps so that a boring job will not have to be a long and frustrating one, too.

First, get all the material together. Besides two gallons of aluminum paint (enough to cover two hundred feet of fence), you will need a wire brush, a two-inch paint brush, a four-inch paint brush or a roller and a paint tray, and a few old rags.

Once you have collected the materials, check your work site. If the grass is overgrown around the bottom of the fence, clip the grass so it won't get in your way. Then begin wire-brushing the entire fence, stroking the brush vigorously against the metal. This process will remove any flaking paint or spots of rust so that the new coat of paint will stick to the surface better. This part of the job is time-consuming, but it will ensure that the job will not have to be repeated again very soon.

After the fence is wire-brushed, stir the paint to be sure that the color is even. Five minutes should be long enough. Once the paint is mixed, begin painting the posts with the two-inch brush. This smaller brush will allow you to get around the wire so that more paint gets on the post.

Next, begin to paint the chain-link itself, using the four-inch brush. Paint diagonally, from the top of the fence down, so that you get the maximum coverage out of each stroke. You may find this part a little tedious, but there should be no spots to be touched up after.

If you use a roller, follow the same order—diagonally, from the top down. Pass the roller over the fence slowly so that you cover the surface fully. Remember to make sure the roller isn't too full of paint because it will splatter all over the place. Of course, whether you use a brush or a roller, you will have to repeat the same steps for both sides of the fence. Once you have cleaned everything up according to the paint manufacturer's directions on the back of the can of paint (usually they call for soaking the brushes in turpentine or mineral spirits), your job is complete.

If these simple steps are followed, the job of painting a chain-link fence can become a great deal easier. As long as you have to suffer in the hot sun painting, you might as well make the job as simple and effective as possible. Done carefully, your paint job should last for several years, during which time you should be able to forget how irritating the thought of doing the job was in the first place.

Follow-through

A "how-to" paper always has great potential for success. The key lies in first specifying exactly what the process is and then presenting the steps in specific, easy-to-understand terms.

The starting point for a set of directions is the specific subject. The obvious choice is something you know how to do well; don't try to explain how to groom a horse, for instance, unless you've done it or have the time to do the necessary research to find out how to do the job. In the case of this paper, the starting point was the task itself, a relatively common household task: painting a chain-link fence. The prewriting on this topic produced this information:

• *can be a messy job, need plenty of rags*

- *a roller is easier, but you have to be careful not to splatter paint all over — that's why I hate to paint a ceiling with a roller — you end up polka-dotted*
- *need a wire brush, too — that's the worst part of this job — takes a lot of elbow grease to get the rust and flaking paint off — I wonder if the flakes of paint are dangerous, like abestos or lead?*
- *need to cut the long grass and weeds, too — otherwise, the grass gets in the way and you end up painting the grass instead of the fence*
- *when I painted our fence last year, I used about 2 gallons of aluminum paint for 200 feet*
- *paint the posts separately — use a two-inch brush*
- *if the chain link is vinyl-coated, you don't paint it — maybe just the posts*
- *rather than buying a roller and tray, you can use a four-inch brush*
- *it's best to paint diagonally from the top down — that way, any excess paint will drip down and hit some of the rest of the fence*
- *boring job, no matter what you do — I've painted four different ones so I should know*
- *have to paint both sides, of course*
- *clean up is pretty standard — should I mention it?*

This list features most of the information used in the final draft, although it appears there in a different form. But before it can appear in this final form, a number of steps must be taken.

For example, you must establish the sequence. Doing so will help ensure that the subject will indeed be a process rather than a list of guidelines. In the case of this paper, for instance, the initial writing produces the following main steps:

- 2 *need a wire brush, too — that's the worst part of this job — takes a lot of elbow grease to get the rust and flaking paint off — I wonder if the flakes of paint are dangerous, like abestos or lead?*
- 1 *need to cut the long grass and weeds, too — otherwise, the grass gets in the way and you end up painting the grass instead of the fence*
- 3 *paint the posts separately — use a two-inch brush*
- 4 *it's best to paint diagonally from the top down — that way, any excess paint will drip down and hit some of the rest of the fence*
- 5 *have to paint both sides, of course*
- 6 *clean up is pretty standard — should I mention it?*

The initial listing never contains all the information needed to complete a final draft. Therefore, it's no surprise that this prewriting doesn't contain one of the steps that appears in the final draft: stirring the paint. Gaps such as this one are filled in with the necessary details as you compose and revise.

As these steps show, painting a chain-link fence is definitely a process. The steps must be performed in the set order (numbered in the prewriting) to achieve the result: a painted chain-link fence.

The steps of any process must be made as simple and understandable as possible. Remember, your reader is a beginner, dependent on you to explain how to perform the process. In the case of this paper, the process is fairly simple to begin with. Basically the painter must gather the necessary materials, prepare the job site by clipping grass and wire-brushing the fence, paint the posts, paint the chain link, and clean up. But the steps are clearly divided and explained so that a beginner could easily follow them.

For instance, look at this paragraph from the final draft:

```
    If you use a roller, follow the same order—diagonally,
from the top down. Pass the roller over the fence slowly so
that you cover the surface fully. Remember to make sure the
roller isn't too full of paint because it will splatter all
over the place. Of course, whether you use a brush or a
roller, you will have to repeat the same steps for both
sides of the fence. Once you have cleaned everything up
according to the paint manufacturer's directions on the
back of the can of paint (usually they call for soaking the
brushes in turpentine or mineral spirits), your job is
complete.
```

This paragraph contains information that will definitely help the beginner. Even experienced painters sometimes give themselves a quick "spray painting," thanks to a too-full roller; a beginner would certainly splatter paint unless warned.

In addition, this paragraph reminds the reader of another step that may possibly be forgotten: painting the opposite side of the fence. Because the instructions call for a careful, complete painting of the first surface of the chain link, a beginner may forget to paint the opposite side as well.

Rather than providing a multitude of possible directions for cleanup, the paragraph suggests following the instructions provided by the manufacturer. This makes great sense; different brands and types of paint require different types of cleanup. Rather than presenting information that could be inappropriate for a particular brand of paint, this section simply provides a general parenthetical explanation of what cleanup usually entails and then notes where to find the specific instructions to perform this final step.

In a set of directions, the second person is usually appropriate. You are, after all, addressing your reader directly. This paper would be much longer and less direct without the use of *you*. Look, for instance, at this brief paragraph, in which the second person has been replaced by the third person — *you* replaced by *worker*:

```
    After the fence is wire-brushed, the worker must stir
the paint to be sure that the color is even. Five minutes
should be long enough. Once the paint is mixed, the worker
must begin painting the posts with the two-inch brush. This
smaller brush will allow the painter to get around the wire
so that more paint gets on the post.
```

Now look at the same paragraph as it looked in the final draft:

```
After the fence is wire-brushed, stir the paint to be
sure that the color is even. Five minutes should be long
enough. Once the paint is mixed, begin painting the posts
with the two-inch brush. This smaller brush will allow you
to get around the wire so that more paint gets on the post.
```

The first version is longer: sixty-one words versus fifty-four words in the final draft version. A more serious problem, however, is that the first version doesn't talk directly to the reader. The final draft version is both shorter and more direct, and therefore more effective.

If it is going to fulfill its purpose—to enable a reader to perform the task—a "how-to" paper must be clear, understandable, and direct. You make your process paper effective by first providing a specific introduction for your reader; then a sequence of the process, in steps small and simple enough for the beginner to handle; and finally, a conclusion restating the essence of the process. A process paper fulfilling these requirements will be successful because a reader will be able to perform the task it sets forth. In a process paper, that's the sign of success.

Checklist

Use the answers to the following questions to help you revise your first draft:

1. Does your paper have a thesis? Write it down.
2. Check the sequence of the steps. Is your paper actually a process, or is it a list of suggestions?
3. Have you addressed your reader directly?
4. Is each step simple and clear? Could any step be further divided?
5. Have you noted any potential problems or special equipment needed to complete the task?
6. Does your introduction provide a clear direction for your reader?
7. Does your conclusion restate the essence of the process?

ASSIGNMENT 6

In a 400- to 600-word essay, take some process—one occurring naturally or one that is the basis for some device or machine, for example—and explain it.

Reason

Whether it's a device, a phenomenon, or cycle of the world around us, process is an everyday concern. People want to understand how things work: how the human eye functions, how flowers grow, how thunderstorms occur, how internal combustion engines work. Therefore a paper that explains one of those processes has built-in appeal.

In a paper that explains a process, you present the various steps so that your reader is able to follow the progression. Most things are far more complex than they seem at first glance, even for a person who has a working knowledge of the subject. For someone new to it — and basically that's your audience — the complexity can be overpowering unless you separate the process into smaller, simpler units.

Imagine, for instance, that you are explaining how the standard household dehumidifier works. Most people have heard of the device; many own dehumidifiers themselves to remove dampness from cellars or other excessively damp spots. Dehumidifiers work by drawing humid air across cold coils. As the humid air hits the coils, it condenses — turns to liquid — and collects in a tray or is carried through a hose to some drain.

Understanding how such a device works can be important for the homeowner, for one reason in particular: if the temperature in the affected area drops below sixty-five degrees Fahrenheit, most units will not function, and the moisture that collects on the coils will freeze. If the unit continues to run with ice on the coils, the motor that drives the fan may be damaged; at the very least, the appliance will waste electricity that the homeowner will still be paying for.

Knowing how an expensive household appliance like a dehumidifier works would help owners get the most for their money; the value of this information basically underscores the importance of such a paper. If the introduction prepares the reader for the steps that follow, if the sequence itself is simple, clear, and understandable, and if the conclusion restates the significance of the process, your paper will be effective.

What Your Reader Needs

When you explain a natural or manufactured process, you have an advantage because the process that is the basis for the paper is right there in front of you. What your reader needs is a version of that process that takes the complex set of steps and presents it in terms that someone unfamiliar with the process could understand.

Let's say you are explaining how the average household septic system works. As you write, you should normally assume that your reader knows little or nothing about private septic systems. Sometimes, of course, you will be writing for an audience that shares a fairly advanced level of knowledge, for example, in a paper to be presented aloud to your astronomy class explaining how a star first develops, glows, and then finally burns out. In this case, you'll be writing for a group of individuals who already have a base of information about the stars; you can therefore feel comfortable talking about **novas** and **supernovas** and **black holes**.

Most of the time, however, you won't be writing to other experts; in these cases, you must write for the beginner. With a private septic system as your subject, you should present the basics. That means explaining the main parts of the system — the plumbing that carries the waste water out of the house, the holding tank that is the first stop for the waste water, and the distribution tanks (sometimes called *beehives*) that distribute the waste water — as well as how these parts of the system carry out the process.

Basically your reader needs to know what happens to the waste water, and tracing the pathway it follows explains this: (1) the waste water leaves the house and is collected in the holding tank; (2) it then flows to the distribution containers; (3) it leaches out into surrounding soil; and (4) it gradually filters through the earth. The result is a writing that meets your reader's needs.

A paper that effectively explains how some process occurs is both practical and valuable. You can make sure your paper is effective by sizing up your reader and your reader's needs. You'll be writing a paper about some process that you understand. Remember, however, that most of the time your reader won't share your knowledge; if you adjust your presentation with this fact in mind, the paper that results will be successful.

Model

THE DEATH OF A SMILE

Take a look in the mirror and smile. If your gums look pink, firm, and attractive, chances are that your smile is healthy. But if your reflection lacks any of these characteristics, you could be suffering from some stage of periodontitis, a disease that turns healthy gingiva, commonly called <u>gums,</u> into a breeding ground for bacteria that will wage a war on your teeth. Unchecked, periodontal disease will make your smile a casualty.

In the first stage of periodontitis, the gums become tender and sensitive to the touch. They swell up, bleed, and even begin to recede, exposing the more sensitive underlying surfaces of the teeth. Instead of a healthy pink, the gums take on an angry red hue. This stage can occur within one year, even with brushing, unless the teeth are regularly flossed and professionally cleaned and examined. Of course, things like poor eating habits and smoking can accelerate the process.

Without treatment, the advanced stage of periodontitis can set in within five years. At this point, the gums recede permanently and the teeth become loose as the supporting bone begins to disintegrate. All along the gums, infected pockets appear. The mouth becomes greatly inflamed and sore.

If dental care is still put off, the final stage of periodontal disease can begin within ten years. In this stage, the bone that supports the teeth is completely and irreversibly destroyed. Because they are no longer anchored in bone, the teeth that remain become very loose and useless. At this point, the only solution is to pull the remaining teeth and then replace them with a set of false teeth. A healthy smile has died. Its porcelain-and-plastic substitute, greatly inferior to the original, flashes in the mirror now.

Of course, a smile doesn't have to die. Proper dental

care is a matter of habit. Daily brushing and flossing.
along with regular visits to a dental hygienist for
cleanings and examinations, keep periodontal disease in
check. Improving diet and eliminating smoking also help to
keep a smile healthy. A smile is a beautiful gift. With a
little care and attention, it will last a lifetime.

Follow-through

The first step to success in a process paper is to choose a topic that you
understand well. The second step is to separate that process into steps that
someone lacking your experience — someone with the level of knowledge you
had **before** you learned that particular process — will be able to understand.
Basically that's your goal.

The process outlined in this paper is periodontitis, the medical name for
what is commonly referred to as *gum disease*. Once the process is identified, the
preliminary stage of the writing process begins. Take a look at this preliminary

*gum disease — periodontitis — starts with bad hygiene — ten years after it
starts, your teeth are all shot — gums swell up, bleed, etc. — it's too bad — after
the eyes people notice a smile first — rotten teeth are a real turnoff — you see a
lot of people walking around like that — the health instructor said that there are
plenty of cases among educated people and people with money — not just poor
people — you can tell by looking at their gums when they smile — if your gums
are healthy, they're pink and they don't bleed — flossing is important — a lot of
people think brushing is enough, but it isn't — regular cleanings, too — what
you eat really affects it, so does smoking — can even happen if you brush, but
you'd have to do a pretty poor job — when it starts, the gums hurt if you touch
them, and you can see some of the root exposed — bacteria get in and an infection
begins — I'll bet it must make for horrible breath — Bucky at work had it — he
had these big buck teeth but you could tell they were loose — everybody hated to
talk to him face to face because his breath stunk — he's had rotten teeth for a long
time but the books says it only takes five years or so before real damage starts —
bone underneath the gums begins to break down permanently and teeth loosen
up — all the roots start showing — real sensitive — mouth hurts all the time — if
nothing is done, after a few more years all the bone underneath is gone — the
teeth kind of float around, no good for chewing, etc. — they have to be pulled —
it's funny, but I'll bet some of the teeth that have to be pulled don't even have bad
cavities — it's the bone underneath and the gums that are the worst*

The preliminary writing basically presents the main steps in order:

   *1. starts with bad hygiene; 2. when it starts, the gums hurt if you touch
them, and you can see some of the root exposed — bacteria get in and an
infection begins; 3. it only takes five years or so before real damage starts —
bone underneath the gums begins to break down permanently and teeth loosen*

up — all the roots start showing — real sensitive — mouth hurts all the time;
(4) if nothing is done, after a few more years all the bone underneath is gone —
the teeth kind of float around, no good for chewing, etc. — they have to be pulled

As you can see, the list also produces information that is not used — the details about the co-worker, for instance, and the comments by the health instructor. That's common in the writing process. But the preliminary writing does include information that eventually supports the main steps — the material about regular cleanings, for example, and the acknowledgment that diet and smoking can affect the development of the disease.

This paper about periodontitis is clearly process. Without treatment, the disease becomes progressively worse over a ten-year period, with various stages occurring in sequence: poor hygiene leads to the first part of the infection, which leads to an increasing disintegration of supporting bone, and so on. Each step of this process is presented in simple and understandable terms, exactly what's called for in this type of paper.

In a set of instructions, the second person — *you* — is usually appropriate. In the explanation of this process, however, the second person is definitely not called for; using *you* would inadvertently indicate that the reader suffers from a disease resulting from poor oral hygiene, as this example shows:

> Without treatment, the advanced stage of periodontitis can set in within five years. At this point, your gums recede permanently and your teeth become loose as the supporting bone begins to disintegrate. All along your gums, infected pockets appear. Your mouth becomes greatly inflamed and sore.

As you can see, the underlined words make the paper far less appealing to the reader; it suggests that the reader has periodontitis. Make sure that if you do use the second person, you don't accidentally use it in an indefinite sense. *You* is, however, the correct choice when you address the reader directly.

Because this is not a "how-to" paper, there is no presentation of special equipment. The paper does occasionally present some complex terminology, but these terms are explained or defined. *Periodontitis,* for instance, and *gingiva* are both defined; even *recede* is explained as it relates to teeth. As a result, the process is much clearer for the reader.

The sum of all these points is a paper that explains a process in clear, understandable terms. It explains how a relatively common condition develops; more important, it also explains how such a disease can be prevented. The result is a successful paper because it brings the process across clearly to the reader.

Checklist

Use the answers to the following questions to help you revise your first draft:

1. Does your paper have a thesis? Write it down.

2. Check the sequence of the steps. Is your paper actually a process or is it a list of suggestions?
3. If you've used the second person, is it appropriate?
4. Is each step simple and clear: Could any step be further divided?
5. Have you explained or defined any special terms or equipment?
6. Does your introduction provide a clear direction for your reader?
7. Does your conclusion restate the essence of the process?

FOR FURTHER STUDY

If you don't know how to swim or if you've worried about what might happen if you were somehow unable to swim as you normally do, you will truly appreciate Carla Stephen's "how-to" paper, "Drownproofing." In a clear, step-by-step fashion, Stephens simplifies the seemingly complex task of staying afloat so that even a nonswimmer might well be able to survive until help arrives.

Drownproofing

CARLA STEPHENS

If your warm-weather plans include water sports, there's one thing you should do to make this summer safe as well as enjoyable for your family: Drownproof them!

Drowning is the second leading cause of accidental death for people between the ages of 4 and 44, according to the American National Red Cross. Twenty-eight percent of those drowned are children under 15 years old. Seven out of ten of them are boys.

Even more shocking is the fact that many of the seven thousand annual drowning victims *know how to swim*. In fact, swimmers face several hazards that non-swimmers don't. First, they may overexert themselves — especially in May and June when they're likely to expect out-of-condition bodies to perform as well as in summers past. They may also get into a situation beyond their skills. If panic takes over, tragedy may follow.

With drownproofing, on the other hand, a poor swimmer or even a non-swimmer can survive in the water twelve hours or more — even when fully clothed and in rough water.

Developed by the late Fred Lanoue, drownproofing relies on the body's ability to float when air fills the lungs. Picture yourself bobbing restfully just under the surface of the water. With a few easy movements you come up to breathe as often as necessary. That's the basic idea of drownproofing, a technique endorsed by the Red Cross, the National Safety Council and the YMCA. It's easy to learn, even for some three-year-olds. You can teach yourself and your family.

Here's how it's done: First, take a breath through your mouth. Then, holding your breath, put your face into the water and float vertically with your arms and legs dangling. Don't try to keep your head up; it weighs fifteen pounds.

When you're ready for another breath, slowly raise your arms to shoulder height. At the same time bring one leg a little forward and the other back into a position somewhat like the scissors kick. (If injury makes it necessary, drownproofing can be done with either the arm or the leg movements.) Then gently press your arms down to your sides (not backward) and bring your legs together. Keep your eyes open and raise your head until your mouth is out of the water. Exhale through your nose, your mouth or both.

Inhale through your mouth while continuing to press your arms down. But don't press too hard, for you want to keep your chin at, not above, the surface of the water. Finally, return to the resting position with your face in the water. If you sink too far, a small kick or a slight downward push of your arms will return you to the surface.

When teaching your children, it's advisable to stand with them in shoulder-deep water. Have them bend forward to practice the breathing and arm movements. If they swallow water, be patient and encourage them to try again. Once they're comfortable with the procedure, move into deeper water near the side of the pool to coordinate the floating, breathing and body movements. Water just deep enough for them to go under is sufficient. Remember, all movements should be easy and relaxed.

If your child needs to work at the vertical float, let him practice at the side of a pool or some other spot where he'll be able to hold on. At first you might even help hold him up by placing a hand just beneath his shoulder. Have him take a breath, put his face into the water and then remove his hands from the side. As soon as he has some experience in floating remove your hand and watch.

While practicing, youngsters usually spend only about three seconds under water at first. That time should gradually increase—depending, of course, on their age. Older children may reach ten seconds, the period recommended for adults.

With a little practice your family will be drownproofed and truly ready for fun in the water.

Questions for Study

1. Stephens's initial paragraph is short—a single sentence—but is it still effective? Explain your answer in a few sentences.
2. The thesis for this essay is actually "spread out" over the first four paragraphs. Paraphrase the thesis.
3. Make a list of the steps in the drownproofing sequence.
4. Stephens was addressing both experienced swimmers and nonswimmers. Are there any steps in the paper that need to be explained in more complete detail, especially for nonswimmers? Answer in a brief paragraph.
5. Stephens's paper ends somewhat abruptly. Prepare a more traditional conclusion for this essay.

ALTERNATE ASSIGNMENT G

Carla Stephens's essay deals with staying safe while involved in a leisure-time activity. For this assignment, take another leisure-time activity and explain how to perform some part of it. For instance, how do you throw a curve ball? Perform a magic trick? Toss a frisbee? Throw a dart? Shoot a foul shot? Each of these activities involves a complex series of steps; explain each step so that a newcomer to the activity will be able to perform the process.

———————

Process frequently appears in your writing as a supporting technique. This is the case in this excerpt from Frank DeFord's book *Alex: The Life of a Child*, which tells the story of his daughter and her struggle with cystic fibrosis, which robbed Alex of her vitality and eventually her life. In this writing, DeFord used process in a few different ways, including to illustrate how cystic fibrosis affects the afflicted child and what he and his wife used to have to put Alex through each day so that she could breathe.

Cystic Fibrosis

Frank Deford

Cystic fibrosis is, notwithstanding its name, a disease primarily of the lungs. It has nothing to do with cysts. It was not identified as a distinct clinical entity until the midthirties, and not until some years later was the full pathology comprehended. Inexplicably, the disease attacks not only the lungs but other disparate parts of the body: the pancreas, the major digestive organ; and, in males, the testes. So it undermines breathing, eating, reproduction — all of life itself.

The common agent in all cases is mucus. The cystic fibrosis victim's body manufactures too much mucus, or the mucus is too thick, or both. So baffling is the disease that nobody knows for sure which basic factor is the issue. Whatever, the mucus obstructs the airflow in the lungs and clogs the pancreas and the testes. Adding to the perplexity is the fact that no two patients have the same history, except in the sense that CF is always progressive, always terminal.

The luckiest patients are those born without lung involvement. Others have such mild cases that they go undetected for years; quite possibly there are even some CF patients who never know they have the disease, but die relatively young of some misunderstood pulmonary involvement. At the other end of the spectrum, some infants are essentially born dead, their tiny bodies so ravaged by the disease that they cannot even begin to draw breath.

As events proved, Alex was toward the worse end of the spectrum. While she died at eight, half of the children now born in the United States with cystic fibrosis who are diagnosed and treated live to the age of eighteen. Be grateful for small favors. Back in the midfifties, when the Cystic Fibrosis Foundation was started, a child with CF could not even expect to live to kindergarten. Regrettably, early steady advances stopped just about the time Alex was born. Until the early seventies almost every passing year saw another year of life expectancy added for a CF kid, but these advances were somewhat illusory. They were largely prophylactic, stemming almost entirely from better maintenance and more powerful antibiotics.

The longer life span in no way indicated an approaching cure, nor even a control (as, for example, insulin keeps diabetes under control). In a sense, it isn't accurate to say that we kept Alex alive—we merely postponed her dying.

Alex's day would start with an inhalation treatment that took several minutes. This was a powerful decongestant mist that she drew in from an inhaler to loosen the mucus that had settled in her lungs. Then, for a half hour or more, we would give her postural drainage treatment to accomplish the same ends physically. It is quite primitive, really, but all we had, the most effective weapon against the disease. Alex had to endure eleven different positions, each corresponding to a section of the lung, and Carol or I would pound away at her, thumping her chest, her back, her sides, palms cupped to better "catch" the mucus. Then, after each position, we would press hard about the lungs with our fingers, rolling them as we pushed on her in ways that were often more uncomfortable than the pounding.

Some positions Alex could do sitting up, others lying flat on our laps. But a full four of the eleven she had to endure nearly upside down, the blood rushing to her head, as I banged away on her little chest, pounding her, rattling her, trying somehow to shake loose that vile mucus that was trying to take her life away. One of her first full sentences was, "No, not the down ones now, Daddy."

Psychologists have found that almost any child with a chronic disease assumes that the illness is a punishment. Soon, the treatment itself blurs with the disease and becomes more punishment. Sick children have highly ambivalent feelings about their doctors, on the one hand hating them for the pain and suffering they inflict, on the other admiring them, wanting to grow up and be doctors. Wendy Braun and Aimee Spengler, Alex's best friends, told me after Alex died that whenever the three of them played doctors and nurses, Alex participated with enthusiasm, but when she played the doctor, it was always cancer she was seeking to cure. She could not bring herself to be a cystic fibrosis doctor. As much as she adored and trusted her specialist, Tom Dolan, she must have associated too much pain with him ever to want to *be* him.

In cystic fibrosis a child must transfer this attitude toward the parents, as well, for we were intimately and daily involved in the medical process. Imagine, if you will, that every day of your child's life you forced medicines upon her, although they never seemed to do any good; you required her to participate in uncomfortable regimens, which you supervised; and then, for thirty minutes or more, twice a day, you turned her upside down and pounded on her. And this never seemed to help either. I have been told that parents let their self-conscious resentment of the illness surface during the treatments, and I must face the fact that this was sometimes surely true of me too. In some moments I must have thought that I was also being punished.

And say what you will, explain to me intellectually all you want about how much the postural drainage helped Alex—still, when every day I had to thump my little girl, pound away on her body, sometimes when she was pleading with me, crying out in pain to stop, something came over me, changed me. I guess, over eight years, I did therapy two thousand times, and Carol many more, probably three thousand, having to manage both times each day when I was traveling. I never understood how she managed. But still, me: Two thousand times I had to beat my sick child, make her hurt and cry and plead—"No, not the down ones, Daddy"— and in the end, for what?

After the therapy was finished, we had to start on the medicines. I recall how exciting it was during one period—Alex was two and a half—when she *only* had to take one antibiotic. How glorious that was, just one antibiotic every day. Usually it was two, and Dr. Dolan had to keep changing them, as Alex's body built up immunities.

She had to take many other medications, too, including, relentlessly, an enzyme preparation named Viokase. The bulk of Viokase is animal enzyme, which Alex needed because her pancreas couldn't produce sufficient enzymes of its own. Relative to the medicines that dealt primarily with her lung problems, Viokase was pretty effective. The minority of CF patients who don't have lung involvement initially can get by with the pancreas problem as long as they diligently take their enzyme substitutes. Alex had to take Viokase every time she ate anything. Of course, considering her lung condition, this seemed like small potatoes. Carol and I didn't even think about it much.

For most of her life, before she learned to swallow pills, Alex took the Viokase as a powder, mixed into apple sauce, which was an inexpensive carrying agent that could transport the drug into the system without its breaking down. And so, before every meal she ever ate, Alex had a plate of apple sauce with the enzyme powder mixed in. It was foul-tasting stuff, a bitter ordeal to endure at every meal. "Oh, my appasaws," she would moan, "my appasaws," always pronouncing it as if it were a cousin to chain saws or buzz saws.

"Come on Alex, eat your Viokase," I would say, and rather impatiently, too. After all, she had already been through an inhalation treatment, a half hour of physical therapy, several liquid medications — so what was the big deal with the apple sauce. *Come on, let's go.* Alex had had a great appetite when she was younger, but a few years later she'd just pick at her food. It occurred to me then that if all your life eating was a project, and you couldn't eat a lot of the delicious things everybody else enjoyed, eventually eating would bore you. Imagine having to start off with apple sauce every time you ate anything — and not getting much sympathy for it, either.

Later, doctors and nurses or other people would say, "Alex seems to have lost her appetite," and I would nod gravely, being pretty sure by then that it was psychological. Eating, like everything else for Alex, had become strictly a matter of staying alive.

When she was very young, before she began to comprehend how pointless it all was, Alex was wonderfully accepting of all that was demanded of her. At first, like any baby, she wasn't in any position to quibble; she just seemed to go along, assuming that inhalation, apple sauce, and all that were things all babies endured. When she played with her dolls, she would give them therapy, putting off the down ones if the dolls behaved. After a time Alex began to notice that her brother was not required to endure what she did every day, but that didn't bother her too much either. Since she was the only baby girl around, she simply assumed that therapy was something that all babies and/or all girls must go through.

Only slowly did the recognition come that she was singled out for these things. Then she began to grope for the implications. One spring day when she was four, Alex came into my office and said she had a question. Just one was all she would bother me with. All right, I asked, what was it. And Alex said, "I won't have to do therapy when I'm a lady, will I?"

It was a leading question; she knew exactly where she was taking me.

As directly as I could I said, "No, Alex" — not because I would lie outright about it, but because I knew the score by then. I knew that she would not grow up to be a lady unless a cure was found.

Questions for Study

1. DeFord defined cystic fibrosis in the first sentence, and from that point he used process as one of his main techniques to tell the story of his daughter Alex. Take any of the sections of process and make a list of the steps within that section.
2. Which use of process has the most effect? Why? Explain in a paragraph.
3. How did the various processes required for treatment affect Alex? Her parents? Make a list of the effects for Alex and for her parents.
4. If DeFord had not included any process in the essay, would it still be as effective? Explain your point of view in a paragraph of about a hundred words.

ALTERNATE ASSIGNMENT H

DeFord was primarily writing about his daughter Alex and the severe discomfort and pain caused by cystic fibrosis. But at the same time, he explained the process of the disease. For this assignment, choose a disease or condition you know and explain its cycle. If you lack the necessary information about a disease or condition, head to the library and do a little research; then you'll have the information you'll need to explain the process.

Chapter 10

EXAMPLE

INTRODUCTION

You've probably said it hundreds of times yourself: "For example, . . ."
You've said it when you've made a statement and you wanted to make sure
that the other person understood what you meant. Basically that's the definition of example: writing that uses an instance to bring home some point to a
reader. As a writing technique, example is very common; if you've written
effectively, you've done so because you've used examples.

Take a look at this passage about prime-time soap operas — without the
necessary examples:

> The plots on the shows are unrealistic. Nobody could
> have that many near tragedies. A lot of the situations are
> based on coincidence. One person plots against and tries to
> ruin another. The formulas are the same: one devious
> character keeps trying to control the rest of them. It's
> the same plot; just the characters and settings change.

Confused? You should be. If you have watched any of the nighttime soap
operas, like "Dallas," "Knots Landing," "Dynasty," or "Falcon Crest," you
know there is truth in that paragraph. The problem is that this paragraph
doesn't explain or illustrate. Take a look at these paragraphs, which provide
the necessary examples:

> The plots on nighttime soap operas are unrealistic.
> Nobody could have that many near tragedies. On ''Dynasty,''
> Krystle Carrington had every problem you could imagine
> with her pregnancy, including a premature birth—at home,
> of course. The baby wasn't breathing either, but her
> husband, Blake Carrington, saved the baby with the worst-
> acted CPR you ever saw.
> So many of the little twists in the plot are based on
> coincidence, also. On ''Dallas,'' Pam was going to marry
> Mark Graison, and then he caught some rare disease and
> apparently died in a plane crash. Then she was going to
> remarry Bobby Ewing, but he was killed by her jealous

```
sister. But that was all right, because Mark wasn't really
dead-and a year later, neither was Bobby.
     On ''Dynasty,'' Blake Carrington just happens to have a
long-lost brother Ben who works with the evil Alexis Colby
to try to ruin him; just as J. R. Ewing tries to bury Cliff
Barnes season after season. One year J. R. had Cliff nearly
dead broke after getting him to invest all his money in some
offshore oil rigs. Cliff, who seems to live only to get back
at J. R., got lucky; the oil wells hit. Alexis Colby and
Blake Carrington fight for control of everyone on
''Dynasty''; J. R. fights for that control on ''Dallas.''
It's the same plot; just the characters and settings change.
```

These paragraphs give examples from two of the shows, "Dallas" and "Dynasty." They give the example of Krystle Carrington to explain the near trage-dies, the situations of Pam Ewing and Ben Carrington to illustrate coincidence, and the manipulations of J. R. Ewing and Alexis to show the constant plotting.

Although example is a writing technique that appears in all types of writ-ing, sometimes you will be called on to write a paper that relies more heavily on examples than any other technique as the main support for your thesis. If, for instance, your thesis is that the writing on prime-time soaps is poor, you would use several paragraphs with specific examples from "Dallas" and "Dynasty" to support that thesis. Or if you were writing about the typical television villain, you might illustrate that stereotype by giving various examples of the actions of J. R. Ewing as portrayed by Larry Hagman. In fact, you may find an example paper relatively easy to write. Once you have established your thesis, you build a frame of examples to support it and then restate the significance in a concluding paragraph.

THE MAKEUP OF AN EXAMPLE PAPER

Imagine for a moment that you are playing a game like "Family Feud" at home with some friends. The object of the game is to match the responses that people have given to a survey question, and your team has one minute to answer the following: "Name four recent fads."

Immediately your team starts talking. "Designer jeans," somebody says. "No, no, designer jeans are still in — a fad is something like hula hoops," someone else says. "How about pet rocks?" "Nah, it says 'recent.' Pet rocks went out years ago!" After forty-five seconds of frantic talking, your team comes up with the following: multicolored hair, sunglasses on a string, Bo Derek–style hair (hair that is braided and beaded, as she wore hers in the movie *10*), and camouflage clothing. Your team loses — pet rocks were listed, along with Brooke Shields dolls, mood rings, and home video games — but suddenly you have the basic subject for a fine paper: fads in fashion.

Fashion designers seem to conspire to keep us looking foolish year after year. Are the lapels wide or narrow this year? Should you buy leather pants or polyester skirts? Is it "in" to have long hair, curly hair, or moused hair? Mark Twain said that if you don't like New England weather, wait a minute — it'll

Example   **151**

change. The same is true of fashion. Before you're used to one style, another replaces it.

To turn this information into an effective paper, first develop a thesis such as this: "With fashion today, you can never be sure if what you have in your wardrobe is "in' or 'out.'" Next, devote a paragraph each to these examples: multicolored hair, sunglasses on s string, beaded hairdos, and camouflage clothing. In each paragraph, explain how quickly these items fall out of fashion. Then, once you've added a concluding paragraph, you have a nice neat package called an *example paper.*

USING THE TECHNIQUE

In an example paper, as in any writing, you need a clear thesis and information that supports that thesis. To make your paper effective, follow through on the following points:

1.   Include enough examples.

When you write, how much is enough is always a concern. In an example paper, the answer is crucial to your effectiveness.

Imagine, for instance, that you are writing about the work associated with caring for a dog or cat. If you've ever owned one, you know how much work is involved. From cleaning up after your pet to taking your pet to the veterinarian, you have your hands full.

But what if your wrote your paper with only those two examples? Although tasks like cleaning up after your pet and taking it for shots or other treatments is time-consuming, the work doesn't seem very overpowering. As a result, your examples don't support your thesis because they give a limited and inaccurate picture of the amount of work associated with owning a pet.

One type of paper that has traditionally been taught in college classrooms is the five-paragraph essay. The formula is simple: Present a thesis in the first paragraph that suggests or actually states three supporting points, then present those three points—each in its own paragraph—and finally sum up the significance of your ideas in a concluding paragraph.

In the paper about the work associated with owning a pet, for example, the two reasons already suggested—cleaning up after the pet and taking the pet to the veterinarian—are not sufficient. If you added a third—exercising the pet daily, perhaps, or grooming the pet—you'd have at least a generally recognized minimal amount of support.

Of course, don't shoot for the minimum only. If you can provide four, five, or more examples, do so; the more sound examples you can give, the better picture your reader will have.

If, for instance, you add the bother of arranging for a kennel or a pet-sitter every time you'll be away from home for a while and the responsibility of keeping your pet locked up during mating season (or the bother and expense of having the animal spayed or neutered), your reader won't rush off to the pet store without giving a little more serious thought to what owning a pet truly means.

2.   Make the examples relevant.

"Irrelevant!" any number of television and movie lawyers yell when the argument being presented in the courtroom isn't directly connected to the rest of the discussion. Like those lawyers, you have to be concerned with relevance when you choose your examples.

If you were writing about some frustrating household chores, for example, you might choose dusting, vacuuming, and washing windows. If you've ever spent fifteen minutes or so washing both the outside and the inside of the picture window in your living room, only to find that as soon as you've finished, your dog has its wet nose nuzzled against the formerly clean pane, you know the feeling of frustration.

But if you've also included an example about sweeping up at work, your example is no longer relevant or appropriate. Yes, sweeping is a thankless duty that you sometimes have to do at home, but the example deals with sweeping up at work. Instead, remember to choose examples that have a direct connection to your thesis.

3.   Make your examples specific.

One of the biggest dangers in writing is assuming that your reader will understand what you say just because you understand it. In an example paper, you can fall into this trap when you don't make your examples specific enough.

Let's say you are writing about inconsiderate drivers. After you complete the prewriting stage of your writing, your thesis is something like this:

```
On any day on any street in this city, you can find
inconsiderate drivers.
```

As examples, you first mention people who drive aggressively — pass at every opportunity, cut off any other drivers, run yellow lights, and so on. Next, you mention drivers who are speed demons — exceed speed limits, ignore school zone signs, speed off from traffic lights, and so on. Then you deal with drivers who are inept or careless — change lanes without looking, fail to use signals, and apparently don't notice one-way or yield signs.

So far so good, right? The problem is the fourth example: drivers who are rude and insensitive. You say that they do whatever they want to and don't care about others. They never give others a break on the road.

The problem here is that *rude* and *insensitive* are abstract terms. You should make these two words more specific by either defining them or illustrating them. Are these drivers roadhogs, straddling two travel lanes and never yielding to a driver from the other direction attempting to cross the road? Do they take a parking space even after you have begun backing into it? Do they ride your back bumper, flash their high beams, and honk the horn so that you'll get out of their way on the highway? These are specific examples: they show what you mean by *rude* and *insensitive,* and so they fulfill your reader's needs.

4.   Arrange your examples effectively.

Example **153**

You have a number of choices available when it comes to setting up your writing. In a narrative or process paper, for instance, you often follow a chronological order — the order of time — if you are telling a story in the order in which it happened or how a process was or should be performed. In a descriptive writing, you often use spatial organization — the order of one part in relation to the others.

Another order, one frequently used in example papers, is least-to-most-significant organization. Basically you start with a strong example and move to stronger and stronger examples until you end the body with your strongest example.

In a paper about the advantages of owning a VCR, for instance, you might begin with the flexibility of taping and then watching all your favorite television shows at a time convenient for you. That is a strong example; many of the more popular shows are on at inconvenient or conflicting times.

Then you might mention the advantage of being able to catch up on all the movies you may have missed or of reseeing, for a nominal fee, the ones you particularly enjoyed. Tapes of movies are available for sale, and renting movie tapes is relatively inexpensive and convenient, so this is an even stronger advantage.

Then you might follow this example with one about the convenience of being able to watch a taped movie or event over a series of nights or at whatever times you wish. The advantage of being able to stop a long movie when you've become tired and then start it up again when you're better rested is a very strong point in favor of VCRs.

But certainly the strongest point about having a VCR is that you can enjoy all the advantages in the comfort of your own home. No matter what the show, you don't have to go any farther than your living room to enjoy it.

Least-to-most-significant order isn't the only way to arrange an example paper. You might, for instance, begin with the strongest example to "hook" your reader's interest. Or if the examples are about equal in importance or significance, you might try arranging your examples in different combinations to see which order has most appeal. Remember, however, that the least-to-most-significant arrangement is particularly effective in an example paper; it draws your reader all the way through your paper because each strong point leads to an even stronger one.

Because it enables you to support and illustrate your thesis, example is a valuable technique to master. All you have to do to ensure that you will use the technique effectively is to provide enough examples and make sure that those examples are specific, relevant, and effectively arranged.

ASSIGNMENT 7

In a 500- to 750-word essay, explain some frustrations or pet peeves you face regularly.

Reason

"Abigail Van Buren" and "Ann Landers" are the pen names for twin sisters who earn their living by writing syndicated advice columns that appear in hundreds of newspapers nationwide. Both Abby and Ann are popular with the reading public because of the answers they provide to a variety of questions, both serious and not so serious.

One not-so-serious area they've discussed from time to time is the "Great Toilet-Paper Debate." Should toilet paper unroll over or under? What's amazing is not that so many people would take the time to respond; the truly amazing thing is that most people honestly *do* have an opinion on seemingly unimportant matters.

Yes, people do have strong opinions about such minor things as where a tube of toothpaste should be squeezed, how a newspaper should be read, and whether glasses or plates should be washed first. A paper that features these minor points, sometimes called *pet peeves*, can result in interesting reading because people enjoy seeing the very irrational, very human side of others. Recognizing the foibles of others makes it easier to accept their own irrational humanness.

Of course, people face legitimate frustrations every day, too. Imagine, for instance, that you are a recent college graduate seeking your first job. What kind of frustrations might you face? Initially would come a variation of the eternal which-came-first-the-chicken-or-the-egg dilemma: How can you gain the experience the employer wants if no one will give you a job without experience? Once you get that first job, there is the question of learning the system, including the politics of the office. Then there is the frustration of being looked on by fellow workers as an outsider, a "college kid" full of idealism but lacking practicality. Also there is the frustration of trying to adapt your book learning to the pile of paperwork that awaits you each morning — and this list is far from complete.

Whether your subject is frivolous or serious, it will have appeal. What you find frustrating will no doubt interest a reader because your reader probably has dealt with or is still dealing with some of the examples of frustration, serious or silly, that you present.

What Your Reader Needs

When you write about your daily frustrations, first make sure that your thesis is clear. Your reader will always depend on your thesis as well as the rest of your introduction to provide a preview of what is to come.

In an example paper, your preview is particularly crucial. Without a clear thesis, your paper might seem merely to be a grocery list of examples without any reason behind it.

Take the idea of household pet peeves. Given only those three examples — where you should squeeze a tube of toothpaste, in what order a newspaper should be read (or how you should fold one to read it), and which should be washed first, glasses or plates — your reader wouldn't be able to grasp the full significance of what you want to say. But once you add a thesis like the

Example **155**

following, your reader will be prepared for the body of information that follows:

> My fiancée and I are headed for trouble once we're married because she doesn't know how to do the simplest things around the house the right way: <u>my</u> way.

Your reader needs direction in order to understand the significance of the examples. Use your thesis to provide that direction, and then use the examples to follow through on your thesis.

Model

IT DOESN'T PAY TO BE A GOOD BOY

With all the corruption around us in politics, business, and government, you'd think that a person would get a little respect for being honest and following the rules. But based on my experiences, I think the opposite is true. From what I've found, if you follow the rules everybody is supposed to uphold, you are penalized. Today, it doesn't pay to be a good boy.

When I was in high school, I was the last guy cut from the basketball team. My father had gone to high school with the coach and he offered to call the coach to ask him to give me a break, but I told him that if I wasn't good enough to be chosen on my ability, I didn't think I should be on the team. About halfway through the season, I found out that two of the kids I thought I was better than had had their parents call the coach before the season; those calls were probably the reason I was cut. What made it worse was that the team won the state championship that season and was rewarded with a week-long, all-expense-paid trip to Disneyworld as a reward. I played by the rules and sat home; those other two players used influence to get on the team and they went to Florida.

I ran into a similar problem this year with my car. I knew that my car probably wouldn't pass the emissions testing around inspection time. My mechanic told me the engine needed a ring job; four hundred dollars was the cheapest estimate I could get. I knew that without the repair, the car would continue to run poorly and send all that pollution out into the atmosphere, so I spent the money. My cousin had the same problem with his car, but he didn't bother with the ring job. He simply slipped the man doing the emissions test twenty dollars and he got his inspection sticker.

It's the same thing at work at the supermarket. Every night, ten of us are given the job of reloading as much as possible of different aisles during the first three hours of a shift. Then each of us is supposed to spend the last

hour of our shift ''squaring down'' the products—pulling
all the packages forward so that the shelves look full. One
night last week, I had managed to replenish almost the
entire canned-vegetable section, the hardest section in
the store to keep up with. The girl in the next aisle,
however, hadn't put up half as much stuff in her three-hour
shift, and she had the paper-goods section, the easiest in
the store to fill. But because she spent an hour and a half
squaring down, her aisle looked fuller. As we left for the
night, the boss complimented her and then criticized me for
being slow and sloppy. I tried to explain that if I had done
less loading and more squaring down, my aisle would look
better but actually be in worse shape, but he just turned
away.

Even here in college it doesn't pay to follow the rules.
Last semester, in my American government class, we all had
to turn in a ten-page term paper about the workings of the
U.S. Senate. It was hard to meet the deadline; everybody in
class had to use the same books, which had been put on
reserve. I spent five nights in a row in the library. When I
got the paper back, I had received a ''B,'' which made my
overall average ''B+.'' The kid who sat next to me had the
same average without the paper, but rather than handing the
paper in on time, he asked for an incomplete. He told me he
finished the paper during the semester break, submitted
it, and received an ''A+'' for the paper. He ended up with
an ''A−'' for the course. If I had an extra month to do the
paper, I think I could have done a better job, too. Instead,
I handed it in on time because that was the rule, and
somebody that broke the rule ended up getting a better grade.

I guess I'm not sorry I do what I know is right. Rules are
important because they provide guidelines to follow for
all of us. Furthermore, by following the rules, I know that
whatever reward I get at work or school I've earned. But
it's never easy to watch somebody else who hasn't worked as
hard as you have get the same or a better reward because that
person has somehow got around the rules.

Follow-through

When you write about things that frustrate you, your job is to make sure that
your examples truly express the frustration you feel. You do this by providing
enough specific, relevant examples and arranging them effectively.

Whether you are writing about serious frustrations or insignificant ones,
you must first generate some ideas from which you can develop a thesis and
draw supporting examples. In the case of this paper, the initial information
included these ideas:

*my sister stays out late and my parents don't say anything; they used to ground
me—at work people who cut corners do a lousy job, but cover it up—Carol does*

Example **157**

half the work she's supposed to but she makes it look good but I get yelled at — if cops see a decal for a police association, they never give the car a ticket — people who are kept on a team only because their fathers knows someone — do all your work in class but unless you kiss the professor's feet, you don't get a break — People always show up at the 12 and under register with more than 12 items — People who take incompletes and get better grades — politicians take advantage of their power — get special privileges, etc. — People who find inspection stations that falsify findings rather than keeping their car up-to-date.

All these pieces of information either state or suggest that other people get ahead by breaking or ignoring rules that you choose to follow. The thesis, then, is easy to develop:

```
From what I've found, if you follow the rules everybody is
supposed to uphold, you are penalized.
```

The next step is to decide which examples will be most effective. There is no automatically correct number of examples. However, the generally recognized minimum support would be three examples; therefore choose at least three, four — or more — if you have suitable examples. In the case of this initial listing, these four pieces of information become the supporting examples:

1. People who are kept on a team only because their father knows someone.
2. People who find inspection stations that falsify findings rather than keeping their car up-to-date.
3. People who cut corners at work — do a lousy job, but cover it up.
4. People who take incompletes and get better grades.

Some of the other examples are good; for instance, *"if cops see a decal for a police association, they never give the car a ticket"* is an example of the abuse of the system of justice, as is the example about politicians taking unfair use of their power.

The problem is that they don't directly affect the writer; they aren't relevant, not to the same degree that the examples eventually chosen are. Nor is the example about the people who take unfair advantage of the speedy checkout line at the supermarket directly relevant. This situation is annoying, yes, but the connection is not quite as strong as it is with the examples featured in the final draft.

The detail about the writer's sister is potentially a strong example. Yet it doesn't have the same universal appeal that the chosen examples have. In other words, the special treatment she receives at home affects the writer within that particular household. The other examples affect the writer in the world at large, and because of this common element, it's easier for the writer to tie them together and easier for the reader to see the connection.

Once you've decided on the number and relevance of the examples, you need to make sure they are specific enough. This is particularly important because what annoys or frustrates one person may not immediately seem bothersome to another. Yet, when you explain in detail why the point frustrates you, it is more that your reader will understand.

Look, for instance, at this example from the final draft:

> I ran into a similar problem this year with my car. I knew that my car probably wouldn't pass the emissions testing around inspection time. My mechanic told me the engine needed a ring job; four hundred dollars was the cheapest estimate I could get. I knew that without the repair, the car would continue to run poorly and send all that pollution out into the atmosphere, so I spent the money. My cousin had the same problem with his car, but he didn't bother with the ring job. He simply slipped the man doing the emissions test twenty dollars and he got his inspection sticker.

Now look at the information that this example is based on:

> *People who find inspection stations that falsify findings rather than keeping their car up-to-date.*

Up-to-date and *findings* are unclear terms. But the final draft explains the significance of these words by explaining that the testing was for auto emissions and the car needed repair so that it could pass this specific test. The cousin, of course, dispensed with all this stuff by bribing the person giving the test. With this information, the reader can understand the frustration involved in spending four hundred dollars because it was the correct thing to do while at the same time watching somebody else avoid the expense — and continue to break the law by polluting the air — by slipping the inspector an extra twenty dollars. The final version is clear and specific because it is fleshed out; it is amplified.

Once you've identified the bits of information you plan to use, you then must decide how to arrange them. You have a number of alternatives available, but the least-to-most-significant order is generally effective.

In the case of this paper, the first example is a strong one: fellow high-school students who used connections to remain part of a championship basketball team. It is followed by a stronger example, one that involves a shifty deal with an automobile inspector. This example is followed by an even stronger and more annoying example: the co-worker who concentrates more on having her work look good than on performing the task assigned. And this is followed up by an example of a particularly annoying and unfair instance: a student who gets a higher grade by taking unfair advantage of a professor's generosity. As the final draft shows, this organization is effective.

In an example paper, you always have the potential for a strong essay because you basically use the examples to hammer home your thesis. To follow through on that potential, remember to include enough examples, and then make sure that the examples are clear, connected, and effectively arranged.

Example **159**

Checklist

Use the answers to the following questions to help you revise your first draft:

1. Does your paper have a thesis? Write it down.
2. Which examples have you used to support your thesis? List them.
3. Are these examples specific?
4. Are these examples relevant?
5. Is the arrangement of the examples effective?
6. Does your introduction provide a clear direction for your reader?
7. Does your conclusion sum up the significance of your thesis and the examples?

ASSIGNMENT 8

In a 500- to 750-word essay, take some common belief, axiom, or proverb and give some examples that prove it.

Reason

Day after day we hear the same old sayings, like "A penny saved is a penny earned" and "A stitch in time saves nine." Are these sayings true or are they just convenient phrases? In reality, they are probably a little bit of both fact and fiction.

Take something like Murphy's law, for example: "Whatever can go wrong will." Now think of your own day-to-day activities: Have you had days when everything that might possibly go wrong did?

Consider when you woke up fifteen minutes late on the morning of a big examination. You rushed through a shower and breakfast and then went out to your car; it wouldn't start. At the last minute, you managed to get a ride with your neighbor, but you were five minutes late for the exam. You were expecting an objective test, but your instructor had decided to go with an essay test. When you took out your pen, it wouldn't write; the ink had leaked out in your jacket pocket — and it was only 9:15 A.M. You still had to face the rest of the day.

Maybe your day wasn't quite this bad, but there's no doubt that a day of miscues provides plenty of examples to prove Murphy's law.

In this case, the thesis — "The people who came up with Murphy's law knew what they were talking about" — would be supported by the various examples of things that went wrong, all in one morning. Therefore the individual problems — waking up late, facing a car that wouldn't start, arriving late for the examination, finding that the instructor had changed the type of test, and discovering that your pen didn't work because all the ink had leaked out and ruined your jacket — become the frame that explains and illustrates your thesis.

What Your Reader Needs

All things considered, you'll probably find a writing based on an axiom or a popular belief somewhat easy to write because the proverb or belief itself is a great starting point; it's a built-in thesis. Your most difficult job is accumulating and arranging examples that are clear and that are connected to that thesis.

Take "A stitch in time saves nine," for instance. Too often we let things go that we should attend to right away. As a result of our own laziness or procrastination, we end up doubling or tripling our work or expense. What your reader needs to see is a series of good, clear, connected examples to support the proverb.

First, of course, your reader needs to see that proverb expressed in a thesis: "Several incidents that have happened to me in the last three months have proved to me that 'a stitch in time saves nine.'" Once you have provided this direction for your reader, your job is to support the thesis with a sufficient number—at least three—of clear, connected examples.

In this case you can muster plenty of examples. For example, you failed to collect the leaves you had raked into piles earlier; in the spring you discovered that the grass underneath the piles had died. Repairing the damage took a weekend of work and cost you fifty dollars for supplies.

Then there was the time when your car needed a tune-up, but you ignored the problem for months until the day you got stuck in an intersection. The combined cost for the road service and the major overhaul was over two hundred dollars, and you were without a car for a week.

And then there was the time when your good suit needed to be cleaned, but you conveniently forgot about it until you received a last-minute invitation to a function for which your suit was perfect. You spent thirty minutes on the phone trying to find a place that does same-day cleaning. A five-dollar cleaning turned into a fifteen-dollar headache.

Finally there was the time when you needed a weekend off from work so that you could travel to an out-of-town wedding, but you put off making arrangements to change your hours until the week before. After much haggling and begging, you managed to convince one of your co-workers to fill in for you, but you had to agree to work the next four weekends in return.

These examples are specific and connected. They clearly support the thesis, and it is this clear support that your reader needs in an example paper.

Model

1984 IS HERE NOW

Among the most famous political satires is George Orwell's 1984. In this book, written in the late 1940s, Orwell presented a world of the future that has some pretty frightening changes from our own. But the truly ironic

Example   **161**

part of Orwell's predictions is that many of them have come true. In some ways, 1984 is here today.

For example, in 1984, there are three superpowers, Eurasia, Eastasia, and Oceania. The alliances between the three nations change from time to time. Similar things have happened in the real world between the three major superpowers, the United States, Russia, and China. For example, during World War II, the United States and Russia were allies. But following World war II, the United States and Russia became enemies; as an emerging communist nation, China shared this animosity for the United States until the mid-1970s, when Richard Nixon brought the United States and Communist China together. Now the United States and China have peaceful relations, but both nations have shaky relationships with Russia.

But this shifting in alliances isn't the only one of Orwell's predictions that rings true today. In 1984, the government has a special agency called the Ministry of Truth. One of the things this agency does is to go back and change the news. Things are not quite that bad today, but we often see attempts to cover up or change something that some government official has said or done. In Russia, whenever a leader dies, it's weeks before they officially announce it to their own people and the rest of the world. Here in the United States, it seems as if after every press conference that President Reagan has given during his two terms, one of his aides has had to ''clarify'' what the President said. According to the information I learned recently in my government class, former presidential candidate George McGovern wasn't much better. In the 1972 presidential campaign, when someone revealed that George McGovern's vice-presidential selection Thomas Eagleton had once been treated for a mental disorder, McGovern announced that he was ''1000 percent'' behind Eagleton. A few days later, apparently forgetting what he had said earlier, McGovern dropped Eagleton as his running mate.

The government in 1984 manipulates the information it lets the people hear. At least in the United States, thanks to an active, aggressive press, the government can't completely hide the truth. Sometimes it does a pretty good job, however. When the space shuttle Challenger blew up, the NASA officials kept crucial information out of the news until they had to admit it during the hearings after the tragedy. For example, they didn't immediately admit that the makers of the rocket booster had warned them about the danger of a launch in cold weather and about various other weaknesses in the space shuttle's operation. When the nuclear emergency happened at Three-Mile Island and radioactive gas was released, it was weeks before we learned the truth about the danger. When Russia had that terrible near-meltdown at Chernobyl, it was months; the people living in Kiev, which is about fifty miles from the plant, knew less about the nuclear accident than the rest of the world did. When it comes to revealing the truth completely and willingly, today's world governments have something in common with the government in 1984.

Another prophesy that seems to have been fulfilled is how important television would become. In 1984, it is called a telescreen; like our televisions, it projects pictures and sound. Unlike our television sets, however, it is against the law to turn the telescreen off, as the government can monitor you as well. Obviously we are free to turn the television on and off as we wish and nobody can watch us through the television. But there is no doubt about how much time people spend sitting in front of a television set rather than reading a newspaper to get a fuller picture of what is happening around them. Furthermore, like the telescreen in 1984, the television can be used for propaganda purposes. Here in the United States, for example, successful politicians become as adept in front of the cameras as actors and news anchors.

Thank goodness today's world isn't exactly the way Orwell predicted it would be in 1984. We shouldn't be too smug, however; the world may not be exactly the way Orwell suggested it might be, but there are enough predictions about the governments of the superpowers that come close to being true to make us all think. From the relationships between the world powers and how they dispense the truth to the effect of television on our lives, Orwell's prophesies seem pretty close to reality.

Follow-through

Using a popular belief or axiom as a starting point for your paper should simplify things for you. Basically your job is to use that saying as your thesis and then to provide examples to support it.

The basis for this paper is George Orwell's classic political satire, *1984*, a text frequently part of high-school and college reading lists. Orwell used his protagonist, Winston Smith, to show the evils of authoritarian government. One of the slogans from the book, "Big Brother Is Watching You," symbolizes what can happen when people let government wield too much control in their lives. People still occasionally use the term *1984* to express loss of personal freedom or too-severe government control. The belief that some of Orwell's predictions have come true today is a good basis for an example paper.

For any writing, your first job is to generate a working basis of information. For a paper that draws on a text, as this model does, you can draw part of that working list from the book itself.

Example **163**

For example, for this paper, the prewriting included this information:

Winston Smith works at Ministry of Truth — they're in charge of lies — he has to hide to write in a diary — like book censorship now? Big Brother Is Watching You was the big slogan — nothing like that today except maybe television ads during political campaigns — telescreen; one in every room I think — couldn't turn it off either because they were looking at you — you can turn off the television today but people watch so much — how many hours I wonder? — manipulations at presidential news conferences — aides explaining what Reagan meant to say — in class last week they talked about George McGovern — 1000% behind Thomas Eagleton — next day drops him — Nixon destroyed him — I wonder if there's a connection? — Government controls what official information they give out. Space shuttle blows up, Three-Mile Island or Love Canal information — bit by bit — Russians were worse when their power plant almost melted down — it could never happen in the US they kept saying, but Three-Mile Island happened — don't think anybody died with TMI — that's another thing, three superpowers — two were allied against the third, and then they changed it and the history that went with it — same thing today, they don't change the history but they try to lie about it and there are three superpowers, too — now we're friends with China, but we used to be friends with Russia — Rocky IV was so anti-Russian, like propaganda — they say the Russians use propaganda, how about the opening of the Olympics in Los Angeles with all the balloons or doves or whatever it was?

As you can see, this initial list contains information from the book, but it also contains ideas inspired by the bits of textual information. Of course, not everything from the initial list appears in the final draft, and not all the bits of information that are used appear in the same form. The examples you include in your final version must, of course, be specific and relevant, not general as they are in their prewriting state.

Take a look at this section from the prewriting:

Government controls what official information they give out. Space shuttle blows up, Three-Mile Island or Love Canal information — bit by bit — Russians were worse when their power plant almost melted down — it could never happen in the US they kept saying, but Three-Mile Island happened — I don't think anybody died with TMI

Most of the information here is relevant to a discussion about governments' withholding information, but other parts — "could never happen in the US they kept saying, but Three-Mile Island happened — I don't think anybody died with TMI" — are directly connected.

Of course, as it appears here, the remaining information is still not nearly specific enough to communicate your ideas to your reader. Notice how the information that is used — the space shuttle disaster and the nuclear accidents at Three-Mile Island and Chernobyl — is made specific in the final draft.

> Sometimes it does a pretty good job, however. When the
> space shuttle Challenger blew up, the NASA officials kept
> crucial information out of the news until they had to admit
> it during the hearings after the tragedy. For example, they
> didn't immediately admit that the makers of the rocket
> booster had warned them about the danger of a launch in cold
> weather and about various other weaknesses in the space
> shuttle's operation. When the nuclear emergency happened
> at Three-Mile Island and radioactive gas was released, it
> was weeks before we learned the truth about the danger.
> When Russia had that terrible near-meltdown at Chernobyl,
> it was months; the people living in Kiev, which is about
> fifty miles from the plant, knew less about the nuclear
> accident than the rest of the world did.

Obviously, the final version is far more specific than the preliminary notes
were. Important and necessary details about the shuttle disaster and the
nuclear problems are presented so that the example clearly supports the thesis.

Because the examples are all about equal, the order of paragraphs in the
body could probably be changed without a lessening in the effectiveness of the
paper. Of course, a change like that would require some changes in wording
and transition, but a competent writer could make the switch and still have an
effective paper.

When you write an example paper, you use several specific, relevant examples, effectively arranged, to support your thesis. With a conclusion that restates this thesis included, you have an example paper that fulfills the needs of
your reader.

Checklist

Use the answers to the following questions to help you revise your first draft:

1. Does your paper have a thesis? Write it down.
2. Which examples have you used to support your thesis? List them.
3. Are these examples specific?
4. Are these examples relevant?
5. Is the arrangement of the examples effective?
6. Does your introduction provide a clear direction for your reader?
7. Does your conclusion sum up the significance of your thesis and the
   examples?

FOR FURTHER STUDY

Because of Ed Lowe's humorous treatment of the world of sailing, both the
experienced sailor and the landlubber will enjoy this essay. Lowe educates his
readers about sailing by peppering his essay with examples of sailing terminology that is confusing to a person new to sailing.

Example **165**

Adrift on a Sea of Words

ED LOWE

The language of sailing, laced as it is with history, romance, tradition and technology, is basically ridiculous.

Nothing on a sailboat is called by a name that describes it, or its exact equivalent in English. For example, in the real and practical world on earth, the noun "pulley" describes a simple bracketed wheel whose perimeter is grooved to accommodate a rope, string, chain or line of some kind, so that you can pull down to make an object at the other end of the line go up. Pulleys are standard equipment on sailboats, where they are called "blocks." They neither block anything, nor do they resemble in form anything cube-shaped or even squared-off, like a city block. They are simply called blocks, and if you ask a sailing instructor why, he will not know the answer.

My sailing instructor, an English teacher on earth, shrugged off the question during my first lesson and moved quickly into the physics of sailing, presumably to escape further discussion of the linguistics. The escape, we soon discovered, was impossible.

He opened the lesson by explaining that in sailing, all verbal references to the location of things, whether on the sailboat or in the world at large, were based on the direction from which the wind was blowing at the time of utterance. The side of the boat closest to the source of the wind at any given time, he said, was called windward; the other side was called leeward. These sides switched if the wind changed direction, or if the boat turned in relation to the wind. So, if the port side (the left side, if you stood aft and faced the bow) was the windward side when we were traveling west, it became the leeward side the instant we turned the boat around and went the other way. Starboard, the opposite side from port, then became the windward, and port, *lee*ward.

Waves of pain slashed against the back of my right eyeball. I had already suffered enough trying to learn port from starboard. They changed sides if I stood at opposite ends of the boat. These new sides literally changed with the weather. It seemed impossible to avoid confusion in this mental maze. What if I walked foreward (from aft) backwards, stood at the bow (front) of the boat, facing the stern (back), and suddenly the wind changed direction? My starboard would be port, my windward, leeward; my aft would be foreward and my bow, aft, or at least half-aft. Up might be down, and I might find that I'd changed into a flounder.

Moreover, the instructor pronounced leeward "looward," (just as he pronounced gunwale "gunnel," and bowline "boe-lin"). But "lee," he said, on oft-used abbreviation of leeward ("looward") was pronounced "lee," not "loo."

"I soo," I said, meaning, "I see," and we shoved off ("oof").

As he turned the sailboat into the wind, or was we "came about," the instructor said, rather ritualistically, "Ready about!" then hesitated before adding, "Hard-a-lee!" He told me to push the tiller out, while he held the "sheet." I assumed the sheet to be the sail, since the sail was mostly white and could have passed for a sheet, but the sheet was not that—it was the line that controlled the sail.

"Hard-a-lee," I learned, meant a lot: (1) that I should duck my head to avoid being hit by the "boom." As the boat turned, the sail was going to swing from one side to the other, just missing my head, if I ducked, and changing the relationship between the wind and the boat, thus necessitating an immediate redistribution of passenger weight. This meant (2) that, continuing to duck, I should go sit on the opposite side of the boat as quickly as possible, lest I unwittingly conspired with the wind to capsize the craft. This change, combined with the turn, meant that I had moved from the leeward side to the windward side just as the windward side was becoming the leeward side. The truth, then, was that when somebody said, "Hard-a-lee" I really moved from leeward to leeward ("looward" to "looward"), or from lee to lee ("lee" to "lee").

I described the hard-a-lee part of the lesson to my neighbor, Philip, and inadvertently relieved him of a great and vexing riddle. He, too, had taken up sailing and had gone out with somebody who knew all the words. Whenever that person said "Hard-a-lee" fast and without clarification, Philip's sensitive but nautically ignorant faculties heard "Heartily."

Willing to go along with what he assumed was an old, oral, sailing tradition but baffled by his skipper's insatiable appetite for vigor and happy spirits in his one-man crew, Philip opened his eyes wider and smiled brighter each time the captain repeated the order. With every tack, Philip tried to summon up more enthusiasm, as he bounded joyfully from windward to leeward and back again, more heartily each time. By the end of that first sail, Philip was so tired of grinning and bounding, so weary of staged enthusiasm and feigned joy, he relaxed, and his family took him for morose. The next time he sailed, he brought along his son, Andrew. Whenever they were about to tack, he told Andrew, "I'm going to turn now. Duck! And then switch sides." He said that it worked well.

I learned new semantic somersaults each time I talked to sailors about their exclusive hobby. A rope was a rope until you took it aboard a sailboat, when it became a line. A cable purchased under its own name stayed that way until a sailor got hold of it; he called it "a rope." My friend Kevin had a large sailboat (he called it a sloop), and said that inside its cabin, the ceiling was not the ceiling—it was "the overhead." The walls were called "ceilings," he said, the floor was a "cabin sole," and the timber running beneath the floor was "the floor."

My eyes spun. "You can lean against the ceiling in your cabin," I snapped, "but you can't stand on the floor! Is that right?"

"Right," Kevin said.

Questions for Study

1. Lowe's thesis is expressed in the initial sentence: "The language of sailing, laced as it is with history, romance, tradition and technology, is basically ridiculous." Which examples do you think best support his thesis?
2. Lowe explained why some terms have their names—*windward* as the side of the boat closest to the source of wind at any time, for instance—but he didn't explain some of the others. Make a list of the terms he didn't explain. Choose one, and using a dictionary, explain its meaning in a paragraph.
3. Did Lowe arrange his examples in least-to-most-significant order, or did he arrange them otherwise? Identify the order, listing the examples.
4. Lowe didn't provide a conclusion, at least not in the traditional sense of restating the thesis and recapping the examples. Yet his concluding two paragraphs are connected to the thesis, because the paper ends with an example that proves that the language of sailing is ridiculous. Is the absence

Example **167**

of a formal conclusion in this essay a serious flaw? In a paragraph or so, explain how you feel.

ALTERNATE ASSIGNMENT I

It's easy to sympathize with Lowe because we have all been through an experience during which we were faced with terms unfamiliar to us. Maybe it was the first night at a new job or a checkup at the doctor. For this assignment, give examples of terminology in any field (or in several fields) that you have found confusing or illogical.

Among the most-read sections of *Time* magazine is the weekly essay that regularly appears on the last page, and among the names appearing more frequently at the bottom of those essays for the last several years is that of Roger Rosenblatt. In the following essay from that series, Rosenblatt gave various examples of verbal misuses and indicated the effects that these mistakes have on both the speaker and the listener.

Oops! How's That Again?

ROGER ROSENBLATT

"That is not what I meant at all. That is not it, at all."
—*T.S. ELIOT, The Love Song of J. Alfred Prufrock*

At a royal luncheon in Glasgow last month, Businessman Peter Balfour turned to the just-engaged Prince Charles and wished him long life and conjugal happiness with Lady Jane. The effect of the sentiment was compromised both by the fact that the Prince's betrothed is Lady Diana (Spencer) and that Lady Jane (Wellesley) is one of his former flames. "I feel a perfect fool," said Balfour, who was unnecessarily contrite. Slips of the tongue occur all the time. In Chicago recently, Governor James Thompson was introduced as "the mayor of Illinois," which was a step down from the time he was introduced as "the Governor of the United States." Not all such fluffs are so easy to take, however. During the primaries, Nancy Reagan telephoned her husband as her audience listened in, to say how delighted she was to be looking at all "the beautiful white people." And France's Prime Minister Raymond Barre, who has a reputation for putting his *pied* in his *bouche,* described last October's bombing of a Paris synagogue as "this odious attack that was aimed at Jews and that struck at innocent Frenchmen"—a crack that not only implied Jews were neither innocent nor French but also suggested that the attack would have been less odious had it been more limited.

One hesitates to call Barre sinister, but the fact is that verbal errors can have a devastating effect on those who hear them and on those who make them as well. Jimmy Carter never fully recovered from his reference to Polish lusts for the future in a mistranslated speech in 1977, nor was Chicago's Mayor Daley ever quite the same after assuring the public that "the policeman isn't there to create disorder, the policeman is there to preserve disorder." Dwight Eisenhower, John Kennedy, Spiro Agnew, Gerald Ford, all made terrific gaffes, with Ford perhaps making the most unusual ("Whenever I can I always watch the Detroit Tigers on radio"). Yet this is no modern phenomenon. The term *faux pas* goes back at least as far as the seventeenth century, having originally referred to a woman's lapse from virtue. Not that women lapse more than men in this regard. Even Marie Antoinette's fatal remark about cake and the public, if true, was due to poor translation.

In fact, mistranslation accounts for a great share of verbal errors. The slogan "Come Alive with Pepsi" failed understandably in German when it was translated: "Come Alive out of the Grave with Pepsi." Elsewhere it was translated with more precision: "Pepsi Brings Your Ancestors Back from the Grave." In 1965, prior to a reception for Queen Elizabeth II outside Bonn, Germany's President Heinrich Lübke, attempting an English translation of *"Gleich geht es los"* (It will soon begin), told the Queen: "Equal goes it loose." The Queen took the news well, but no better than the President of India, who was greeted at an airport in 1962 by Lübke, who, intending to ask, "How are you?" instead said: "Who are you?" To which his guest answered responsibly: "I am the President of India."

The most prodigious collector of modern slips was Kermit Schafer, whose "blooper" records of mistakes made on radio and television consisted largely of toilet jokes, but were nonetheless a great hit in the 1950s. Schafer was an avid self-promotor and something of a blooper himself, but he did have an ear for such things as the introduction by Radio Announcer Harry von Zell of President "Hoobert Heever," as well as the interesting message: "This portion of *Women on the Run* is brought to you by Phillips' Milk of Magnesia." Bloopers are the lowlife of verbal error, but spoonerisms are a different feetle of kitsch. In the early 1900s the Rev. William Archibald Spooner caused a stir at New College, Oxford, with his famous spoonerisms, most of which were either deliberate or apocryphal. But a real one — his giving out a hymn in chapel as "Kinquring Kongs Their Titles Take" — is said to have brought down the house of worship, and to have kicked off the genre. After that, spoonerisms got quite elaborate. Spooner once reportedly chided a student: "You have hissed all my mystery lectures. In fact, you have tasted the whole worm, and must leave by the first town drain."

Such missteps, while often howlingly funny to ignorami like us, are deadly serious concerns to psychologists and linguists. Victoria Fromkin of the linguistics department at U.C.L.A. regards slips of the tongue as clues to how the brain stores and articulates language. She believes that thought is placed by the brain into a grammatical framework before it is expressed — this in spite of the fact that she works with college students. A grammatical framework was part of Walter Annenberg's trouble when, as the newly appointed U. S. Ambassador to Britain, he was asked by the Queen how he was settling in to his London residence. Annenberg admitted to "some discomfiture as a result of a need for elements of refurbishing." Either he was overwhelmed by the circumstances or he was losing his mind.

When you get to that sort of error, you are nearing a psychological abyss. It was Freud who first removed the element of accident from language with his explanation of "slips," but lately others have extended his theories. Psychiatrist Richard Yazmajian, for example, suggests that there are some incorrect words that exist in

Example **169**

associative chains with the correct ones for which they are substituted, implying a kind of "dream pair" of elements in the speaker's psyche. The nun who poured tea for the Irish bishop and asked, "How many lords, my lump?" might therefore have been asking a profound theological question.

On another front, Psychoanalyst Ludwig Eidelberg made Freud's work seem childishly simple when he suggested that a slip of the tongue involves the entire network of id, ego and superego. He offers the case of the young man who entered a restaurant with his girlfriend and ordered a room instead of a table. You probably think that you understand that error. But just listen to Eidelberg: "All the wishes connected with the word 'room' represented a countercathexis mobilized as a defense. The word 'table' had to be omitted, because it would have been used for infantile gratification of a repressed oral, aggressive and scopophilic wish connected with identification with the preoedipal mother." Clearly, this is no laughing matter.

Why then do we hoot at these mistakes? For one thing, it may be that we simply find conventional discourse so predictable and boring that any deviation comes as a delightful relief. In his deeply unfunny *Essay on Laughter* the philosopher Henri Bergson theorized that the act of laughter is caused by any interruption of normal human fluidity or momentum (a pie in the face, a mask, a pun). Slips of the tongue, therefore, are like slips on banana peels; we crave their occurrence if only to break the monotonies. The monotonies run to substance. When that announcer introduced Hoobert Heever, he may also have been saying that the nation had had enough of Herbert Hoover.

Then too there is the element of pure meanness in such laughter, both the meanness of enjoyment in watching an embarrassed misspeaker's eyes roll upward as if in prayer — his hue turn magenta, his hands like homing larks fluttering to his mouth — and the mean joy of discovering his hidden base motives and critical intent. At the 1980 Democratic National Convention, Jimmy Carter took a lot of heat for referring to Hubert Humphrey as Hubert Horatio Hornblower because it was instantly recognized that Carter thought Humphrey a windbag. David Hartman of *Good Morning America* left little doubt about his feelings for a sponsor when he announced: "We'll be right back after this word from General Fools." At a conference in Berlin in 1954, France's Foreign Minister Georges Bidault was hailed as "that fine little French tiger, Georges Bidet," thus belittling the tiger by the tail. When we laugh at such stuff, it is the harsh and bitter laugh, the laugh at the disclosure of inner condemning truth.

Yet there is also a more kindly laugh that occurs when a blunderer does not reveal his worst inner thoughts, but his most charitable or optimistic. General Ford's famous error in the 1976 presidential debate, in which he said that Poland was not under Soviet domination, for instance. In a way, that turned out to contain a grain of truth, thanks to Lech Walesa and the strikes; in any case it was a nice thing to wish. As was U.N. Ambassador Warren Austin's suggestion in 1948 that Jews and Arabs resolve their differences "in a true Christian spirit." Similarly, Nebraska's former Senator Kenneth Wherry might have been thinking dreamily when, in an hour-long speech on a country in Southeast Asia, he referred throughout to "Indigo-China." One has to be in the mood for such a speech.

Of course, the most interesting laugh is the one elicited by the truly bizarre mistake, because such a mistake seems to disclose a whole new world of logic and possibility, a deranged double for the life that is. What Lewis Carroll displayed through the looking glass, verbal error also often displays by conjuring up ideas so supremely nutty that the laughter it evokes is sublime. The idea that Pepsi might actually bring one back from the grave encourages an entirely new view of experience. In such a view it is perfectly possible to lust after the Polish future, to watch the Tigers on the radio, to say "Equal goes it loose" with resounding clarity.

Still, beyond all this is another laugh entirely, that neither condemns, praises, ridicules nor conspires, but sees into the essential nature of a slip of the tongue and consequently sympathizes. After all, most human endeavor results in a slip of the something—the best-laid plans gone suddenly haywire by natural blunder: the chair, cake or painting that turns out not exactly as one imagined; the kiss or party that falls flat; the life that is not quite what one had in mind. Nothing is ever as dreamed.

So we laugh at each other, perfect fools all, flustered by the mistake of our mortality.

Questions for Study

1. Rosenblatt certainly provided plenty of examples of people not quite saying what they wanted to say. Choose the example that most tickled your funny bone, and in a paragraph, explain why you found it funny.
2. List the sentence or sentences that express the thesis.
3. Pretend you are the editor, who has decided to cut some of the examples. Make a list of the examples you would cut, and in a brief memo to Rosenblatt, explain why you have cut them.
4. Rosenblatt suggested that to some psychologists, slips of the tongue are not completely accidental; rather, these mistakes are really statements from our subconscious selves of how we really feel. What do you think? Express your ideas in a paragraph.

ALTERNATE ASSIGNMENT J

Rosenblatt's essay is entertaining because he showed famous and prominent people making the same kinds of mistakes the rest of us make every day. For this assignment, give some examples of instances when you've put your foot in your mouth or you've experienced others saying what they don't mean at all.

Chapter 11

═══════ DEFINITION ═══════

INTRODUCTION

It's standard equipment for any college student. It's a mini-encyclopedia, the starting point for some answers and the deciding point for others.

What is it? It's a dictionary, a collection of words and their meanings — their definitions. A dictionary is particularly important because it enables us to discover what we don't know about words as well as to clarify what we already know about them. Words are symbolic forms of the world around us; definitions of individual words give us a better understanding of our world. For this reason, definition is an invaluable technique for you as a writer.

Actually, looking at a dictionary is probably the easiest way to understand the operating principle of definition. A dictionary definition is generally set up this way: take an item, put the item into its appropriate specific class, and then show how it differs from other items in its class. For example, a dodo (item) was a large bird (class) characterized by an inability to fly (difference from others in its class). Most terms can be classified, and because the items within the class have different qualities, distinguishing one idea from another is often easy.

Although a dictionary is an invaluable resource when dealing with definitions, in fact we define various words, phrases, concepts, ideas, and so on, each day without using a dictionary. For example, we often define something by telling what it is similar to — "Well, a comet is like a giant sloppy ice-ball, with the tail like the spray of water following behind" — or by telling what it isn't like — "A croissant isn't like a muffin or doughnut at all. It's much flakier and not as sweet." Obviously these kinds of definitions are not as precise as those available in a dictionary or encyclopedia, but they allow you to deal with some subject because they give you a range within which to place that subject.

In many cases, a brief definition such as that available in the average pocket dictionary is not enough to create a clear picture. In those cases, you'll need to generate an extended definition — a far more detailed explanation of a word, a phrase, an idea, or a concept, for example. This is particularly the case when you are dealing with abstract concepts or ideas that have different meanings in different circumstances.

Imagine, for instance, that you've received an invitation to a party and at the bottom of the invitation are these words, "Appropriate Dress Required."

What does this phrase mean? Part of the problem has to do with the word *appropriate*. The dictionary defines it as "fit, suitable, proper, conforming to a standard, etc." This definition is clearly correct, but it still doesn't tell you what you need to know. What's appropriate for one party (a bowling banquet) is inappropriate for another (a dinner party in honor of the governor).

An extended definition such as this meets the needs of your reader:

> The clearest part of the invitation was the line at the bottom: ''Appropriate Dress Required.'' I know my boss, so I knew exactly what she meant by <u>appropriate</u>. She meant dresses for the women–not skirts and definitely not slacks – and dark suits with white shirts and plain ties for the men. But <u>appropriate</u> didn't refer only to clothes. She meant hairstyles, too. Shorter hair was her preference for women, although she would allow longer hair as long as it was swept away from the face and tied up. For the men, she also wanted shorter hair; any man with hair over his shirt collar could expect to get an icy greeting at the party and the worst assignments for a month back at work. She expected the men to be clean shaven, too, and if they dared to have moustaches or beards, these had to be neatly trimmed.

This extended definition explains that, in this case *appropriate* meant fulfilling the edicts of an employer who had very specific ideas of what she felt was correct dress and apparently the power to make sure that her demands were met.

Whether it's a one word definition or a more detailed explanation, definition is a valuable technique for you to master. It allows you to explain in specific terms what you mean; as a result, it increases the chances that your reader will understand your ideas as you mean them to be understood.

THE MAKEUP OF A DEFINITION PAPER

No doubt you have already used definition to explain or clarify some point you've made in some paper. As the paragraph on "appropriate dress" shows, you often use definition to help explain some special circumstances. The woman who required such dress was obviously pretty single-minded and demanding; without a paragraph to explain exactly what she meant by *appropriate*, the reader might not have seen her as she really was (or as you the writer saw her, anyway).

Sometimes, however, you will face a subject that requires a more elaborate, extended definition or an entire essay devoted to defining something. Imagine, for example, that you are dealing with the subject of the drive for happiness in our society today. As you look around you, talk to family and friends, and consider your own values, you make a few disheartening discoveries. For too many people today, happiness is tied to things, to possessions, to vanity, to monetary success. The right car, the right clothes, the right friends, the right places, the right look — people don't seem to be happy unless they have them, even if obtaining them means being selfish or abandoning old places and friends who no longer fit in the picture.

Maybe you could talk about what, in your view, happiness should be based on. Your thesis might be something like this:

```
No matter what television and fancy magazines try to tell
us, being happy has much more to do with learning to
understand and like the person that you are than it does
with owning a twenty-five-thousand-dollar car or having
the biggest wardrobe in town.
```

Then, in the body, you would go on to define happiness by explaining how people come to terms with their inner selves and what it means when they do; first, recognizing that sometimes you seek money, power, fame, and so on, to compensate for some quality you feel is lacking; then, identifying and focusing on those admirable qualities you possess — generosity, compassion, gentleness, confidence: finally, identifying and accepting and controlling those negative qualities — greed, cruelty, selfishness — that come with being a human being.

In this case, you define happiness by first explaining what it isn't: conspicuous consumption. Then you present the two main components of happiness: an accentuation of positive personal qualities and an acceptance and mastery of negative personal qualities.

Sometimes, of course, your subject will be more clear and concrete, as would be the case if you were defining an infectious disease such as mononucleosis for a science class or a surveying device such as a transit for a civil or construction engineering class. A definition paper on such concrete topics as these would be far more precise. A transit, after all, is a transit; it is a universally recognized device, so your job in a definition paper on a transit will be to explain what the component parts are and how they function as a unit. Maybe you could also explain the history of the device, the history of the name, and so on.

In a definition paper, your job is fairly straightforward. No matter if your subject is abstract or concrete, you must present the term or concept in your introduction, use the body of your paper to explain and specify it, and then restate the significance of that definition in your conclusion. Fulfill these requirements, and your definition paper will be effective.

USING THE TECHNIQUE

No matter what you are writing about, your job is to communicate your ideas clearly to your reader. In a definition paper, you'll find it easier to meet this goal if you follow through on the following guidelines:

1. Take advantage of a dictionary, but don't rely exclusively on it.

A good dictionary is a fine place to begin a definition paper. After all, you can look up any term and find an excellent, encapsulated explanation. The problem is, however, that most terms have a multitude of meanings, some differing only a shade from the others. You need to present your definition in such a way that your reader will see what meaning you attach to the word.

For example, imagine you are defining *optimist*. The dictionary says that an optimist is "one who believes that good ultimately prevails over evil." Sometimes, however, optimists tend to see good even in the worst situations and hope against hope that something good will happen. Some optimists are also unrealistic in that they fail to take into account the evil and unfairness that exist in the world. And some optimists complicate their own lives needlessly because they carry the unnecessary burden of trying to make sense out of some of life's senseless realities, like promising students who nevertheless fail and young, healthy people who nevertheless die. You won't find these examples in the dictionary, yet you might well use this type of illustration to define *optimist*.

The dictionary fuels your fire; it provides a start, a point of clarification or delineation, which you must amend and adapt so that it reflects a more correct definition as you see it. Sprinters crouch down and put their feet against special devices called *starting blocks* to gain the fastest possible start in a race, but for the other 99 percent (or more) of the race, they have no device to help them. A dictionary is your starting block; feel free to take advantage of it, but remember that it is useful to you at the start. After that, you're on your own.

2.   Provide a working definition early in the paper.

If you want your reader to understand your points thoroughly, you should make sure that what you are talking about is presented early enough. If, for instance, your subject is a loner, your main job is to provide an extended definition of the term, a task that will take several paragraphs.

But in order for your reader to understand the various paragraphs that make up your extended definition of a loner, you need to provide a brief definition of *loner* early in the paper, preferably in the introduction:

> But a loner isn't someone who is painfully shy or someone who hates other people; instead, a loner is an individual who, rather than joining with others to draw from a sense of community, draws on inner resources to find peace, happiness, and fulfillment.

With this direction, your reader is prepared to see that, in your view, being a loner does not mean being odd or deficient or weird. Without this brief declaration in the introduction, your reader might have been misled into thinking that your paper would deal with these negative qualities, often associated with being a loner.

3.   Provide both limited and extended definitions.

In some cases when you write, you will be able to provide a simple definition. For example, you might define a spatula as a tool or implement used to turn or spread food or paint. That would pretty much take care of the definition.

Many of the subjects you'll have to define will be far more abstract and complex, however, and will thus need far more in the way of definition. If, for instance, if you were defining humor, you would need to provide both a limited definition and a more extended definition. Initially you would define the subject — "Humor is the state or condition of recognizing what is funny or amusing" — but then you would provide a more detailed illustration. After all, what makes some people nearly fall out of their chairs laughing might simply confuse or annoy the next person; humor is a far more complex concept than the one covered by the simple definition.

For this reason, your definition paper would be complex, too. For instance, for this paper on humor, you might divide the subject into physical humor and psychological humor, explaining each in detail. Your explanations of these two types of humor would contain both limited and extended definitions. This paragraph from the extended definition of physical humor is a good example:

> When some people think of physical humor, they immediately think of slapstick humor. The appeal of this type of humor, which involves such violence as hitting, punching, slapping, slipping, and falling, is difficult to justify. Hit your own thumb as you work on some project, and you might bleed, swear, or pass out; watch a television comedian hit his thumb with a hammer, however, and you'll probably laugh. Everyone knows that a person could slip on a banana peel and be seriously hurt, maybe even die, yet people still break up over a slip on a banana peel.

This part of the extended definition of humor deals with one aspect of physical humor: slapstick humor. But within this portion of the **extended** definition, which uses two examples of this type of humor — hitting one's thumb and slipping on a banana peel — as well as our reactions to them, is the **limited** definition of slapstick humor, which appears underlined. This balance makes the overall definition more effective because it not only presents plenty of examples explaining what makes us laugh but also spells out in specific detail the various elements making up the larger topic.

4.   Recognize all the possible meanings of the terms you use.

As you write, make sure you are aware of both the denotations and connotations of terms. **Denotation** is the actual, literal dictionary definition without any of the additional, subjective meanings that we often attach to a term. **Connotation** refers to the various meanings that the term evokes.

Immature, for instance, literally means "not yet fully developed"; that's its denotation. If you try referring to a sixteen-year-old as immature in that individual's presence, you'll be in for a fight, despite the obvious truth of the statement; after all a sixteen-year-old is hardly fully developed. The sixteen-year-old will be objecting to the connotations associated with the term *immature,* like *irresponsible* or *disrespectful* or *undependable.*

Denotation and connotation are always important concerns for you as a writer. In a paper on definition, they are especially important concepts because an effective definition depends so much on the terms you use to explain, support, or illustrate it.

    5.   Make your examples clear, specific, and detailed.

No matter what you write about, you need to explain your ideas in complete detail. A definition paper is no different, and the examples you choose will help you present your ideas clearly.

In a paper about personal popularity, for example, your thesis might be something like this:

> A truly popular individual is a person who has a balance of honesty, sincerity, friendliness, and good looks.

This thesis presents a limited definition of personal popularity, and it divides it into four main elements. Your job as the writer is to amplify each of these elements by providing clear, specific, and detailed examples; if you don't, your reader won't get the full range of your ideas. Look at this paragraph, which lacks sufficient detail:

> A crucial element in personal popularity is good looks. People are attracted to people who look good. Looking good affects your personality, probably because people like to be near happy people, so personal popularity and good looks have a reciprocal relationship.

This paragraph has potential, but it is not at all clear for the reader. For instance, what exactly is meant by *good looks?* And how are personal popularity and good looks reciprocal? Once the examples are amplified, however, the paragraph does fulfill its potential:

> A crucial element in personal popularity is good looks. But <u>good looks</u> doesn't necessarily mean looking like a model in a fashion magazine. <u>Good looks</u> means careful grooming–neat and clean hair, skin, and clothes–and it also means the pleasant, smiling demeanor of a person who has confidence. Looking good affects your personality; if you're happy with the way you look, you feel good about yourself. People are attracted to people who are happy about how they look, probably because we all like to be near happy people, so personal popularity and good looks have a reciprocal relationship.

This second version is much more effective because it defines *good looks* and their effects in thorough detail. The key is to amplify all your examples; that's what your reader needs:

    6.   Arrange the elements of your paper effectively.

In order to make your definition paper as effective as possible, focus on the arrangement of the examples and illustrations. In the paper on personal popularity, for example, the elements that make up personal popularity are set forth in the thesis: honesty, sincerity, friendliness, and good looks.

If, after you examined your first draft, you decided that honesty is the most important part of personal popularity, you might follow a least-to-most-important arrangement, setting the elements up in increasing order of importance, with honesty as the final element in your presentation. But if these four qualities are equal in importance, you might experiment with different ones.

If, however, you were defining guilt, you might define it by tracing its development and its effects on the guilty individual. In this case, your arrangement would be chronological, presenting the various examples in the order in which they occurred.

As always, the arrangement you choose for your paper depends on your subject and the points you are trying to make about it. Because an effective arrangement means a more effective paper, pay particular attention to this part of your work.

Definition is an important writing technique for you to master. Very little in the world around us is simple and clear, so explaining and specifying exactly what you mean is vital if you are going to communicate your ideas to your reader.

ASSIGNMENT 9

In a 500- to 750-word essay, present the elements that make up the ideal form of something, for example, a lecture, a concert, a friend, a society, or a government. Or take the opposite approach and define the elements of a bad lecture, concert, and so on.

Reason

Maybe one of the few things that people can agree on is that people generally can't agree on much — and the more controversial or open-ended the topic, the wider the range for disagreement. For this reason, a paper that presents a definition of the ideal form of something has great potential because most people have a very definite idea of what makes up an outstanding event or presentation, and they are generally interested in seeing another view, if for no other reason than to defend their own view or to tear yours down.

Take the example of the ideal vacation. What are its components? Basically your job is to state these components in your initial limited definition and then to amplify this initial definition in the body of the paper. In this case, your thesis might read this way:

```
The ideal vacation begins with a special destination that
provides plenty of activity and entertainment at a
reasonable price.
```

You would follow this thesis with the components of the ideal vacation — a

special destination, special activities and entertainment, and reasonable cost
—and then close up with a conclusion that restates the significance of the
paper. The result is a clear, understandable definition of something in its ideal
state.

What Your Reader Needs

When you write a paper defining something in an ideal state, you must present
it in clear, specific terms. That's what your reader needs.

An introduction providing a clear thesis is vital; it provides a direction for
your reader. In this case, that direction includes your limited definition of the
subject. For instance, if you are defining a good restaurant, your reader first
needs to know the specific focus of your paper.

A paper about a good restaurant, for example, might begin with an introduction like this:

> Most people count going out to dinner as one of the joys of
> living. After a hard day of working to meet the needs of
> others, sitting down and having someone meet your needs is
> a pleasure well worth the money. No matter what kind of food
> you prefer—steak, seafood, Italian, Chinese, or Cajun—or
> what budget you are working from, there's a restaurant that
> meets your needs. But the type of food or its cost isn't what
> makes up a good restaurant. Rather it's the quality of that
> food, the courtesy with which it is served, and the
> atmosphere in which it is served that define the ideal
> restaurant.

This introduction lets your reader know what will follow in the body. The
thesis, shown underlined, specifies the three main components of the definition of a good restaurant—good food, excellent service, and outstanding
atmosphere—and sets the scene for what will follow.

Of course, the examples that make up the body of the definition must be
explained in specific detail too. *Atmosphere,* for instance, is a highly subjective
term; in order to make your reader understand what you mean by it, you must
provide a thorough explanation, as this paragraph shows:

> Atmosphere, the feeling created by the setting, is very
> much an element in the ideal restaurant, and it is the
> combination of a number of elements. No matter what style
> of restaurant, the furnishings should be elegant and in
> good repair. Wooden furniture and any brass or silver
> accessories should be sturdy and well-polished. Carpeting
> should be bright and clean, as should table linens.
> Curtains should be carefully matched and arranged, and
> windows should be sparkling. If there is music, it should
> be live and subdued. Lighting should be sufficient to read
> the menus but no brighter. And there should be enough room
> between tables so that people can converse without being

distracted or worrying about being overheard. The idea is
to make people feel as if they are dining in a beautiful
private dining room.

This paragraph provides a specific explanation of this element of the definition of a good restaurant: atmosphere is achieved when the furnishings are top quality and well maintained, when music and lighting are subdued, and when privacy is ensured.

Your reader first needs a clear direction, which you provide with an effective introduction. Then your reader needs clear examples that specify the components of your subject. These you provide in the body of your paper. Finally, your reader needs a restatement of the significance of your paper, which you present in your conclusion. Once you have met these needs, you'll have an effective paper because your reader will have a clear view of your ideas.

Model

BAD TEACHERS

The influence of great teachers lasts for a lifetime.
Their caring, enthusiasm, commitment, and competence
leave their students with at least the awareness that they
have experienced people who know what to teach and how to
teach it. Fortunately, everyone can name at least one
teacher who fits this description. Unfortunately, though,
everyone can also name at least one teacher who lacked
these vital characteristics. These individuals, the bad
teachers, imparted lessons that had none of the clarity of
purpose and action that students need. Instead, bad
teachers gave their students memories of empty lessons and
wasted time. Sadly, these lessons last a lifetime, too.

Caring about students is one of the primary requirements
for teachers. They must demonstrate that their concern is
the students' welfare. But poor teachers indicate clearly
that the students' needs are not very important to them.
Therefore, both the nursery-school teacher whose tone of
voice signals her perpetual annoyance with chattering
voices and the college professor whose attitude indicates
that students distract her from her research send out a
clear message: Don't bother me.

Of course, closely connected with caring about students
is enthusiasm for teaching. Teachers who enjoy their jobs
are no doubt in a better position to interest their
students. Immediately, the students see that their
teachers believe that learning is important and fun. But
when teachers lack this enthusiasm, the message that
students receive is different: Learning is tedious work.
Bad teachers don't lead discussions; they mechanically
read lecture notes or, worse, write the lecture on the

blackboard and have the students waste time merely copying these facts. Homework is assigned by these teachers, but its connection with the classroom work isn't demonstrated; sometimes it is collected and thrown away without any evaluation. Bad teachers show little interest in their profession. When the spark of enthusiasm is missing, where will the students in that classroom find the inspiration to achieve?

To be truly successful, teachers must also be committed to their profession. This means a continual striving toward excellence in their various fields of study. Their lesson plans must be a blend of careful study and innovative teaching approaches. Bad teachers, however, care little about teaching as a profession. There is no growth in a subject area for them. Sometimes they don't even bother to discuss new developments in their subject area, maybe because they don't care to learn any more themselves. Period after period, year after year, the same tired lessons are repeated with the same mediocre results. These teachers show no commitment to teaching; their careers consist of counting the days between vacations.

Perhaps the most vital characteristic of successful teachers is competence. Certainly, enough attention has been given to the incompetence of teachers in the last few years. For example, the State Board of Education published a study recently that included a copy of a letter of recommendation written by an English teacher with a master's degree. The letter was a shameful mass of errors, clearly written by someone who lacks competence. Although the term implies the mastery of a subject area, competence also means the ability to pass on that information. Many times, brilliant researchers or scholars become bad teachers because they lack communication skills. Therefore bad teachers aren't incompetent only when they are illiterate; incompetence also means having a problem communicating the subject matter to students. As a result, poor teachers don't do the most basic job required of a teacher: teaching.

Becoming a teacher means far more than going to college and receiving a degree. Beyond this basic education, teachers must show that they genuinely care about their students, their subject matter, and their profession, and then they must learn to demonstrate this sincere interest. Most important of all, however, they must be able to communicate with their students. Bad teachers don't have these attributes, nor do they try very hard to develop them. The crime in all of this, of course, is that bad teachers have the opportunity to influence so many students, perhaps permanently giving them a negative attitude about learning.

Follow-through

When you write a paper that defines the ideal state of something, your starting point is the subject you choose. Once you've decided exactly what subject you want to define, you must begin to break it down into the key elements, because the combination of those elements makes up the subject and thus provides the definition.

In the case of this subject, bad teachers, the first step is to specify what elements make up a bad teacher. The prewriting produced the following information:

> *Mrs. Welch was a bad teacher—lazy, cruel comments, real sarcastic—never admitted she made a mistake even when everybody could prove it—that English teacher—what was his name?—he was so smart, you could tell it, but he was way over our heads—he used to say, "You understand, right," over and over—the more he'd say it the more confused I'd be. Ms. Sullivan—she cared a lot—used to ask about personal stuff, your family and stuff at school but it wasn't because she was nosy—she'd stay after school just to talk—she really made you understand, too, a great communicator—Feller!!—what a creep—and lazy—gave the same tests year after year and they were always the standardized kind—he was too lazy to make up his own—never corrected our homework—I saw him throw it out one day at the end of class—he didn't even look at it—pathetic—he really hated the job, as if it was our fault—always stayed out sick on parents' night so he wouldn't have to defend himself—he didn't seem to care about anybody in his classes—Ms. Winfield was great, though—so enthusiastic—nobody ever cut her class—she cared, too—if you messed up a test and had a good reason, she'd make up a special test and average the grades—smart, too—she was getting a doctorate, I think, but you'd never know it—she wasn't an egghead, but every week she'd bring in new articles and stuff that was just being discovered—regular person—Mr. Henderson was really dumb—it's too bad, really, but the notes he writes—one day when he sent me to the office with a note, the principal started goofing on him—and he was a pain, too, really insulting—the worst ones are the ones who hate what they're doing—if they don't want to work with kids, they shouldn't—school's hard enough, so you need someone who is really exciting, who loves being a teacher.*

This prewriting provides both general and specific details about teachers; further, it provides details about both bad teachers and good teachers. Identifying what the teacher *should* be like makes it easier to show how a bad teacher shortchanges students.

According to this prewriting, a good teacher is a person who cares about the job and the students, who communicates well, and who is enthusiastic, compassionate, and ambitious; a bad teacher is someone who dislikes the job and the students, who can't get ideas across in class, and who is dull, insulting, and lazy. As the final draft shows, even though the focus of the paper is on bad teachers, the attributes of good teachers are also presented in order to give the reader a more complete definition.

In order to provide a clear direction for your reader, you must provide an introduction with a thesis. In the case of this paper, the introduction first gives the reader a point of reference—a limited definition—by presenting some of the attributes of good teachers: "Their caring, enthusiasm, commitment, and competence leave their students with at least the awareness that they have experienced people who know what to teach and how to teach it." Once this limited definition is given, the focus switches to bad teachers. This limited definition is actually expressed in a few sentences:

> Unfortunately, though, everyone can also name at least one teacher who lacked these vital characteristics. These individuals, the bad teachers, imparted lessons that had none of the clarity of purpose and action that students need. Instead, bad teachers gave their students memories of empty lessons and wasted time.

The thesis, which also depends on the definition of good teachers, can be paraphrased this way: "Unlike good teachers, bad teachers lack caring, enthusiasm, commitment, and competence." With this listing of elements, the reader is prepared for the extended definition that follows in the body.

Each element in the extended definition should be amplified so that it presents a clear picture for your reader. The examples in this paper fulfill this requirement. "Tone of voice" and "attitude" are used to explain lack of concern for students' well-being; "repeated lessons" and "mediocre results" illustrate lack of commitment to the teaching profession.

How you arrange information is always important. In the case of this paper, the order is least to most significant. Competence, identified as the "most vital characteristic" of an effective teacher and therefore as the most serious failing of the bad teacher, is presented last in the body of the paper, following lack of caring, lack of enthusiasm, and lack of commitment. Although this order is obviously subjective, it is nonetheless effective.

The key to success in a paper defining the ideal state of something is to present your definition in clear detail. You start with an effective introduction, followed by elements of the definition spelled out in the body. Then, once you've restated your definition in the conclusion, you've met the needs of your reader; you've written an effective paper.

Checklist

Use the answers to the following questions to help you revise your first draft:

1. Does your paper have a thesis? Write it down.
2. Have you presented at least a limited definition early in your paper?
3. Have you made the various elements of the definition clear, specific, and detailed?

4. Does your introduction provide a clear direction for your reader?
5. Does your conclusion restate the significance of your paper?

ASSIGNMENT 10

Take a quality or a characteristic, and, in a 500- to 750-word essay, define it.

Reason

There is no doubt that the world is complex. Each individual has a separate personality, and each personality affects the relationships we have with each other. Our personalities—and the world around us—are combinations of hundreds of different characteristics that are often difficult to define. A paper that takes one of these attributes has appeal because the essay helps us understand some part of a personality or the world it is part of.

Imagine, for example, that you are going to write about freedom. Among the qualities of life, probably none has been thought about, spoken about, or written about more often than freedom. Individuals and nations thirst after it; the United States is founded on it. But what exactly is it?

To answer the question, you must first come up with an acceptable brief definition. A good starting point is a dictionary, which in most cases will provide a brief encapsulation of the various meanings of a word. The average dictionary would no doubt give you several different meanings for the word *freedom* from which you can develop a brief definition: "Freedom is the state of exemption from unfair control."

Next, you provide examples that will support or illustrate this brief definition. Perhaps you will support this definition by giving examples of personal freedom (choosing your own career, spouse, neighborhood, and so on), political freedom (voting, supporting a particular candidate, or becoming a candidate yourself), and philosophical freedom (thinking, reading, and watching whatever you wish as long as doing so doesn't harm anyone or keep other people from pursuing their interests).

Not everyone will agree with your assessment of a subject, of course. For example, to some people, freedom may mean absolute lack of control, the state of being able to do exactly what they please regardless of consequences. To other people, freedom may mean living under a system of government such as our own.

In short, there will always be some controversy over the definition of qualities or characteristics. And it is precisely because of this disagreement that people will be interested in reading your definition.

What Your Reader Needs

When you write a paper defining an attribute or characteristic, your reader needs to see that term explained and supported in specific terms. The setup is fairly simple: first, you provide a limited definition of the quality, and then you provide an extended definition through clear, specific examples.

One source for that limited definition is a dictionary. For most subjects, you will have a basic understanding. You know, for example, what nervousness is; you have felt it yourself sometimes and you recognize it in others. Your reader shares this basic understanding. But these definitions are generally unspoken; using the dictionary is a way for you to clarify the definition and make sure that you have voiced your unspoken definition in universal terms.

An appropriate limited definition of *nervousness* — "the state of being anxious, tense, or fearful" — meets the needs of your reader because it verbalizes what your reader understands but has probably never quite put into words. It is a start, a common point of reference. It prepares the reader for your extended definition of nervousness. Nervousness is recognizable through physical actions (like sudden movements, shaking, pacing, and biting nails), physical discomfort (like upset stomach, headaches, and nausea), and emotional upset (rapid speech, sudden mood swings, confusion, and so on).

The limited definition in the introduction provides the direction. Then the various examples support this definition, and the conclusion restates the significance. The result is a paper that meets the needs of your reader. And no matter what quality or attribute you are writing about, that's your primary responsibility.

Model

CONFIDENCE

Among the most important components in our relationships with each other is confidence. Whether the situations involve telling someone a secret or buying a car or taking an exam, they all require confidence, a sense of complacency and trust that means whatever choice was made was the right one. In our day-to-day living, perhaps no other trait is as important.

In any definition of <u>friendship</u>, the word <u>confidence</u> is likely to appear because the knowledge that one's deepest secrets can be expressed without fear that they will be repeated is probably the most important attribute a friend can have. This type of confidence is vital to existence because all of us need to be able to share our most private thoughts and ideas. Other personal relationships depend on confidence in some part, too. Some of these relationships— for example, patient-to-doctor and client-to-lawyer—are protected by a code of ethics to ensure confidentiality. Without the confidence that these people can be trusted, our ability to function would be seriously impaired.

Confidence in products and services is so valuable that millions of dollars a year are spent cultivating it through advertising. Companies know that their reputations depend on the confidence people have in them, and they expend much time, effort, and money to maintain it. A striking example of what can happen when the public loses that confidence is the first scare involving Tylenol

Extra-Strength Capsules. Because of a few deaths caused not by the product itself but by poison that was added by someone <u>after</u> it left the manufacturer, all Tylenol products were briefly taken off the market and then repackaged in tamper-proof boxes. Because Tylenol is produced by a multi-million-dollar corporation that can afford to spend massive amounts of money to advertise, the pain reliever managed to recapture its position as one of the best-selling products of its type and to handle the other scares that have occurred since. The cost of recovering the public's confidence, however, is probably beyond the ability of smaller firms to pay; a lack of confidence in their products would put them out of business fast.

But the kind of confidence that means the most to us is self-confidence. If there is one attribute that separates the successful person from the person who just misses the mark, it is self-confidence. It is no substitute for raw talent or intellect; rather, it enhances these traits. Sometimes figures in the public eye, like sports broadcaster Howard Cosell or baseball star Reggie Jackson, take self-confidence a step further until they seem arrogant or conceited. But true self-confidence is not overconfidence; it is instead a quiet sense that fills individuals with the knowledge that they will do their best because that is what they are capable of.

Confidence, then, qualifies as one of the central threads of life. It is vital in relationships between individuals, and it is central in the workings of business. But confidence is most important in the way people view themselves. With confidence, they can go through life comfortable in the sense that they have done their best. Without it, they must look over their shoulders and wonder how long it will be before inevitable failure overcomes them.

Follow-through

A paper that defines a quality or characteristic already has a head start toward success. After all, it covers a subject that your reader no doubt has an interest in. But to take advantage of this head start, you need to provide a limited definition of your subject and then support it with an extended definition featuring clear, specific examples.

In the case of this paper, the starting point is the subject — "confidence" — and the limited definition: "a sense of complacency and trust that means whatever choice was made was the right one." This was the focus for prewriting, during which the following information was produced.

- *Need to have confidence in doctors, surgeons because they cut you open — they have to have confidence, too, because of all the malpractice suits — one mistake and they're out of business.*

- *like the Tylenol murders — I'm surprised they didn't go down the drain — once people lost confidence in a product, it's all over — Chrysler was an exception, too — all these companies spend all kinds of money on advertising just to earn confidence.*
- *confidence — special between friends — you know they'll keep a secret — a doctor keeps secrets, too, private personal things — they can't testify against a patient, I don't think, or a lawyer against a client or a priest against somebody who confesses — I think it's a law — code of ethics they swear to.*
- *pro athletes have all kinds of confidence — rock stars, movie stars, stand up on stage and know they'll give a great performance.*
- *self-confidence — like a little voice in your head that says you can do it — you can only do your best, though — confidence won't give you anything you don't have.*
- *you have to watch it too — sometimes you can sound too confident, get cocky.*

This list has information that can be lumped in three general categories: (1) confidence in business and industry; (2) confidence in friends and associates; and (3) confidence in yourself. As the final draft shows, these three elements have become the basis for the extended definition.

Once the elements of confidence are established, the main idea — the thesis — can be developed. In the case of this paper, the thesis is presented at the end of the introduction. First however, the types of situations in which confidence plays an important part, as well as the limited definition of the quality, are presented:

> Whether the situations involve telling someone a secret or buying a car or taking an exam, they all require confidence, a sense of complacency and trust that means whatever choice was made was the right one.

This information sets the scene for the thesis — "In our day-to-day living, perhaps no other trait is as important" — and specifies the direction of the paper for the reader.

Of course, in order for the paper to be effective, the extended definition — the supporting examples — must be spelled out in complete detail. To spell out what you mean, you draw on the initial information that you've generated. The final draft shows that plenty of the prewriting information ended up in the supporting examples.

But this information is seldom in a usable form as it first appears. For example, look at this information that eventually became the supporting examples in the third paragraph:

> *like the Tylenol murders — I'm surprised they didn't go down the drain — once people lose confidence in a product, it's all over — Chrysler was an exception, too — all these companies spend all kinds of money on advertising just to earn confidence.*

Now look at the information as it appeared in the final draft.

> Confidence in products and services is so valuable that
> millions of dollars a year are spent cultivating it through
> advertising. Companies know that their reputations depend
> on the confidence people have in them, and they expend much
> time, effort, and money to maintain it. A striking example
> of what can happen when the public loses that confidence is
> the first scare involving Tylenol Extra-Strength
> Capsules. Because of a few deaths caused not by the product
> itself but by poison that was added by someone <u>after</u> it left
> the manufacturer, all Tylenol products were briefly taken
> off the market and then repackaged in tamper-proof boxes.
> Because Tylenol is produced by a multi-million-dollar
> corporation that can afford to spend massive amounts of
> money to advertise, the pain reliever managed to recapture
> its position as one of the best-selling products of its
> type and to handle the other scares that have occurred
> since. The cost of recovering the public's confidence,
> however, is probably beyond the ability of smaller firms to
> pay; a lack of confidence in their products would put them
> out of business fast.

Clearly this final version is markedly different—and better—than the original information. The first version touches just a fraction of what happened as a result of the unfortunate poisonings involving the pain reliever Tylenol. But the final version recounts some of the actual effects; all Tylenol products had to be pulled from the shelves, new designs for tamper-proof packaging had to be developed, and millions of dollars had to be spent—all to reclaim the confidence that might have been lost.

The initial information also includes a reference to the dramatic resurrection of the Chrysler Corporation. But the connection between this comeback and confidence isn't clear; there doesn't seem to be evidence that the public had ever lost confidence in the automaker. The corporation was simply losing money, at least in part because of poor business practices. The Tylenol case is more directly related to the topic of confidence, and the connections are more easily shown; therefore, the Tylenol case, not the Chrysler case, is amplified to become one of the main examples in the extended definition.

In addition to deciding which examples to use in your extended definition, you must decide how to arrange those examples. If the elements are all about equal in importance, you might try different orders to see which is most effective; another reader can be a big help in this case because that reader provides a fresh view. If the elements of the definition build on each other— (as with a fad, for instance)—you might use chronological order. This model follows a least-to-most-significant order. Confidence as a building block in personal relationships is presented first, followed by confidence as the foundation of a successful business, and finally confidence as the main component of a successful individual. The paper moves from a strong example, to a stronger example, to the strongest example, with this strongest component being clearly designated: "But the kind of confidence *that means the most to us* is self-confidence." Your choice of subject will dictate what order to follow. But no matter what order you set, it must be clear and logical for your reader.

A paper defining a quality or characteristic has natural appeal. In this type of paper, you provide a clear, understandable definition of a complex concept, but you also provide a chance for your reader to compare that definition with his or her own definition of that same concept. Once you produce a definition paper with a clear thesis, supporting examples, and an effective conclusion, your reader will have that chance.

Checklist

Use the answers to the following questions to help you revise your first draft:

1. Does your paper have a thesis? Write it down.
2. Have you presented at least a limited definition early in your paper?
3. Have you made the various elements of the definition clear, specific, and detailed?
4. Does your introduction provide a clear direction for your reader?
5. Does your conclusion restate the significance of your paper?

FOR FURTHER STUDY

Progress: What does it mean to you? This is precisely the subject that Charles Osgood, news anchor for the "CBS Sunday Night News" and editor and anchor of "Newsbreak" and "The Osgood File" on CBS Radio, tackles in this essay. The examples that make up his definition point out this ironic fact, something new and improved isn't always better, at least for the average person.

It's New! It's Improved! You Get to Carry It Yourself!

CHARLES OSGOOD

I recently saw an ad for a commuter airline about a new "improved" baggage service. The improvement is that instead of an airline employee carrying your luggage out to the plane, YOU get to carry the bags out to the plane.

This is typical of what passes for improved service these days.

In the bank, you used to hand your checks and deposit or withdrawal slips to a teller, and the teller would sort out the slips, push different buttons and then hand you the cash or receipt. Now they have improved banking service so much that nobody does anything for you. Instead of waiting in line for a teller, you wait in line for a machine. Then you push all the buttons and sort out all the slips. If there is any mistake, you have only yourself to blame. This may not be better for you, but it's better for the bank.

It started with the supermarkets. I can remember when you'd go to the grocery store and tell the grocer what you wanted and he'd find it, take it down from the shelves and put it in a paper bag for you.

Now things have improved a lot. You find it. You lift it into the shopping cart. You put it on the checkout counter. About half the time, you bag it yourself and you carry it out to the car yourself. I don't mind doing all this, you understand, but I fail to see how it is better.

To make a long distance phone call, you used to tell the operator what city and phone number you wanted. That was all you had to do. She would get the number for you. Sometimes you'd hear her talking operator talk to another operator, with codes and all that. Now you are your own operator. This may not be easier for you, but it's easier for the phone company.

There used to be an elevator man in our building. His name was Bill. Bill knew what floor I got off on. I never had to tell him. Bill ran the elevator, opened and closed the door, and we would exchange a word or two about the weather. Several years ago Bill was replaced by a panel of buttons. The doors open and close by themselves now. Sometimes they close on somebody. The doors don't care. They don't care about the weather either. They are the new improved doors that go with the new improved elevators.

A fellow at the gas station used to pump the gas into your car. He also would volunteer to check your oil and always would wipe your windshield. Now under the new improved filling station, unless you want to pay more for the gas, you pump it yourself. If you want the oil checked, you check it. If you are lucky, they will lend you a greasy rag for wiping the dipstick. If you expect to see through the windshield, you had better wipe it yourself. They will lend you another rag—or the same rag.

I'm not sure I can stand many more of these improvements. It is clear now that when companies say they are doing things better, they don't mean better for you. They mean better for them.

Questions for Study

1. Although the second paragraph provides a sentence that might be considered the thesis—"This is typical of what passes for improved service these days"—you need the example in the initial paragraph to understand Osgood's point. Take these two paragraphs and paraphrase the main idea of this essay.
2. List the examples that Osgood used to make up his extended definition.
3. Which example do you feel best supports his definition? In a brief paragraph, explain your reasons.
4. Is the order Osgood chose effective? Briefly explain any changes you would suggest.
5. Which expresses the thesis better—the introduction or the conclusion?

ALTERNATE ASSIGNMENT K

In Charles Osgood's view, hearing that something is "improved" should make you a little suspicious. As his examples show, sometimes when things are touted as "better," your question should be "In what way?" or "For whom?" Now it's your turn. For this assignment, provide an extended definition of *progress*, a variation of the subject Osgood wrote about.

There's a fine line between individuals who devote all their working time to a career and those who devote all their time to work. The first group are champions of work; the second are victims of it. In this essay, Ellen Goodman has provided an extended definition of this second group—the workaholics —by examining what a life of this kind means for the individual and his or her family.

The Workaholic

ELLEN GOODMAN

He worked himself to death finally and precisely at 3 A.M. Sunday morning.

The obituary didn't say that, of course. It said that he died of a coronary thrombosis—I think that was it—but everyone of his friends and acquaintances knew it instantly. He was a perfect Type A, a workaholic, a classic, they said to each other and shook their heads—and thought for five or ten minutes about the way they lived.

This man who worked himself to death finally and precisely at 3 A.M. Sunday morning—on his day off—was 51 years old and he was a vice-president. He was, however, one of the six vice-presidents, and one of three who might conceivably —if the president died or retired soon enough—have moved to the top spot. Phil knew that.

He worked six days a week, five of them until 8 or 9 at night, during a time when his own company had begun the four-day week for everyone but the executives. He worked like the Important People. He had no outside "extracurricular interests," unless, of course, you think about a monthly golf game that way. To Phil, it was work. He always ate egg-salad sandwiches at his desk. He was, of course, overweight, by 20 or 25 pounds. He thought it was okay though, because he didn't smoke.

On Saturdays, Phil wore a sports jacket to the office instead of a suit, because it was the weekend.

He has a lot of people working for him, maybe 60, and most of them liked him most of the time. Three of them will be seriously considered for his job. The obituary didn't mention that.

But it did list his "survivors" quite accurately. He is survived by his wife, Helen,

48, a good woman of no particular marketable skills, who worked in an office before marrying and mothering.

She had, according to her daughter, given up trying to compete with his work years ago, when the children were small. A company friend said, "I know how much you will miss him." And she answered, "I already have."

"Missing him all these years," she must have given up part of herself which had cared too much for the man. She would be "well taken care of."

His eldest of the "dearly beloved" children is a hard-working executive in a manufacturing firm down South. In the day and a half before the funeral, he went around the neighborhood researching his father, asking the neighbors what he was like. They were embarrassed.

His second child was a girl, who is 24 and newly married. She lives near her mother and they are close, but whenever she was alone with her father, in a car driving somewhere, they had nothing to say to each other.

The youngest is 20, a boy, a high-school graduate who has spent the last couple of years, like a lot of his friends, doing enough odd jobs to stay in grass and food. He was the one who tried to grab at his father, and tried to mean enough to him to keep the man at home.

He was his father's favorite. Over the last two years, Phil stayed up nights worrying about the boy.

The boy once said, "My father and I only board here."

At the funeral, the 60-year-old company president told the 48-year-old widow that the 51-year-old deceased had meant much to the company and would be missed and would be hard to replace. The widow didn't look him in the eye. She was afraid he would read her bitterness and, after all, she would need him to straighten out the finances — the stock options and all that.

Phil was overweight and nervous and worked too hard. If he wasn't at the office, he was worried about it. Phil was a Type A, a heart-attack natural. You could have picked him out in a minute from a lineup.

So when he finally worked himself to death, at precisely 3 A.M. Sunday morning, no one was really surprised.

By 5 P.M. the afternoon of the funeral, the company president had begun, discreetly of course, with care and taste, to make inquiries about his replacement. One of three men. He asked around: "Who's been working the hardest?"

Questions for Study

1. Is the opening sentence a definition of a workaholic? Explain your answer.
2. Make a list of the characteristics of a workaholic according to Goodman's definition.
3. What kind of person was Phil? Did Goodman provide enough detail? Explain your answer in a few sentences.
4. What example in the essay has the most impact? Why? Answer in a paragraph of a hundred words or so.
5. Although Goodman's essay lacks a formal conclusion, the final paragraph is powerful and effective. In a brief paragraph, explain how Goodman managed to hammer home her definition of a workaholic.

ALTERNATE ASSIGNMENT L

In this essay, Ellen Goodman defined a stereotype: a workaholic. But she made the definition of the stereotype come alive by telling the story of one workaholic: Phil. For this assignment, take another stereotype, like a politician, a business executive, a lawyer, an athlete, a mental patient, a member of the clergy, or a drug user — and define that stereotype by telling the story of one individual who fits it.

Chapter 12

COMPARISON ══ AND CONTRAST ══

INTRODUCTION

Maybe it's an oversimplification to say so, but life begins to get complicated as soon as you face your first choice. Making a choice means looking at alternatives and then deciding which one is more appropriate for you. In other words, you **compare** and **contrast** and make your decision based on what you learn. Comparison means examining the similarities of subjects, and contrast means studying the differences. Comparison and contrast are thus types of analysis that you both see and use more than you probably realize.

In fact, all of us decide what to eat, what to wear, what to do, and so on by examining alternatives. Magazines such as *Consumer Reports*, for instance, are successful because they specialize in comparing and contrasting products and services and then presenting the results so that the public can make decisions.

Much advertising also relies on comparison and contrast, but unlike the *Consumer Reports* approach, advertisements often present more than mere facts. A good advertisement is designed to persuade someone to make a particular choice, and ad makers use a number of different techniques — including comparison and contrast — to do their selling. Some ads, for example, attack the competition directly. Burger King versus McDonald's and Pepsi versus Coke are the better-known examples, but the list is seemingly endless.

Others are less direct in their approach; for instance, Ivory Dishwashing Liquid versus the "leading brand" or Nissan versus the other imported cars. In any case, whether the subject is fast food or fast cars, these types of advertisements use comparison and contrast to try to convince us that one product is better than another.

As a writer, you will often use comparison or contrast as a supporting element in a paper. In an essay about rock music, for example, you might examine Mick Jagger of the Rolling Stones and Ray Davies of the Kinks as a way of illustrating the influence of British rockers from the 1960s on today's musical world:

Because of Mick Jagger and Ray Davies, both the Rolling Stones and the Kinks still maintain much of their appeal

even today. These two stars, who led their groups to America
during the early 1960s, represent different types of
attractions. Jagger is the hard-rocking bad boy who ''can't
get no satisfaction''; Davies is the rock-and-roll
philosopher who gave the musical world Lola, its first
transsexual. Yet for all their differences, they share one
point: they are both survivors of a lifestyle that has
claimed many of their peers.

As this paragraph shows, comparison and contrast support the overall theme
of the paper — rock music and its influence — because they illustrate the example of two rock stars who differ in style but who still strongly influence popular
music.

   When you use comparison and contrast, you basically plot one thing next to
another on the basis of some common ground or common points. And because
examining alternatives is something we do frequently, comparison and contrast are valuable techniques to master.

THE MAKEUP OF A COMPARISON AND CONTRAST PAPER

Although you frequently use comparison and contrast as supporting techniques, you also often devote an entire paper to comparison and contrast and
use other techniques to support them. In some of your college classes, for
instance, you may face essay questions like the following, which call for comparison and contrast as the main technique:

In Of Mice and Men, George and Lennie are obviously
different, maybe complete opposites. But at the same time,
are they also similar? Based on your reading and our
discussions in class, compare George and Lennie. What
points are common to both characters?

or

   In Chapter 2, ''Women—The Story Is Still the Same,'' Mae
Foster stated that women are not much better off today than
they were twenty-five years ago. In class, most of you
disagreed; you felt that women today enjoy a much better
situation overall. In a brief essay, present some specific
evidence showing in what ways today's women are better off
than their mothers.

The answer to the first question might point out that both Lennie and George
rely on dreams to exist, both need the other man completely, and both are
basically good men. There are other potential similarities, too.

   The answer to the second question might focus on changes in educational
and employment opportunities in the last twenty-five years. Maybe it would

also note society's increasing awareness of the domestic roles of both men and women today in relation to earlier years.

Of course, essay questions such as these aren't the only kind of assignments calling for a comparison and contrast treatment. You might, for instance, write a paper for an economics class that contrasts two different alternatives for using savings: buying treasury notes that earn steady interest or investing in real estate and gambling that your investment will pay off.

No matter what your subject, your comparison and contrast paper must follow some logical order. Like any good writing, it should have a beginning, a middle, and an end, that is, an introduction, a body, and a conclusion. And the paper must contain various points of comparison or contrast that you establish based on your prewriting. Basically, your job is to arrange your information so that your reader will be able to understand your points. Although there are a number of different ways to present your paper, there are two main methods of arranging the material you generate in prewriting so that you will communicate your ideas to your readers.

Block Format

In the block format, you first discuss all the points about one subject and then, in the same order, all the same points about the second subject. In other words, you deal with the first one completely before you start with the second.

Take a look at this informal sentence outline illustrating the block format for a paper contrasting running with swimming:

1. Thesis: Although swimming and running are both excellent forms of exercise, swimming is probably better for complete physical fitness.
2. The initial cost for running shoes and other gear can be excessive.
3. Few indoor facilities exist for running, so runners are at the mercy of the weather.
4. Runners risk serious injury, particularly to the ankles, shins, and knees.
5. Running ranks high as an aerobic exercise, but it can also lead to a slight weakening of the upper body.
6. Swimming also has some hidden costs, like the fee for health club membership, but a swimmer gets more for the money.
7. In bad weather most swimmers have access to a nice, safe pool.
8. Except for some risk of shoulder strain, swimming injuries are rare.
9. Swimming is a better choice for both its aerobic value and its overall conditioning effect.
10. So although both running and swimming are great forms of exercise, swimming is the better investment of time.

As you can see, the same points — cost, convenience, risk, and benefits — are presented, first for running and then for swimming. The points appear in the same order for both subjects: Paragraphs 2, 3, 4, and 5 cover these subjects as they relate to running, and Paragraphs 6, 7, 8, and 9 cover these same subjects in the same order for swimming. The result is a balanced paper.

But balance doesn't mean you shouldn't take a side in the discussion. In fact, in many writings, you use comparison and contrast to decide which alternative is more — or less — appropriate; in a paper that examines leasing a new car versus owning one, for example, your reader is waiting for your findings about which alternative is better. In short, you can still express an opinion while maintaining that balance. Just make sure that the same elements are part of your discussion of each subject.

Alternating Format

In the alternating format, you move from subject to subject based on the elements under discussion. In other words, you "seesaw" from one subject to the second and then back again for the next point. The same model outline is modified here to illustrate this format.

1. Thesis: Although swimming and running are both excellent forms of exercise, swimming is probably better for complete physical fitness.
2. The initial cost for running shoes and other gear can be excessive.
3. Swimming also has some hidden costs, like the fee for health club membership, but a swimmer gets more for the money.
4. Few indoor facilities exist, so runners are at the mercy of the weather.
5. In bad weather most swimmers have access to a nice, safe pool.
6. Runners risk serious injuries, particularly to the ankles, shins, and knees.
7. Except for some risk of shoulder strain, swimming injuries are rare.
8. Running ranks high as an aerobic exercise, but it can also lead to a slight weakening of the upper body.
9. Swimming is a better choice for both its aerobic value and its overall conditioning effect.
10. So although both running and swimming are great forms of exercise, swimming is the better investment of time.

Like the block format, the alternating format also presents all the same points for both subjects — cost, convenience, risks, and benefits — but they are arranged differently: Paragraphs 2, 4, 6, and 8 cover the main points for running; 3, 5, 7, and 9 cover the same points, in the same order, for swimming. In simple terms, the alternating format switches from one subject to the next as it goes through the material point by point. And like the block format, the alternating format still allows you to take a stand without distorting the balance of the paper.

Deciding Which Format Is Better

How you arrange your paper depends on your subjects and your choice of focus. If, for example, you have several points of discussion, use the alternating format because your reader will be less taxed to remember all the points.

For instance, if you were writing a paper examining high school and college on the basis of social life, convenience, level of difficulty, level of responsibility, and level of independence and you used the block format, your reader might easily forget what you had to say about social life for high school by the time the material about social life for college is presented.

But in the alternating method, the specific material about high school would appear head-to-head with the material about college, and it would be easier for the reader to follow your ideas. In addition, transition is easier to maintain because the paragraphs on the same point are back-to-back.

In a paper that has few elements of discussion, however, use the block format, particularly if these points don't require much amplification. For example, if you were contrasting actual computer games in an arcade with the home versions, you might discuss special effects, level of difficulty, and response of the equipment. If you used the alternating methods for these subjects, the Ping-Pong effect could be distracting for your reader, as the paper goes from special effects for one subject to special effects for the next and back again for level of difficulty and response of the equipment for each subject. Using the block method, though, you could make all your points about each subject without the danger of distracting your reader.

Considering the Exceptions

Of course, you can prepare a comparison and contrast paper without following either format. In fact, you wouldn't have to read for long before you discovered several great comparison and contrast essays that follow neither format. Some papers compare the two subjects and then contrast them. Other papers switch from comparison to contrast and then back, depending on the thesis of the paper. In the hands of an experienced writer, comparison and contrast can appear in any number of forms.

As you skills develop, experiment; try different combinations. As a beginning writer, though, make your job simpler by following one of these formats so that you can then concentrate on expressing your ideas clearly.

USING THE TECHNIQUE

Although preparing a comparison and contrast paper may seem difficult at first, the task is not necessarily any more complex than preparing other writing assignments. To make your overall job more manageable, follow these suggestions:

1.   Begin with a thesis that focuses on two subjects.

In a comparison and contrast paper, you can of course compare or contrast any number of items, and as you gain experience, do so. But for the sake of simplicity and clarity, choose two for now.

Consider, for instance, this thesis from a paper examining the news departments of the three major television networks.

In terms of such features as effective news anchors, broad international news coverage, and top-notch

```
correspondents, ABC News is by far the best of the three
major-network news departments.
```

For a balanced study, you would have to examine ABC, CBS, and NBC as they relate to each other. You would thus have to compare Peter Jennings first to Dan Rather and then to Tom Brokaw. Then you would have to compare ABC's international news coverage with CBS's coverage and then with NBC's. As you can see, with more than two subjects, preparing a comparison and contrast can become quite a complex job.

Of course, this doesn't mean that a good comparison and contrast essay can't deal with more than two subjects. Sticking to two subjects, however, simplifies your task, so it's a good idea for a beginning writer.

2.   Make sure the subjects have some common ground.

When you choose the subjects for a comparison and contrast, it's important that you make that choice based on some common point. This doesn't mean, however, that writing that examines things with little in common has no value.

For example, similies and metaphors are figures of speech that compare two obviously dissimilar things. A simile is a comparison between two different things, usually including the words *like* or *as* ("The foam from the waves lay on the beach like the lace on a wedding garment") and a metaphor is a comparison between two dissimilar things without the works *like* or *as* ("The foam from the waves was the lace for the ocean's wedding garment"). Likewise, an analogy is an extended comparison of two unlike subjects: "Being pregnant is like running a marathon. At first you feel sick but it is still exciting. But after a while, you get more and more tired until all you want to do is finish. Then, when it's all over, you're glad you did it." These devices are certainly valuable parts of any writer's repertoire, but even the best writer would find it difficult to develop an extended comparison and contrast based solely on these figures of speech. Focus instead on subjects with some built-in connections to draw on.

For example, a comparison of sailing trips to Tahiti and to Bermuda as two vacations would make sense. Both trips are recreational, both involve cruises, and both have a beautiful island as a destination. But changing one of the subjects to a business trip to Boston makes the task much more difficult because the common ground is no longer as apparent.

Don't feel that these suggestions mean that you should choose subjects to compare or contrast that don't challenge you. Avoid the obvious; unless you have some novel points, don't, for example, compare one ordinary day at the beach with another ordinary day there. Consider your audience: What will they view as exciting or interesting? That's your starting point. Once you've made your initial choice, then follow through point-by-point. By doing so, you automatically limit your thesis, a primary requirement for good writing. When your basis for comparison is clear, your reader is more likely to understand your point of view. And that's what you're after.

3.   Concentrate on either comparison or contrast.

Obviously no two subjects are exactly alike or exactly different. The key is to examine the subjects and decide whether there are more points that are similar or more that are different, and then to direct the focus of your paper accordingly.

For instance, if you choose college and technical school as subjects, you would find that they have many similar attractions. Both provide advanced training by professionals, both award recognized diplomas or certificates, and both charge reasonable tuition and provide financial aid. These points thus become the focus of the paper.

Of course, for the essay to be successful, you must also note that the objectives of these two types of postsecondary education are vastly different. Your task is simplified because the emphasis is on the similar points, and your paper is also accurate because you have acknowledged the obvious major difference.

4.   Have at least three major points to compare or contrast.

For your paper to be effective, it must be adequately developed. Therefore you should provide at least three major points of similarity or difference and discuss each point in relation to each subject.

If, for example, you study the overall efficiency of United Parcel Service (UPS) and the U.S. Postal Service, you should at least consider price, speed, convenience, and reliability for both subjects. Once your have established this basis for comparison, it becomes the blueprint that will lead to an effective paper. Certainly a comparison and contrast essay doesn't always fit into a neat compartment, but a point-by-point presentation does simplify your task by giving you a clear plan to follow.

5.   Arrange the elements of the paper effectively.

How you will arrange the elements of your comparison and contrast paper depends in part on the elements themselves. If, for instance, you are examining traveling by bus compared to traveling by train, and the elements — convenience, expense, speed, and accommodations — are about equal in importance, you might experiment with different arrangements. Try out different orders on another reader; fresh insight is always helpful.

Sometimes, however, you won't feel that the elements in the discussion are equal. For example, if you were writing a paper comparing bottle feeding and breast feeding on the basis of cost, psychological bonding between mother and child, nutritional value, and convenience for the mother, you might feel that the biggest advantage of breast feeding is the psychological bonding that develops through the close physical relationship between the mother and the child. In this case, you should use least-to-most-significant order in order to build reader interest — first convenience, then cost, then nutritional value, and finally bonding.

Look closely at the elements of your comparison or contrast. An effective arrangement makes those elements illustrate your thesis and thus communicate your ideas to your reader — and that is always your goal.

It makes no difference whether you are looking at similarities or differences. If you want to communicate your ideas clearly to your reader, you must make sure that your reason for writing — your thesis — is clear and direct. Then you must make sure that there is a legitimate basis for comparison between the subjects, as well as adequate support for the comparison. Finally, you must make sure that you arrange the elements so that they best communicate what you have to say. The result will be a paper that meets the needs of your reader.

ASSIGNMENT 11

Choose two individuals who have some points of similarity or differences and write a 500- to 750-word essay comparing or contrasting them.

Reason

This assignment is basically an exercise in analysis, one that we perform each day whether the subjects are professors, athletes, or friends. We all have opinions and make judgments about the individuals around us. And because we are all generally interested in what other people feel about those same individuals, a comparison and contrast paper dealing with two individuals has appeal.

For instance, imagine that you are writing a paper about two presidential candidates. If you feel that presidential nominee Senator Michaels is superior to his opponent Governor Charles based on intelligence, personal charisma, and political experience, you have the basis for your paper.

But don't feel that you are restricted to writing about famous individuals only. If you have two sisters, for instance, who are as opposite as can be in terms of their attitudes toward school, their sense of fashion, and their taste in music, you probably have the basis for a fine paper. Remember; even though the subject is the surprising differences between your sisters — individuals your reader is unlikely to know — your reader will most probably know two individuals very much like your sisters.

In any case, your paper will have appeal. After all, it will feature the kind of analysis that we all perform every day. Therefore, although the two individuals you choose to examine may not be well known to your reader, your paper will still be appealing because it will represent exactly the kind of reasoning that your reader regularly exercises.

What Your Reader Needs

In order to understand your point of view, your reader will first want to know why you are taking your stance. Who are the individuals? What points make them similar or make them different? Remember, we compare actors, politicians, waitresses, teachers, and so on, everyday, but too often the basis of comparison is not clearly stated.

For instance, if you feel that the overall medical care that you've received from the local emergency-room doctor is inferior to the treatment you normally receive from your own physician, your paper will begin with a thesis that telegraphs that point clearly and directly:

> No matter what the hospital advertising says, the care I received from the emergency room doctor last month was nowhere near as good as the care I normally receive from my doctor.

Once this thesis is presented, your reader needs to see the point supported. In other words, you use comparison and contrast to show on what basis your personal physician is superior to the emergency room physician.

In this case, if you feel that your own doctor has an excellent bedside manner, superior medical credentials, and proven expertise, then these points will become the framework on which to support your thesis. Basically your job is to examine each doctor on each of these points. It's this kind of analysis that your reader needs.

Once you've presented each point for each subject — that is, once you've discussed bedside manner for the emergency room physician and for your own physician, medical credentials for the emergency room physician and for your own physician, and proven expertise for the emergency room physician and for your own physician — you must add a concluding paragraph restating the significance of your analysis.

No matter what subjects you are comparing and contrasting, you must always fulfill some basic requirements if your paper is to be effective. You must provide a clear direction for your reader in the introduction (a thesis), and, after you provide support for that thesis in the body, you must restate it in a conclusion. By doing so, you ensure that your ideas will be expressed clearly; in other words, you will make sure that you meet the needs of your reader.

Model

PETE ROSE, THE TY COBB CLONE

Among the greatest baseball players of all time was Ty Cobb, an individual who dominated the game in his time. Cobb was an all-around star, noted for his defensive abilities, his hitting for power and batting average, and his overall aggressive play. For years no one could come close to the stature of Ty Cobb, at least until Pete Rose came on the baseball scene. He, too, is an all-star, a man prized for his defensive versatility and consistent hitting. But Rose is most like Cobb if you compare their styles of play. In this regard, Pete Rose could be called a Ty Cobb clone.

Of course, calling Rose a clone of Cobb is an exaggeration because no player has been able to match Cobb's achievements. For example, look at the differences between Cobb and Rose. Cobb batted left-handed and Rose is a switch-hitter. Cobb spent nearly his whole career as an outfielder; Rose has played the outfield and first, second, and third bases. Maybe the most important difference between the two players is that they played in different eras, Cobb from 1905 to 1928 and Rose from 1963 to the present; there is an ongoing debate about which period was the better one for baseball. Despite all these differences, however, the record book shows some striking similarities between Cobb and Rose.

Among Ty Cobb's strengths was his outstanding defense. Although he played a handful of games in other positions, Cobb was an outstanding outfielder. His career fielding average of .961 indicates that for twenty-four years, any ball hit to Cobb was nearly always an out.

But if Cobb's fielding was outstanding, his hitting was extraordinary. According to the Baseball Encyclopedia, his batting average was over .300 in all but his first season, and for four seasons, he batted over .400; .420 in 1911 was his best average. He led the American league in batting for twelve years—seven of them consecutive. Although he never hit many home runs, he is among the top three players in baseball history for doubles and triples.

But maybe what Ty Cobb is best remembered for is his aggressive style of play. A gazelle on the basepaths, he held the record for the most stolen bases in a season until 1962, and he is still listed among the leaders for career stolen bases. One telling anecdote about Cobb relates how he would sit on the dugout steps before a game and sharpen his spikes in front of his opponents. It was apparently his way of telling them that if they stood in his path, he would slice his way through them to the base.

Although Cobb's overall effect on the game has never been matched, Pete Rose has proved to be a modern-day Ty Cobb in several respects. Like Cobb, he is noted for his defense. For example, in 1974 his fielding average was .992, a league record for outfielders, even though he broke into the major leagues as a second baseman. During his career he has also played first and third base, all with defensive consistency.

Like Cobb, Rose is also noted for his hitting. Although he recently overtook Cobb in career hits, his batting statistics can't match Cobb's. But his lifetime batting average is over .300, and he has earned the National League batting title three times in his more-than-twenty-year career. He is also among the all-time leaders in doubles.

But the strongest similarity between Ty Cobb and Pete Rose is style of play. Rose is known as ''Charles Hustle,'' a nickname he earned for his aggressive, physical brand of baseball. One incident that illustrates Rose's hard-driving style occurred in the 1975 All-Star Game. Many players view the All-Star Game merely as a meaningless exhibition that gives the fans a chance to see all their favorite players on the field at the same time. But in that 1975 game, Rose showed that he is not like most players; on a close play at the plate, Rose slammed into Boston's Carlton Fisk, knocking the catcher flat and the ball loose as he scored a run. Some critics accused Rose of taking the All-Star Game too seriously, but he probably didn't think much about it. He always plays that way.

There will never be another Ty Cobb. His all-around outstanding play marked him as one of the best baseball players ever. He was, after all, the first player selected to Baseball's Hall of Fame. Pete Rose is certainly no Ty Cobb, but he comes as close to matching him as anyone has. Rose's defensive and offensive skills have ranked him among the best players in modern times, so much so that Philadelphia willingly signed him to an $800,000 contract in 1979 when he was nearly forty years old. But it is in playing style that Rose most resembles Cobb. Ty Cobb is remembered as the fiercest competitor of his time, perhaps of all time. Pete Rose has proved that, at least in that category, he and Cobb belong in the same league.

Follow-through

Probably the hardest work you will have on this paper will occur before you actually do any of the composing. A successful comparison and contrast paper requires a good deal of planning. Once you've done your initial prewriting and planning, however, you may even find the composing easy.

First of all, you must pick the two individuals and decide whether you will emphasize the similarities or the differences. Remember; both similarities and differences exist for any two subjects with a common ground.

In the case of this model, Ty Cobb and Pete Rose are naturals for a comparison and contrast paper because even at first glance, they seem to have much in common. The prewriting for this paper contained the following information:

Pete Rose always said he wanted to be like Ty Cobb — he finally passed him in career hits a few seasons ago — sometimes he plays like he's Cobb's reincarnation, like a clone — he's a player manager now; Cobb was, too — the Georgia Peach, that's what they called Cobb — Charlie Hustle is Rose's nickname — he's a real hot dog — he slammed into Fisk at that '75 All-Star Game, knocked him down, scored a run — people said he was grandstanding, a show-off, but he doesn't care whether it's an exhibition game or the World Series — Cobb was a wildman, too — he used to sharpen his spikes while the other team took batting practice to scare them — he'd use them, too, sliding in spikes high — I think he was one of the highest paid players of his time — they used a dead ball then, I'm pretty sure — maybe that's why he didn't hit many home-runs — I'll recheck all this stuff in the baseball encyclopedia — Cobb's best batting average was .420, almost a hit every other time at bat – no all-star games then — Rose was a regular in the All-Star games when the players and sportswriters used to pick the teams — pros today make the all-star team if they only bat close to .300 — Ted Williams is the last player to bat .400, and that was at least 20 years ago — Cobb could run, too — he had the record for stolen bases until Maury Wills (?) broke it in 1960 or so — Rose isn't all that fast but he hustles his way — makes up for it by working harder than the rest — Cobb was unbelievable, led the league in batting for 12 years, a lefty — Rose, a switch-hitter, did it 3 times, not bad for modern-day players — Rose and Cobb were both excellent fielders — have to check the record book for exact numbers and positions, but I know it's Hall of Fame quality — Cobb was the first player selected for the Hall of Fame, and he wasn't really very well liked, so he must've been good — a lot of people can't stand Rose either because he seems like an arrogant show-off — it'd be tough to have either Cobb or Rose as a manager — both played in the outfield mostly — Rose was originally an infielder but made the switch to the outfield when he broke into the majors — that's a big adjustment from infield to outfield — I think Cobb even pitched one game — some people think it was harder to play during Cobb's time and others think it's harder today — the money's better today — before he went back to Cinncinati as player manager, Rose signed with the Phillies for almost a million bucks, and the guy was almost 40 — I wonder what Cobb could've earned today with his statistics.

The information here clearly shows some strong similarities between Cobb and Rose. The preliminary writing also indicates some of the differences between the two players, which eventually make up the second paragraph in the final draft:

> Of course, calling Rose a clone of Cobb is an exaggeration because no player has been able to match Cobb's achievements. For example, look at the differences between Cobb and Rose. Cobb batted left-handed and Rose is a switch-hitter. Cobb spent nearly his whole career as an outfielder; Rose has played the outfield and first, second, and third bases. Maybe the most important difference between the two players is that they played in different eras, Cobb from 1905 to 1928 and Rose from 1963 to the present; there is an ongoing debate about which period was the better one for baseball. Despite all these differences, however, the record book shows some striking similarities between Cobb and Rose.

Getting these points out of the way early is important. The prewriting referred to Cobb as a "reincarnation, a clone" of Cobb; yet a check of the record book clearly shows that Cobb was by far the better player. Because the prewriting also mentioned some of the major differences between Cobb and Rose — for example, the eras in which they starred and the positions that they played — the presentation of this information early in the paper makes it clear that Rose is not being drawn as the exact duplicate of Cobb. As a result, the reader has a clear view of the writer's intent: to show that the talents, skills, and achievements of Pete Rose are similar — but not equal — to those of Ty Cobb.

Although the preliminary writing provides the seeds for most of the material appearing in the final draft, these initial pieces of information must be amplified and clarified. *The Baseball Encyclopedia* is the source of the statistics that back up the preliminary information about batting averages, batting titles, positions played, records held, and so on. You won't always have to provide this type of statistical support; your subject will dictate whether you'll need to consult record books. A paper such as this one about professional athletes would be greatly weakened without this factual support. If you were comparing two of your uncles on the basis of their personalities, career choices, and attitudes toward family life, however, you wouldn't have to head to the library to look anything up.

In a comparison and contrast paper, you should provide at least three points of similarity or difference and then discuss each point in relation to each subject. In this paper, there are three points — offense, defense, and playing style — and each is discussed in relation to each player.

One of the strongest attributes of the final version of the paper is the arrangement of the elements in the body. The closest similarity — playing style — is presented last. The arrangement of points within an essay is vital; in this case, if playing style had not been the final point, the essay would have fallen flat. The statistics show that playing style is the only area where Rose could be considered Cobb's equal. Batting average, stolen bases; and extra-base hits — Cobb beats Rose in each category. There is legitimate basis for comparison between the players, but the paper might have been less effective if one of the other points had been used as the anchor in the essay because the similarity is just not strong enough.

This paper follows the block pattern; that is, first Cobb is discussed in relation to defense, offense, and style of play, and then Rose is discussed in relation to the same points in the same order. This format is an appropriate choice here because only three main points of similarity are presented. Therefore the reader is unlikely to forget what has been said about Cobb's style of play before Rose's style of play is presented because the paper is not very long. The alternating format could also work with this paper; in many cases, the choice of format is a judgment call, so experiment a bit to see which format best communicates your ideas to your reader.

Maybe this essay isn't quite ready for *Sports Illustrated,* but the final version of the paper is clear, informative, and direct. In short, it is well written, and it meets the needs of the reader.

Checklist

1. Does your paper have a clearly defined thesis? Write it down.
2. What is the basis for comparison? List the points; remember, you need at least three.
3. Is the arrangement for your points effective? List your anchor point.
4. Have you discussed each point in relation to each individual (example: defense for Ty Cobb, defense for Pete Rose; offense for Cobb, offense for Rose; style of play for Cobb, style of play for Rose)?

5. Have you consistently followed a particular method of arrangement (block method or alternating method)?
6. Does your introduction provide a clear direction for your reader?
7. Does your conclusion restate the significance of what you have told your reader?

ASSIGNMENT 12

Take two devices, activities, places, or periods of time, and compare or contrast them in an essay of 500 to 750 words.

Reason

If practice truly makes perfect, then we should be particularly skilled concerning comparison and contrast. Daily we study the alternatives the world offers us and decide which ones are best for us on the basis of our examination. Are the Celtics or the Yankees the greater sports dynasty? Is capitalism superior to communism? Which is better, aerobic dance or bicycling? These are the types of questions that people regularly consider. Therefore a writing about two activities, places, or periods of time has considerable appeal.

Imagine, for example, that you are contrasting a traditional stereo with a compact-disk player. You would need to consider price, availability, and sound quality. In terms of price, compact-disk players, which use a laser beam to "read" the music without any of the scratching, popping, and whistling common with ordinary records and tapes, are generally more expensive — up to a hundred dollars more than a comparable traditional unit — and so are the disks that must replace the records used on a traditional system. Therefore cost involves not only the unit itself but the replacement cost of one's current album collection, which cannot be used on the CD system.

Furthermore, because compact-disk players are relatively new items, they have been in short supply from time to time. Open any newspaper, however, and you will see advertisements proving that traditional stereo units are always abundant. Furthermore, compact-disk players represent an entirely different technology, so finding someone to repair one might be more difficult than finding someone to repair a traditional stereo unit.

But the quality of sound! That's what makes the expense and difficulty of owning a compact-disk player worthwhile. On a compact-disk recording, you hear all the music, with none of the distortions that you hear with traditionally recorded music.

This information is a fine basis for a comparison and contrast paper. First, however, you must provide a clear thesis:

> Even though you can buy a regular stereo immediately and at less cost, a compact disk player is worth the wait and the extra expense because you'll finally be able to hear recorded music as it was intended to be heard.

What remains is to amplify each of these points — availability, expense, and sound quality — and finally to add a concluding paragraph. The result will be a fine paper.

Remember: people are generally interested in the subjects you present. Therefore, follow through on this interest by expressing your main idea about those subjects — your thesis — clearly; then support and illustrate it in the body of your paper, and finally, restate it in your conclusion.

What Your Reader Needs

In the analysis of any two subjects, your reader needs to know the specific subjects and the points that you are making about them. These are the crucial points in any successful paper. In other words, once the thesis is established, your reader needs to be able to see points of analysis, that is, the basis for comparison.

If your subject is television comedy — specifically, a recent situation comedy like "Family Ties" and its vast inferiority to a situation comedy of a generation ago, "The Mary Tyler Moore Show" — your reader needs to see that point of view expressed clearly in a thesis.

```
When it comes to quality television, a situation comedy
like ''Family Ties'' is poor in comparison to a classic show
like ''The Mary Tyler Moore Show.''
```

Once you've made this main point clear, your reader needs to be able to see your basis for comparison. If you feel that, compared to "The Mary Tyler Moore Show," "Family Ties" is badly acted, poorly written, and unimaginative, you have a basis for comparison.

Of course, you must discuss both shows on the basis of acting, writing, and creativity or freshness, and you must arrange these elements in some logical order — either the block order or alternating order. Further, you must explain each of these points in plenty of detail because your reader needs a complete picture. Saying that "Family Ties" is unimaginative is not enough; you must show that it is unimaginative by providing specific examples of stereotypical characters, repetitive plot lines, and so on.

Your reader always needs a clear direction and plenty of support for that direction. Therefore, your goal is to provide a thesis and then to give examples that illustrate it. Once you've done this, your paper will be successful because it will meet the needs of your reader.

Model

The Good Old Days?

```
Every once in a while I hear people talking about how
good life was in the ''old days.'' Most of the time people
don't specify exactly that they mean by the good old days,
but usually I take them to mean the time when the speakers
```

were young. Let's take the turn of the century as an
example. Many people would claim that life was much better
eighty years ago, but I'm afraid they are just being
nostalgic. When living conditions, working conditions,
and health matters are considered, there is no such thing
as the good old days.

Eighty years ago living conditions for many people were
poor. Certainly the rich had beautiful places to live;
some of their mansions still stand today. But for the
working class, home often meant an overcrowded tenement
with none of the facilities that we, in the 1980s, view as
essential. Obviously electric service was rare. Gas lit
many homes, and coal or wood heated them. The plumbing was
primitive by our standards. Bath water was heated on the
stove, kettle by kettle. Those who were lucky had a ''water
closet''; for the rest, the privy was outside.

Today much of our housing is at least adequate. Of
course, there is still a crying need for good housing for
all citizens. Anyone who has seen the bombed-out look of
parts of New York City and other major cities knows that
the problem is still nowhere close to being solved. But in
much of the country, the housing conditions are adequate,
with electricity, heat, and indoor plumbing.

Back at the turn of the century, business was good—if
you owned one. But if you were a worker, life was not
necessarily good. Wages were poor and the hours were long.
Further, the safety regulations we know today didn't
exist, so workplaces were often dangerous. Many
millworkers died as a result of needless industrial
accidents, and many others had their lives shortened by
the effects of the substances they worked with.

In the 1980s the plight of the worker is still serious,
but it is certainly an improvement over the past. Today
wages everywhere are generally better, and the forty-hour
work week is pretty much standard. More important, safety
regulations are now in effect in most industries, so
workers overall have a better chance of surviving in one
piece to collect their pensions. Although many people
might argue that unions sometimes cause problems, these
organizations, which were only in their infancy eighty
years ago, have been the saving grace for American workers.

How many people who had tuberculosis around 1900 lived
to tell about it? How many children died of childhood
diseases that are considered minor today? Medicine has
always been an imprecise science; unfortunately, doctors
simply don't know all the answers. This was more true
eighty years ago. Sanitary conditions were much poorer
then. Further, even routine surgery was life-threatening
because not enough was known about anesthesia and its
effects. A minor matter such as having a tooth pulled
became a major incident of danger and discomfort.

Today illnesses like tuberculosis are under control. In our day we have also seen one of the greatest killers of humans – smallpox – actually practically eliminated. Children rarely die of measles or other childhood illnesses anymore. Immunizations have checked their spread. Surgery, although never a blessing, is generally safer because of various advances in medicine. A trip to the dentist today means a relatively painless treatment.

Somehow yesterday always seems a bit better than today. Maybe this illusion accounts for the many remarks about the good old days. But when people take the time to examine those good old days in relation to today's world, they should find that for all its problems, our present time is a better period to work and to live in.

Follow-through

Planning is an important component of all writing. In a comparison and contrast paper, it's particularly vital. The planning includes prewriting about two subjects, sifting through that information to establish the basis for comparison, and deciding what format to follow. Then all you face is fleshing out this material and refining the draft, a process much easier to say than to do. Still, your work becomes easier once you choose your subjects, complete your prewriting, draft out a thesis, and decide on the points you will cover.

This model examines today's world in relation to yesterday's — more specifically, to the time around the turn of the century. The prewriting for this paper produced this information:

- *You always hear people talking about the "Good Old Days," old people especially, like my grandfather and his buddies — "this or that was cheaper or easier or cleaner" — but I think it's a lot of baloney.*
- *Old Mrs. Sheehan has two missing fingers from an accident at the mill when she was only a teenager — then she said they fired her for getting injured — you could never do that today — at least employers have to be fairer — unions help, too — Gramps forgets about stuff like that, but he had two brothers die from lung diseases that the doctors said were related to the stuff they worked with years before.*
- *I think people forget about the improvements in medicine — today kids get shots for all kinds of diseases — you hardly ever hear of measles or diphtheria any more — you used to have to worry about all of that stuff plus killers like polio or tuberculosis — polio has been making a comeback — a lot of the people who were affected as kids are suffering again, a relapse — no more smallpox, it was just about wiped out and I read somewhere that the only virus left is in a test tube somewhere — a visit to the dentist was really painful because they didn't have anything in deaden the pain — operations were really serious because all they had was ether.*
- *Housing, too — there are still a lot of shacks and ghettos — but those pictures*

Gramps has of where he grew up are really awful — no electricity, no central heat, and no bathroom!!! — and he lived in a good place — a lot more people have adequate housing today — some places in big cities are still a national disgrace — we're the richest nation on earth, but look at the way we let people live — it's still better today, though — except for the poor homeless nobody has to chase after wood or coal — you can take a bath and watch television and cook so much easier.

- *Same thing at work — OSHA and other government agencies monitor stuff like asbestos — they require safeties on machinery — there are rules about work hours, lunch hours, breaks, etc. — most places have 40-hour work week — if you work more you get overtime — Gramps never got overtime in his whole life — and he worked for about $5 a week — of course, things were cheaper, but compared to today, even a guy at minimum wage with benefits is better off than a foreman like Gramps was.*

Some of this prewriting information can be arranged into three separate groupings — living conditions, working conditions, and health care.

- Living conditions: *Housing, too — there are still a lot of shacks and ghettos — but those pictures Gramps has of where he grew up are really awful — no electricity, no central heat, and no bathroom!!! — and he lived in a good place — a lot more people have adequate housing today — some places in big cities are still a national disgrace — we're the richest nation on earth, but look at the way we let people live — it's still better today, though — except for the poor homeless nobody has to chase after wood or coal — you can take a bath and watch television and cook so much easier.*

- Working conditions: *Old Mrs. Sheehan has two missing fingers from an accident at the mill when she was only a teenager — then she said they fired her for getting injured — you could never do that today — at least employers have to be fairer — unions help too — Gramps forgets about stuff like that, but he had two brothers die from lung diseases that the doctors said were related to the stuff they worked with years before.*
  Same thing at work — OSHA and other government agencies monitor stuff like asbestos — they require safeties on machinery — there are rules about work hours, lunch hours, breaks, etc. — most places have 40-hour work week — if you work more you get overtime — Gramps never got overtime in his whole life — and he worked for about $5 a week — of course, things were cheaper, but compared to today, even a guy at minimum wage with benefits is better off than a foreman like Gramps was.

- Medical care: *I think people forget about the improvements in medicine — today kids get shots for all kinds of diseases — you hardly ever hear of measles or diphtheria any more — you used to have to worry about all of that stuff plus killers like polio or tuberculosis — poli has been making a comeback — a lot of the people who were affected as kids are suffering again, a relapse — no more smallpox, it was just about wiped out and I read somewhere that the only virus left is in a test tube somewhere — a visit to the dentist was really painful because they didn't have anything to deaden the pain — operations were really serious because all they had was ether.*

As the final draft shows, not all the information here was used; and the information that became part of the final draft was also amplified and made more specific. But these categories — living conditions, working conditions, and health care — became the basis for comparison.

Any good writing begins with a clear direction — a thesis, in the final draft, there is no doubt about the direction of the paper because of the thesis:

> When living conditions, working conditions, and health
> matters are considered, there is no such thing as the good
> old days.

A comparison and contrast paper should follow a consistent order, with either the block order or the alternating order as the likely choice. This paper follows the alternating order: first, living conditions in 1900 are presented, and then living conditions today; working conditions in 1900, then working conditions today; and medical care in 1900, and then medical care today. Each point is thus discussed for each subject in a consistent order.

The information about the turn of the century is consistently listed first. The reader thus first sees how difficult circumstances were at the turn of the century and then how much better those same circumstances are today. As a result, the various advances seem even more stunning in comparison to the earlier conditions.

A careful arrangement of the elements of your comparison and contrast paper will make your paper more effective. In the case of this draft, the points of the basis of comparison are about equal; therefore which point — medical care, housing conditions, or working conditions — is placed as the anchor point is a matter of judgment. A skillful writer could no doubt change the order of this final draft and not lessen the effect of the paper.

Whenever you write, your job is to tell your reader what you are writing about and then to develop and explain that idea. In a comparison and contrast paper, you first provide a clear thesis in your introductory paragraph, then discuss each of the subjects in relation to each of the points in the basis of comparison, and finally sum up that main idea in a concluding paragraph. The resulting paper will effectively communicate your ideas about those subjects to your reader. That's always your target when you write.

Checklist

1. Does your paper have a clearly defined thesis? Write it down.
2. What is the basis for comparison? List the points. Remember: you need at least three.
3. Is the arrangement of your points effective? State your anchor point.
4. Have you discussed each point in relation to each subject (example: living conditions in 1900, living conditions today; working conditions in 1900, working conditions today; medical care in 1900, medical care today)?
5. Have you consistently followed a particular method of arrangement (block method or alternating method)?
6. Does your introduction provide a clear direction for your reader?

7. Does your conclusion restate the significance of what you have told your reader?

For Further Study

Award-winning writer Andy Rooney is best known for his "A Few Minutes with Andy Rooney" essays appearing at the end of CBS's "60 Minutes." In these pieces and in his syndicated newspaper column, Rooney handles both the lightweight and heavyweight issues of the day. In this essay, he used comparison and contrast to point out the foolishness of political labels.

Republican or Democrat

Andy Rooney

If I say I am neither a Republican nor a Democrat, it seems to me it shouldn't make anyone angry. It does, though. What seems to happen is that when I say that, *everyone* gets mad at me. My Republican friends think I've lost my marbles and my Democratic friends think I've sold out to the enemy.

The fact is, though, I am neither. I have absolutely no inclination to sign up with any party or to vote their ticket right down the line, either. I'm against whoever is in office. That's not a party.

I can usually spot a liberal Democrat or a conservative Republican at one hundred feet, and I have no trouble at all when they come close enough so I can hear them talk. It doesn't matter whether the subject is sports, fashion, oil, politics, religion or breakfast food. I know one when I hear one. I credit my perception to my neutrality. I'm neutral against both extremes.

Most Democrats are considered to be liberals and most Republicans are thought of as conservative, but a strange thing has happened in relation to the word "conservative." In the first place, liberals are more conservative in matters of the land and our total environment. They want to save it. The traditional political conservatives, on the other hand, are not for conserving much of anything. They think all the trees and oil should be used.

The second paradox in relation to the word "conservative" is that most Republicans no longer fit the classic definition. "Conservatism," Thorstein Veblen said, "is the maintenance of conventions now in force."

In the 1930s, when Franklin Roosevelt was trying to curb our free enterprise system by imposing government on capitalism, Republican conservatives fought him. They wanted to maintain the status quo. They lost, though, and things did change. We no longer have that same free enterprise system. Government is in on the distribution of money at every level. Republicans want to get the government out. They are the revolutionaries who want change. Liberal Democrats wish to maintain things the way they are. *They* are, by definition, the conservatives.

Not knowing whether I'm a Democrat or a Republican sometimes gives me an insecure feeling of inferiority, and I've often tried to lay out in a clear way what I think Republicans believe and what I think Democrats believe. If I could do that, I might be able to take sides. I like liberals better than conservatives, but conservatives make more sense.

Democrats (I think to myself) are liberals who believe that people are basically good, but that they need government help to organize their lives. They believe in freedom so fervently that they think it should be compulsory. They believe that the poor and ignorant are victims of an unfair system and that their circumstances can be improved if we give them help.

Republicans (I think to myself) are conservatives who think it would be best if we faced the fact that people are no damned good. They think that if we admit we have selfish, acquisitive natures and then set out to get all we can for ourselves by working hard for it, that things will be better for everyone. They are not insensitive to the poor, but tend to think the poor are impoverished because they won't work. They think there would be fewer of them to feel sorry for if the government did not encourage the proliferation of the least fit among us with welfare programs.

Questions for Study

1. Paraphrase Rooney's thesis.
2. Did Rooney follow some order of organization? Make an informal sentence outline of his paper to see if you can trace his use of comparison and contrast.
3. What points did he examine about each subject? List this basis of comparison.
4. Rooney's essay doesn't have a formal conclusion. Reread the essay and then write a concluding paragraph that restates his idea.

ALTERNATE ASSIGNMENT M

In his essay, Rooney took the labels *Republican* and *Democrat* and proved that the characteristics normally associated with these two political-party stances aren't as simple and clear-cut as they have seemed to be in the past. Labels tend to be that way. For example, take the titles *political activist* and *patriot*. What are the differences? Is one a villain and one a hero? Or are they truly different? Obviously, as Rooney's essay about political parties shows, there are no simple answers when one deals with labels.

For this assignment, take two terms—for example, *hero* and *daredevil*, *arrogance* and *self-confidence*, *airhead* and *eccentric*, *apathy* and *fear of becoming involved*, *true love* and *crush*—and write a comparison and contrast paper that deals with the differences or similarities (or both) of the two terms.

Among the most interesting developments in television programming over the last decade has been the surprising popularity of prime-time soap operas. Plot lines that were once solely the property of the daytime serials suddenly showed up after supper and turned these evening counterparts into perennial ratings champs. In this essay, Stephen Birmingham has used comparison and contrast to discuss two of the more popular and enduring of the nighttime soaps, "Dallas" and "Dynasty."

Dallas vs. Dynasty: Which Show is Better?

STEPHEN BIRMINGHAM

Having emerged, somewhat bleary-eyed, from a long, hot summer of reruns on television's two popular prime-time soap operas, *Dallas* and *Dynasty*, all I can say is that I'm glad I'm not rich. Rich folks, if these two shows are to be believed, get themselves in such godawful messes, and the message of both shows is clear: all the oil in Texas and Colorado will not sweeten their little lives.

There are other conclusions to be drawn. For one thing, older rich people tend to be nicer than younger ones. On both *Dallas* and *Dynasty*, most of the trouble-makers are flushed with youth, good looks, health, lust and greed. Generally, the older a rich person is, the less threatening he or she becomes. Barbara Bel Geddes (Miss Ellie on *Dallas*) can only watch with genteel dismay the fiscal and carnal shenanigans of the younger members of her family, just as Blake Carrington (John Forsythe) does on *Dynasty*.

Then, too, on both series, the props a rich person uses can tell you a lot about what he or she is up to. When Joan Collins, Alexis Carrington Colby on *Dynasty*, lights up one of her brown cigarettes (for some reason, no one seems to smoke on *Dallas*), or when she flings herself assertively onto an oversized white sofa and crosses her shapely legs all in one motion, we know that Alexis is out for blood or money, or probably both. When Adam (played by Gordon Thomson) pours him-self a drink and his hand shakes visibly (a "nervous disorder" that may be drug-re-lated), we know that he is a bad guy even before he embarks on one of his underhanded schemes. Watch out for wealthy drinkers and smokers.

Fashion can also tell you a lot about a rich person's character. If Alexis can be considered a role model, then vampish, scampish women wear Lilly Daché-type hats, dresses with Joan Crawford shoulder pads and slit skirts, and are willing to display more than a little bit of cleavage. Nice women, as epitomized by Krystle, wear pale, flowing hostess gowns and cover up their collar bones.

And here's another thing about rich people. They never spend any time *alone*. According to *Dallas* and *Dynasty*, the rich are no sooner seated in a well-appointed room then someone else comes barging in to confront them with some piece of news or gossip, or to propose some devilish scheme. Both shows are fraught with opening and closing doors, with confrontation scenes, with entrances and exits in high dudgeon, while in between these scenes, maids putter around the room with feather dusters. Furthermore, if a rich person *should* actually find himself alone, the phone immediately rings. That's one reason I'm glad I'm not rich. The rich have no privacy. Their friends, enemies and relatives won't give them any.

They also seem to get very little peace and quiet. Crickets seem to dwell in the walls of both the Carrington and Ewing mansions, and both families could use a good exterminator. Whenever these insects begin to buzz off-stage, it's usually a signal that something unpleasant is about to happen. Meanwhile, as in old Bette Davis and Irene Dunne movies, all the characters' emotions are heightened with offstage music—as though without it, we would not get the point. This is particu-larly heavy-handed in *Dynasty*, where solemn drum rolls portend disaster, twitter-ing birds tell us that it's the morning after a night of happy lovemaking and sobbing violins persuade us to be brave—tomorrow may be better.

These similarities between the two shows are, of course, essentially cosmetic.

Though both stories abound in rapes, blackmail, adultery and other forms of sexual hanky-panky, as well as financial skulduggery, they are essentially different. Which, then, tells the better, more convincing yarn? I guess I'd vote for *Dallas*. Somehow, the continuing saga of the Ewing clan of Southfork Ranch is the more plausible. In *Dynasty*, for example, we are asked to believe that a new bride (Jeff's) would willingly consent to live under the same roof as her new husband's ex-wife — an arrangement that, in real life, neither woman would find very appetizing. In *Dynasty*, too, there was something (an episode I happened to miss) about someone trying to poison someone else by having an entire room painted with a toxin-based paint. When they want to kill each other in *Dallas*, they go about it in a much more sensible, straightforward way.

Both stories have villainous hero/heroines — the kind of people we love to hate. In *Dallas* it is J. R. Ewing, and in *Dynasty* it is Alexis. (Blake Carrington might also be considered another villainous hero here, except, you see, he has this thing about creating a family dynasty — which is why he makes everybody live in the same house — and so he has to be partly forgiven for his heavy ways.) Though Joan Collins gives a lively, authoritative performance, her Alexis seems to me to be written as a stock Mrs. Rich Bitch out of Central Casting. *Dallas's* J. R. Ewing is a more subtly written character. Alexis is without redeeming social value. But J.R. — even when he knits his brow and squints his eyes, and we know he is plotting to place flies in the ointments of various of his friends and relatives — is a character we somehow *like*, and even at times feel sorry for.

Perhaps it is Larry Hagman's basically boyish face, and the twinkle of humor that occasionally crosses it, that makes us believe that J. R. Ewing couldn't be all *that* bad. Behind his conniving and his shady multimillion-dollar deals, there lurks a mischievous little boy who's having fun playing the game he knows the best — the double-cross. Often, too, his deals go sour. He mucks them up, and gets his comeuppance. That's satisfying, and it's also somehow endearing. Alexis in *Dynasty* gets knocked down a peg or two from time to time. But her repeated failures to break up Blake Carrington's marriage and to seduce him away from his lovely, fair-haired, hostess-gowned wife, just aren't quite the same thing. She's just a brazen hussy who doesn't seem to know that it takes more than décolletage to get a man between her sheets.

Finally, of the two shows, *Dallas* seems the more secure and self-confident. It has, after all, been around longer, and it seems more sure of what it's doing. To be sure, in the process of maturing it has picked up some mildly annoying habits. For instance, almost every dramatic scene is preceded by what is called an "establishing shot" — the exterior facade of the house or office tower in which the scene is going to take place; then the camera moves inside to the scene itself. After a while, this device, a parade of architectural set pieces, becomes a predictable as those crickets.

Dynasty, by contrast — perhaps because it's still fairly new — seems cautious and uncertain. In each new episode, much of the dialogue — almost half of it, or so it seems to me — consists of expository material, a nervous recounting and rehashing of events that have occurred in previous episodes. It's as though the show had no idea when we might have first tuned in, or how much backfill we might need, or how clear the story is making itself from what we are seeing and hearing on the screen. Real people, when they converse, don't have to keep reminding each other of what happened yesterday. This, plus the fact that all the dark-haired males on the show (not the blond, sympathetic Steven, of course) look as though they had their locks blown dry by the same hair stylist, gives *Dynasty* an air of unreality and confusion.

Of course, in time, *Dynasty* may ripen to the suave self-assurance of its dowager ancestor and prototype on the rival network. Until then, as the two shows battle it out in the popularity polls, and as we watch these rich folks tough it out among themselves, we're grateful that the rich *do* seem to be different from you and me. But there's another, even more comforting, message in both shows. These characters do not represent the *real* American rich, or even the typical American rich. The emotional litterbugs who populate both shows are the trashy rich, whose antics we enjoy reading about and hearing about because we can think: there but for the grace of God go I. And we see something confirmed that we knew all along—that all the money in the world won't buy an ounce of Class.

Questions for Study

1. Birmingham's thesis appears in the first paragraph: "Rich folks, if these two shows are to be believed, get themselves in such godawful messes, and the message of both shows is clear: all the oil in Texas and Colorado will not sweeten their little lives." Make a list of the details he used to support this thesis.
2. In a paragraph, sum up the major differences that Birmingham found between the two shows.
3. List the basis for comparison that Birmingham set for the two shows.
4. Birmingham has decided that "Dallas" is a better show than "Dynasty"; on the basis of the evidence he presented (rather than on your own feelings if you're a fan of either show—or both shows), do you agree? Answer in a paragraph of about a hundred words.

ALTERNATE ASSIGNMENT N

In the entertainment industry, the best new show or movie seems to be an imitation of another successful production. In the world of television, this tendency often results in shows with similar plot lines; "Dallas" and "Dynasty" are good examples, as are "Falcon Crest" and "Knots Landing." For one season police shows will be popular; the next season it will be medical shows or situation comedies—all clear cousins to each other. In the movies, the follow-up to a successful movie is often a sequel ("Jaws" and "Rocky" are examples of this trend, as are the various "Star Wars" movies) or an imitation ("Raiders of the Lost Ark" is a good example of a movie that inspired a number of other adventure movies). For this assignment, take two movies or two television shows like the ones mentioned here and compare or contrast them.

Chapter 13

CAUSE AND EFFECT

INTRODUCTION

If you open a newspaper in a major city on many days, you're likely to see a news story like this:

> Shortly after 6:30 last evening on Interstate 159, seven cars were involved in a chain-reaction accident that apparently occurred when poor visibility due to heavy fog caused the first driver to hit a soft shoulder and overturn. According to police reports, the other six drivers blamed the fog for their inability to see the other operators in time to stop their own cars and avert a crash. Ten people, all residents of Stasion, were taken to Parkside Hospital for treatment. Traffic had to be rerouted for more than an hour as ambulances transported the injured and tow trucks from two cities cleared the wreckage.

This lead paragraph contains both causes and effects. The **causes** of the accident—why the accident happened—are identified as a heavy fog and a soft shoulder; the **effects**—what happened as a result of the accident—are identified as one overturned car, six other cars involved in a chain-reaction crash, ten people injured and taken to the hospital, traffic rerouted for over an hour and so on.

Cause and effect will appear often in your writing because this technique helps you explain why things happen and what occurs when they do. Because effects always have causes and causes always lead to effects, the two appear together, although as this paragraph shows, they don't appear in perfect balance; usually the emphasis is on one or the other. In this lead paragraph, for instance, the emphasis is on effects—several are listed—rather than on causes.

But these next two paragraphs from the same news item show how this balance shifts from paragraph to paragraph—sometimes even from sentence to sentence:

> Mr. Alvin Trales, the driver of the first car, a 1986 Mercury Sable, reported that he had just reduced his speed

to 35 mph on 159, where the posted speed is 50, when he hit a
particularly dense spot of fog. ''Next thing I know, my
front tires hit this mud or something on the side of the
road. I started to spin, so I hit the brakes hard. Then it
was bottoms up—I'm stuck upside down in the middle of the
road. I unhooked my seat belt and got the hell out of that car
fast.''

According to the 46-year-old Trales, as soon as he
reached the side of the highway, the second car, a 1983
Datsun Sentra driven by Ms. Margery Townsend, hit the
overturned car broadside. As Trales helped her from her
vehicle, the third vehicle, a late-model Dodge van, hit the
rear of the Datsun, knocking Trales and Townsend to the
ground.

The second paragraph of the story focuses on the causes, explaining what
initiated the accident, at least according to the first driver. The third paragraph
of the story, however, focuses on additional results: one car after another
plowing into the overturned car, the initial driver and the first victim knocked
to the ground by the third car, and so on.

Cause-and-effect writing deals with why things happen and what results
when they do. Mastering cause and effect as a writing technique is important,
then, because it will enable you to explain more of your subject: what caused
the subject to happen or what resulted from it—or both.

THE MAKEUP OF A CAUSE-AND-EFFECT PAPER

You will often use cause and effect as support in your writing, as they were
used in that news item about the chain-reaction crash. Sometimes, however,
your topic will call for a more detailed application of this technique, and in
these cases, chances are that you will write a paper that focuses either more on
cause or more on effect.

Consider, for instance, a paper about your worst term in high school. You
failed two subjects and dropped from a C average to D in three others. That's
the effect, but what caused it?

For one thing, you missed the first two weeks of that term when you came
down with the chicken pox. In addition, you put in five extra hours a week at
work during the remainder of that ten-week period. Also, it was springtime, a
period when students seem to suffer from "spring fever" and generally perform poorly. One of your friends was going through a difficult time because of
her parent's divorce, and you were giving her a shoulder to cry on. Finally, you
simply became lazy; you figured all along that your teachers would never
actually fail you.

The effect—failing for the term—was caused by a case of chicken pox,
extra hours at work, a dose of spring fever, the needs of a friend, and your own
laziness. The paper that results is a cause paper. Of course, the effect appears as
well. Don't forget that causes and effects are always related.

Now, if you were writing about the recent increase in the number of adults seeking orthodontic treatment (braces), you might begin with the reason for the increase. Maybe it's because dentists are now more aware of the relationship between proper occlusion (bite) and stomach and intestinal problems; or maybe it's because orthodontists are making different, long-term payment plans available for their services.

No matter what the reason, the results — the effects — of adults having their teeth straightened are numerous. For instance, improved self-confidence develops when people perceive that they look better. Also, people pay more attention to overall better dental hygiene; when people are happy with their smiles, they'll take care of them, too. Further, these individuals enjoy overall better health, as a proper bite ultimately means better digestion. Some people even develop better dispositions; no longer self-conscious about their teeth, they are often like different people, full of smiles.

Whether the cause of this paper is a dentist's recommendation, more attractive payment programs, or increased availability of orthodontic services for adults, the paper focuses on the results — the effects — of improved orthodontic treatments for adults, from improved appearance to improved personalities.

Of course, in a cause paper, you may begin with multiple effects, if, for instance, your failure in that term in high school also meant a drop in your class rank, a loss of athletic eligibility and privileges at home, and an eventual letter of rejection from your first choice for college. Likewise, your effect paper may begin with multiple causes; the paper about adults with braces might begin with various reasons for the increase, rather than only one. The key is to spell out both the causes and the effects in detail because doing so will give your reader a more complete understanding of your subject.

USING THE TECHNIQUE

Your cause-and-effect paper will be just as effective as your planning is. Therefore, as you write, adhere to the following guidelines.

1. Don't oversimplify causes or effect.

Consider a serious problem like juvenile deliquency. What causes someone to change into a criminal? Is it a case of "Spare the rod and spoil the child"? In other words, if parents are not overly strict with their children, will the youngsters be deliquent? And if this is true, does this mean that all ill-tempered misfit adults were raised by parents who didn't discipline their children?

You don't have to be a psychologist to know that this statement is simply not absolutely true. Make a list of individuals you know who came from strict homes but who have nonetheless run into problems with authority. Then make a list of those individuals who were raised in homes where discipline was lacking but who somehow have become solid citizens.

Lack of discipline in childhood can certainly contribute to maladjustment in adulthood, but saying that one causes the other is oversimplifying. Instead, lack of discipline is one of a series of potential causes.

Likewise, maladjustment in adults is not the only potential effect of weak discipline in childhood. For instance, perhaps these individuals, having received no direction themselves concerning what guidelines children need, will be ill prepared for parenthood themselves. Furthermore, maybe these individuals will lack self-discipline, a condition that could affect their performance in school or at work. Maybe they'd be unhappy, too, because they were never taught to control themselves.

Or maybe the opposite would result. Maybe these individuals would make great parents because they learned for themselves by themselves what discipline is necessary. Maybe they will make better students and workers because their discipline has been self-learned, not imposed on them. And maybe they will be happier adults, free from the stress that a fierce concern with discipline can bring about.

The point is that you need to be realistic in dealing with either causes or effects. Life is complex. One thing rarely directly causes another. Instead, be prepared to recognize multiple causes and multiple effects.

2.   Distinguish between direct causes or effects and related causes or effects.

Think back to the last cold you had. On the day before you came down with the sniffles, coughing, sneezing, and general uncomfortable feeling, you sat in a draft, maybe walked through some puddles, or forgot to wear your hat or gloves. Did you cause your cold by doing one of these things? No, but none of them helped, either. The direct cause of the common cold is a virus that is carried in the droplets produced when someone sneezes or coughs. Of course, the virus can also be transmitted by touch, so that if people come in contact with the droplets, they can contract the virus and then pass it along.

Your overall physical state is one factor influencing whether you will contract the virus and the degree to which you will contract it. If you are tired and rundown, for instance, you are more likely to catch a cold. If walking in puddles or forgetting to wear your hat affects your overall physical condition, then doing so is a related cause. Both direct and related causes are valid, as long as you make sure that your reader can see the difference. The paragraph about the common cold, for instance, should look something like this:

> Catching a cold is really a matter of your own metabolism. Even if you are in the best of health, you can be victimized by a cold. But if your own bodily defenses are weakened, for instance, if you have recently recovered from another virus or are currently fighting one, you are highly susceptible. If, on top of this weakened condition, your body is exposed to adverse circumstances like extreme cold or dampness, you are a prime candidate. It's easy to catch the virus, too; once somebody who has the virus coughs or sneezes, the virus is lying there waiting to get you. Once you touch a surface that has been contaminated by the virus, even if you simply shake hands with a person who has a cold or who has touched a contaminated surface, the cold virus has found a new home: you.

In this paragraph, **direct** causes (weak bodily defenses and contact with a contaminated individual or surface) and **related** causes (extreme cold or dampness) appear, but both types are clearly identified. This sentence — "If, on top of this weakened condition, your body is exposed to adverse circumstances like extreme cold or dampness, you are a prime candidate" — shows the reader that cold and dampness are problems only if the conditions are right.

Remember that there are both direct and related effects, too. The direct effect of a housing development in your neighborhood may have been an increase in automobile traffic. But an automobile accident would be a related effect. The housing development may have meant more traffic, but accidents had occurred in your neighborhood before the housing development. An increase in automobile traffic, however, definitely would increase the probability of an accident, so it is valid to include this effect as long as you indicate that it is a related effect rather than a direct effect.

Of course, some causes and effects are far less related than others. For example, it's unlikely that you failed high-school calculus because you hated your second-grade math teacher. Therefore, avoid these types of remote causes and effects.

3. Don't mistake coincidence for an actual cause-and-effect relationship.

Sometimes tracing a cause and its immediate effect is easy. If you leave milk unrefrigerated for a day or so, it will turn sour. Or if you fall asleep in the noontime sun, you'll get a sunburn you won't forget for a while.

Other times, however, causes and effects aren't that clear-cut. If, for example, you eat at a restaurant and become sick within the next hour, you might have a case of food poisoning. You might also simply have a case of the flu that coincidentally hit you an hour after you had eaten. How can you tell which is which?

In this case, the proof might be somewhat difficult because both conditions have similar effects. However, if the restaurant reported other complaints about bad food and illness at the same time that you became sick, you probably are a victim of food poisoning. Otherwise, you're probably a victim of coincidence, the accidental occurrence of two or more events at the same time.

Coincidence is often confused with actual cause-and-effect relationships. The Latin term for this logical fallacy is *post hoc, ergo prompter hoc* ("after this, therefore because of this"). Imagine, for example, that you go to a job interview and find two chairs available in the waiting room. You take the one on the left and then another candidate — who eventually gets the job — takes the one on the right. If you conclude that you didn't get the job because you sat in the wrong seat before the interview, you are guilty of the *post hoc* fallacy.

Before you conclude that one thing caused another or that one thing resulted from the other, think of all the possibilities. Surely sitting in the wrong seat couldn't disqualify you for a job, unless of course you sat expressly where you were told not to. Perhaps your jittery presentation hurt your chances; or maybe there was a better candidate.

Some of the cause-and-effect relationships you present won't be absolute; in other words, maybe it was your acceptance of an offer to smoke rather than your jittery presentation that for some reason annoyed the interviewer and cost

you the job. To suggest this type of possibility, use qualifying words such as
*seems, could be, might be, appears , rarely, usually, often, sometimes, some, per-
haps, probably,* and *seldom.* There is only a one-word difference between "I
didn't get the job because I smoked during the interview," and "Maybe I didn't
get the job because I smoked during the interview," but there is a world of
difference in the meaning.

4.   Make your presentation thorough.

Multiple cause and effect is the rule rather than the exception in today's
complex world. Therefore be thorough in terms of tracing causes and effects.
For example, your paper would be limited if you completely blamed the
pollution that regularly blankets major metropolitan areas like Los Angeles or
New York City on the emissions from cars. Yes, cars are responsible for a
sizable amount of that pollution, but you must also credit various industries,
municipal incinerators, sewage treatment plants, buses, trucks, planes, and
even cigarettes—all of which send various amounts of poisons into the
atmosphere.
Besides making sure that you have presented a sufficient number of causes
and effects, you must also provide enough detail about each element that you
include. To say that excessive reading during childhood may cause a person to
become nearsighted is not sufficient; it doesn't tell the entire story. Instead, you
must provide a presentation that gives your reader plenty of specific
information:

> Some researchers have suggested that there is a definite
> connection between the excessive reading some children do
> and the myopia—nearsightedness—that these individuals
> sometimes develop. The theory essentially states that the
> stress on the developing muscles surrounding the eye due to
> great amounts of reading actually causes a permanent
> change in vision. Gradually, distance vision worsens.
> Ironically, the reading that affects vision actually keeps
> the victim from noticing the change right away. Because
> these youngsters have no trouble pursuing their hobby—
> reading—they don't notice the change until they begin
> experiencing trouble reading the blackboard or street
> signs, well after the first changes in vision have probably
> occurred.

This paragraph contains both causes (excessive stress on eye muscles, possibly
causing myopia, which is then masked by the gradual nature of the change)
and effects (worsening of distance vision and difficulty in reading street signs
and blackboards). Rather than a simple statement that one thing causes another, this paragraph gives plenty of detail to support and explain the statement. The result is a much more effective paragraph.

5. Arrange the elements effectively.

The arrangement you choose will depend in large part on the subject you are writing about. In the case of the news item at the beginning of this chapter about the chain-reaction car crash, the arrangement of the elements follows chronological order. The fog caused the first driver to lose control of his car, which overturned and blocked the road; this roadblock, in turn, caused the second car to crash into the first car, and on and on. Cause led to effect; the effect then became the cause of the next segment of the multiple accident.

Sometimes a paper begins with a result. For instance, if you were writing a paper about a professional football team that had battled its way to the Super Bowl only to fall apart in this championship game, you might begin with a thesis stating that this lopsided loss was really the result of a number of problems. Then you would support this thesis with the series of causes; an injury to a key player, a dispute concerning a racial slur allegedly made by a member of the coaching staff, unsettling rumors of the owner's dissatisfaction with the head coach, and disruptive anonymous reports that several key team members were using cocaine.

There are two principles of arrangement at work here. The overall arrangement presents the result — the team's surprising and disappointing loss in the Super Bowl — and then the body of the paper presents the various causes behind that loss. But the arrangement of the causes is least-to-most-significant: the injury to the key player was less a problem than the alleged use of illegal drugs by several team members.

Sometimes a paper begins with a problem of some kind — a cause — as a thesis and then presents various results that can actually or potentially occur. Therefore, if you were writing a paper about spiraling real-estate values, the body of your paper might present such possible results as the renovation of former broken-down buildings in urban areas, the squeeze put on those low- and middle-income families who can't muster enough of a down payment to buy their own homes but who must also face higher rents, a generally increased interest in real estate as an investment, and an improved tax base for the cities and towns enjoying the housing boom because of the increased property valuations.

In this case, the overall arrangement presents the thesis — "Increasing real-estate values can bring about some changes" — and then the body presents the various effects. But because none of these effects directly causes the other, and because they are arguably about equally important, these elements could be arranged in a variety of ways.

The arrangement of the paper can affect its impact. Therefore take some time to set up your paper so that your organization will help to communicate your ideas to your reader.

The technique of cause-and-effect writing is important to master because it will enable you to explain the full range of a subject. Remember; the more your reader understands about your subject, the more likely it is that your reader will understand what you are trying to communicate. And that's always your ultimate purpose.

ASSIGNMENT 13

Take a change or event in your own or somebody else's life, and in a 500- to 750-word essay, explain what led to that change or event.

Reason

Every life is filled with turns, twists, and backtracking, and any one of these bends in the road can occur for a number of reasons. Because everyone experiences a vast number of different turning points, a writing dealing with the cause of that event is sure to have appeal.

Certainly a crucial event such as your leaving a secure job for a far riskier one would make a fine paper. You would first begin with a thesis that tells of your decision:

> When I first told people that I was quitting my job as an administrative secretary to devote my time to selling real estate full time, people thought I was crazy, but they didn't really understand my reasons.

Then your paper would present what motivated you to make the switch — the causes: lack of challenge in your previous job, which mostly involved answering the phone and simple typing; a salary scale that didn't compensate you adequately; your natural talent in persuading people; a strong interest in the world of real estate coupled with a genuine desire to help people find homes and apartments they can afford; and your drive to become your own boss within a few years.

The thesis states that people didn't understand your reasons for the switch. The causes support this thesis because they explain your reasons, and as a result, your reader gets a full view of your motivation to leave one job and head for another.

But traumatic or crucial events aren't your only possibilities for this paper. You could, for example, tell what made you take up collecting baseball cards and comic books as a hobby; there are plenty of reasons that you might. After all, a collection of this type can provide a link to your childhood; your collection will be a legacy to hand on to your own children; and it can be a source of great personal pleasure — it is, after all, a collection of items that you had always enjoyed having, and it can be a fine investment.

Whether your subject is the serious, change-of-life type or the simpler, slight-change-in-direction-or-interest variety, it has potential. Remember; on our roads of life, we all face far more twists and turns than straight paths.

What Your Reader Needs

Your reader always needs a clear direction; you provide that with the thesis you include in your introduction. But a clear thesis is never enough by itself; in a paper concerning some event or change in your own or someone else's life, your reader needs strong support: specific, detailed explanations and illustrations.

In that paper concerning a career change, you need to spell out your reasons clearly. Remember; the thesis stated that people thought you were crazy because they didn't understand your reasons. Basically, your job is to provide a thorough explanation of your reasons for your reader.

For instance, saying that you have a natural talent for persuading people is not enough. Instead, your reader needs a more thorough explanation:

> Also, while I was working as an administrative secretary
> at the insurance company, I handled phone requests for
> information about insurance. Because I took the time to
> explain the coverage and benefits of various policies to
> people, I would regularly sell three or four policies a
> month. The people who bought the policies told me that they
> bought the policies because they could tell how much I
> cared about them. I knew I had a good personality, and I
> figured that if I could sell policies on the phone when it
> wasn't even my job, I could really be successful if I could
> devote all my attention to sales.

This paragraph gives your reader what is needed: a clear explanation of what you mean by using a natural talent and by the gamble involved in making the career change. After all, selling an insurance policy or two on the phone is one thing; making your living exclusively on the basis of sales is an entirely different matter.

Remember, too, that your introduction should probably give some indication of the result. For instance, if your job switch was a success, you might include an additional sentence like this in the introduction:

> When I first told people that I was quitting my job as an
> administrative secretary to devote my time to selling real
> estate full time, people thought I was crazy, but they
> didn't really understand my reasons. A few years later,
> however, they were able to see that my instincts were
> correct.

This sentence lets your reader know ahead of time that you gambled and won; the examples that follow will help to show that your self-confidence was well based.

And if your venture was a failure? You can let your reader know this too, in essentially the same way:

> When I first told people that I was quitting my job as an
> administrative secretary to devote my time to selling real
> estate full time, people thought I was crazy, but they
> didn't really understand my reasons. And after a few months
> of struggling and failing, I began to see that my family and

friends understood the world of real estate far better than
I did.

Your reader needs an introduction that provides a clear direction, but this
direction alone is not enough. You must also make sure to provide specific,
thorough examples to illustrate your reasons or motivations. If you restate your
thesis and these examples in a conclusion, your paper will meet the needs of
your reader.

Model

DAVID: DRUG ADDICT AT EIGHTEEN

Two months ago, a young man named David began serving a
three-year jail sentence in the House of Correction for
selling heroin. This conviction was only the last in a
series of arrests, suspended sentences, probation, and
trips to halfway houses that began more than ten years ago
when he was a high-school junior. By the time he was
eighteen, he was an addict, financing his habit by pushing
the drug. Before he began fooling around with drugs, David
had been a bright student and a decent athlete. When he
walked into the House of Correction two months ago, his
gaze was empty and his body was wasted. The questions that
remain concern how all this happened. Although there are
no clear answers, there are a number of possible reasons
that a pretty decent kid will become the type of figure who
deserves to spend three years of his life in prison.

David's family background certainly has something to do
with his problems. His father was a merchant seaman, and
although his family was not broken in the traditional
sense by divorce, his father was away from home for up to
six months at a time. As a result, David's mother was forced
to be both mother and father to David and his three older
sisters. For David, this was particularly hard. He used to
tell me in study hall how close he and his father were and
how much he missed his father. In fact, David first got
involved with drugs—pot—during one of his father's longer
trips. By the time his father came back, David had already
experimented with many drugs, including LSD and heroin,
and he liked the sensations and the peer admiration too
much to stop.

Another problem for David was money: he had too much for
his own good. His father's job paid well, so David had no
needs. His parents, particularly his father, tried to make
up for what David lacked in attention by giving him plenty
of money. As a result, it was easier for David to get
involved with drugs because he had plenty of money to buy
them.

Besides money, David's own personality enabled him to
get deeply involved very quickly without anyone's paying

much attention. He was intelligent, good-looking, almost charismatic. The knowledge of his drug use was not widespread, but he made it clear to everyone who did know that he could handle it. People knew he was a wise-guy. For example, he used to break into cars and hot-wire them and then drive all over the city just for fun, but he never got caught. He seemed too smart to get tripped up.

Maybe the permissiveness of the time was the biggest contributing factor. We were in high school in the early 1970s when all the standards governing young people came under attack. David organized one of the first student walkouts, this one over the student dress code. As was typical of David, he managed to con his way out of a suspension afterward. During the walkout, however, he met a number of older activists, many of them drug users, and they provided him with drugs to use and sell. Five years before this, David probably never would have been able to lead a walkout; neither would he have met those figures who first interested him in drugs.

David is on methadone now, for the third time. This time, however, he receives his little pill in prison under the supervision of a prison doctor. It's a sad ending for David, but one that he has earned. Although some blame can be assigned to his parents, his friends, and the period of time itself, the fact remains that David did what he did by choice, and at least for the next three years, he has that to think about.

Follow-through

A paper that explains how you or somebody else reached some level or decision in life has appeal because people are generally interested in the "behind-the-scenes" information—not just the event or decision itself, but what brought you to that point, expressed in clear and complete detail.

The preliminary work for a paper such as this is vital. You need first to establish what subject you wish to explain. Once you've come up with the general decision, event, or incident in your own or someone else's life, you must turn back the pages of your memory and rediscover why you or someone else arrived at that particular point.

In this paper, for example, the subject is a friend who has lost years of his life because of drugs. By why did this happen? Why did someone who apparently had so much going for him throw all of it away and turn to drugs? The prewriting for this paper provides a number of answers:

David was always such a wise-guy—he and Linda used to get drunk, break into cars, hot-wire them, drive them all over the city—he said he did it 20 or 30 times, never got caught—his old man gave him plenty of money, too-always the guy who had bucks to buy things—records, tapes, clothes, leather coats—he said he hated living with all girls—three sisters and mother—because his father was away a lot—a merchant marine—but he did all right—they all spoiled him, and the sisters always covered up for him when he came home wrecked—he said the first few times he got high he wasn't worried about getting caught because his old man was away and he could con the rest of them anyway—I think he was the first kid in school to bring pot he got from older guys in the neighborhood in with him and sell it—I remember the day— smiling, he pulled out a plastic baggie full of pot—he used to say he hated it because his father was never around, but it didn't stop him from breaking into his own father's house to steal family stuff to sell for drugs two years ago— maybe he just wanted some more attention from his father, trying to keep him at home instead of out to sea all the time—what a waste—he used to be so smart, was a pretty good basketball player, too—he always had to have all the attention—mostly everybody that knew him liked him—he was so funny—he liked hanging around with those older guys he met during the walkouts—he knew the other kids thought he was a big shot when he used to brag about all the drugs he was doing with the older guys—everybody thought he was cool and never got hung up on the stuff—always had plenty of money to pay for drugs— what a mess he was the last time I saw him—just dirty and his eyes were funny-looking—really sad—everybody knows he's an addict—the judge that finally sent him up gave him all kinds of chances—he'd go for methadone and then shoot up on top of it—they gave him three years straight—he probably deserves it for being so stupid.

This preliminary list provides plenty of details about David. In particular, it provides many possible reasons for David's turn to drugs. With a little re-arranging, these general details can be grouped into categories:

- 1. *David was always such a wise-guy—he and Linda used to get drunk, break into cars, hot-wire them, drive them all over the city—he said he did it 20 or 30 times, never got caught—he always had to have all the attention—mostly everybody that knew him liked him—he was so funny—everybody thought he was cool and never got hung up on the stuff.*
- 2. *His old man gave him plenty of money, too—always the guy who had bucks to buy things—records, tapes, clothes, leather coats—always had plenty of money to pay for drugs, too.*
- 3. *He said he hated living with all girls—three sisters and mother—because his father was away a lot—a merchant marine—but he did all right—they all spoiled him, and the sisters always covered up for him when he came home wrecked—he said the first few times he got high he wasn't worried about getting caught because his old man was away and he could con the rest of them anyway—maybe he just wanted some more attention from his father, trying to keep him at home instead of out to sea all the time.*
- 4. *I think he was the first kid in school to bring pot he got from older guys in the neighborhood in with him and sell it—he liked hanging around with those older guys he met during the walkouts—he knew the other kids thought he was a big shot when he used to brag about all the drugs he was doing with the older guys.*

These groups of information basically make up four general reasons: (1) David's own personality; (2) David's access to plenty of money; (3) David's family situation — an "absentee" father and doting sisters and mother; and (4) circumstances allowing David to become involved with older drug users.

Rearranged a bit — 3,2,1,4 — these reasons become the supporting examples in the paper. The arrangement in the final draft is effective; three of the supporting causes are about equal in importance, and the fourth — identified as "the biggest contributing factor" in the final draft — anchors the presentation.

In a cause-and-effect paper, it is important not to oversimply. Having plenty of money available does not mean that a young person will automatically turn to drugs. Under certain circumstances, however, it can be a contributing factor, an indirect cause as opposed to a direct cause. Probably no single reason actually caused David to become involved with drugs. It was all the factors in combination.

In the second paragraph, for instance, the point about David's family as a factor is presented: "David's family background *certainly has something to do with* his problems." As the italicized words show, his family situation was undeniably part of his problem, but it was clearly not the only part. Each supporting cause is presented as part of the problem, without any effort to oversimplify or draw unfair cause-and-effect relationships.

Attention is also given to the potential for confusing coincidence with actual cause and effect. Did the period of time actually contribute to David's problem? The evidence given in the paragraph — the connection between the student unrest and outside activists with access to drugs — is at least reasonable.

Besides presenting causes, you must also give plenty of specific detail to illustrate each cause. You do this by amplifying the initial information you've generated. Look, for instance, at the group of ideas that was eventually turned into the fourth paragraph of the final draft:

> 1. *David was always such a wise-guy — he and Linda used to get drunk, break into cars, hot-wire them, drive them all over the city — he said he did it 20 or 30 times, never got caught — he always had to have all the attention mostly everybody that knew him liked him — he was so funny — everybody thought he was cool and never got hung up on the stuff.*

Now look at this same information amplified and made more specific in the final draft:

```
    Besides money, David's own personality enabled him to
get deeply involved very quickly without anyone's paying
much attention. He was intelligent, good-looking, almost
charismatic. The knowledge of his drug use was not
widespread, but he made it clear to everyone who did know
that he could handle it. People knew he was a wise-guy. For
example, he used to break into cars and hot-wire them and
```

```
then drive all over the city just for fun, but he never got
caught. He seemed too smart to get tripped up.
```

The final version doesn't settle for telling that everyone liked David; it shows his attractive qualities; intelligence, good looks, and charisma. It doesn't settle for simply telling that David was a wise-guy who would steal cars and take them for joy rides: it shows how he managed to hide the fact that he was out of control. He was, after all, a wise-guy—but a wise-guy who had never really been caught.

The concluding paragraph restates the significance of the paper; in particular, it points out that whatever blame can be placed on the reasons presented, further blame must be placed on David's own shoulders. In essence, the conclusion states that David was not an innocent victim. It reminds the reader once more what the point of the essay is, and as a result, the conclusion truly completes the paper.

Checklist

Use the answers to the following questions to help you revise your first draft:

1. Does your paper have a thesis? Write it down.
2. Have you developed a sufficient number of causes? List them.
3. Have you distinguished between direct and indirect causes?
4. Have you made sure that you have expressed causes rather than coincidence?
5. Have you amplified each cause?
6. Is the arrangement of your causes effective?
7. Does your introduction provide a clear direction for your reader?
8. Does your conclusion restate the significance of your paper?

ASSIGNMENT 14

Take an issue, an experience, or a situation, and in a 500- to 750-word essay, talk about some of the effects it has had (or might have).

Reason

Imagine for a moment what would happen if you were able to change one small part of life. Then think for a minute: What would result from even a slight change? If you did eliminate a disease, for example, what would happen to the thousands and thousands who used to die from that disease? Would something more horrible develop to take its place? Would the increased population deplete world resources? Would life be better—or worse? One situation brings with it multiple probable and possible effects. That's why a writing on this subject has appeal.

Imagine, for instance, that you choose to write about the increasing number of tanning salons in the United States. Your thesis would indicate their popularity and suggest what could happen as a result:

> But this growing wave of tanning salons brings with it a
> number of potential problems for the future that most users
> don't pay much attention to.

The paragraphs of the body of this paper would present the various potential dangers to the skin from excessive exposure to ultraviolet rays: increased wrinkling, a leathery appearance; premature aging and spotting; and a greatly increased risk of developing skin cancer.

Now, even though these effects are speculations (although many dermatologists claim that these effects are nearly guaranteed for the serious sun worshiper, the tanning-salon industry claims that their systems filter out the dangerous effects), they are still suitable examples. After all, the thesis indicates that these are *potential* problems.

In a paper dealing with the effects of some experience, situation, or issue, the idea is to give your subject in the thesis and then indicate the actual or potential effects of it. Remember; even slightly touching one domino in a series can have dramatic effects on the rest. It's those effects that pique our interest.

What Your Reader Needs

In a paper about the various effects resulting from some experience or situation, you need to provide a clear direction and specific examples. Without these two main components, your paper won't communicate your ideas to your reader.

The clear direction is presented in your introduction through your thesis. Take, for instance, the recent trend in our country of two parents going out to work each day. If your reader is going to understand your point, you must set that direction in the introduction:

> Today, maintaining a decent standard of living often means
> that both husband and wife must go off to work each day. The
> situation is difficult enough for childless couples. They
> must try to coordinate working hours, household duties,
> and vacation schedules. But for couples with children, the
> problems brought about when both partners work are even
> more complicated and stressful.

An introduction such as this helps your reader because it leaves no question about what is to follow; the thesis — underlined here — makes it completely evident.

Of course, this introduction is just the beginning of a successful paper. Your introduction promises "complicated" and "stressful" effects; that's what you must deliver. For example, because the number of parents working has increased, one effect is a shortage of qualified day-care centers. Another effect is the increased flexibility in working hours sometimes provided for working parents. Another effect is more independent children or children who learn to become dependent on someone other than Mom and Dad. Yet another effect is the chaos occurring at the end of a working day when parents and children all return home together, each individual scrambling to get a little bit of time with the others.

Each of these effects is indeed stressful or complicated—or both. What your reader needs, however, is a fleshed-out version of each effect, one that is detailed enough to support the thesis. Saying that children learn to become less dependent on their parents is not enough for your reader. Instead, you must provide details like this:

> But it isn't only the working parents who must make some adjustments; their children face some major changes as well. Instead of playing leisurely around their own living rooms with their own toys, they spend their days sharing toys that belong to no one in particular as they play in the large playrooms of day-care centers or in the home of paid sitters. They must learn to get along with other toddlers, and they must learn to take their disputes not to Mom or Dad but to a certified day-care specialist. Instead of spending time with a parent and following a schedule comfortable for both parent and child, these day-care children follow a rigorous community schedule: breakfast at 8:30, snack at 10, lunch at noon, nap at 1, snack at 2:30, and so on. They must learn independence to survive.

This paragraph takes the idea that day-care children learn to be less dependent on their parents and illustrates it with plenty of specific detail to paint a clear picture of the magnitude of change required of preschoolers when their parents go off to work. And it's precisely this kind of detail that your reader needs if you are to follow through on the promise you present in the introduction.

Model

THE EFFECTS OF TELEVISION VIOLENCE ON CHILDREN

With all the dangers to shield children from, too many parents ignore one threat that is right in their own living rooms: the television. Through this medium, the world can almost come alive for the viewers. Unfortunately anyone who watches even a moderate amount of television is exposed to many graphically rendered acts of violence. Children, particularly elementary-school-age kids, are susceptible to the effects of television because many of them have not yet developed the ability to distinguish television's fiction from reality.

Except for the news, most of the violence that appears on television is fictional. For instance, most adults are easily able to understand that the punch thrown by one of the officers or villains on a police or detective show is staged, but children have no way of knowing that the two stunt men who actually performed that scene worked carefully so that no one was hit or hurt. For many children, the scene is real, part of the world created by television for them. This is another instance of the distorted view of life that television promotes; on TV, monumental problems are solved, bad guys are captured, and misguided individuals are helped to see the wrong direction of their lives, all within twenty-five minutes or so. Thanks to television, many children expect instant solutions, which can make the harshness of the real world more difficult to handle. These youngsters, like their television heroes, may try to use violence to eliminate their frustrations.

Excessive television violence can have other effects as well. For instance, watching television is a passive experience, but the material watched is anything but passive. When children watch the members of the ''A-Team'' dangling from a helicopter or tackling and beating up some bad guy, they can be overwhelmed by the excitement. As week after week, Mr. T and the rest of the heroes on different shows walk away from these confrontations with only a few scratches, they may inadvertently encourage kids to imitate them. The result can be more aggressive behavior.

Perhaps the worst danger of excessive violence on television is that its presence may help to create a tolerance for violence. After a while, some children don't even notice it. What happens each week on shows like ''Knight Rider'' or ''Hardcastle and McCormick'' is a good example. On every show, the stars squeal tires, smash cars, and do whatever they have to do, including fighting, in order to solve the crimes and get the bad guys. Instead of being noticed, the violence often just blends in. The real danger here is that children may accept this attitude and apply it to the real world. Then, like their heroes, they may take this vigilante attitude seriously and try to solve their own problems through violence.

Several years ago, the networks heeded the public's request and began to make their shows less violent. But even though the instances of physical violence per show have dropped, the reruns of the more violent shows are still on the air in many places. Cable television and other innovations have complicated the problem further, as they enable children to view more types of television programming, some of which contains violence.

To help their children handle television violence, parents should supervise more closely the shows their children watch. If a program is too violent, perhaps the simplest solution is not to let them watch it. Parents should also take the time to explain that the action on most shows is make-believe; this could be especially helpful for younger children. Finally, parents should stress that violence seldom solves any problem, regardless of what television heroes do or say.

Follow-through

A paper that presents the effects of some incident or situation, like all good writing, requires planning. The key is to use that initial planning to focus more

directly on your subject—to develop your thesis—and then to provide supporting paragraphs illustrating specific effects.

In the case of this paper, the general subject—what television violence
does to children—is the starting point. The prewriting for this subject produced the following information:

- *Kids watch the "A-Team" or "Dukes of Hazzard" and think all the stunts are
  real and you can't get hurt if you do it—how about that story of the kid who
  jumped off his garage like the "Greatest American Hero"?—they seem to get
  all wired up when they sit around watching this stuff.*
- *Whenever stars get cut up or beat up they recover overnight.*
- *Kids watch people take the law into their own hands—like Rambo—and
  think they can, too—vigilantes, like that Goetz guy in New York who shot the
  kids on the subway.*
- *Reruns are the worst—kids can watch "Hawaii Five-O" every afternoon and
  see any kind of violence you want—the "Fall Guy," too, and "CHIPS."*
- *Little kids like in elementary school don't really know the difference—adults
  know it's all pretend on TV, but little kids can't tell so how will they know how
  much they can hurt somebody?*
- *All these television heroes solve their problems as much by fighting as they do
  by talking—that's a great example.*
- *How about the way kids imitate? If the guys on "Hardcastle and McCormick"
  —and one of those guys is an ex-judge, another great example—can belt
  people around and get away with it and get praise, why shouldn't kids do the
  same?*
- *The shows are supposed to be less violent now, but look at the "A-Team" or
  "Knight Rider"—those people are always fighting—after a while the kids
  don't even notice it—they probably just figure that's the way it's supposed to
  be.*
- *"Miami Vice" and "Hill Street Blues" are really violent, but kids shouldn't be
  up that late—what happens when they go into reruns during the day?*
- *Even when somebody dies after being blown up or shot, it doesn't seem
  real—if it happened in real life it would be horrible agony but on TV it's as if
  you're detached—kids learn to ignore it.*

As you can see, not all the information here was used in the final draft, but this
prewriting provides a good deal of the material appearing in the final draft. In
the final draft, three main effects are presented: (1) because of their inability to
understand that television violence is contrived, children get the incorrect idea
that violence solves problems; (2) the violence on television can so excite
children that they imitate it; and (3) the more violence children see, the more
they learn to accept it as an ordinary part of life.

Take a look at the initial prewriting, this time with numbers referring to
these three categories in front of the appropriate pieces of information used in
the essay:

- *1. Kids watch the "A-Team" or "Dukes of Hazzard" and think all the stunts*

are real and you can't get hurt if you do it. 2. They seem to get all wired up when they sit around watching this stuff.
- 2. Whenever stars get cut up or beat up they recover overnight.
- 3. Kids watch people take the law into their own hands — like Rambo — and think they can, too — vigilantes, like that Goetz guy in New York who shot the kids on the subway.
- 1. Little kids like in elementary school don't really know the difference — adults know it's all pretend on TV, but little kids can't tell. 2. So how will they know how much they can hurt somebody.
- 1. All these television heroes solve their problems as much by fighting as they do by talking — that's a great example.
- 3. How about the way kids imitate? If the guys on "Hardcastle and McCormick" — and one of those guys is an ex-judge, another great example — can belt people around and get away with it and get praise, why shouldn't kids do the same?
- 3. The shows are supposed to be less violent now, but look at the "A-Team" or "Knight Rider" — those people are always fighting — after a while the kids don't even notice it — they probably just figure that's the way it's supposed to be.
- 3. Even when somebody dies after being blown up or shot, it doesn't seem real — if it happened in real life if would be horrible agony but on TV it's as if you're detached — kids learn to ignore it.

Of course, as the final draft shows, these groups of ideas were filtered, amplified, and made more specific during the composing and revising stages.

Thorough development is also crucial to the success of your paper. Remember, your reader depends on the specific information you provide in order to understand your point. The prewriting for this paper produces three solid results of television violence, and it also produces enough specific detail to support these results.

In addition, however, a fourth paragraph in the body deals more with a cause: the fact that reruns and cable television are among the reasons that so much television violence is available for children. The prewriting provides information about this factor, too:

> Reruns are the worst — kids can watch "Hawaii Five-O" every afternoon and see any kind of violence you want — the "Fall Guy" too, and "CHIPS" . . . "Miami Vice" and "Hill Street Blues" are really violent, but kids shouldn't be up that late — what happens when they go into reruns during the day?

Of course, the fifth paragraph of the final version presents the information differently, but the idea is still the same — that some of the most violent television programs are still available to impressionable children.

The overall arrangement of elements of the paper helps to make it effective. Following the introduction, the three main effects are presented to bolster the case that violence on television can indeed affect children. The placement of the paragraph on reruns and cable television — basically a cause paragraph — after the three effect paragraphs is particularly effective because it helps to underscore the magnitude of the problem: even if we work to stop television violence on newer shows, we still face the problem of the rebroadcast of the earlier objectionable shows. Cause and effect are constant companions, so using them together is a perfectly natural step.

This paper is effective because all the necessary elements for success are present. It has an introduction that presents a thesis; it has a body featuring examples of results spelled out in specific detail; and it has a conclusion that restates the significance expressed in the paper. Together, these elements communicate your ideas to your reader — and that's exactly what a successful paper must do.

Checklist

Use the answers to the following questions to help you revise your first draft:

1. Does your paper have a thesis? Write it down.
2. Have you developed a sufficient number of effects? List them.
3. Have you clearly expressed the connection between the effects and your subject?
4. Are the effects explained in specific detail?
5. Is the arrangement of your effects effective?
6. Does your introduction provide a clear direction for your reader?
7. Does your conclusion restate the significance of your paper?

FOR FURTHER STUDY

What does the future hold for humankind? If we consider the seemingly daily advances in technology that help to prolong our lives and improve their quality, most of us would assume that the world of tomorrow will be a paradise, a place of more comfort and less pain. In this paper, Isaac Asimov, noted science-fiction writer and essayist, has presented a vastly different future world, one that we may well create for our descendants through our own ignorance and apathy.

The Nightmare of Life Without Fuel

ISAAC ASIMOV

So it's 1997, and it's raining, and you'll have to walk to work again. The subways are crowded, and any given train breaks down one morning out of five. The buses are gone, and on a day like today the bicycles slosh and slide. Besides, you have only a mile and a half to go, and you have boots, raincoat and rain hat. And it's not a very cold rain, so why not?

Lucky you have a job in demolition too. It's steady work. Slow and dirty, but steady. The fading structures of a decaying city are the great mineral mines and hardware shops of the nation. Break them down and re-use the parts. Coal is too difficult to dig up and transport to give us energy in the amounts we need, nuclear fission is judged to be too dangerous, the technical breakthrough toward nuclear fusion that we hoped for never took place, and solar batteries are too expensive to maintain on the earth's surface in sufficient quantity.

Anyone older than ten can remember automobiles. They dwindled. At first the price of gasoline climbed — way up. Finally only the well-to-do drove, and that was too clear an indication that they were filthy rich, so any automobile that dared show itself on a city street was overturned and burned. Rationing was introduced to "equalize sacrifice," but every three months the ration was reduced. The cars just vanished and became part of the metal resource.

There are many advantages, if you want to look for them. Our 1997 newspapers continually point them out. The air is cleaner and there seem to be fewer colds. Against most predictions, the crime rate has dropped. With the police car too expensive (and too easy a target), policemen are back on their beats. More important, the streets are full. Legs are king in the cities of 1997, and people walk everywhere far into the night. Even the parks are full, and there is mutual protection in crowds.

If the weather isn't too cold, people sit out front. If it is hot, the open air is the only air conditioning they get. And at least the street lights still burn. Indoors, electricity is scarce, and few people can afford to keep lights burning after supper.

As for the winter — well, it is inconvenient to be cold, with most of what furnace fuel is allowed hoarded for the dawn; but sweaters are popular indoor wear and showers are not an everyday luxury. Lukewarm sponge baths will do, and if the air is not always very fragrant in the human vicinity, the automobile fumes are gone.

There is some consolation in the city that it is worse in the suburbs. The suburbs were born with the auto, lived with the auto, and are dying with the auto. One way out for the suburbanites is to form associations that assign turns to the procurement and distribution of food. Pushcarts creak from house to house along the posh suburban roads, and every bad snowstorm is a disaster. It isn't easy to hoard enough food to last till the roads are open. There is not much in the way of refrigeration except for the snowbanks, and then the dogs must be fought off.

What energy is left cannot be directed into personal comfort. The nation must survive until new energy sources are found, so it is the railroads and subways that are receiving major attention. The railroads must move the coal that is the immediate hope, and the subways can best move the people.

And then, of course, energy must be conserved for agriculture. The great car factories make trucks and farm machinery almost exclusively. We can huddle together when there is a lack of warmth, fan ourselves should there be no cooling breezes, sleep or make love at such times as there is a lack of light — but nothing will for long ameliorate a lack of food. The American population isn't going up much any more, but the food supply must be kept high even though the prices and difficulty of distribution force each American to eat less. Food is needed for export so that we can pay for some trickle of oil and for other resources.

The rest of the world, of course, is not as lucky as we are. Some cynics say that it is the knowledge of this that helps keep America from despair. They're starving out there, because earth's population has continued to go up. The population on earth is 5.5 billion, and outside the United States and Europe, not more than one in five has enough to eat at any given time.

All the statistics point to a rapidly declining rate of population increase, but that is coming about chiefly through a high infant mortality; the first and most helpless victims of starvation are babies, after their mothers have gone dry. A strong current of American opinion, as reflected in the newspapers (some of which still produce their daily eight pages of bad news), holds that it is just as well. It serves to reduce the population, doesn't it?

Others point out that it's more than just starvation. There are those who manage to survive on barely enough to keep the body working, and that proves to be not enough for the brain. It is estimated that there are now nearly 2 billion people in the world who are alive but who are premanently brain-damaged by undernutrition, and the number is growing year by year. It has already occurred to some that it would be "realistic" to wipe them out quietly and rid the earth of an encumbering menace. The American newspapers of 1997 do not report that this is actually being done anywhere, but some travelers bring back horror tales.

At least the armies are gone—no one can afford to keep those expensive, energy-gobbling monstrosities. Some soldiers in uniform and with rifles are present in almost every still functioning nation, but only the United States and the Soviet Union can maintain a few tanks, planes and ships—which they dare not move for fear of biting into limited fuel reserves.

Energy continues to decline, and machines must be replaced by human muscle and beasts of burden. People are working longer hours and there is less leisure; but then, with electric lighting restricted, television for only three hours a night, movies three evenings a week, new books few and printed in small editions, what is there to do with leisure? Work, sleep and eating are the great trinity of 1997, and only the first two are guaranteed.

Where will it end? It must end in a return to the days before 1800, to the days before the fossil fuels powered a vast machine industry and technology. It must end in subsistence farming and in a world population reduced by starvation, disease and violence to less than a billion.

And what can we do to prevent all this now?

Now? Almost nothing.

If we had started twenty years ago, that might have been another matter. If we had only started fifty years ago, it would have been easy.

Questions for Study

1. This essay doesn't begin with a formal introduction, nor does it have an explicit thesis. Yet there are a number of hints in the opening paragraph that indicate what the essay deals with. Make a list of the details that help set up the story.

2. Although the introduction doesn't specifically provide direction, the conclusion definitely states that thesis: "If we had started twenty years ago, that might have been another matter. If we had only started fifty years ago, it would have been easy." In a few sentences, paraphrase what Asimov is telling his readers in this concluding paragraph.

3. Make a list of the various effects that Asimov has used to illustrate his vision of the future.

4. Are there any good points in the future world Asimov has presented? Explain your answer in a brief paragraph.

5. In a paragraph, explain the lesson Asimov was trying to teach.

ALTERNATE ASSIGNMENT O

As frightening as Isaac Asimov's vision is, his paper is speculation, an essay about what *could* happen. For this assignment, speculate about what could happen based on something that doesn't yet exist. What if we could use genetic engineering to "build" perfect children or at least to "build in" special talents or qualities? Or what if guilt could somehow be eliminated from our thinking processes? Whatever subject you choose, plot all the possibilities — the effects — that could result.

"Why?" It's a question that can have some disturbing and frustrating answers. Sometimes, however, there don't seem to be any answers, at least any answers that make sense. That's pretty much the point in this writing by Rabbi Harold S. Kushner, a *Reader's Digest* condensation of a section of his book, *When Bad Things Happen to Good People*. In this excerpt, Kushner has presented both cause and effect as in dealing with the age-old concept that terrible personal tragedies are somehow forms of punishment sent by a Supreme Being.

Why Do Bad Things Happen to Good People?

HAROLD S. KUSHNER

Our son, Aaron, a bright and happy child who could identify a dozen varieties of dinosaur, had just passed his third birthday. My wife and I had been concerned about his health because he stopped gaining weight at the age of eight months, and a few months later his hair started falling out. Yet prominent doctors had told us that while Aaron would be very short as an adult, he would be normal in all other ways.

When we moved from New York to a Boston suburb, we discovered a pediatrician who was doing research in problems of children's growth. We introduced him to Aaron. Two months later he told us that our son's condition was called progeria, rapid aging. He said that Aaron would never grow much beyond three feet in height, would have no hair on his head or body, would look like a little old man while he was still a child, and would die in this early teens.

How does one handle such news? What I felt was a deep, aching sense of unfairness. I had been a good person. I had tried to do what was right. I was living a more religiously committed life than most people I knew. How could this happen to me?

Even if I deserved the punishment, on what grounds did an innocent child have to suffer? Why should he have to endure physical and psychological pain every day of this life? Why should he be condemned to grow into adolescence, see other boys and girls dating, and realize that he would never know marriage or fatherhood? It simply didn't make sense.

Why do bad things happen to good people? Virtually every conversation I have had on the subject of God and religion has gotten around to this question. The misfortunes of good people are a problem to everyone who wants to believe in a just and fair world.

I try to help my congregation of 2,500 through the wrenching pain of their divorces, their business failures, their unhappiness with their children. But time and again, I have seen the wrong people get sick, the wrong people be hurt, the wrong people die young.

I was once called on to help a family through an almost unbearable tragedy. This middle-aged couple had one daughter, a bright nineteen-year-old college freshman. One morning they received a phone call from the university infirmary: "We have bad news. Your daughter collapsed while walking to class. A blood vessel burst in her brain, and she died before we could do anything. We're terribly sorry. . . ."

I went over to see them that same day. I expected anger, shock, grief, but I didn't anticipate their first words: "You know, Rabbi, we didn't fast last Yom Kippur."

Why did they think that they were somehow responsible for this tragedy? Who taught them to believe in a God who would strike down a gifted young woman as punishment for someone else's ritual infraction?

Assuming that somehow our misfortunes come as punishment for our misdeeds is one way to make sense of the world's suffering. But such an answer has serious limitations. It creates guilt where there is no basis for guilt.

Often, victims of misfortune try to console themselves with the idea that God has reasons that they are in no position to judge. I think of a woman I know named Helen.

She noticed herself getting tired easily. She chalked it up to getting older. Then one night, she stumbled over the threshold of her front door. The following morning Helen made an appointment to see a doctor.

The diagnosis was multiple sclerosis, a degenerative nerve disease. The doctor explained that Helen might find it progressively harder to walk without support. Eventually, she might be confined to a wheelchair, and become more and more of an invalid until she died.

Upon hearing the news, Helen broke down and cried: "I have a husband and young children who need me. I have tried to be a good person. I don't deserve this."

Her husband attempted to console her: "God must have his reasons for doing this, and it's not for us to question him. You have to believe that if he wants you to get better, you will, and if he doesn't, there has to be some purpose to it."

Helen wanted to be comforted by the knowledge that there was some purpose to her suffering, but her husband's words only made her feel more abandoned and more bewildered. What kind of higher purpose could possibly justify what she would have to face?

We have all read stories of little children who were left unwatched for just a moment and fell from a window or into a swimming pool and died. Why does God permit such things to happen? Is it to teach parents to be more careful? That is too trivial a lesson to be purchased at the price of a child's life. Is it to make the parents more sensitive, more compassionate people? The price is still too high.

Well, then, is tragedy a test? I was the parent of a handicapped child for fourteen years, until his death. I was not comforted by the notion that God had singled me out because he recognized some special spiritual strength within me. I may be a more effective pastor, a more sympathetic counselor than I would ever have been without Aaron's death, but I would give up all those gains in a moment if I could have my son back.

Does God then "temper the wind to the shorn lamb"? Does he never ask more of us than we can endure? My experience has been otherwise. I have seen people crack under the strain of tragedy. I have seen marriages break up after the death of a child. I have seen people made noble and sensitive through suffering, but I have also seen people grow cynical and bitter. If God is testing us, he must know by now that many of us fail the test.

These various responses to tragedy all assume that God is the cause of our suffering. But maybe our suffering happens for some reason other than the will of God. The Psalmist writes, "I will lift up mine eyes unto the hills, from whence cometh my help. My help cometh from the Lord, which made heaven and earth." He does not say "My tragedy comes from the Lord."

Could it be that God does not cause the bad things that happen to us? Could it be that he does not decide which families shall give birth to handicapped children but, rather, that he stands ready to help us cope with our tragedies?

One day, a year and a half after Aaron's death, I realized that I had gone beyond self-pity to accepting what had happened. I knew that no one ever promised us a life free from disappointment. The most anyone promised was that we would not be alone in our pain, that we would be able to draw upon a source outside ourselves for strength and courage.

I now recognize that God does not cause our misfortunes, but helps us — by inspiring other people to help. We were sustained in Aaron's illness by people who made a point of showing that they cared: the man who made Aaron a scaled-down tennis racket; the woman who gave him a small handmade violin; the friend who got him a baseball autographed by the Boston Red Sox; the children who overlooked his limitations to play stickball with him. These people were God's way of telling our family that we were not alone.

In the same way, I believe that Aaron served God's purposes, not by being sick but by facing up so bravely to his illness. Aaron's friends and schoolmates were affected by his courage and by the way he managed to live a full life despite his limitations. Others who knew our family were moved to handle the difficult times of their own lives with more hope and courage by our example.

Let me suggest that the bad things that happen to us in our lives do not have a meaning when they happen. But we can redeem these tragedies from senselessness by imposing meaning on them. In the final analysis, the question is not why bad things happen to good people, but how we respond when such things happen. Are we capable of accepting a world that has disappointed us by not being perfect, a world in which there is so much unfairness and cruelty, disease and crime, earthquake and accident? Are we capable of forgiving and loving the people around us, even if they have let us down? Are we capable of forgiving and loving God despite his limitations?

If we can do these things, we will be able to recognize that forgiveness and love are the weapons God has given to enable us to live fully and bravely in this less-than-perfect world.

I think of Aaron and all that his life taught me, and I realize how much I have lost and how much I have gained. Yesterday seems less painful, and I am not afraid of tomorrow.

Questions for Study

1. The thesis for this writing appears in the fifth paragraph: "Why do bad things happen to good people? . . . The misfortunes of good people are a problem to everyone who wants to believe in a just and fair world." Do the first four paragraphs help to explain the thesis? Present your view in a brief paragraph.
2. This essay contains both causes and effects. Make two lists, one for causes and the other for effects, and then classify the paper as either a cause or an effect paper.
3. Kushner uses three main examples of tragedies: 1. his own son Aaron; 2. the 19-year old college freshman; 3. and his acquaintance Helen. Which tragedy would you find hardest to bear? Give your answer in a paragraph.
4. How does Kushner explain the cause of these tragedies? In two or three sentences, paraphrase his answer.
5. List the various effects that Aaron's illness has for Rabbi Kushner.

ALTERNATE ASSIGNMENT P

Have you yourself suffered through a serious illness or personal tragedy or watched as someone else did? What brought the tragedy about? What happened as a result? For this writing, explain the background of the unfortunate situation and the various causes and effects associated with it.

Chapter 14

DIVISION AND
—— CLASSIFICATION ——

INTRODUCTION

Take a mental stroll through an imaginary campus library. Walk inside the door and you'll see the reference section, for example, to the left, and the periodical section to the right. The rest of that first floor is devoted to the stacks in which the books are stored. Half of the second floor is devoted to the audiovisual section; the other half houses the microfilm section. The computer section takes up the whole third floor.

Now take a walk to that second floor and head into the audiovisual department to look at the records. What you'll discover are classical albums, jazz albums, and rock-and-roll albums, all arranged in categories. Further, the albums within these categories are also arranged in categories. For instance, the rock and roll albums are arranged by years: 1950–1959, 1960–1969, 1970–1979, 1980–present.

The first example—the organization of the library building—is **division.** The second example—the arrangement of albums in the audiovisual department—is **classification.** Both are types of **analysis,** the process of taking something large or complex and dealing with it in a simpler, more easily understood form.

Although there are many differences between these two types of analysis, the major difference is in number. Division deals with one subject, which is separated into its components. Therefore a complex device like a television is easier to understand if it is presented piece by piece. Classification deals with many items, which are categorized. Thus a study of cars is often more practical if the subject is arranged in groups—full-size, mid-size, compact, and subcompact, for instance.

Of course, a study of cars could also be arranged differently: luxury cars, mid-priced cars, and economy cars, for example, or eight-cylinder, six-cylinder, and four-cylinder cars. Each system of classification gives different information; which you choose depends on your intent as the writer.

Analysis is a process we complete every day. From morning to night, we are faced with problems, some minor and some major, and all of which require us to reason our way through until we reach an answer.

You use these types of analysis in writing, too. Imagine for a moment that you are writing a paper about hunger in the United States. After doing some research, you might be able to illustrate the inadequacy of the two hundred dollars that many food-stamp recipients receive per month by dividing the check into what items it pays for and what is left over.

In that same paper, you might also classify the types of poor people: the wholly indigent — "bag" people who have no homes and who live in subway or bus stations; the highly subsidized poor — individuals who are nearly wards of the state in that they receive free or subsidized housing, food, and medical care; and the unrecognized poor — people who make enough money to exceed the guidelines for assistance but who are nevertheless going without because they must pay for housing and food without assistance.

Writing that is simple and clear is effective because your reader understands it. Division and classification are both means of clarifying and simplifying a subject. As a result, they are valuable techniques for you to master.

THE MAKEUP OF A DIVISION OR A CLASSIFICATION PAPER

Sometimes, when you write, you will use division and classification as supporting techniques. Other times, however, the subject you are writing about will call for a more thorough division or classification approach.

Of the two types of analysis, you'll use division far less often than classification for an entire paper; however, you will still occasionally use division as the main technique in your writing. If you were asked to write about a labor-saving device — a food processor, for instance — you would use division to make it easier for your reader to understand the appliance.

    There are basically three main parts in most food
    processors: the housing, the inverted bowl, and the
    chopping blades. Each part must be kept in working order
    for the unit to run properly.
    The housing is the largest part of the food processor. It
    contains the circuitry and the motor that drive the blades.
    Furthermore, the front of the housing has a series of
    buttons that control what the machine does. For
    example, . . .

But you'll use classification much more often as the main technique in your writing. Imagine, for example, that you are writing a paper in which you state that the type of sales clerk in a clothing store actually affects the sales in the store. You would then present the types or categories of clerks: the too-aggressive salesperson who nearly attacks you as you walk in the door and who nearly smothers you with attention; the invisible salesperson who offers no help and actually seems to be avoiding any opportunity to answer a question or to look in the back room for some item you want; and the helpful salesperson who has mastered the subtle balance between too much and too little attention. A section of that paper would read this way:

The invisible salesperson is probably more annoying
than the pesty salesperson. With the pest, you can't move
around freely or browse, but at least help is available if
you need it. Yet with the invisible salesperson, you are on
your own. If you want to know whether an item is available in
another size or color, you might as well guess because
there is no one around to answer your question. If there
aren't any signs indicating where the dressing room is or
how many garments you may take into the dressing room at a
time, don't expect any help; nobody is on the floor. If
you'd simply like another opinion about how something looks
on you, you had better ask your reflection in the mirror
because there'll be nobody else around.

In paragraphs devoted to each of the other two categories, you would support your thesis: people feel more comfortable shopping for clothes when they are served by salespeople who deliver service rather than annoyance or frustration.

Very little in life is actually simple. Dealing with a subject in manageable units or pieces makes your ideas easier to understand for your reader. For that reason alone, division and classification are techniques worth spending time on.

USING THE TECHNIQUE

In an analysis based on division or on classification, you will ensure your success if you adhere to the following guidelines:

1. Remember that in dealing with a single item or individual, you will generally use division; in dealing with multiple items or individuals, classification.

The important point to remember is that both division and classification are forms of analysis. You simply go in slightly different directions with each. With division, you break a whole into parts; with classification, you take those parts and put them in categories based on some common ground.

2. Remember that the categories you set when you classify are general and not all-inclusive.

In life there are no absolutes. If, for instance, you went to a professional wrestling match and decided that the crowd could be classified as fans who believe the sport is genuine, those who think some of the action is real, and those who are there for the laughs, you've obviously overlooked some who "fall between the cracks," who don't quite fit in the categories you've established.

There is nothing wrong with generalizations, as long as you don't present your reader with a series of absolute categories that don't allow for the exceptions. In the paper on wrestling, for example, you should phrase your thesis this way:

> At the last wrestling match I attended, most of the crowd
> seemed either to believe the action was real, to believe it
> was a little real, or to completely disbelieve it.

The words *most of the crowd* and *seemed* allow for those who don't fit into the various classes established. As a result, the classification is both fair and accurate.

3. Keep the various portions and classes distinct and logical.

One potential problem in either a division or a classification paper is that you may overlap the segments. If, for instance, you use division to explain a gas lawn mower, you may divide it into the engine, the housing, and the handle assembly. In each case, of course, you would further subdivide. The handle assembly, for example, includes the power control and the starting cord.

If, however, you divided the lawn mower into engine, carburetor, housing, and handle assembly, your division wouldn't be logical because the carburetor is part of the engine. It should therefore be listed as a subsection of the engine.

Generally you face a bigger potential for error with classification because it is easy to make classes overlap. For example, let's say you are writing a paper about types of pollution that are endangering our survival on this planet. After some thought, you come up with the following categories: air pollution, water pollution, and ground or soil pollution. The problem here is that the categories overlap: waste that pollutes the soil contaminates both groundwater when it is buried and air when its fumes escape into the atmosphere. To solve this problem, you could present two classes — air pollution and water pollution — and subdivide each so that you present a number of types of air pollution and a number of types of water pollution.

Or you could change your principle of classification, that is the basis on which you set up the classes. Instead of organizing around two general types of pollution, for example, you could change the principle of classification to sources of pollution: fossil fuel exhaust, nuclear waste, chemical or industrial waste, untreated effluent from individual and city waste-water treatment centers, and so on.

Of course, each of these classes could be divided as well; fossil fuel exhaust could be separated into exhaust from cars and buses, exhaust from power-generating plants fueled by oil or coal, and exhaust from homes heated by wood or fossil fuel. Remember: whether you are dealing with division or with classification, the smaller, clearer, and more understandable the sections, the easier it will be for your reader to understand your point.

4. Be consistent in your sections and categories.

No matter what type of analysis you use when you write, you need to be consistent in its use throughout the paper. You shouldn't begin the division of that lawn mower based on function and then switch to a division based on size. Instead, depending on the needs of your reader, separate the machine on the basis of function or on the basis of size.

The same is true of classification: the principle of classification you begin with must be the principle you apply throughout your classification. If you classify the visitors you see on a beach as beach bums, semiregular visitors, pale-faced strangers, and fat, out-of-shape sun seekers, you have not been consistent in your principle of organization. The first three categories are based on some sign—probably the degree of tan or the level of familiarity the individuals show with the area and the people around them. But the fourth category—fat, out-of-shape sun seekers—is based on a different principle: the physical condition of people on the beach. Stick with one principle throughout your classification paper.

5.　Make your division and classification reasonably complete.

If you were doing a paper for a health or biology class on one of the new electronic prostheses (artificial limbs) being developed to replace the human hand, you wouldn't be very successful if you divided the human hand into skin, bones, and blood vessels. One of the reasons scientists have had such difficulty developing practical replacement parts for the human body is the tremendous complexity of the real thing. Besides skin, bones, and blood vessels, your hand is composed of, among other things, nerves, tendons, ligaments, muscles, and cartilage. No matter what the subject of the division, you must make sure to be as thorough as is reasonably possible to meet the needs of your reader.

You must also be thorough when you set up a classification. If you decide to write about what is currently popular in movie theaters and you used the classic division of comedy and tragedy only, you would obviously be presenting a classification that is too limited. What about all the adventure films? Musicals? Horror films?

In order to have a classification, you must have at least two classes. Of course, you aren't limited to two classes. Remember, the clearer and more manageable the classes, the easier it will be for your reader to understand your point. The purpose of your paper and the needs of your reader will dictate how many classes you should set up. In most cases, however, rather than limiting yourself to two classes, adjust the principle of classification and set up more, smaller classes.

6.　Arrange the sections of your paper effectively.

How you set up your writing is important, no matter what you are writing about. In a division or classification paper, your paper will become even more effective if it is carefully set up.

In a division paper, you need to section off your subject in some logical order. A device might be divided in spatial order—so that one part is put in relation to another—from the inside out, from the outside in, or from one end to another. A corporation might be divided in order of authority—from the company president to the various vice-presidents to the mid-management executives, and so on. The key is to arrange your division so that someone unfamiliar with the item will understand it—and that means clarity and simplicity.

In a classification paper, you have a choice of types of arrangement. You could, for instance, arrange your paper in a least-to-most-significant order. Imagine you have developed the following categories for television shows: children's shows, documentaries, situation comedies, soap operas, variety shows, and police or medical dramas. Because your thesis is "Television programming on both educational and commercial networks offers plenty of quality entertainment for all ages," you decide to make the final category one that stresses quality:

> But the best shows available on both educational and
> noneducational channels are the documentaries, which
> appear frequently. For instance, in one week last month,
> there was a special on ABC about life in detention camps for
> Japanese-Americans during World War II, another in the
> series of shows about Jacques Cousteau's ocean research,
> and an NBC ''white paper'' study on street people in our
> major cities. Each of these shows is like a mini-college-
> course in history, science, psychology, or sociology.

By using this category as the last one in your paper, you move from strong category to stronger category until you finally provide the strongest evidence that quality television programming is a reality.

Of course, if all the classes are about equal in importance, you can try different arrangements to see which combination flows best. Check with another reader; most of the time an objective view helps.

Division and classification are valuable techniques for you to master because they allow you to take complex issues and situations and to deal with them in more manageable units. Dealing with more understandable portions makes your job as a writer easier. More important, however, a clear and simple presentation of a complex topic makes things easier on your reader — and for that reason, division and classification are particularly important writing techniques.

ASSIGNMENT 15

Take an object, device, or organization, and in a 500- to 700-word essay, divide this topic.

Reason

Curiosity is one of the strongest human drives. Whether the subject is a compact-disk player, the human eye, or the FBI, people are interested in understanding how something is put together. For this reason, a division paper holds great potential.

As long as it has several parts, any device, object, or organization will probably be suitable. A common rubber ball, for example, would be a poor choice because it is composed of two halves of colored rubber bonded together. If, however, you had worked at the plant where these balls are made and were familiar with the various chemicals and materials used to make these rubber balls, you would have a suitable subject for a division paper.

Imagine, for instance, that you are writing a paper explaining how a top-quality running shoe protects the foot of the long-distance runner. A good running shoe is composed of a combination of different materials set in a specific design. Between the sole (a piece of semihard, synthetic rubber) and the bottom of the shoe (often a combination of nylon and leather) is a sandwich of two or more different types of foam rubber. This sandwich is angled outward to cut down on the wobble of the runner's legs.

Dividing the shoe into parts allows you to discuss the various elements of the shoe that, in combination, help to absorb a great deal of the tremendous pounding that the runner's foot would otherwise be subjected to. For the reader who knows little about running, your division paper would illustrate the modern-day marriage between athletics and technology. For the experienced runner, your paper would provide a concrete illustration of the special design or materials that keep him or her out on the road rather than in the trainer's room. In either case, the division would serve the needs of the reader because it would satisfy that curiosity natural to all of us.

What Your Reader Needs

When you write a division paper, you must develop it with the idea that you are introducing something new to your reader. Therefore you must express your reason (your thesis), the logic of your division, and the various segments of the subject in simple, clear, and understandable terms. Certainly not all your readers will be new to your topic, but more experienced readers will not suffer because you present a thorough division.

To comprehend the subject of your division, your reader needs a clear thesis as well as a sufficient number of manageable and logical segments of that subject. And the reader needs to see those segments arranged in such a way that they make sense.

If, for instance, your subject is a volunteer suicide-prevention group and your thesis is "The public has no idea of how complex an organization like 'Please Call' suicide prevention group is," your reader needs to see that complexity simplified through your use of clearly divided segments.

Thus, you might separate the hundred-member organization into a number of smaller units of people. The executive unit, for example, raises funds and lobbies for governmental support. The phone unit counsels the despondent individuals and their families or friends. The outreach unit visits the individuals and families to offer some in-person comfort. And the intervention unit goes to the scenes of threatened suicides and attempts to somehow convince the individuals not to take their lives.

Breaking a complex organization into sections like these makes your reader's task easier. You use the various portions of the division to support your thesis and, as a result, draw a more complete and accurate picture of the organization. Rather than seeing a huge group of faces working at a common goal, your reader sees that this organization is actually a combination of four units, each working toward a common goal but each working in a different way.

In a division paper, your reader clearly needs the direction that a thesis provides, and your reader needs segments of that division that are clear, understandable, detailed, and logical. Once you've provided this thesis and presented the segments, all that remains is to add a concluding paragraph restating the significance of your paper, and you'll have met the needs of your reader.

Model

THE HOME COMPUTER

Anyone wanting to join the growing number of individuals who own home computers should have a basic understanding of the components that make up the unit. Although some personal computers have been on the market for around a hundred dollars, their capabilities are limited to such simple tasks as keeping track of the balance in a checkbook. A more advanced computer that has many of the same capabilities as an office or business computer is a major investment sometimes totalling a thousand dollars or more. As companies such as IBM, Tandy, and Apple market similar computer systems, it is important that consumers know the components they are paying for.

Like their big brothers in industry, home computers can be separated into two main parts: the hardware and the software. The hardware is basically the machinery of the computer. The terminal itself with the various units connected to it is hardware, as are the disks on which information is stored. The software consists of the various programs that tell the computer how to run.

The most important part of the hardware is the central processing unit—the CPU. This is the brain of the computer, although it is nonfunctional without the software. The other parts of the hardware tie into this unit and perform according to its orders.

The video display unit is also part of the hardware, and it consists of a televisionlike screen and a standard keyboard. Sometimes the television screen or the keyboard is separate from the CPU, connected by a wire that looks very much like the cord that connects the receiver to the rest of the telephone. These parts are the most visible and familiar parts of the home computer. Users communicate with the CPU by typing the message, and they read the response on the video screen in front of them.

Another important part of the hardware is the disk drive. Seeming a little like a record player, the disk drive holds the various disks from which the computer reads information and on which it records information.

Sometimes the hardware also includes a printer, which produces hard copy of the documents stored on the disk or in the computer. The most common types of printers are dot-matrix printers, which print characters that are a series of tiny dots, and letter-quality printers, which produce a normal typewriter script. Often the paper in these printers is in folded sheets, but the paper is perforated page-by-page and along each edge so that it can be separated into standard-size sheets.

The software consists of the program or the series of commands that tells the computer how to run. This information is stored on a disk. In spite of all the elaborate hardware, a computer cannot run without the all-important software. If the CPU is the brain of a computer system, then the software is the brain within the brain, the part that tells the CPU—and, consequently, the rest of the system—what to do and how to do it.

The name home computer sounds simple enough, but in fact the device is quite complex. A practical home computer is much more than a simple electronic game system or an overgrown calculator. A good home computer is actually an elaborate system consisting of a CPU, a video terminal, a typewriter keyboard, a disk drive, computer programs, and, in many cases, a printer. If someone actually needs a home computer, chances are that person's needs will be served by a system made up of these components.

Follow-through

A division paper allows your reader to see something taken apart, the idea being that seeing the portions separately will foster a better understanding of the whole. Therefore, to meet the needs of your reader, you must present the parts in such a way that they clearly add up to the whole.

As always, establishing the thesis is vital because you use the information you generate to support that thesis. Because you are working with a single subject, your field of information will probably be pretty narrow to begin with. The parts are all there; it's a matter of remembering all of them and then dividing them in a logical fashion.

But before you can establish your thesis, you must first do some preliminary study of the object or organization. In the case of this paper, the prewriting produced this information:

• *television screen*	• *typewriter keyboard*	• *power surge guard*
• *command keyboard*	• *printer? not always*	• *disk drive*
• *software/programs*	• *computer itself/CPU*	• *modem*
• *disks*	• *graphics*	• *memory*

As this list shows, a home computer is no simple matter. Basically there are two main divisions—hardware and software—each of which must be subdivided. Breaking the computer down this way will make it easier for your reader to understand the computer as a whole.

Besides being complex, a home computer is expensive; although floppy or semihard disks are relatively inexpensive, the other components cost from one hundred dollars to several hundred. The thesis, which appears in the last two sentences of the introductory paragraph in the final draft, states that a home computer is a major investment and that therefore a consumer should know all its components.

Once this point is established, the next step is deciding which bits of the initial material should be used. In the case of a home computer, the major parts are the computer itself (the central processing unit, or CPU), a video screen of some kind, a disk drive, and a typewriter keyboard. In some cases, these components are separate pieces connected by electrical cables; at other times they are housed in one unit. The initial list includes these components.

But the initial list also mentions components or capabilities that are not clearly and logically divided. For instance, graphics and memory are capabilities or functions of the computer system, one (graphics) available only if you have the proper software or commands for the computer, and the second (memory) dependent on the level that the particular computer is designed to handle.

A modem is a device that allows the user to use telephone lines to tie into other computer systems. It is not, however, standard equipment. The same is true of a command keyboard. Some home computers have an additional keyboard with a series of special keys; others feature a few additional keys on an otherwise ordinary-looking typewriter keyboard. It's simpler, then, to leave this potentially confusing detail out.

In today's world of electronic devices, a surge depressor — a device that protects against sudden increases in electrical current that could damage delicate electronic components — is fairly common. But this device is not necessarily part of the average home computer unless it is a built-in feature. Therefore, this detail should be left out.

Although the other components mentioned here are standard parts of most home computers, a printer is not. It is common enough, however, to be included. After it has been edited, that original prewriting list looks like this:

- *television screen*   - *printer? not always*   - *typewriter keyboard*
- *disk drive*   - *computer itself/CPU*   - *software/programs*
- *disks*

Once the specific details to be included have been selected, they must be arranged so that the division is clear and understandable to the reader. A computer can be divided many ways; one way is to separate the machine (the hardware) from the instructions that allow it to perform (the software). That's the principle illustrated in this paper, as the second paragraph points out:

```
    Like their big brothers in industry, home computers can
be separated into two main parts: the hardware and the
software. The hardware is basically the machinery of the
computer. The terminal itself with the various units
connected to it is hardware, as are the disks on which
```

```
information is stored. The software consists of the various
programs that tell the computer how to run.
```

This paragraph prepares the reader for the analysis to follow; it specifies how the device is going to be divided.

Beginning with the hardware is a good decision because it is what most people think of when they hear the word *computer*. The subdivision of the hardware begins with the part that isn't really noticeable because it doesn't look like anything special from the outside: the CPU. In this case, beginning with the most important part makes sense because all the other parts of the hardware tie into the CPU and are thus dependent on it. The other parts — the video display unit, the keyboard, and the disk drive — are each presented and each explained so that the whole of the hardware is clear for the reader. The printer is presented at the end because it is not always part of the home computer package.

The software is explained but not subdivided. Although software could be divided by function — instructions for word processing or accounting, for instance — all software is sets of instructions. Illustrating how that information is encoded on a disk or is used by the computer would change the focus of the paper and might well confuse the reader. As a result, explaining that software as "the brain within the brain, the part that tells the CPU — and, consequently, the rest of the system — what to do and how to do it" serves the needs of the reader; it is simple and clear.

Once the division is complete, the concluding paragraph reaffirms the thesis of the paper: a person should know what makes up a home-computer system before purchasing one. Basically that's the plan when you write a division paper. You state your thesis, use the division to illustrate and support that thesis, and restate it all in the conclusion. If your division is clear, complete, and understandable, you'll have done what you set out to do; you will have met the needs of your reader.

Checklist

Use the answers to the following questions to help you revise your first draft:

1. Does your paper have a thesis? Write it down.
2. Is your division logical? List the parts.
3. Have you divided your subject into enough sections?
4. Have you thoroughly explained each portion and its relationship to the other portions?
5. Are the various parts arranged logically and effectively?
6. Does your introduction present a clear direction for your reader?
7. Does your conclusion restate the significance of your paper?

ASSIGNMENT 16

Take a group of persons, places, things, or experiences with some points in common, and in a 500- to 700-word essay, classify them.

Reason

Walk into an old-fashioned hardware store sometime and ask to buy some nails. The counter clerk will undoubtedly ask you what kind and size and then head to the back room. If you peek in the back room, you'll see a series of buckets or bins, each labeled and holding a certain type and size of nail. It's a great system; all the nails are arranged in classes, so it is much easier for personnel to find what the customers want.

That's what classification does; larger subjects are easier to understand because they are arranged in smaller chunks. For instance, imagine that you are writing about the popularity of fast-food restaurants in America. One way to organize a subject like fast-food restaurants is to classify them by type. There are the burger places, the chicken places, the pizza places, the doughnut places, the taco places, and so on. By taking fast-food restaurants and arranging the many restaurants in categories, you give your reader a concrete view of how widespread the popularity of such places is. Take this paragraph from a paper on fast-food restaurants, for example:

```
    In many cities, if you get sick of hamburgers or chicken,
you can simply drive down the road to a pizza place. In my
city, for example, there is a Pizza Hut diagonally across
from a Papa Gino's; both places offer a similar menu at
similar prices, and they both seem to have plenty of
business. Within two blocks of this main strip are five
other pizza shops. These aren't national chains like the
other two places; they are more ''mom-and-pop''
operations, but this lack of national exposure doesn't
seem to hurt them. On a Friday or Saturday night, you have to
wait in line to be served.
```

Each paragraph in the body of the paper talks about a particular type of restaurant; the whole paper thus gives a fuller view of the vast popularity of fast-food restaurants. And the view is much clearer for your reader, thanks to the arrangement, which presents the information in smaller, more manageable units.

What Your Reader Needs

A successful classification paper simplifies a subject because it arranges that subject in categories based on some common principle. Basically that's what your reader needs; a thesis as well as a clear principle of classification supporting that thesis.

If, for instance, your thesis states that the types of cars people drive tell something about those people, you must present classes that clearly support that thesis. If people own four-wheel-drive vehicles, does that mean they're fun-loving and anxious for adventure? If they drive fancy European sedans, does that mean they're upwardly mobile and interested in appearances? If they drive station wagons, does that mean they're conservative and family-oriented? Whatever theory you propose, your reader needs your follow-through to understand your point.

At the same time, your reader depends on your consistency of presentation in order to understand what you mean. If, for example, you begin by talking about the types of cars people drive as reflections of their personalities, you can't switch in the middle of your presentation to the condition of those cars as a reflection. If it is the high-performance Corvette that makes the statement, whether the car is dirty or clean, polished or dull, dented or flawless shouldn't affect the class you've assigned it to.

Of course, you could change the principle of organization for the entire paper so that it reflected this point. In this case, your thesis would state that the condition people keep their cars in says something about their personalities; then your classes might be people who never clean or maintain their cars, people who maintain some part of their car (tires, convertible tops, or chrome-work), and people who are meticulous in caring for their cars. Remember: your reader is counting on a consistent presentation, so follow through on the principle of organization you set.

Remember, too, to make your classification thorough. It's unreasonable to expect that you'll be able to fit all of the items of a subject into an appropriate class. Certainly there are people who have bought a four-wheel-drive vehicle because it is practical or because it was on sale. The same would be true of every other class. To overcome this built-in problem, try to establish enough different classes — at least three — so that you provide classifications for at least the majority of the individual parts of your topic.

Your reader needs a clear, thorough, consistent study in order to understand the point you set forth in your thesis. And it's the classification you set up that will help you meet your reader's needs.

Model

VACATION RESORTS

The word <u>vacation</u> means different things to different people. For some, a vacation can be spent happily at home, resting from the normal activities of life. For others, a vacation means a quiet sightseeing tour of places of historical or cultural significance. But for millions of Americans, vacation time means a trip to a resort. There are different types of vacation resorts that cater to the desires of different people, and three of the most popular types are island resorts, honky-tonk resorts, and theme-park resorts.

Island resorts have among their chief appeals beautiful beaches and a slow-paced lifestyle. Therefore some famous islands, such as Hawaii's Oahu, are not part of this category because they are simply too developed and fast-paced. The other islands in the chain—including the so-called big island, Hawaii—do fit in because they have unspoiled beaches and slower lifestyles. Probably the most popular of these island resorts are Bermuda, the Virgin Islands, and the Canary Islands. Although these places are separated by vast tracts of water, they share a reputation as places to go for rest, relaxation, sun, and nightlife. On these islands, great food, luxurious accommodations, friendly people, and great fun await the travelers.

For those who want their fun with a slightly more garish twist, however, there are the honky-tonk resorts. Unlike island resorts, these places are not marked by undeveloped landscapes or slow lifestyles. Instead, the resorts are crammed with various hotels, businesses, fast-food joints, and, of course, people. Old Orchard Beach in Maine and Daytona Beach in Florida are two good examples of this type of resort area. Connected to the beach area at each of these resorts is an amusement park and a pier that juts out into the ocean. There are plenty of shops and eateries lining the pier, and the crowds strolling along attest to the popularity of the resorts. Maybe the premier honky-tonk resort, at least on the East Coast, is Atlantic City in New Jersey. Take Daytona Beach, multiply it, and add gambling casinos and big-time entertainment, and you have Atlantic City.

Another type of resort area, the theme park, got its start over thirty years ago when Walt Disney opened Disneyland in California. The trend toward this type of resort really accelerated, though, when Disneyworld in Florida opened in 1972. In Disneyland and Disneyworld, as well as in other theme parks such as Knotts Berry Farm, Busch Gardens, and The Old Country, the old amusement park blueprints have been replaced with plans that incorporate the most modern technical innovations. The results are imaginative rides and attractions that are cleaner, safer, and more exciting. The parks themselves are huge but incredibly well managed. The workers are neatly clad and courteous, the food is good, and the grounds are nearly spotless. The comfort of the guests of the park is the chief priority, so that even though admission to these theme parks is expensive, most people agree that the parks are worth every penny.

As all this shows, there is no single answer to the question of how Americans like to spend vacation time. However, one of the most popular alternatives is to travel to a vacation resort. Whether Americans want to lie on the beach on a quiet island, eat greasy French fries on a boardwalk, or ride upside down on a roller coaster, there is a vacation resort to entertain them.

Follow-through

A classification paper presents a large subject in simplified fashion. You use classes of information to support some idea you propose; if your groupings are clear, logical, and thorough, your reader will understand your point. The key to success, then, is to present a thesis and then to support it with a sufficient number of understandable classes.

As for any paper, the initial step for a classification paper is the prewriting stage. Once you have established a general topic, you need to generate some information from which you will eventually build your paper. For this paper, the starting point is the subject of vacation resorts. The prewriting produced this list:

Old Orchard Beach and places like that — lots of lights and pizza places, French fries on the pier — beautiful beach, old and new hotels — loud is probably the best word — Daytona is like that, too — beautiful beach and everything but plenty of cheap shops and hot dog stands, Burger King under the pier — tacky, but if you like it, so what? — now you could probably die in Bermuda and people wouldn't notice for a few days — it's so low key — great food and entertainment — beautiful beaches — we rode that moped all over the island in the rain — had to pop the clutch by pushing it up this big hill and pedaling like crazy down — we went through the Poconos when we were kids — boring — wonder what those Club Med places are like? — Karen says that St. Croix in the Virgin Isles is like Bermuda — Canary Islands are, too — I like more excitement — I loved Knotts Berry Farm — the rides were great — it wasn't cheap, though. Neither was Busch Gardens in Tampa — beautiful animals there — a real Middle East flavor in the park — I saw pictures of a dude ranch — I wonder what people see in those places? — Atlantic City, popular, too — all shine and bright lights but just a honky-tonk like Daytona — there are poor neighborhoods only a few blocks from the casinos and hotels.

This preliminary listing contains the seeds for the paper, but before it can be useful in a classification paper, this information must be arranged into some general groups. The following vacation spots are mentioned: Old Orchard Beach, Daytona Beach, Bermuda, the Poconos, Club Med, St. Croix, the Canary Islands, Knotts Berry Farm, Busch Gardens, a dude ranch, and Atlantic City. Now the job is to come up with some kind of groupings.

The prewriting puts Old Orchard Beach and Daytona Beach together initially; then Atlantic City is joined to Daytona at the end of the list under the label *honky-tonk*. These three vacation spots thus make up one category.

Bermuda is linked with St. Croix and the Canary Islands on the basis of scenery and lifestyle. That's a second category: *slow-paced island resorts*. And Knotts Berry Farm is linked with Busch Gardens as exciting vacation spots, eventually called *theme-park resorts*.

But the original list involves other vacation spots, too: the Poconos, Club Med, a dude ranch. However, they don't fit into any of the other categories, nor can they all be combined into one category. Further, the preliminary list shows that the writer doesn't know as much about these places. Therefore it makes more sense to amplify the three categories with other information rather than to try to develop another category based on one of these other places.

Look first at these preliminary details for the island resorts:

Now you could probably die in Bermuda and people wouldn't notice for a few days — it's so low key — great food and entertainment — beautiful beaches — we rode that moped all over the island in the rain — had to pop the clutch by pushing it up this big hill and pedaling like crazy down — Karen says that St. Croix in the Virgin Isles is like Bermuda — Canary Islands are, too.

The information here isn't useful yet because it needs to be amplified. First, some definition and illustration of the category *island resort* is necessary, and that is provided in the final draft through details like "unspoiled beaches" and "slower lifestyles." Further, an example of a well-known island that doesn't fit — Hawaii's Oahu — is presented. Besides the initial vacation spots that do fit into the category, another one — the "big island" of Hawaii — is given in the final draft, and additional details concerning the attractions of these resorts are presented: rest, relaxation, sun, and nightlife — great food, luxurious accommodations, friendly people, and great fun. The result is a clear, understandable presentation of a class of resorts:

```
    Island resorts have among their chief appeals beautiful
beaches and a slow-paced lifestyle. Therefore some famous
islands, such as Hawaii's Oahu, are not part of this
category because they are simply too developed and fast-
paced. The other islands in the chain-including the so-
called big island, Hawaii-do fit in because they have the
unspoiled beaches and slower lifestyles. Probably the most
popular of these island resorts are Bermuda, the Virgin
Islands, and the Canary Islands. Although these places are
separated by vast tracts of water, they share a reputation
as places to go for rest, relaxation, sun, and nightlife.
On these islands, great food, luxurious accommodations,
friendly people, and great fun await the travelers.
```

As the preliminary list shows and common sense indicates, these three categories outlined in the final draft fall far short of summing up all the vacation possibilities. The thesis notes this point:

```
There are different kinds of vacation resorts that cater to
the desires of different people, and three of the most
popular types are island resorts, honky-tonk resorts, and
theme-park resorts.
```

This thesis provides a clear direction for the reader, and the same three general categories of resorts mentioned in the thesis are then presented in the body of the paper, but the thesis also acknowledges that these types of resorts represent only some of the available vacation possibilities.

None of the categories seems to have any greater appeal than the others; no information in the paper indicates that an island resort is necessarily more or less popular than a honky-tonk resort or a theme-park resort. Therefore the arrangement is a matter of choice. If you were revising this paper, you could no doubt rearrange the order of the classes without affecting the effectiveness of the paper. If, however, the information in the paper stated that theme-park resorts attract 20 percent of American vacationers, island resorts 25 percent, and honky-tonk resorts 30 percent, you might well want to present the classes in that order.

Your job in a classification paper is to support a thesis with classes of information. To ensure that your paper will communicate your ideas clearly, follow a consistent principle of classification and make sure your classes are reasonably thorough, clearly defined, and effectively arranged. Add an introduction containing a clear thesis and a conclusion restating the significance of your paper, and your classification paper will be effective.

Checklist

Use the answers to the following questions to help you revise your first draft:

1. Does your paper have a thesis? Write it down.
2. Is your principle of organization consistent throughout the paper?
3. Have you provided enough classes to support your thesis?
4. Do the classes overlap?
5. Have you provided enough details to illustrate each class?
6. Does the arrangement of the classes follow a particular order?
7. Does your introduction present a clear direction for your reader?
8. Does your conclusion restate the significance of your paper?

FOR FURTHER STUDY

To become a professional athlete is the secret dream of many Americans. Even though most of us don't have the natural ability necessary, we still dream; occasionally, we may even try to bring a little sport into everyday life. In this essay, Jonathan Walters has highlighted this seemingly natural impulse to challenge ourselves. His subject is throwing and he has illustrated the playful side of people by classifying types of throws. His approach is humorous, and his classes include plenty of examples that most readers can relate to.

To This Hurler, Throwing Is an Art Form, Not a Hit-or-Miss Proposition

Jonathan Walters

You've got tosses, flips, flings, slings, lobs, heaves and Hail Marys. You can do it sidearm, underhand, overhand and behind the back. When you try a tough one and hit it, it can be one of the sweetest feelings in the world — or one of the worst.

Throwing. Next to running it is probably the most natural athletic impulse we know. In a checkered career of chucking everything from dirt bombs to long bombs, I've come to know three basic types of tosses.

I unloaded a Type III one hot summer day at Crane's Beach in Ipswich, Mass. My father was 100 feet away, beyond two softly swept sand dunes, and moving. I heaved an ice cube. Threw it as hard as I could. The ends of my fingers hurt. My shoulder yelped. I watched with growing disbelief as it twirled and glinted toward its target, catching bits of the afternoon sun in its sweeping arc. It landed dead center on my father's hair-free pate. I escaped personal injury only because he couldn't believe I'd thrown it.

Type III throws, understand, are the most dangerous. You try them because you figure you haven't a chance in hell of making them. Not even a presidential motorcade is off limits.

My friend Paul recalls a Type III he let fly in his employer's parking lot. The sun was setting on one of those rare balmy February days in New England. A co-worker was pulling out of the lot, rolling open his sun roof as he went. Paul packed a snowball, subconsciously calculated trajectory and force, and cranked it from about 40 yards away. "All I remember," he recalls, "is seeing the snowball explode all over the inside of this poor guy's windshield. It must have snuck in through about a six-inch opening."

The distinguishing and unfortunate feature of Type III throws is that you have no defense to offer for your action. True, you did mean to drop one through that sun roof, but you never figured you could do it. This is the feature that separates a Type III toss from a Type II. Type II's are merely mistakes; you aimed at one thing and hit another. Although Type II's can make for unpleasant surprises, when confronted with the evidence you can — weakly — claim you were aiming at something else.

Once my father and a friend were tossing a balled-up jacket around the Greyhound bus station in Bridgeport, Conn. Between them was a flashing neon greyhound, its front and back paws churning for a finish line it would never reach. With one particularly hard throw, my father clipped the hound's back legs. In a spray of sparks and a wisp of smoke, the animal was crippled. My father and his friend sprinted past it and onto the bus. But they'd been spotted. A frantic porter leaped on after them, saw them hunkered down in their seats a few rows back and, pointing at my father, began yelling, "You killed the greyhound! You killed the greyhound!"

"I never was a natural athlete," my father says.

The outcome of Type II throws doesn't have to be bad. Another friend of mine was sitting at his desk one morning when a fellow employee threw him a cherry tomato, expecting him to catch it. The amazing thing wasn't that she was 30 feet away when she threw it, but that my friend was on the other side of a five-foot-high partition, completely out of view. As if guided there by Mission Control in Houston, the little red orb landed neatly in the breast pocket of his shirt.

As dazzling as a good Type II can be, the most satisfying throws are Type I's. You want to make them, and you do. Hit your target with a Type I and you feel a surge of power and confidence that can turn your whole rotten week around.

A few years back, my friend Bill was teaching high school English in Madison, Va. Being the liberal sort, he allowed gum chewing in class, but no bubble blowing. One student in particular had been flouting the rule regularly — and loudly. "The kid was sitting in the center of the last row," Bill recalls. "I turned to write something on the backboard and caught him out of the corner of my eye blowing another one — a big one. I picked up a piece of chalk, spun around and whipped it.

Now, I can't throw. You know I can't throw. Well, the bubble just exploded all over this kid's face, and the class went bananas."

Although such Type I's may serve a valuable social purpose, the most uplifting ones are undoubtedly those you unload just for fun. A high school buddy of mine was on the second floor of the Smith College library peeling an orange in lieu of studying applied mathematics. The woman he was with leaned over, asked him for a piece of peel and said, "Watch this." With a neat sidearm flip, she sent the skin spinning the width of the library's central atrium toward a wastebasket one floor below. Bingo. She hit it. "And an orange peel isn't that aerodynamic an object, either," my pal points out.

A throw like that is positively therapeutic. It elevates you. For a second, you're Johnny Unitas, Cy Young and John Havlicek rolled into one.

In the summer of 1972, I was working at a boatyard on a lake in New Hampshire, and one day I was fantasizing about my Celtics. I had a three-quarter-inch bolt in my hand. There were two seconds left in Game 7 of the world championship. Overtime. The Celtics were trailing 102–101. I twisted past one Philadelphia defender and looked to the basket. I fired. The bolt rolled out of my hand with a neat backspin. It twirled away in a hypnotic arc. The buzzer sounded. With a sharp "clang" and an unequivocal "plop," the bolt ricocheted off the I-beam backboard and into the rusty blue Maxwell House coffee can 50 feet away. I did a five-second victory dance: hands held high, a little workboot shuffle thrown in. As a fellow worker looked on bemused—and slightly amazed—I spun on my heel and headed out to the dock to pump a little gas.

Questions for Study

1. Walters' thesis appears in the last sentence of the second paragraph: "In a checkered career of chucking everything from dirt bombs to long bombs, I've come to know three basic types of tosses." But his introduction provides other important details that help set the scene and provide a clear direction. Make a list of the details in the introduction that direct the reader, and in a few sentences, explain how they provide that direction.
2. Walters has divided tosses into three classes and has then provided examples to support each definition. List each class and briefly paraphrase the definition he gave.
3. The essay begins with Type III throws and finally works to Type I throws. Is this arrangement effective, or would you suggest that the order be changed? Explain your answer in a few sentences.
4. This essay lacks a conclusion. Instead, Walters ended with another example. Compose a conclusion that restates the significance of the essay.

ALTERNATE ASSIGNMENT Q

Jonathan Walters took an activity common to people — throwing — and illustrated how we use it to amuse ourselves, perhaps to break up the monotony of life. For this assignment, choose another activity common to people — for example, talking, laughing, arguing or debating, walking, or singing — and classify this activity.

Fairy tales may tell us that all those Prince Charmings and Sleeping Beauties find sweethearts, marry, and live happily ever after, but real-life marriages are usually less like storybooks. The ideal marriage would have duties split evenly and equally, but as Judy Syfers has shown through her classification of the types of work often expected of a wife, tradition dictates a far less ideal setup.

I Want a Wife

Judy Syfers

I belong to that classification of people known as wives. I am A Wife. And, not altogether incidentally, I am a mother.

Not too long ago a male friend of mine appeared on the scene from the Midwest fresh from a recent divorce. He had one child, who is, of course, with his ex-wife. He is obviously looking for another wife. As I thought about him while I was ironing one evening, it suddenly occurred to me that I, too, would like to have a wife. Why do I want a wife?

I would like to go back to school so that I can become economically independent, support myself, and, if need be, support those dependent upon me. I want a wife who will work and send me to school. And while I am going to school I want a wife to take care of my children. I want a wife to keep track of the children's doctor and dentist appointments. And to keep track of mine, too. I want a wife to make sure my children eat properly and are kept clean. I want a wife who will wash the children's clothes and keep them mended. I want a wife who is a good nurturant attendant to my children, arranges for their schooling, makes sure that they have an adequate social life with their peers, takes them to the park, the zoo, etc. I want a wife who takes care of the children when they are sick, a wife who arranges to be around when the children need special care, because, of course, I cannot miss classes at school. My wife must arrange to lose time at work and not lose the job. It may mean a small cut in my wife's income from time to time, but I guess I can tolerate that. Needless to say, my wife will arrange and pay for the care of the children while my wife is working.

I want a wife who will take care of *my* physical needs. I want a wife who will keep my house clean. A wife who will pick up after my children, a wife who will pick up after me. I want a wife who will keep my clothes clean, ironed, mended, replaced when need be, and who will see to it that my personal things are kept in their proper place so that I can find what I need the minute I need it. I want a wife who cooks the meals, a wife who is a *good* cook. I want a wife who will plan the menus, do the necessary grocery shopping, prepare the meals, serve them pleasantly, and then do the cleaning up while I do my studying. I want a wife who will care for me when I am sick and sympathize with my pain and loss of time from school. I want a wife to go along when our family takes a vacation so that someone can continue to care for me and my children when I need a rest and a change of scene.

I want a wife who will not bother me with rambling complaints about a wife's duties. But I want a wife who will listen to me when I feel the need to explain a rather difficult point I have come across in my course of studies. And I want a wife who will type my papers for me when I have written them.

I want a wife who will take care of the details of my social life. When my wife and I are invited out by my friends, I want a wife who will take care of the babysitting arrangements. When I meet people at school that I like and want to entertain, I want a wife who will have the house clean, will prepare a special meal, serve it to me and my friends, and not interrupt when I talk about the things that interest me and my friends. I want a wife who will have arranged that the children are fed and ready for bed before my guests arrive so that the children do not bother us. I want a wife who takes care of the needs of my guests so that they feel comfortable, who makes sure that they have an ashtray, that they are passed the hors d'oeuvres, that they are offered a second helping of the food, that their wine glasses are replenished when necessary, that their coffee is served to them as they like it. And I want a wife who knows that sometimes I need a night out by myself.

I want a wife who is sensitive to my sexual needs, a wife who makes love passionately and eagerly when I feel like it, a wife who makes sure that I am satisfied. And, of course, I want a wife who will not demand sexual attention when I am not in the mood for it. I want a wife who assumes the complete responsibility for birth control, because I do not want more children. I want a wife who will remain sexually faithful to me so that I do not have to clutter up my intellectual life with jealousies. And I want a wife who understands that *my* sexual needs may entail more that strict adherence to monogamy. I must, after all, be able to relate to people as fully as possible.

If, by chance, I find another person more suitable as a wife than the wife I already have, I want the liberty to replace my present wife with another one. Naturally, I will expect a fresh, new life; my wife will take the children and be solely responsible for them so that I am left free.

When I am through with school and have acquired a job, I want my wife to quit working and remain at home so that my wife can more fully and completely take care of a wife's duties.

My God, who *wouldn't* want a wife?

Questions for Study

1. Syfers began her paper with the declaration that she is "A Wife," and then she presented the example of a recently divorced male friend who appeared at her door. This example is her starting point for her classification. What details about him in that paragraph support her point that a wife is often unfairly burdened?
2. Make a list of the classes of work or duties Syfers set up, and then, under each, present any subclassifications.
3. Syfers has offered plenty of examples to illustrate her classes. In a paragraph, tell which example you feel provides the strongest support.
4. Imagine that you were debating Syfers. What types of examples could you use to dispute her case? Or is it hopeless—is her case too strong? In a paragraph of a hundred words, provide your answer.

ALTERNATE ASSIGNMENT R

Syfers used the classification of a wife's duties to zero in on the inequality that often characterizes marriage in America. Her paper points out that the job of being a wife is far from simple, easy, or fair. For this writing, take another job and classify the types of duties required. Your approach can be humorous or ironic: rather than Syfers's job description of a wife, you could classify the "duties" of a parent, a boyfriend or girlfriend, or a babysitter. Or you could seriously classify the various tasks undertaken daily by a nurse, a musician, or a social worker.

Chapter 15

═══════ ARGUMENT ═══════

INTRODUCTION

"I'm sorry, I just don't agree. Here's how I see it. First of all, . . ." These words are typical of what you might say and hear in your day-to-day discussions of topics open for speculation or debate. When these discussions become heated, they are usually called **arguments.** In writing, the discussion doesn't have to become heated to be referred to as an argument. When you write to persuade your reader to accept your point of view as valid, the paper that results is an argument. Writing an argument paper essentially means taking a stand on some issue and supporting it.

When you write an argument paper, your intent—your purpose—is to persuade your reader. Argument isn't a type of writing; it's your aim or plan. As the writer of an argument paper, you use whatever means necessary to persuade your reader to accept your point of view; the modes are your means.

Imagine, for example, that you were writing a paper about the current desire, especially among young professionals, to rush their preschool children into early educational experiences. From what you've read and heard on this subject, this practice has as much potential for harm as for good. That's your stance, the point of view that you'll present and support. Your thesis would look like this.

> But the potential gains can't replace the hours of
> spontaneous creativity stolen from these children nor wipe
> out the tremendous stress put on them when their parents
> enroll them in nearly nonstop lessons to develop their
> talents to the greatest degree.

Your intent is to convince your reader to accept this thesis: saturating young children with educational opportunities can have serious consequences. Your success will depend on the evidence you use to support your thesis, and you'll use the modes to present that evidence.

Sometimes you primarily use one technique to present your case. For instance, you might use example as the primary mode in the argument paper about children and early educational experiences. You could provide examples of children losing out on valuable, unstructured free time, thanks to well-intentioned but overbearing parents, as well as examples of the physical effects, like ulcers, chronic headaches, and depression, seen in youngsters under such parental pressure for early success.

But you are just as likely to use a variety of modes to support your thesis and to persuade your reader. In a paper arguing against this type of early education, you might use classification to show the different types of lessons available. In the same paper, however, you might also use definition to specify the stress that some of these youngsters might suffer from, cause and effect to explain the connection between the activities and the physical illnesses that sometimes develop, and so on. In an argument paper, you must use whatever combination of modes will help you fulfill your purpose: to persuade your reader to accept your point of view.

CHOOSING VALID INFORMATION

Your argument will be valid as long as the information that supports it is. You can classify information into three general categories: fact, opinion, and personal feeling. A **fact** is a verifiable truth—something you can prove. For example, that the incumbent in a Senate election won by 200 votes in contrast to the 20,000-vote winning margin in the previous election is a fact.

Opinion is reasoning based on fact. A statement that the Senator's actions during the last terms somehow affected his or her popularity is an opinion. This statement is not fact, although it is based on a fact—the documented difference in the two margins of victory.

Personal feeling is reasoning with no factual support. To say that the Senator will no longer be effective because of the election results is personal feeling; no proof exists to support it. For instance, if the election put a real scare into the Senator, the lawmaker might return to Washington committed to work harder and as a result might become more effective. Because personal feeling has no facts to back it up, it doesn't belong in your argument paper—unless you provide facts to support it, in which case it becomes opinion.

A presentation dealing wholly with facts leaves no room for discussion; facts are truths, after all. But because opinion is reasoning based on those truths, there is room for discussion. Take the subject of book censorship, for example. One person might argue that certain books are unacceptable because they contain material that attacks the government and therefore might inspire youngsters to become less patriotic. Somebody else might present an opposite point of view: because those books attack the government, children should be exposed to them so that they will read the books, discover the flaws in them, and thus become more patriotic. Both arguments are based on the same fact— that certain books contain material that attacks the government—but the opinions are completely opposite.

Your argument paper must be a mixture of fact and opinion. Therefore, persuading your reader that laws mandating the wearing of seatbelts should be enacted means relying not only on statistics from a government study showing that wearing seatbelts dramatically reduces the chances of being thrown from a car during an accident but also on the idea that these laws might well eventually lead to a reduction in the cost of insurance premiums.

The first point is a fact; the statistical evidence is verifiable. The second is an opinion. It isn't fact — not yet anyway — but it is still valid because it has some basis in fact.

How successful you are in persuading your reader will depend on the information you use to prove your argument. Therefore make sure that you support your thesis with facts and opinions; that support is what makes an effective argument.

PREPARING AN ARGUMENT PAPER

Preparing argument papers ranks as among the most frequent writing tasks you'll face. Whether it's an essay test in an American government class, a research paper in an introduction to psychology, or a writing assignment for your English class, you'll find the argument you prepare more effective if you follow these guidelines.

1. Make sure your thesis clearly directs your reader.

No matter what you're writing about, your reader needs to know right from the beginning what point you are making. In an argument paper that point is the position you are taking on an issue. The introduction to your argument paper, then, should contain a clear direction — a thesis — for your reader.

Imagine, for instance, that you are writing about the issue of euthanasia — specifically whether families, in consultation with their doctors, should have the legal right to "pull the plug" on terminally ill family members. This is certainly a volatile issue, one that people have strong feelings about. You must make sure that your stance on the issue is clear from the start, so that your reader can be prepared for the reasoning that will support it. Look, for example, at this introductory paragraph.

> What would you do if one of your close relatives was in a coma from a bad accident or a terminal illness and the doctors told you that there was no hope of recovery? That's a question that more and more families have to face. Today, life-support systems can keep people alive almost indefinitely, even when their brains register no activity. Whether to disconnect the machines and let the individuals die or to keep them connected, maintain the treatment, and hope for a cure or recovery is a difficult question.

An introduction like this one would be ineffective because it doesn't express where you stand. But after you amplify the introduction and specify your stance, your reader will know right from the start how you feel about a subject. For instance, if you support the idea of euthanasia, you could change the introduction this way:

> What would you do if one of your close relatives was in a coma from a bad accident or a terminal illness and the doctors told you that there was no hope of recovery? That's

```
a question that more and more families have to face. Today,
life-support systems can keep people alive almost
indefinitely, even when their brains register no activity.
But keeping people alive in this way does them no service
and it prolongs the grief and adds astronomically to the
financial burden that the families suffer. Therefore, once
doctors have indicated that there is no real hope for
improvement, families should be able to order that life
support be disconnected from terminally ill patients.
```

The new sentences clearly indicate your stance in favor of euthanasia. If, however, you were against euthanasia, you could change the introduction this way:

```
     What would you do if one of your close relatives was in a
coma from a bad accident or a terminal illness and the
doctors told you that there was no hope of recovery? That's
a question that more and more families have to face. Today,
life-support systems can keep people alive almost
indefinitely, even when their brains register no activity.
Many people take this type of reading as an indication that
there is no hope of recovery, but this is simply not always
the case. Revolutionary treatments and cures are being
developed daily, and the human body has an amazing, almost
miraculous capacity for healing itself. Therefore no one
should have the right to decide when another person should
die.
```

This introduction also clearly presents your stance: euthanasia should not be allowed. In either case, you've met the needs of your reader because you've indicated what side of the issue you'll be presenting. As a result, your reader is prepared for the reasoning that will support the thesis.

2.   Acknowledge the strengths as well as the weaknesses of opposing views.

No doubt when you choose to write about a side of some issue, you feel strongly about your stance. But you shouldn't feel so strongly that you overlook the validity of some of the points of the opposing views.

In the matter of euthanasia, for example, even if your opinion is that families should have the right to turn off life-support equipment when no apparent hope for recovery exists, you must recognize that some people object to euthanasia because "pulling the plug" on a person dependent on life-support equipment means death. In your view, keeping someone alive without tangible hope for recovery might seem unfair and incorrect for everyone concerned. But someone else might well argue that keeping a person alive is the sacred responsibility of the family, or that life is not something people should take into their own hands.

Rather than ignoring an opposing view with some validity, you might present a summary of it. You might even concede the particularly strong points and then go on to show that your side of the argument is still the stronger one.

If, for example, you were writing an argument against public smoking, you would provide an introduction including a thesis something like this:

```
Only one alternative is fair for the majority of people,
and that is to ban smoking in all public places.
```

After reading this statement, your reader will certainly know where you stand on the issue—clearly against smoking. Yet smokers are people, too, and banning smoking in public places would definitely inconvenience them. Rather than ignoring this point, you should face it head on:

```
    A ban on smoking in public would be a burden for smokers.
No longer could they light up whenever they wished; some of
them might even say that such a ban would be a violation of
their rights. But nobody has the right to physically harm
somebody else. Smokers might be inconvenienced by not
being able to smoke whenever they wanted to, but they
wouldn't suffer any physical injury. Yet a smoker can harm
a nonsmoker; studies have shown that secondhand smoke is
dangerous to nonsmokers. Therefore the rights of the
majority to good health are more important than the rights
of smokers.
```

In this case, you have admitted that banning smoking might be a hardship for smokers. You've also shown, however, that legitimate reason exists for this hardship. You've conceded a point you couldn't win anyway—that smokers would be inconvenienced if public smoking were banned—and turned it to your own advantage. As a result, your argument is strengthened.

3.   Avoid using absolute terms.

The saying "Never say never" isn't completely accurate. Certainly you should never step in front of a speeding bus or dive into water over your head if you can't swim.

When you write an argument paper, however, you'll probably find absolute terms such as *never, always, every,* and *all* less useful than the more moderate versions *maybe, sometimes, often,* and *a few* or *some.* The difference between "Spanking is always a mistake on the part of parents" and "Spanking is often a mistake on the part of parents" is only one word, but the difference in the impression created is drastic. The first version condemns any use of spanking, a point of view that many parents might find too extreme. The second version doesn't condemn spanking; neither does it endorse the practice. It indicates that spanking may not be the best alternative for disciplining a child, but it also recognizes that on occasion a slap on the hand may reinforce some point a parent has made.

A more moderate version still makes the point but also allows for the different alternatives that may be necessary, depending on the circumstances. Therefore, unless you have positive evidence that absolute terms are appropriate, use qualifying terms.

4.   Avoid mistakes in logic.

In order to be successful, an argument paper must be logical, that is, correctly and reasonably thought out. Formal logic can be divided into two types: induction and deduction. Induction involves coming to a general conclusion after studying specific instances. For example, if the only time your car stalls is when it rains, you could conclude that moisture somehow affects your engine. That is inductive reasoning.

Deduction involves examining general examples to arrive at a specific observation. Imagine, for instance, you've recently been encountering poor television reception between 7 and 8 P.M. If you know that short-wave radio signals can disrupt television signals and that your neighbor has a new short-wave radio that he has been using in the evening hours, you can conclude that the short-wave radio is ruining your television reception. That's deduction.

Your concern shouldn't necessarily be whether your argument is inductive or deductive — or both. Rather, your concern should be whether your argument makes sense. If it does, it is logical.

In an argument paper, you must guard against anything that will keep some portion of your paper from making sense. For this reason, you need to be aware of these mistakes, commonly referred to as *logical fallacies.* Here are some of the most common errors in logic:

Post Hoc, Ergo Prompter Hoc.   This Latin phrase means "after this, therefore because of this," and it is mistaking coincidence for a legitimate cause–effect relationship. For instance, concluding that you developed the flu from walking across the wet grass hours earlier would be incorrect; wet grass does not cause flu. When you write, make sure that you can prove that one thing actually caused another; don't oversimplify.

Hasty Generalization.   Just as it is wrong to mistake coincidence for a legitimate cause–effect relationship, it is also incorrect to come to a conclusion on the basis of too little or unrepresentative evidence.

For example, if you come out to the mall parking lot to find your car stereo stolen and you talk to two other friends who have had similar experiences in the last year, you might conclude that the mall parking lot has a higher-than-average crime rate. Yet a little research might show that the burglary rate in the mall parking lot is actually low in comparison to that of the rest of the city. Make sure that you base your opinions on a broader basis than the experiences of a few of your friends.

Also, avoid stereotypes. All brilliant people aren't bookwormish, all artists aren't eccentric, and all graduation exercises aren't dull and boring. Be fair: the drug-overdose death of one rock musician or professional basketball player doesn't mean that all rock musicians or professional basketball players use drugs.

Make sure, too, that the evidence you use comes from a reliable source. You can't say, for instance, that the glow from a computer screen causes eye damage because your roommate told you. It's unlikely that your roommate is an expert in the field, so that opinion is unqualified. If you want to include this information, you must first verify it. You could, for instance, ask your room-mate to show you the textbook in which the information appears. Or you could speak with an expert—a computer specialist or an eye doctor. Then this information would be valid; you would have verified its accuracy. No matter what the subject, make sure you back up your point of view with valid information.

Either/Or Reasoning.   A common mistake in logic is to presume that there are only two possible sides in an argument. Take this statement, for example:

> Either governments must ban nuclear energy or the world
> faces the certainty of widespread radiation poisoning.

Yes, the possibility of widespread radiation poisoning exists, but it is also possible that there may never be a serious radiation problem or that the poi-soning won't be greatly widespread. If you recognize that a number of sides exist for most subjects, you'll avoid this type of error.

Ignoring the Question.   Sometimes it's easy to turn away from the main point you're dealing with, that is, to ignore the question. There are a number of ways to commit this error.

Sometimes, for instance, you turn from the subject to the actions of an individual associated with it. This error, referred to by its Latin name *argumen-tum ad hominem,* meaning "argument to the man," appears often in discussions about public figures, as in this example:

> Governor Newman suggests that mandatory sentences be
> imposed on people convicted of drunk driving, but what does
> she have to say about the fact that she was arrested for
> drunk driving as a teenager?

The fact that the governor had once been arrested for drunk driving has nothing to do with a proposed law that would automatically jail convicted drunk drivers. Stick to the issue, not the individual.

Also, you must avoid unfair attacks on individuals who hold opposing views. This is what happens when you make the mistake of setting up a straw man. In this fallacy, you first credit individuals who hold opposing views with saying or doing something they haven't said or done, and then you attack them for the offense. As this example shows, setting up a straw man can really distort the main issue:

> By speaking out against the actions of our government
> and our democratic allies, supporters of organizations
> like Greenpeace are endorsing communism. If these
> environmentalists think these democratic governments are
> so full of flaws, they should set up their headquarters in
> Moscow.

Greenpeace and other organizations like it have been known to run their ships in front of fishing fleets seeking endangered species of whales, for instance, or to bring lawsuits to try to block actions involving perceived dangers to the environment. But objecting to some of the actions of a democratic government and objecting to democracy and, at the same time, embracing communism are vastly different matters. Unless you can prove that your opposition has actually said or done something, stick with the truth.

Another way to ignore the question is to beg the question, that is, to state what you feel is true as truth. Look at this example:

```
I'll never understand why the public can't see through a
rabble-rouser like Phil Donahue who tries to
sensationalize every topic he discusses.
```

The problem here, of course, is that although you've offered no proof that television talk-show host Phil Donahue is a rabble-rouser, you've stated it as fact. Remember the distinction between fact and opinion or personal feeling. Don't become sidetracked by confusing fact with opinion or an individual's personality or personal life with that person's public stance.

When you write an argument paper, your job is to make sure it is logical, that it makes sense. As you write and revise, make sure there are no weaknesses in your reasoning. Avoiding the logical fallacies presented here will not guarantee that your paper will be successful, but doing so will definitely strengthen your presentation.

5.   Arrange the elements of your argument paper effectively.

In many cases, the arrangement of your paper can be the deciding factor in its success. This is particularly true of an argument paper.

An argument paper presents your stand on some issue composed of a thesis—a summary of your stand—and various examples or elements that support this thesis. Although you have a variety of arrangements to choose from, the most natural way to present these supporting elements is to start with a strong element, move to a stronger one, then move to an even stronger one, and so on. By arranging your paper this way, you'll build interest on the part of your reader.

Imagine, for example, that you were arguing that the drinking age nationwide should be twenty-one versus the eighteen to twenty standard in many states, and imagine that you were using these elements to support your thesis: a higher drinking age would cut down on the number of drunk driving incidents; a higher age limit would cut down on the number of younger students— sometimes as young as middle-school age—obtaining alcoholic beverages; and people twenty-one years old and older are generally better prepared to moderate their use of alcohol.

This supporting information would be more effective if it were arranged differently, however. First, present the material concerning a twenty-one-year-old drinking age as a means of cutting down on drinking by younger people. Although high-school-age people often have friends or younger brothers and sisters in junior high or middle school with whom they have a relatively close relationship and from whom they could get alcoholic beverages, college-age people don't generally maintain relationships with individuals in this much younger age group. This is clearly a strong reason to raise the drinking age.

Stronger, however, is the point concerning readiness to handle alcohol. Although maturity isn't directly connected to age, people are generally more responsible at twenty-one then they were at eighteen or nineteen. Further, even if they haven't attended college, twenty-one-year-old individuals are more educated because of various life experiences and contacts with other people. As a result, if teenagers are forced to wait until they turn twenty-one to drink, they will probably be better prepared to handle the responsibility that goes along with the privilege.

The strongest point, however, is that a higher drinking age would reduce the number of deaths and injuries due to drunk driving. Numerous national studies have shown that alcohol-related auto fatalities are among the major causes of death for teenagers. Many of these deaths could be prevented if these young people didn't have such ready, legal access to alcoholic beverages.

Arranging your paper this way allows you first to present a strong reason for your reader to accept your thesis. Then, once you've caught your reader's attention, you present a stronger reason. Finally you hammer home your case by presenting the strongest reason. This progression will result in effective support for your thesis.

An argument paper presents a stance and then provides support for that thesis. To make your argument paper effective, however, you must make sure that your thesis — your stance on the issue — is clear to your reader. You must also consider opposing views and use qualifying terms when they're appropriate. Your supporting ideas must be logical — they must make sense — and they must be arranged so that they build interest on the part of your reader. An argument paper that fulfills these requirements will be effective. It will meet the needs of your reader, and that's always your primary goal.

ASSIGNMENT 17 *

Take a controversial topic associated with school — some issue you're concerned about here in college or some problem in education at large — and, in a 500- to 750-word essay, take a stand and support one side of the issue.

Reason

Few people would dispute that learning is vital to success. And fewer still would claim that the educational systems available in this country are without flaw or couldn't benefit from some changes. And it is for precisely this reason that an argument paper dealing with some aspect of education will have appeal.

Think for a moment about your experiences in college so far. How are courses assigned, classes conducted, faculty evaluated, and so on? Have you found something in your collegiate education so far unfair or incorrect?

For example, imagine that your college is among those that have a mandatory attendance policy for all freshmen; if you miss six class hours of any course, your instructor must remove you from the roster. College officials maintain that this policy is important to the success of incoming freshmen, who are often overcome by the freedom of college life. Without this policy, officials explain, some students would miss more classes than they could afford to miss without truly being aware of the eventual consequences: a failing grade for the course, a poor start on a college education, possible academic probation or dismissal from school, and so on.

You feel that this policy is definitely unfair for a number of reasons. For one thing, some students can afford to miss more classes than other students can. A person who has previously studied physics or has shown a natural aptitude for the subject obviously needs less time in a required introductory physics course than someone with less experience in the subject area. Furthermore, there are some legitimate reasons to miss class, such as illness and obligations to work or to occasional time-consuming academic projects. Finally, there is the matter of maturity; college is a place for adults. Individuals who don't have the maturity to know when they belong in class are clearly not ready for college. Thus your stance is against the policy, and your statement of these reasons against the policy becomes the information supporting your stance.

But you are not restricted to writing about college issues. For instance, should we abandon graded systems and teach children at their educational levels rather than at their age levels? Should all students be required to take computer courses before they leave elementary school? Should separate elementary schools be set up for students who display some special ability or talent? Should teachers face national competency-testing? Should students with deadly diseases like AIDS be denied access to public classrooms? Should prayer be returned to the classroom? Should homosexuals be banned from teaching?

No matter what side you take on any of these questions — or on others you develop yourself — people will be interested. Learning is an important part of life, and people naturally have strong feelings about different aspects of education. To follow through on this appeal, think your stance through carefully and then provide strong support. A clear thesis and strong support for it will persuade your reader that your point of view is valid — and that's your goal in an argument paper.

What Your Reader Needs

No matter what subject you are writing about, your reader always has the same basic needs: a clear direction and information that fulfills that direction. In an argument paper, as in any other paper, you provide that direction with a clear thesis. Then you support this thesis with instances or examples proving that your stance makes sense.

Imagine, for instance that your subject is sex education — specifically, whether students should receive sex education classes from the fifth grade on. You believe they should, and to make sure that your reader understands your stance right from the beginning, you must say so clearly and directly in your thesis.

> No matter what opponents say, however, statistics showing that youngsters as young as ten are becoming sexually active are proof all by themselves that sex education classes should start by the time students begin the fifth grade.

Besides a clear, direct thesis, your reader needs proof that your point of view is legitimate. That means you must present evidence supporting your stance. In the case of this subject, several strong reasons bolster your point of view. For one thing, plenty of documentation exists showing that young people are becoming sexually active well before high school. In addition, the rate of teen-age pregnancy has continued to rise alarmingly. Finally, the physical and psychological well-being of sexually active youngsters is at risk as they face the possibility of pregnancy, venereal disease, and so on.

Of course, the opposition has some strong arguments, too. For example, if you instruct youngsters, won't you also be encouraging them to experiment? And shouldn't a subject as serious and personal as this be handled by parents rather than by teachers? By acknowledging that yes, student may experiment, and that yes, parents should be educating their children about sex, but by then pointing out that kids are experimenting now *without* the proper knowledge and that many parents are apparently either unprepared or unwilling to educate their young people, you give your reader valid responses to the main arguments of your opponents and thus strengthen your own point of view.

As you write an argument paper, your job is to persuade your reader that your stance on some subject is valid. To do this, you must express your point of view — your thesis — clearly and directly in the introduction. Then you must provide strong support for that thesis. Finally, you must restate that thesis in your conclusion. Once you've fulfilled all these requirements, you've met the needs of your reader, and you've made a persuasive presentation that proves the validity of your stance.

Model

LIBERAL ARTS <u>IS</u> A LEGITIMATE MAJOR

In today's tight economy, a college degree no longer ensures that a person will get a good job. Consequently, students are more selective about their choices of majors, and as a result, some areas of study are suffering. Among the hardest hit is liberal arts, often considered an easy, unchallenging area. But it's a mistake to abandon an area of study so valuable to the students and to the world of work they will soon join.

Liberal arts has traditionally been the target of
critics who claim that, in pragmatic terms, a degree in
liberal arts is nearly worthless. To them, the liberal arts
curriculum is not challenging enough. Further, these
critics believe that because the course offerings are so
varied, the knowledge gained about specific areas is too
general to be useful. Finally, in terms of marketable
skills, these critics suggest that liberal arts study
provides little help because it lacks focus. Yet what these
critics fail to see is that for these same reasons, a degree
in liberal arts may be especially valuable to the worker
embarking on a career.

Actually, rather than being too easy, a program in
liberal arts may be too challenging. Besides the normal
electives that a person pursuing a more specialized
associate's or bachelor's degree faces, individuals
majoring in liberal arts must choose many other electives—
up to half the program of study in some cases. Having to
choose between so many different courses creates a double
burden. First, the students must decide which of a large
listing of courses will serve their needs. Then they have
to begin study in that discipline, one that may be new to
them. Therefore the popular stereotype of a liberal arts
degree as a ''Mickey Mouse'' program concentrating on
basket-weaving and theory-of-golf classes is seldom true.

Also, the knowledge gained from the variety of courses
isn't necessarily general. Even with a wide variety of
courses to choose from, some overlap will no doubt occur.
For example, if liberal arts students take a liking to
business theory courses, they may well take a number of
courses in this field. Further, even introductory courses
provide specific information. Therefore liberal arts
students are potentially richer in knowledge; they have
received specific information in a greater number of
subject areas than the average student encounters.

Admittedly, students with a degree in liberal arts may
have few marketable skills; that is, they don't have
diplomas that say journalist or engineer or nurse. But a
diploma doesn't come with marketable skills. As anyone who
has been part of the work force for a short time can testify,
being a good worker has little to do with any degree. A
person who graduates with training in a specific discipline
is ready to begin a new job or, rather, to learn a new job.
Obviously, someone with a degree in marine biology is
theoretically better prepared to work in a fish hatchery,
especially if that company needs some sort of specialist.
But the liberal arts graduate may have sufficient
theoretical background to learn to work in the hatchery as
well as to learn to manage the plant and to write the company
newsletter.

Particularly in the last few years, the liberal arts

degree has received a great deal of criticism. But what critics fail to see is that liberal arts education does help to prepare people for the working world. Because this is the case, schools may be doing a disservice to their students by eliminating or weakening liberal arts programs. Some students require more freedom of choice in their courses. When we deny them the right to make those choices, we also undermine one of the attributes that successful people need: the ability to reason effectively. Because a study of liberal arts encourages this, it should be promoted, not attacked.

Follow-through

Your argument paper on some educational issue begins with your choice of subject. From this starting point, you will generate information that will help you solidify and support the stance you have taken on the issue.

The prewriting you do on an argument paper actually helps you develop your stance on the issue. When you first begin, you may understand in some personal way why you feel as you do about some subject, but when you put those ideas down on paper, you will be able to specify the reasons for your position.

The subject is the liberal arts degree. The particular focus in the final draft is that a liberal arts degree has much more educational value than critics grant it. The route to this specific focus begins with the prewriting, which produced the following information:

- *Mickey Mouse courses—that's what they always say about liberal arts—you hear them talk about how all the jocks on scholarship take liberal arts because it's so easy—sure some of them do, but there are a lot that take business, too, and get by—LA is just like other majors—it's as hard as you make it—How about that Lyons kid?—he was an LA major and now he's cruising through med school.*
- *Some of the specialized majors think they're so superior—LA majors almost have to set up their own course of study—much harder to do than following somebody else's plan.*
- *Don't graduate with "specialized" training—companies have to invest extra money training—makes LA grads less marketable, no real skills, a liability? —but everybody needs training when they get out of school, even specialists, so that shouldn't be all that big a deal.*
- *Courses for LA majors aren't easy, either—most times, you end up taking advanced course in a few areas—whatever you're interested in—probably learn more than the people majoring in engineering or nursing do—the only thing they can do is the one thing they're trained for, but somebody with an LA background has a really broad background—that's probably important to a company—you've had a lot of experience in a lot of areas but at least a little in other areas.*

- *Lee was like that — took a lot of biology and business courses, and was then hired at that salmon farm or whatever it was — now she spends half the time in the plant doing the actual biological-type work and running the personnel department.*
- *My adviser had a whole folder of LA grads working in all kinds of fields — she said many companies don't always care about what theories you remember because they want people whom they can train — they want a person who has received an advanced education but who isn't limited to one area — Joe specialized in political science, history, and English, and he ended up as a technical writer with a major corporation — not always so easy, though — sometimes companies need a specialist.*

This prewriting shows reasons for and against Liberal Arts as a valuable major. As you can see, however, the overwhelming evidence is in favor of Liberal Arts — evidence that solidifies the initial idea that Liberal Arts is a legitimate major to pursue. This idea is expressed in the thesis from the final draft:

```
But it's a mistake to abandon this area of study so valuable
to the students and to the world of work they will soon join.
```

With this thesis in the introduction, the reader knows right from the start the stance the paper will present.

The initial writing also presents some of ideas that buttress opposing views:

- *1. Mickey Mouse courses — that's what they always say about Liberal Arts — you hear them talk about how all the jocks on scholarship take Liberal Arts because its so easy.*
- *2. Don't graduate with "specialized" training — companies have to invest extra money training — makes LA grads less marketable, no real skills, a liability?*
- *3. Not always so easy, though — sometimes companies need a specialist*

The material about easy courses is disputed by showing that someone majoring in Liberal Arts may well take more difficult courses in various different fields, a potentially more difficult educational choice, especially if the material is new to the student.

The other two objections, however, can't be easily dismissed. Yes, there will be occasions when a company will need to hire a specialist. The final draft presents this fact; at the same time, though, it uses the strong support from the prewriting — the story of the girl who was hired to work at a fish hatchery because of her varied background — to point out that it's not a "specialists-only" world awaiting the college graduate. The result is a paper that acknowledges the strong points of opposing arguments but that nevertheless manages to rise above these points.

The logic of the paper is basically sound. Certainly an opponent might dispute some of the points. For instance, does the hypothetical example of the fish hatchery, developed from that prewriting material about the girl and the fish hatchery, qualify as evidence of the interest of the business world in people with a liberal arts background? Obviously the case of one person doesn't prove anything. However, the example isn't stated as fact; rather, it is presented as a reasonable idea, a theory that makes sense. The positions of the opponents—and not the opponents themselves—are attacked, and fact is kept separate from opinion.

The arrangement of the elements is effective, too. Following the introduction, the paper begins with a summary of the main points of the opposition: liberal arts is unchallenging, general, and unfocused. But these complaints also become the basis for the defense of liberal arts, which follows in the next three paragraphs.

The third paragraph illustrates that a liberal arts curriculum is not necessarily unchallenging, certainly an important point in the discussion. And the fourth paragraph deals with a point similar in importance: the knowledge gained is far from general. This element is presented as the second point in the argument, however, because it is more crucial to the topic of a liberal arts education as a step toward a career; the paragraph talks about the overall impact of education in terms of a person's importance to a business. The fifth paragraph presents the strongest support for the thesis: a liberal arts degree provides such a broad base of education that its bearer may be more attractive to employers than other applicants.

All of this is followed up by a conclusion that restates the thesis, that the study of liberal arts helps to develop thinking, possibly the most important attribute of the successful individual. As obvious as this point may seem by now, the importance of liberal arts to the working world is restated as well.

An effective argument paper is a carefully arranged series of elements. The result of this combination of a clear thesis, supporting examples, and a restated thesis is an argument that makes sense. No matter what your subject or your reason for writing, that's always your goal.

Checklist

Use the answers to the following questions to help you revise your first draft:

1. Does your paper have a clear thesis? Write it down
2. Have you acknowledged the strengths of the opposing arguments?
3. Are all the points in your argument logical?
4. Have you arranged the elements of your argument effectively?
5. Does your introduction provide a clear direction for your reader?
6. Does your conclusion restate the significance of your argument?

ASSIGNMENT 18

Take some controversial issue associated with entertainment (show business, sports, the arts, and so on), and in a 500- to 750-word essay, take a stand and support one side of the issue.

Reason

Fun and diversion — that's what entertainment provides for us. Whether it's a television show, a movie, a game, a concert, or a play, people are interested in various aspects of each subject — including the controversial sides. Should the movie rating system be tightened up or made less restrictive? Should professional athletes be subjected to random drug testing? Should major television programmers like CBS, NBC, and ABC be forced to allot more time to educational and public-service broadcasting? Should works of art featuring nudity be kept in a separate, restricted area of museums? No matter what the question, people are interested; many already have strong opinions about these issues. As a result, a paper presenting a stand on some side of a controversial issue associated with the world of entertainment will definitely have appeal.

For example, how much support should the government provide for educational television? Under the current system, public broadcasting stations are chronically short of money. The equipment of the stations is often second-rate — or worse — and the personnel are underpaid in relation to their commercial counterparts. All in all, the offerings on educational channels are simply too valuable and entertaining to entrust to voluntary contributions and second-class broadcasting conditions. Therefore, some people feel that the government should provide full financial support for educational channels.

In your judgment, however, full government support would be the worst thing that could happen to educational television. For one thing, you believe that the major corporations that now support public broadcasting stations owe something to the consumers, a responsibility that, thus far, the corporations have accepted. Once the government intervenes, however, you feel that these corporations will have one more reason to forget about the needs of the public.

You also feel that the regular on-air fund-raising that occasionally seems like public begging is also important. Taking things for granted is too easy for most of us, and educational television is one of those things. Like corporations, individuals have responsibilities, too. If people want to be able to watch fine shows and specials like "NOVA," "The Macneil/Lehrer Report," "Masterpiece Theatre," "Sesame Street," and "National Geographic," they should help support them. The pleasure and education they gain from the broadcasts are certainly worth a small contribution.

Finally, there is the point of control. Holding the purse strings generally means exercising some editorial power. If the government provided the financial support, educational stations would lose independence from government control they now have. Maybe they would no longer be able to broadcast programs critical of the government; and if these programs were shown, perhaps they'd be broadcast in a heavily censored form. Turning educational television over to the government is simply not worth the risk.

Your thesis is that educational television should be supported by private and corporate sponsors rather than by the government treasury, and you've followed through on this thesis by providing arguments that back it up. Thus you illustrate the validity of your point of view.

The world of entertainment — show business, the arts, or athletics — has great appeal for most people. Along with this appeal comes an interest in many different sides of each subject. A paper on a controversial aspect or one of these subjects, then, will have appeal because it will offer the reader one more point of view on a subject about which the reader has probably already developed an opinion.

What Your Reader Needs

With a controversy associated with entertainment, you already have the interest of your reader in your favor. To capitalize on this interest, you need to prove that your stand has validity. In other words, you need to provide a clear thesis and then back it up with strong support — you need to meet your reader's needs.

First of all, your reader needs to know right from the start what the issue is and what your stance on it is. Imagine, for example, that your subject is the video cassette recorder (VCR). Many people feel that the VCR may well spell the end of movie theaters. These individuals suggest that rather than going to the movie theaters, people will stay home and watch movies in the convenience of their own homes. And the widespread — though illegal — practice of copying movie tapes, they suggest, will eventually bring about widespread financial disaster for the movie industry, which, in turn, will affect the number and quality of movies in the future.

In your view, however, the VCR explosion will neither wipe out the theaters nor negatively affect the movie business. For one thing, watching a movie at a theater is very different from watching one at home. It's a night out, one of the most time-honored social outings, and you don't believe that people will radically change their social habits. Television was supposed to wipe out movie theaters back in the 1950s and 1960s; theaters changed, yes, but they didn't disappear.

Furthermore the movie theaters have a lock on the newest movies, which are generally not available on cassette until six months or more after their release date. As you see it, people will still be more likely to pay the extra money to see a new movie on its release than to wait months until the cassette is available.

Although you admit that copying tapes is a widespread practice, you feel that most people are more interested in seeing movies than in owning them. Also, with rental rates so inexpensive, you believe that fewer people will continue to go to the trouble of copying movie tapes.

In fact, as you see it, the growing popularity of VCRs will make the movie industry stronger. First, people who enjoy a movie in a theater will be more likely to rent or buy the cassette. This trend, in turn, will help the movie as a entertainment form; moviemakers will benefit from this double interest. In addition more VCRs mean a larger market for and a larger interest in movies. Rather than facing a recession, the movie industry may have to begin making more movies to satisfy the growing audience.

To meet the needs of your reader, your introduction must clearly convey your stance. Otherwise your reader would be misled and confused, as would happen if this were the opening paragraph.

It used to be that the only ways you could see a movie were
to go to a neighborhood theater or to watch an edited
version with plenty of commercials on one of the networks.
But these are no longer your only alternatives; now you can
watch a movie uncut, in the convenience of your own home.
All you need is a video cassette recorder—a VCR—a cassette
of the movie, and a compatible TV. These VCRs are bringing
about the biggest revolution the movie industry and movie-
goers have ever seen.

The problem with this paragraph is that it doesn't let the reader know your
stance. This second version, however, provides this needed element.

It used to be that the only ways you could see a movie were
to go to a neighborhood theater or to watch an edited
version with plenty of commercials on one of the networks.
But these are no longer your only alternatives; now you can
watch a movie, uncut, in the convenience of your own home.
All you need is a video cassette recorder—a VCR—a cassette
of the movie, and a compatible TV. Some people have said
that the mushrooming VCR sales will put movie theaters out
of business and cost the movie industry millions, but it's
more likely that the increasing popularity of VCRs will
actually be a major benefit for everybody concerned.

This introduction is effective because it provides a direction for the reader—a
specific thesis. With this thesis, the various supporting reasons make sense for
your reader—and that's your primary goal.

In order for your reader to understand your argument paper, it must be
logical. A logical argument paper begins with a clear thesis, with strong examples supporting it, and ends with a conclusion restating your stance. Once your
paper fulfills these requirements, it will make sense for your reader, which is
always your main objective.

Model

RESTRICTING OFFENSIVE TELEVISION COMMERCIALS

If there is an area of television programming that needs
further attention, it is the commercials. Far too many of
the ads on television today are objectionable for any
number of reasons. Some of the commercials are annoying,
some of them are demeaning, and some of them, if not
dishonest, are deceptive to some degree. Because
television commercials reach an enormous number of
viewers, including impressionable children, something
should be done to restrict the objectionable ones.

Of course, not all commercials are objectionable. Some
companies that do the hardest selling, like Maxwell House
Coffee or AT&T, have ads that put across their message

without alienating the public. Unfortunately, in today's programming, there are too few of this type.

The commercials most people label offensive are the idiotic ones. Who doesn't know, for instance, that Mr. Whipple secretly squeezes the Charmin tissue or that Wisk combats that terrible condition called ''ring around the collar''? Mention ''Ginsu'' and people will answer ''knives''; say ''K-tel'' and people will say ''records.'' From beginning to end, from character to jingle, these types of commercials are annoying and ridiculous. Ironically, though, they are effective because the audience does remember the names of the products being sold. Certainly some people will be so annoyed that they won't buy the product, but the many commercials using this tactic prove that the risk is obviously worth taking.

Sex in advertising is among the most unfair and demeaning techniques used. Besides the subliminal sexual message, there is the insulting use of the human body, usually a female body, to sell some product. A good example of this practice is a recent Diet Pepsi commercial that quickly focuses on a woman from the neck down, with the camera shot finally centering on her crotch. The message here is clear: Diet Pepsi is sexual excitement in a can. Bon Jour jeans and Nair hair remover are two other products whose commercials exploit women. Like the annoying characters and jingles in other ads, sex in commercials is all too common.

Commercials geared to children, however, should be subject to the biggest reform because kids are perhaps the least equipped people to deal with the temptations these commercials present. The magic of television can make sugary breakfast cereals, for example, even more attractive. The young actors and actresses who sing and dance about Apple Jacks and the cartoon wizard who tells kids that the little cookies in Cookie Crisp are great for breakfast are usually too much to resist for a young audience. Fast-food giants like McDonald's and Burger King operate on the same principle: Eating there is so much fun, what kid could refuse? Companies should have a right to advertise, but taking advantage of trusting children just isn't fair.

By far the most offensive commercials for children are the ads for toys. Although there are more of them on during the Christmas season, toy commercials are a daily component of television programming. These commercials present the toys in the best possible situations. But young children generally aren't able to understand that the Mattel toy motorcycle that looks like so much fun as it jumps from one giant pile of dirt to the next on television will look pretty tame in their houses unless they also happen to have two giant piles of dirt. Although the commercial for the Snoopy Sno-Cone Machine does say that some assembly is required, it doesn't explain how much actual physical strength will be needed for a child to grind an ice cube by hand with the machine. Both commercials, and many more like it, leave children wide open for disappointment and frustration.

No one is suggesting that advertisers be denied a chance to sell their products to the public. However, techniques that patronize, demean, or deceive the audience should be curtailed. The buying public could play a major part in this reform if they simply sent word to the companies that they object to these types of commercials. When profits are concerned, companies can be very attentive to their customers. It is unrealistic to suggest that everything objectionable can immediately be eliminated from television commercials. Still, television advertising can be made more acceptable so that neither children nor adults have to wonder if they are being tricked.

Follow-through

In an argument paper on a controversial subject from the world of entertainment, the topic will already have appeal. To capitalize on this appeal, you must first identify your subject and your stance. Then you must present evidence strong enough to support that thesis and thus persuade your reader to accept your point of view.

Once you've chosen your topic, you must generate the material from which you will construct a logical argument. In the case of this paper, the topic is obviously a good choice: television viewers are bombarded every several minutes by commercials, many of them offensive for a variety of reasons. The prewriting for this paper produced the following information:

Worst commercials are for toys — they suck the kids in, make them think the toys will do all the stuff they show — cars jumping over hills — they'd never really do that — and you can hardly understand the talking dolls — that Sno-Cone machine I bought for Aaron — I thought my arm would fall off after turning that stupid crank for five minutes to get one cup of mush — no way any kid could do that — it needs an adult's power — Saturday morning is filled with commercials for toys and cereals too — all that sugary junk and they sell it like a Hollywood show — I hate the toilet paper ads, especially Charmin with that stupid store manager Whipple — it makes you remember the product, though — same thing for Wisk with "Ring around the collar" — even the ones for K-tel records and Ginsu knives — they look as if they were made by some amateur in his basement but you remember them — I don't think we'll be seeing Ginsu ads anymore, bankrupt, I think, but it wasn't from paying for those terrible commercials — some commercials are pretty good though — the phone company ones about long distance are super — coffee, too — I read that they use molasses to make the coffee look richer and darker on television — I wonder if that's legal? — nobody ever puts cream or milk in it, at least not so that you can see it — some of the fast-food ads are entertaining but they try to con kids, too — adults get conned, too, like when that girl in the commercial for jeans almost beats the guy with a whip — weird — they've got a right to sell things, but they really shouldn't trick people or confuse or shock them — those soda commercials do it, too — that one with the girl coming out of the water — you never see her face — they focus on the top of her suit as she walks until finally all you can see is her crotch — it's like a porno movie, and it's on regular television — what's that got to do with soda, anyway? — other ads like that too, nylons, health clubs, hair remover — "Do this, take this, wear this, and you'll be sexy, too" and we're as bad as the kids because we buy that junk, too.

In particular, the prewriting provides the basis for a clear thesis, which, in the final draft, appears at the end of the introduction.

```
Because television commercials reach an enormous number of
viewers, including impressionable children, something
should be done to restrict the objectionable ones.
```

Once the thesis is established, the next step involves drawing support from the information generated. The prewriting contains the seeds for the final draft; the information, however, must be amplified and clarified. Look, for instance, at this passage from the freewriting:

I hate the toiler paper ads, especially Charmin with that stupid store manager Whipple — it makes you remember the product, though — same thing for Wisk with "ring around the collar" — even the ones for K-Tel records and Ginsu knives — they look as if they were made by some amateur in his basement but you remember them — I don't think we'll be seeing Ginsu ads anymore, bankrupt, I think, but it wasn't from paying for those terrible commercials.

The information is the basis for the third paragraph of the final draft, but as it is in the prewriting, the information is confusing. Once it is amplified and clarified, however, this same information is transmitted into the clear, coherent, effective paragraph that appears in the final draft:

```
    The commercials most people label offensive are the
idiotic ones. Who doesn't know, for instance, that Mr.
Whipple secretly squeezes the Charmin tissue or that Wisk
combats that terrible condition called ''ring around the
collar.'' Mention ''Ginsu'' and people will answer
''knives''; say ''K-tel'' and people will say ''records.''
From beginning to end, from character to jingle, these
types of commercials are annoying and ridiculous.
Ironically, though, they are effective because the
audience does remember the names of the products being
sold. Certainly some people will be so annoyed that they
won't buy the product, but the many commercials using this
tactic prove that the risk is obviously worth taking.
```

As the prewriting shows, ideas dealing with the positive side of advertising were also generated. This information isn't conveniently overlooked in the final draft, however. Certainly advertisers have the right to sell their products, and some commercials are tasteful and entertaining. These points are clearly acknowledged in the final draft; the second paragraph mentions two specific companies that air effective and nonobjectionable commercials, and the fifth and seventh paragraphs reaffirm the rights of advertisers. As the final draft shows, however, these points don't weaken the argument; they instead make it all the more valid.

In order to make your argument effective, you must arrange the various elements so that they have the biggest impact on your reader. This paper, for example, first presents the thesis—that something should be done to restrict offensive television commercials—and then admits that some commercials are *not* objectionable. It is a fine lead-in to the discussion of the commercials that are offensive. In the third paragraph, examples are presented of commercials that are objectionable because they are silly and idiotic. This is a strong paragraph; people should not be subjected to commercials that insult their sensibilities or intelligence.

The fourth paragraph, however, moves to a more serious point: commercials that are offensive because they use sex and demean women to sell products. Commercials that insult a person's intelligence are one thing; commercials relying on sexual innuendo or treating humans as objects are quite another.

But the final examples are the most serious because they involve children, a group of people who are the least prepared to handle any deceptive advertising. The arrangement is effective because it moves from a serious example, to a more serious example, to the most serious examples in order to build reader interest. Once these examples are presented, the thesis is restated in the concluding paragraph.

```
However, techniques that patronize, demean, or deceive the
audience should be curtailed.
```

The rest of the conclusion suggests a way to deal with the problem of objectionable commercials: when the public find something upsetting about some commercial, they should notify the advertisers. Suggesting a solution in the concluding paragraph is not always appropriate, but as you can see, it is a very effective technique in this draft.

An argument paper is your opportunity to express your stance on some subject. To communicate this stance effectively, you must first let your reader know your position on the issue; that is, you must express your thesis. Then you must provide clear, coherent examples that strongly support that thesis. Once you restate that thesis, your job is complete because your paper has fulfilled its purpose; it has met the needs of your reader.

Checklist

Use the answers to the following questions to help you revise your first draft:

1. Does your paper have a clear thesis? Write it down.
2. Have you acknowledged the strengths of the opposing arguments?
3. Are all the points in your argument logical?
4. Have you arranged the elements of your argument effectively?
5. Does your introduction provide a clear direction for your reader?
6. Does your conclusion restate the significance of your argument?

FOR FURTHER STUDY

All the doubts, frustrations, and questions that death raises are problems we must all deal with. For physician and researcher Allan J. Hamilton, however, death is an ever-present concern. To deal with the question of how far doctors and researchers should go in prolonging life through extraordinary means, Hamilton has focused on the story of David, who, born without any natural protection from diseases, spent his life in a plastic bubble.

Who Shall Live and Who Shall Die

ALLAN J. HAMILTON

The bizarre life and recent death of David, the boy in the bubble, have left me strangely upset. I am a physician and a researcher, and David's story seems to pose serious and fundamental questions about human existence in general and its relation to the medical community.

Within that bubble, I fear, lies the hint of some monstrous metaphor about life itself that both beckons and appalls one at the prospect of its revelation. Perhaps the original sin committed by the medical profession was discovering that one of David's siblings had died of SCID, which is the abbreviation for severe combined immune deficiency syndrome. Armed with this knowledge and anxious to have a candidate for study and research, physicians at Baylor College of Medicine delivered David from the womb and whisked him away from his impending doom into a sterile incubator. Lest I paint the picture too dark, we should realize that David would have died in a matter of days to weeks had doctors not invented some way to preserve his life. So, born defenseless, there was no way to protect him other than to leave him unborn in a sense, to let him live out his days in a perpetual womb of polyethylene.

David's immunological innocence, his fateful inability to fight back, made it necessary for him to shun contact with this world lest it kill him. He commands our attention, like some divine emissary sent down from heaven in the purest state of grace who is therefore unable to withstand the bacterial bickering and microbial murders of our wantonly pestilent world. Like fervent priests, the scientists and physicians attended to him and labored for years to preserve him in his state of immunological grace.

The price that David paid to live among but isolated from us no one will truly comprehend but the boy and those who loved him. For the majority of his life David never felt the vital and comforting warmth of a fellow being's soothing touch. Up until the very end he had never heard the human voice arriving at his ear undistorted by the electronic gadgetry that zealously protected him within the plastic domain. All of his food, his clothes, the paper he wrote on, the sheets he slept on, the books, the toys, all the material objects of his life passed through vacuum-sealed doors, through huge, hissing autoclaves, under disinfecting beams of ultraviolet light before they could reach him. It is testament to our technology and the devotion of David's doctors that they were able to maintain him for such a long time within the bubble. No germ had yet reached him. Still, your heart never stopped aching as you saw him striving against all odds to be a little boy like any other lad his age. You also felt yourself cheering for every medical and scientific advance that permitted David to approach what we all know as real life outside of the bubble.

Then there came a real hope, a real chance. David was now 12 years old. In some traditions that is an age when a child assumes his adult identity and with the help of his elders assumes the mantle of the warrior. So the great men of medicine in their long white coats gathered and tried to find a suitable donor from whom David might get the right white cells to defend himself, to become a true immunological warrior within his tribe. No exact match could be found, as if David's innocence once again placed him alone among his fellow men. The physicians at Baylor College of Medicine transplanted bone-marrow cells from David's sister, who was the closest tissue match they could find. The greatest fear was that his sister's white cells might try to attack David's body once they were injected within him. We may never know if this valiant experiment worked, for David did not live long enough for us to see a definitive result. Within a few days David began to get quite sick and it was necessary to take him out of the bubble. Like the hero in a mythological tale, he emerged from his womb a grown man of 12, pushing himself bravely into our deadly world of microbes and disease. For a brief lifespan of two weeks he lived truly among us. For the first time he felt his mother's kiss, her arms around him and his around her.

One cannot ask David or his family if living inside a bubble for 12 years was worth it. They do not need to justify themselves to us but rather we, in the research and medical communities, must ask that question of ourselves. If our own children were to be doomed to a lifetime of deprivation and isolation, could we justify it as a laudable scientific effort? We might also ask if SCID-syndrome patients should be kept alive at extravagant expense to the public. For the same hundreds of thousands of dollars it has taken to keep a mere handful of SCID-syndrome patients alive (none of whom has lived as long as David), how many thousands of healthy children could have been saved who died of simple things like a burn, an infection or malnutrition — simple things that a few thousand dollars in judicious programs might have prevented.

As a researcher, I am haunted by David's life and death. I share in a common guilt to which all of us within academic medicine must admit, an ambitious hunger for new discoveries. While we do truly labor for the common good, we also strive for personal recognition; our own egos bob embarrassingly to the surface of swelling altruism. In a way, David was a pawn in this game of discoveries because he was one of the guinea pigs. He would have died had he not been maintained in isolation; he also lived to be the object of research.

All research applications must begin somewhere, and so it is with SCID syndrome or artificial hearts or liver transplants. Ultimately, one human being has to come forward to be an experimental subject. I am sure that there is a great deal about SCID syndrome and the function of the immune system to be learned from David's life and that the knowledge acquired may be worth the emotional and the financial cost of the experiment. The nagging doubt that I have about David was that he was never offered the option of volunteering to be part of the experiment; he was born into it.

Questions for Study

1. Write a short paragraph summing up Hamilton's stand on this issue.
2. Hamilton's initial paragraph doesn't provide a clear direction. In fact, his thesis is spread out over the first three paragraphs. Prepare a more traditional introduction for his argument.
3. Hamilton used a description of David's lifestyle to help make his point. Make a list of the details of David's difficult life that you feel have the most impact.
4. In a few sentences, paraphrase the researcher's dilemma that Hamilton identified.
5. In the sixth paragraph, Hamilton raised the question of expense, specifically whether it makes more sense to spend the money on a vastly greater number of children suffering from less exotic conditions or diseases rather than to spend tremendous amounts of money on a "mere handful" of individuals who are probably doomed to die anyway. In a hundred-word paragraph, give your stance on this controversy.

ALTERNATE ASSIGNMENT S

Hamilton summed up the basis of this controversy when, toward the end of his essay, he asked, "If our own children were to be doomed to a lifetime of deprivation and isolation, could we justify it as a laudable scientific effort?" For this writing, present your stance on this issue: Is experimentation that results in prolonging the life of an individual worthwhile, regardless of the quality of life it produces?

Before a heart condition forced him from the ranks, Arthur Ashe was one of the world's top tennis players. Natural talent, hard work, and determination marked Ashe as one of the great athletes of his time. Further distinguishing Ashe is the fact that he made his mark in tennis, a game that seems still to have an invisible color line. Yet, as a black man who had made his living as a professional athlete, Ashe took a stand that might surprise some people about sports as a road to success.

An Open Letter to Black Parents: Send Your Children to the Libraries

ARTHUR ASHE

Since my sophomore year at University of California, Los Angeles, I have become convinced that we blacks spend too much time on the playing fields and too little time in the libraries.

Please don't think of this attitude as being pretentious just because I am a black, single, professional athlete. I don't have children, but I can make observations. I strongly believe the black culture expends too much time, energy and effort raising, praising and teasing our black children as to the dubious glories of professional sport.

All children need models to emulate—parents, relatives or friends. But when the child starts school, the influence of the parent is shared by teachers and classmates, by the lure of books, movies, ministers and newspapers, but most of all by television. Which televised events have the greatest number of viewers?—Sports—the Olympics, Super Bowl, Masters, World Series, pro basketball play-offs, Forest Hills. ABC-TV even has sports on Monday night prime time from April to December. So your child gets a massive dose of O. J. Simpson, Kareem Abdul-Jabbar, Muhammad Ali, Reggie Jackson, Dr. J. and Lee Elder and other pro athletes. And it is only natural that your child will dream of being a pro athlete himself.

But consider these facts. For the major professional sports of hockey, football, basketball, baseball, golf, tennis and boxing, there are roughly only 3,170 major league positions available (attributing 200 positions to golf, 200 to tennis and 100 to boxing). And the annual turnover is small. We blacks are a subculture of about 28 million. Of the 13½ million men, 5 to 6 million are under 20 years of age, so your son has less than one chance in 1,000 of becoming a pro. Less than one in a thousand. Would you bet your son's future on something with odds of 999 to 1 against you? I wouldn't.

Unless a child is exceptionally gifted you should know by the time he enters high school whether he has a future as an athlete. But what is more important is what happens if he doesn't graduate or doesn't land a college scholarship and doesn't have a viable alternative job career. Our high school dropout rate is several times the national average, which contributes to our unemployment rate of roughly twice the national average.

And how do you fight the figures in the newspapers every day? Ali has earned more than $30 million boxing, O. J. just signed for $2½ million, Dr. J. for almost $3 million, Reggie Jackson for $2.8 million, Nate Archibald for $400,000 a year. All that money, recognition, attention, free cars, girls, jobs in the offseason—no wonder there is Pop Warner football, Little League baseball, National Junior Tennis League tennis, hockey practice at 5 A.M. and pickup basketball games in any center city at any hour.

There must be some way to assure that the 999 who try but don't make it to pro sports don't wind up on the street corners or in the unemployment lines. Unfortunately, our most widely recognized role models are athletes and entertainers—"runnin'" and "jumpin'" and "singin'" and "dancin'." While we are 60 percent of the National Basketball Association, we are less than 4 percent of the doctors and lawyers. While we are about 35 percent of major league baseball, we are less than 2 percent of the engineers. While we are about 40 percent of the National Football League, we are less than 11 percent of construction workers such as carpenters and bricklayers.

Our greatest heroes of the century have been athletes—Jack Johnson, Joe Louis and Muhammad Ali. Racial and economic discrimination forced us to channel our energies into athletics and entertainment. These were the ways out of the ghetto, the ways to get that Cadillac, those alligator shoes, the cashmere sport coat.

Somehow, parents must instill a desire for learning alongside the desire to be Walt Frazier. Why not start by sending black professional athletes into high schools to explain the facts of life? I have often addressed high school audiences and my message is always the same. For every hour you spend on the athletic field, spend two in the library. Even if you make it as a pro athlete, your career will be over by the time you are thirty-five. So you will need that diploma.

Have these pro athletes explain what happens if you break a leg, get a sore arm, have one bad year or don't make the cut for five or six tournaments. Explain to them the star system, wherein for every O. J. earning millions there are six or seven others making $15,000 or $20,000 or $30,000 a year.

But don't just have Walt Frazier or O. J. or Abdul-Jabbar address your class. Invite a benchwarmer or a guy who didn't make it. Ask him if he sleeps every night. Ask him whether he was graduated. Ask him what he would do if he became disabled tomorrow. Ask him where his old high school athletic buddies are.

We have been on the same roads—sports and entertainment—too long. We need to pull over, fill up at the library and speed away to Congress and the Supreme Court, the unions and the business world. We need more Barbara Jordans, Andrew Youngs, union cardholders, Nikki Giovannis and Earl Graveses. Don't worry: we will still be able to sing and dance and run and jump better than anybody else.

I'll never forget how proud my grandmother was when I graduated from U.C.L.A. in 1966. Never mind the Davis Cup in 1968, 1969, and 1970. Never mind the Wimbledon title, Forest Hills, etc. To this day, she still doesn't know what those names mean. What matters to her was that of her more than thirty children and grandchildren, I was the first to be graduated from college, and a famous college at that. Somehow, that made up for all those floors she scrubbed all those years.

Questions for Study

1. Ashe's first two paragraphs present his thesis. Paraphrase it in a sentence.
2. In many ways, Ashe's conclusion may be the most effective of all his examples. In a brief paragraph, explain how the story about his grandmother restates the significance of his argument.
3. Make a list of the facts and statistics that Ashe used to support his argument, and identify which one you think has the most impact.
4. Ashe made his living as a professional athlete; furthermore, as he has admitted in the second paragraph, he has no children. Do you feel that these facts somehow weaken his case?
5. Although in this essay Ashe specifically addressed black parents and provided specific evidence directly related to black families, he also included

information appropriate for all families. List the evidence Ashe presented having universal appeal.

ALTERNATE ASSIGNMENT T

Arthur Ashe's argument deals with a crucial issue: child rearing. In his view, black parents are dead wrong when they cultivate success in athletics above all else for their children.

Whether Ashe's view is correct or incorrect, raising children is an imprecise science; parents make mistakes every day. Some parents, for instance, base their child rearing on extreme permissiveness or extreme discipline, excessive pressure for academic success, emphasis on material goods, and so on, with the hope of helping their children achieve success and happiness. For this assignment, write an essay persuading these well-intentioned but mistaken parents to change their point of view.

HOW I WROTE IT

Aleksandr Who?

WILLIAM J. KELLY

Not too long ago, a farmer in a rural Rhode Island community initiated a fight to remove Aleksandr Solzhenitsyn's book, *The Gulag Archipelago,* from the reading list at his son's high school. His actions are not rare; unfortunately, book censorship is on the rise nationally. More unfortunate is the fact that he may eventually succeed.

Recently, I took an informal survey among my high school freshmen. When I counted hands, I found that 67 of 93 had their own television sets over which *they* exercise absolute control.

Amazing, isn't it? While courts debate the corrupting power of a mere book, this video generation spins the dial to catch yet another rerun of "Gilligan's Island." The real absurdity here is that the farmer's drive to ban the book may well be unnecessary. With television so readily available to them, how many students will be disciplined or practiced enough to read and understand this text? How many would even blink their eyes if told that Solzhenitsyn is just another washed-up movie star making a guest appearance on "The Love Boat" or "Fantasy Island"?

Instead of raiding the shelves of our school libraries, parents should redirect their efforts and take a closer look at their children's favorite pastime. In the last few years, television has received its share of broadsides, and rightfully so. For a medium with so much promise, its product is miserable.

At least partially to blame for this is the current ratings system—it stifles creativity. Since ratings dictate scheduling, a program must gain and maintain an audience or it is axed. In the prime-time battle, new shows, regardless of quality or value, must compete with established programs. Too often, imaginative new offerings have little chance. Therefore, the networks respond by giving the public pale imitations of the more successful shows. The result is prime-time fare that is neither challenging nor entertaining — ubiquitous blandness from channel to channel.

Daytime television also deserves attention, particularly the daytime dramas which have enjoyed such a surge in popularity. Every day, the sex and violence exorcised from prime-time programming appear, readily available to the very population from whom they were removed in the first place. For instance, the most popular of the soaps celebrated for awhile the questionable adventures of a thief/ rapist and a murderess (and his victim, turned lover), Luke and Laura. In a perversity peculiar to television, they were featured, along with their counterparts from the other network soap operas, in a promo entitled, "Love in the Afternoon." So much for the battle for morality on television.

Of course, all this is underwritten by advertisers who hawk their wares in the tradition of mountebanks and carnival barkers. Recently, a judge ordered the major makers of pain-relievers to admit that the active ingredient in each brand is simply aspirin. This follows an earlier case after which a mouthwash manufacturer was forced to inform the public that its product did nothing to combat the common cold. Both cases suggest that, in the world of television, you can make an advertisement say whatever you like, as long as you don't get caught.

Add the newscasts that sometimes distort, exaggerate, or even misreport the news (witness the "late" James Brady), the numerous specials with little special about them, and the various game shows and reruns, and you have a quick portrait of a broadcasting day.

However, don't view this as a proposal to censor television. Actually, the content of the shows is not the problem. Instead, it is the amount of time that students spend viewing mediocre material that should be the greatest concern.

Watching television is a passive experience; it doesn't require the viewer to *do* anything. No imagination is needed, since one is provided, in living color, complete with artificial emotions and atmosphere. The only active participation possible is when the network shows are off and a computer game is attached to the set. Then a person can, for example, practice blowing up planets and destroying millions of aliens. Would that one could do that to t.v. executives.

At best, the actual effects of watching too much television are difficult to measure, as the murder defendant who claimed he overdosed on "Kojak" found out. However, it *is* reasonable to assume that, unsupervised, students will sit and watch television because it is simply easier to do than more complex homework, which brings us back to the original point. Regardless of what any censor says, books are not a menace. At least reading stimulates thinking; no such guarantee is issued with a television set. Instead of slapping a lock on the library door, parents should shut off the television and encourage reading.

Not too long ago, a mother in a rural Maine town began a fight to remove Ronald J. Glasser's book, *365 Days*, a text which deals with the Vietnam War, from the reading list at her step-daughter's high school. Her actions are just further evidence of the rise of censorship.

Still, perhaps I am the one over-reacting. After all, students can probably learn about that episode in recent American history some other way.

I think I saw something about it in *T.V. Guide*—or was it on a commercial?

Two news items, one about an attempt in a Rhode Island town to ban Solzhenitsyn's *The Gulag Archipelago* and the other about an attempt in a Maine town to ban Glasser's *365 Days*, first brought me to write this argument paper. I personally feel students are better off reading these so-called objectionable books in the classroom, where a teacher can explain the significance, rather than in secret without any explanation or guidance.

I was again motivated a few days after reading these articles when I was covering a ninth-grade study hall of thirty or so students, most of whom came with nothing to do. Out of curiosity, I asked how many of them had their own televisions. The results so surprised me that I surveyed the rest of my ninth-grade students. The results of my survey showed that more than two out of every three claimed they had their own personal television sets and could watch whatever they wanted—including the cable programming many of them had—whenever they wanted.

"Why in the world would people bother trying to ban books?" I thought. Two out of three of my students spent most of their free time with television. When these students see adults essentially saying, "Don't read," they simply have one more excuse to turn on their personal television sets.

That became my focus, set forth in the third paragraph:

> With television so readily available to them, how many
> students will be disciplined or practiced enough to read
> and understand the text?

I had plenty of examples of unimaginative programming to draw on from shows like "The Love Boat" and "Fantasy Island." I blamed this situation in part on an industry that shies away from change. Furthermore, I had soap operas, commercials, and newscasts to pick on.

And pick on them I did. When I sat down to write, I remembered the specific examples that appear in the final draft: the promo for soap operas featuring two characters from my ninth-graders' then favorite soap opera, "General Hospital"; the stories of those two companies forced to change their deceptive advertising; the incorrect report that Presidential Press Secretary James Brady, severely wounded in the attempted assassination of President Ronald Reagan, had died; and the law case in Florida involving the defendant who claimed he had overdosed on television watching.

Despite these complaints about television, my intent was not to censor television. I'm opposed to censorship, period. My point was that young people, especially high-school-age students, waste valuable time watching television, time they could be using to read. I used my complaints about the quality of television to underscore my original point: parents shouldn't be banning books because that action discourages reading.

Because I had the two book-banning stories to work with, I chose to begin and end with an example. I intended the ironic reference to *TV Guide* in the final paragraph as a restatement of the thesis in the third paragraph. And I arranged the various complaints about television in what I felt was a least-to-most-significant order so that these examples would encapsulate my thesis. Parents shouldn't ban books; they should encourage reading and discourage watching mindless television programming.

ALTERNATE ASSIGNMENT U

This argument paper is based in part on two news items concerning attempts by parents to force school systems to ban books. Where do you stand on this issue? Do individual parents, on the basis of their own social, religious, or political views, have the right to dictate to school departments what books should or should not be read? For this assignment, present your stance on this controversial issue.

Index

Spatial order
  defined, 153
  within a division paper, 247
  within an example paper, 153
Spelling, 55–56
Statement of purpose
  defined, 12
  examples of, 12–13
Stephens, Carla
  "Drownproofing," 143–144
Stream-of-consciousness, 4
Strunk, William
  Elements of Style, The, 48
Style, 51
Subject, 21
Subject/verb agreement
  defined, 57
  examples of, 57
  ways to correct faults with, 57
Subjective description
  defined, 101
  versus objective description, 101
Summary
  defined, 34
  example of, 35
  versus paraphrase
Syfers, Judy
  "I Want a Wife," 262–263

Tense
  defined, 56
  maintaining consistency with, 56
Thesis
  as the common thread, 24
  defined, 15
  development of, 15–16
  editing as you revise, 17
  identifying its effectiveness, 17–18
  limited definition as part, 178, 182
  versus statement of fact, 17
  versus statement of purpose, 15, 17
  versus title, 17–18
  use of
    within alternating format, 196
    within argument paper, 265–266, 267–268, 269, 272, 274–275, 278, 280, 281, 282, 284–285
    within block format, 195
    within cause and effect paper, 223, 224–225, 230, 231, 234
    within classification paper, 245–246, 248, 251, 254–255, 257, 258

within comparison and contrast paper, 195–196, 197–198, 200, 201, 206–207, 209, 211
within a definition paper, 173, 174, 176, 177–178, 182, 183–184, 186
within a descriptive paper, 99, 103, 105, 107–108, 110
within a division paper, 249–250, 251, 252
within an example paper, 150, 151, 152, 154–155, 156–157, 159, 160, 162
within a narrative paper, 79, 83, 88, 90
within a process paper, 126, 127, 132, 133
Tightening
  defined, 51
  examples of, 51–53
Topic Sentence
  defined, 21
  examples of, 21–22
  placement of in a paragraph, 21–22
Transition
  defined, 39
  list of elements, 39
  use of, 39

Validity, 266

Walters, Jonathan
  "To This Hurler, Throwing Is an Art Form, Not a Hit-or-Miss Proposition," 259
White, E. B.
  "Once More to the Lake," 111–116
Working Definition
  defined, 174
  examples of, 174
Writer-centered Writing
  defined, 16–17
  versus reader-centered writing, 16–17
Writing Process
  defined, 2
  illustrated, 2
  recursive nature of, 49
  three stages of
    composing, 3, 20–31, 32–41
    prewriting, 3, 4–7, 9–19
    revising, 3, 42–62
Writing Rituals, 7